THE DARK SIDE
OF PERSONALITY

THE DARK SIDE OF PERSONALITY

Science and Practice
in Social, Personality,
and Clinical Psychology

Edited by
Virgil Zeigler-Hill and David K. Marcus

American Psychological Association • Washington, DC

Published by
American Psychological Association
750 First Street, NE
Washington, DC 20002
www.apa.org

To order
APA Order Department
P.O. Box 92984
Washington, DC 20090-2984
Tel: (800) 374-2721; Direct: (202) 336-5510
Fax: (202) 336-5502; TDD/TTY: (202) 336-6123
Online: www.apa.org/pubs/books
E-mail: order@apa.org

In the U.K., Europe, Africa, and the Middle East, copies may be ordered from
American Psychological Association
3 Henrietta Street
Covent Garden, London
WC2E 8LU England

Typeset in Goudy by Circle Graphics, Inc., Columbia, MD

Printer: Sheridan Books, Inc., Chelsea, MI
Cover Designer: Mercury Publishing Services, Inc., Rockville, MD

The opinions and statements published are the responsibility of the authors, and such opinions and statements do not necessarily represent the policies of the American Psychological Association.

Library of Congress Cataloging-in-Publication Data

The dark side of personality : science and practice in social, personality, and clinical psychology / Virgil Zeigler-Hill and David K. Marcus, [editors].
    pages cm
  Includes bibliographical references and index.
  ISBN 978-1-4338-2187-5 — ISBN 1-4338-2187-7 1. Personality. 2. Personality disorders. I. Zeigler-Hill, Virgil, editor. II. Marcus, David K., editor. III. Title.
  BF698.3.D37 2016
  155.2—dc23

                                    2015033473

British Library Cataloguing-in-Publication Data
A CIP record is available from the British Library.

Printed in the United States of America
First Edition

http://dx.doi.org/10.1037/14854-000

CONTENTS

CONTRIBUTORS

Tammy D. Barry, PhD, Department of Psychology, University of Southern Mississippi, Hattiesburg

Danielle S. Berke, MS, Department of Psychology, University of Georgia, Athens

Robert F. Bornstein, PhD, Department of Psychology, Adelphi University, Garden City, NY

Timothy A. Brown, PhD, Department of Psychology, Boston University, Boston, MA

Ayca Coskunpinar, MS, Department of Psychology, Indiana University–Purdue University Indianapolis

Melissa A. Cyders, PhD, Department of Psychology, Indiana University–Purdue University Indianapolis

Sindes Dawood, BS, Department of Psychology, Pennsylvania State University, University Park

Kristy M. DiSabatino, MS, Department of Psychology, University of Southern Mississippi, Hattiesburg

Katherine L. Dixon-Gordon, PhD, Department of Psychological and Brain Sciences, University of Massachusetts, Amherst

Emily A. Dowgwillo, MS, Department of Psychology, Pennsylvania State University, University Park

Donald G. Dutton, PhD, Department of Psychology, University of British Columbia, Vancouver, British Columbia, Canada

Joyce Ehrlinger, PhD, Department of Psychology, Washington State University, Pullman

Alex Eichenbaum, MS, Department of Psychology, Washington State University, Pullman

Brian Enjaian, MS, Department of Psychology, Oakland University, Rochester, MI

Lauren R. Few, MS, Department of Psychology, University of Georgia, Athens

Karin Fisher, MS, Department of Psychology, University of Southern Mississippi, Hattiesburg

Gordon L. Flett, PhD, Department of Psychology, York University, Toronto, Ontario, Canada

Kim L. Gratz, PhD, Department of Psychiatry and Human Behavior, University of Mississippi Medical Center, Jackson

Paul L. Hewitt, PhD, Department of Psychology, University of British Columbia, Vancouver, British Columbia, Canada

Christopher J. Holden, MA, Department of Psychology, Oakland University, Rochester, MI

Daniel N. Jones, PhD, Department of Psychology, University of Texas at El Paso

Ellen M. Kessel, MA, Department of Psychology, Stony Brook University, Stony Brook, New York

Daniel N. Klein, PhD, Department of Psychology, Stony Brook University, Stony Brook, New York

Scott O. Lilienfeld, PhD, Department of Psychology, Emory University, Atlanta, GA

Steven Ludeke, PhD, Department of Psychology and Political Science, University of Southern Denmark, Odense

Jessica L. Maples-Keller, MS, Department of Psychology, University of Georgia, Athens

David K. Marcus, PhD, Department of Psychology, Washington State University, Pullman

Joshua D. Miller, PhD, Department of Psychology, University of Georgia, Athens

Alyssa L. Norris, MS, Department of Psychology, Washington State University, Pullman

Amy E. Noser, MS, Department of Psychology, University of Kansas, Lawrence

Dustin A. Pardini, PhD, School of Criminology and Criminal Justice, Arizona State University, Phoenix

Delroy L. Paulhus, PhD, Department of Psychology, University of British Columbia, Vancouver, British Columbia, Canada

Aaron L. Pincus, PhD, Department of Psychology, Pennsylvania State University, University Park

Noah C. Pollock, MS, Department of Psychology, Oakland University, Rochester, MI

James V. Ray, PhD, Department of Criminal Justice, University of Texas at San Antonio

Anthony J. Rosellini, PhD, Department of Health Care Policy, Harvard Medical School, Boston, MA

Simon S. Sherry, PhD, Department of Psychology and Neuroscience, Life Sciences Centre, Dalhousie University, Halifax, Nova Scotia, Canada

Sarah Francis Smith, MS, Department of Psychology, Emory University, Atlanta, GA

Ashton C. Southard, PhD, Department of Psychology, Oakland University, Rochester, MI

Theodore S. Tomeny, PhD, Department of Psychology, University of Alabama, Tuscaloosa

J. Davis VanderVeen, BA, Department of Psychology, Indiana University–Purdue University Indianapolis

Ashley L. Watts, MS, Department of Psychology, Emory University, Atlanta, GA

Diana Whalen, PhD, Department of Psychiatry, Washington University in St. Louis, St. Louis, MO

Virgil Zeigler-Hill, PhD, Department of Psychology, Oakland University, Rochester, MI

THE DARK SIDE
OF PERSONALITY

INTRODUCTION: A BRIGHT FUTURE FOR DARK PERSONALITY FEATURES?

VIRGIL ZEIGLER-HILL AND DAVID K. MARCUS

The past decade has witnessed a dramatic surge in empirical research dedicated to understanding the dark side of personality. This research has flourished despite the fact that there has not been a clear consensus regarding what is necessary or sufficient for a personality feature to be considered "dark." Consistent with previous scholars (e.g., Paulhus & Williams, 2002), we contend that dark personality features are socially aversive and linked with various sorts of interpersonal difficulties and potentially destructive behaviors (e.g., aggression, manipulation, exploitation). For example, certain dark personality features have been linked with the perpetration of sexual violence (e.g., Mouilso & Calhoun, 2012; Zeigler-Hill, Enjaian, & Essa, 2013). Of course, it is important to acknowledge that many personality features, if not all of them, have the potential to be problematic when taken to their most extreme levels (e.g., Grant & Schwartz, 2011). For example,

http://dx.doi.org/10.1037/14854-001
The Dark Side of Personality: Science and Practice in Social, Personality, and Clinical Psychology, V. Zeigler-Hill and D. K. Marcus (Editors)

conscientiousness is generally considered to be a relatively positive personality feature (e.g., O'Connor, Conner, Jones, McMillan, & Ferguson, 2009), but individuals who are "overly conscientious" may be rigid and inflexible, whereas those who are "not conscientious enough" may be impulsive and undependable. It is relatively easy to imagine scenarios in which nearly any personality feature may be socially aversive. Consequently, we propose that traits be considered "dark" when they are linked with interpersonal difficulties across a variety of contexts even when only modest levels of these features are present.

The purpose of this volume is to provide an overview of the current conceptualizations of a diverse array of personality traits that may have socially aversive, destructive, or dark features. It presents an interdisciplinary approach that extends social and personality psychology to overlap with clinical psychology. In doing so, each chapter in this book discusses implications for assessment and intervention, as well as future directions for research.

In addition to prototypically dark personality traits, this book covers some traits (e.g., spitefulness) that have been largely overlooked by psychologists, despite being topics of interest in associated disciplines (e.g., economics, evolutionary biology), and other traits (e.g., perfectionism) that have been presumed to be largely beneficial even though they may often be associated with negative outcomes. We review not only the maladaptive features of these dark traits but also the adaptive and beneficial features—such as the potential for altruistic outcomes from spitefulness—to provide a more expansive and nuanced analysis.[1] As a consequence, this volume includes a relatively broad range of dark personality traits that have rarely, if ever, been brought together in the same work (e.g., sadism and distractibility; interpersonal dependency and overconfidence). We do not believe that the dark personality traits reviewed in this volume constitute an exhaustive list of dark personality traits or even that these are the most important. Rather, our goal for the volume was to cover a wide array of personality traits that would have the potential to expand the common understanding of the dark side of personality. We hope this volume will draw attention to a range of personality traits that have dark aspects.

The dark personality features that have received the most empirical attention during the past decade are the *Dark Triad*, which is a constellation of personality traits that includes narcissism, psychopathy, and Machiavellianism

---

[1]Throughout the book, the terms *adaptive* and *maladaptive* are used in their broadest sense as synonyms for functional or dysfunctional or as being associated with positive or negative outcomes. Unless the authors specify otherwise, these terms are not intended to imply biological adaptation.

(for a review, see Furnham, Richards, & Paulhus, 2013). The first component of the Dark Triad is narcissism, which refers to exaggerated feelings of grandiosity, vanity, self-absorption, and entitlement (e.g., Morf & Rhodewalt, 2001). The construct of narcissism takes its name from the character of Narcissus from Greek mythology, who drowned after falling in love with his own reflection in a pool of water. Narcissism tends to interfere with various aspects of interpersonal functioning because others generally become tired of the exploitative, self-centered, and grandiose tendencies of narcissists (for a review, see Dowgwillo, Dawood, & Pincus, Chapter 1, this volume). Psychopathy is often considered to be the most malevolent of the Dark Triad traits (e.g., Paulhus & Williams, 2002; Rauthmann, 2012), and it is characterized by features that include impulsivity, thrill seeking, callousness, fearlessness, and interpersonal aggression (Hare, 1985; Harpur, Hare, & Hakstian, 1989; Lilienfeld & Andrews, 1996; Patrick, Fowles, & Krueger, 2009; see also Chapter 3, this volume, for a review of the fearless dominance component of psychopathy, and Chapter 2, this volume, for a review of the callous component). Not only are these features of psychopathy only loosely associated with one another (Marcus, Fulton, & Edens, 2013; Miller & Lynam, 2012), but impulsivity—one of its core features—is itself multifaceted (Whiteside & Lynam, 2001; see Part II of this volume). The third component of the Dark Triad is Machiavellianism. The term *Machiavellianism* is a homage to Niccolò Machiavelli, who was a political advisor to the Medici family in the 16th century. His most famous work (*The Prince*) described the sort of manipulative and calculating interpersonal strategies that would become his namesake. Machiavellianism reflects an extremely selfish orientation in which an individual is willing to use whatever means are necessary to attain his or her goals (e.g., deception, manipulation, exploitation; see Chapter 4, this volume, for a review).

Interest in the Dark Triad originated with McHoskey, Worzel, and Szyarto (1998), who examined these personality features with special attention given to the similarities between psychopathy and Machiavellianism. The similarities and differences among the Dark Triad personality traits were further expanded and clarified by Paulhus and Williams (2002), who coined the term *Dark Triad*. These authors noted that the Dark Triad traits shared characteristics such as disagreeableness, callousness, deceitfulness, egocentrism, lack of honesty-humility, and tendencies toward interpersonal manipulation and exploitation. It has been argued that one or more of these shared features may capture the true core of the Dark Triad, but the search for this elusive core has led to considerable debate (see Book, Visser, & Volk, 2015, for an extended discussion). The disagreement over the core of the Dark Triad may be due, at least in part, to the fact that these personality traits are "overlapping but distinct constructs" (Paulhus & Williams, 2002, p. 556).

RESEARCH CONCERNING THE DARK TRIAD

Narcissism, psychopathy, and Machiavellianism have each received considerable empirical attention outside their inclusion in the Dark Triad, but it is impressive that nearly 150 articles have explicitly focused on this particular constellation of dark personality features during the past decade (for a review, see, Furnham et al., 2013). Paulhus and Williams (2002) suggested that researchers interested in any one of these traits should assess all three to gain a clearer understanding of the extent to which each trait uniquely predicts particular outcomes (for an extended discussion, see Furnham, Richards, Rangel, & Jones, 2014). To distinguish between the unique contributions of the Dark Triad traits, researchers often use statistical approaches that account for their shared variance (e.g., entering all three Dark Triad traits into a simultaneous regression; e.g., Furnham et al., 2014).

The Dark Triad traits have been found to predict a wide array of behaviors and interpersonal tendencies. We cannot address the breadth of research concerning the Dark Triad in this brief introduction, so we limit our review to some aspects of interpersonal behavior (see Furnham et al., 2013, for a discussion of the connections that the Dark Triad traits have with a much broader range of outcomes). The Dark Triad traits have often been found to be associated with behaviors and qualities that may contribute to impaired social relationship functioning including aggressive tendencies (Jones & Paulhus, 2010), limited empathic abilities (Jonason & Krause, 2013; Jonason, Lyons, Bethell, & Ross, 2013), interpersonal styles reflecting a blend of dominance and hostility (Jonason & Webster, 2012; Jones & Paulhus, 2011; Southard, Noser, Pollock, Mercer, & Zeigler-Hill, in press), a willingness to use coercive strategies to obtain desired resources (Zeigler-Hill, Southard, & Besser, 2014), a focus on self-advancement with relatively little concern for others (Zuroff, Fournier, Patall, & Leybman, 2010), and a tendency to use deception (Baughman, Jonason, Lyons, & Vernon, 2014; Book et al., 2015).

There are clearly important similarities between the Dark Triad traits, but it is also important to acknowledge some of their differences as well. One area of divergence concerns the fact that psychopathy and Machiavellianism are often viewed as "darker" or more "toxic" personality features than narcissism (Rauthmann & Kolar, 2012). This view is supported by the results of studies showing that psychopathy and Machiavellianism have stronger associations with outcomes such as a relative lack of moral concerns (Arvan, 2013; Glenn, Iyer, Graham, Koleva, & Haidt, 2009). Another key difference among the Dark Triad traits concerns their connections with aggressive behavior following provocation. Psychopathy is associated with the use of aggression in response to physical threats (Jones & Paulhus, 2011), whereas narcissism is most strongly linked with aggressive behavior following self-esteem threats (e.g., Bushman & Baumeister, 1998; Jones & Paulhus, 2010; Twenge & Campbell, 2003). In contrast to psychopathy and narcissism, Machiavellianism does not have particularly strong connections with aggressive behavior following any sort of provocation (Chapter 4, this volume). The lack of aggression displayed by individuals with high levels of Machiavellianism may be explained, to at least some extent, by their caution. In contrast to the cautious and deliberate approach that characterizes those with Machiavellian tendencies, both psychopathy (Hart & Dempster, 1997) and narcissism (Vazire & Funder, 2006) are closely linked with impulsivity.

The Dark Triad has provided a valuable framework for considering socially aversive personality traits, and it has clearly generated a great deal of interest and research. However, it is unlikely that only three dark personality features exist. For example, there have been recent suggestions to expand the Dark Triad into the newly christened *Dark Tetrad* with the inclusion of sadism (e.g., Buckels, Jones, & Paulhus, 2013; Chabrol, Van Leeuwen, Rodgers, & Séjourné, 2009). In addition, Miller et al. (2010) suggested that researchers consider a second constellation of personality features that were both dark and emotionally vulnerable, which they referred to as the *Vulnerable Dark Triad* (i.e., borderline personality features, vulnerable narcissism, and secondary psychopathy). We are supportive of attempts to broaden the examination of dark personality features beyond those included in the Dark Triad (or recent expansions such as the Dark Tetrad or Vulnerable Dark Triad), including characteristics that have received relatively little previous attention, such as spitefulness (Marcus, Zeigler-Hill, Mercer, & Norris, 2014) and status-driven risk taking (Visser, Pozzebon, & Reina-Tamayo, 2014). However, we believe that it is simply too early in the process of understanding these dark personality features to attempt to identify the precise number of dark personality features that exist. Will the Dark Tetrad expand at some point to be the Dark Pentad? Would the Dark Hexad be far behind? We contend that this sort of enumeration approach may be overly constricting and may actually lead researchers to ignore other personality features that may be socially aversive or problematic in other ways. It is important to cast a somewhat wider net because the Dark Triad—or the Dark Tetrad—consists of personality traits that are relatively antagonistic, dishonest, and egocentric. We agree that antagonism is a vitally important aspect of dark personality features, but we would like scholars to consider adopting a somewhat broader view of dark personality features that extends beyond those features that are overtly antagonistic. In essence, we contend that there may actually be various types of dark personality features that deserve close consideration even if they are not overtly antagonistic in nature. This broader view of dark personality serves as the impetus for this volume.

A BROADER VIEW OF DARK PERSONALITY FEATURES

A considerable body of previous research has examined the links that certain dark personality features have with basic models of personality such as the Big Five personality dimensions (e.g., Lee & Ashton, 2014), the HEXACO model (e.g., Jonason & McCain, 2012; Lee & Ashton, 2014), and the interpersonal circumplex (e.g., Rauthmann & Kolar, 2013b; Southard et al., in press). These studies have offered insights into these dark personality features. For example, individuals with high levels of narcissism have been shown to possess low levels of agreeableness and high levels of extraversion, which has led to them being described as "disagreeable extraverts" (Paulhus, 2001). This work has also led to the development of assessment instruments for some dark personality features that are derived from basic personality models including the Five-Factor Narcissism Inventory (Glover, Miller, Lynam, Crego, & Widiger, 2012). The most ambitious attempt to integrate basic personality dimensions with the darker side of personality may be the model of pathological personality features that was described in Section III ("Emerging Measures and Models" in need of further study) of the fifth edition of the *Diagnostic and Statistical Manual of Mental Disorders* (DSM–5; American Psychiatric Association, 2013; see Krueger et al., 2011, for a review).[2] This model of pathological personality is concerned with maladaptive variants of the Big Five personality dimensions of extraversion, emotional stability, agreeableness, conscientiousness, and openness (Thomas et al., 2013) and has led to the development of the Personality Inventory for the DSM–5 (PID–5; Krueger, Derringer, Markon, Watson, & Skodol, 2012). The PID–5 is used to capture the following personality dimensions: detachment (which is characterized by introversion, social isolation, and anhedonia), negative affect (which concerns the tendency to experience an array of negative emotions), antagonism (which refers to aggressive tendencies accompanied by assertions of dominance and grandiosity), disinhibition (which includes impulsivity and sensation seeking), and psychoticism (which involves a disconnection from reality and a tendency for illogical thought patterns). In addition to these higher order dimensions, the PID–5 consists of 25 lower order facets including callousness, deceitfulness, depressivity, hostility, submissiveness, and withdrawal. Research concerning the PID–5 is clearly still in its earliest stages but it has already demonstrated considerable potential (e.g., Hopwood, Schade, Krueger, Wright, & Markon, 2013; Noser et al., 2015; Strickland, Drislane, Lucy, Krueger, & Patrick, 2013).

---

[2]The dimensional model of personality pathology is DSM-specific and therefore does not have a counterpart in the *International Classification of Diseases*.

The PID–5 has the potential to expand our view of dark personality features, but it is not without its possible flaws. Although the PID–5 is an important extension of traditional measures of the Big Five personality dimensions, which often assess relatively moderate levels of these personality dimensions without capturing extreme or atypical levels (e.g., Samuel, Simms, Clark, Livesley, & Widiger, 2010), it is still somewhat limited because it focuses only on potentially maladaptive aspects of the Big Five dimensions in a single direction. As we noted earlier, personality traits may be problematic when individuals possess either extremely low levels or extremely high levels of these traits. For example, individuals who possess levels of conscientiousness that are extremely low may be impulsive and undependable, whereas those with levels of conscientiousness that are extremely high may be somewhat rigid and inflexible. The PID–5 model was intended to account for extremely low levels of conscientiousness, but it is limited in its ability to detect extremely high levels of conscientiousness, which may also have dark elements (e.g., authoritarian or obsessive personality features). Similar limitations exist for the other dimensions (e.g., antagonism captures extremely low levels of agreeableness, but there is little attention given to personality features reflecting extremely high levels of agreeableness such as gullibility).

Dark personality features are socially aversive and associated with a range of negative outcomes, but it is important to note that these personality features may be at least somewhat beneficial in some areas of life. One example of the potential benefits that stem from dark personality features is success in short-term mating contexts (Holtzman & Strube, 2011, 2013; Jonason, Li, Webster, & Schmitt, 2009). For example, individuals with higher levels of narcissism and psychopathy report larger numbers of previous sexual partners and preferences for relationships that require little commitment (e.g., Jonason, Luevano, & Adams, 2012; Jonason et al., 2009) and greater willingness to use deceptive and manipulative mating behaviors, such as mate poaching and infidelity (e.g., Jonason & Buss, 2012; Jonason, Li, & Buss, 2010). Interestingly, women consistently evaluate men with narcissistic and psychopathic personality features as being more attractive than other men (Carter, Campbell, & Muncer, 2014b; cf. Rauthmann & Kolar, 2013a). The link between dark personality features and success in short-term mating contexts has been considered from the perspective of life history theory (i.e., a midlevel model from evolutionary biology that provides an explanation for energy and resource allocation across the life span), and it has been argued that some dark personality features—such as the Dark Triad—may represent alternative life-history strategies that are focused on short-term mating (Book et al., 2015; Carter, Campbell, & Muncer, 2014a; Figueredo et al., 2009; Jonason et al., 2012).

The results concerning the short-term mating success of those with some dark personality features suggest the intriguing possibility that certain dark personality features may represent specialized adaptations that allow individuals to exploit particular niches within society (e.g., Furnham et al., 2013; Jonason, Jones, & Lyons, 2013). In addition to life-history theory, several other promising evolutionary approaches have been applied to understanding dark personality features, including costly signaling theory, mutation load, flexibly contingent shifts in strategy according to environmental conditions, environmental variability in fitness optima, and frequency-dependent selection (for a review, see Buss, 2009). A prominent example of these evolutionary explanations is the argument that psychopathy is the expression of a frequency-dependent life strategy that is selected in response to varying environmental circumstances (Mealey, 1995). Frequency-dependent selection involves a dynamic equilibrium in which certain characteristics (e.g., psychopathic personality features) will be advantageous to the individuals who possess them as long as the frequency of those characteristics remains relatively low in the general population. This frequency-dependent model could easily be applied to other dark personality features (e.g., spitefulness, impulsivity), but it is important to note that the original model concerning psychopathy has been criticized on multiple fronts, including the heritability estimates of psychopathy (e.g., Crusio, 1995; Stoltenberg, 1997) and the failure to consider more parsimonious explanations (Crusio, 2004).

OVERVIEW OF THE VOLUME

Our goal for this volume was to expand the appreciation that researchers and clinicians have for what constitutes dark personality traits beyond the ubiquitous Dark Triad (i.e., narcissism, psychopathy, and Machiavellianism; see Furnham et al., 2013, for a review). Consequently, we cast a wide net when identifying potentially dark personality traits that were worthy of review. First, the broad constellations of dark personality features that we included in this volume were informed by the recent work that has been done to develop a stronger connection between pathological personality features and the Big Five personality dimensions (e.g., Thomas et al., 2013). This can be readily seen by our decision to include sections concerning negative affectivity, antagonism, and disinhibition which are all considered to be pathological personality trait domains in the model that is included in DSM–5 (Krueger et al., 2012). We also included a section on rigidity because we believe this is an important domain that has often been ignored by those researchers who are interested in dark personality features.

A second strategy was to include the Dark Triad traits such that we dedicated individual chapters to narcissism and Machiavellianism (as well as sadism, which has recently been included as part of the newly christened Dark Tetrad). In the case of psychopathy, however, there is compelling evidence that it is best understood as a multidimensional construct and that these various dimensions are only loosely associated with one another and often have distinct (and even opposite) associations with various external correlates (e.g., Benning, Patrick, Hicks, Blonigen, & Krueger, 2003; for a meta-analytic review, see Marcus et al., 2013). In other words, psychopathy may be a compound variable (Lilienfeld, 2013) that emerges when its independent components happen to co-occur. Therefore, rather than devote a single chapter to psychopathy, we followed the outline of the triarchic model of psychopathy (Patrick et al., 2009), which conceptualizes psychopathy as the confluence of boldness, meanness, and disinhibition. In the current volume, the chapter on fearless dominance corresponds to boldness, and the chapter on callousness corresponds to meanness. Disinhibition was represented by the traits of sensation seeking, urgency, and distractibility with urgency being the trait that is most closely related to the disinhibition component of psychopathy (Ray, Poythress, Weir, & Rickelm, 2009). Thus, by deconstructing the compound trait of psychopathy into its constituent parts, we expanded the range of dark personality traits. Furthermore, because psychopathy is not a unitary construct, researchers working within the Dark Triad framework should consider assessing and analyzing the components of psychopathy instead of relying on a composite psychopathy score, which may either amalgamate a set of disparate traits or fail to assess the full range of traits encompassed by the psychopathy construct depending on the particular instrument that is used.

A third strategy we used for expanding the realm of dark personality traits was to consider traits that are decidedly dark but that have not been included in the traditional dark personality literature. Given its associations with fascism, prejudice, and scapegoating, authoritarianism (Ludeke, Chapter 11, this volume) may be as interpersonally destructive and potentially dangerous as any of the Dark Triad traits. Furthermore, authoritarianism is only weakly correlated with the Dark Triad traits (Hodson, Hogg, & MacInnis, 2009; Jonason, 2015), so it may independently contribute to the prediction of various negative outcomes. Spite is another unambiguously dark personality trait. Unlike authoritarianism, which has generated thousands of psychological studies (Ludeke, Chapter 11, this volume) even if it has not been included in the Dark Triad, spite has received surprisingly little attention from personality and clinical psychologists (Marcus & Norris, Chapter 6, this volume). There are a variety of other understudied personality traits—such as greed (Marcus & Zeigler-Hill, 2015) and self-righteousness—that might also have been included in this volume, but the research base for these traits is so limited that it would have been premature to review them.

A fourth strategy to expand the range of dark personality traits was to include internalizing traits. Whereas the traditional Dark Triad traits are associated with inflicting harm and misery on others, the traits reflecting negative affectivity are prototypically associated with the misery they bring to their possessors. We believe that there is a benefit to expanding the notion of dark traits beyond antagonistic or externalizing traits, and a trait may also be considered dark if it is associated with self-harm (e.g., suicide, social impairment). Yet it is noteworthy that many of these "internalizing" traits are also associated with aggressive behaviors and harm to others.

Finally, we also included some traits that might superficially be considered neutral or even positive but that also have darker aspects. For example, fearless dominance is considered to be the "right stuff" for bravery and heroism, but it is also a component of psychopathy (Lilienfeld, Smith, & Watts, Chapter 3, this volume). Similarly, perfectionism is a trait that is often assumed to be adaptive and desirable because it inspires people to produce their best work. Yet, as discussed by Flett, Hewitt, and Sherry (Chapter 10, this volume), high levels of perfectionism are associated not only with personal misery, including suicidality, but, in extreme cases, perfectionism can lead to interpersonal violence and even murder. Even overconfidence, a trait that may be considered more annoying than dark, can have harmful interpersonal consequences. As detailed by Ehrlinger and Eichenbaum (Chapter 12, this volume), in some circumstances, overconfidence can result in disastrous and deadly outcomes (e.g., the deaths of more than 800 overconfident but ill-prepared people who have tried to climb Nepali mountains; the Bay of Pigs invasion of Cuba). Similarly, distractibility might also be considered more irritating than dark until one considers, for example, all of the injuries and deaths caused by distracted drivers (Barry, Fisher, DiSabatino, & Tomeny, Chapter 9, this volume).

Part I: Antagonism

Part I (Chapters 1–6) examines a range of personality features that share a common core of antagonism and includes elements of the Dark Tetrad. Chapter 1 (Dowgwillo, Dawood, & Pincus) is concerned with *narcissism*, which reflects feelings of grandiosity, vanity, self-absorption, and entitlement. The authors consider recent developments in our understanding of narcissism including contemporary models of pathological narcissism that incorporate both grandiose and vulnerable aspects of narcissism.

Chapter 2 (Pardini & Ray) focuses on *callousness*, which is a facet of psychopathy that is characterized by an indifference to the pain and suffering of others, a lack of remorse and guilt for wrongdoing, blunted emotional responses, and a failure to develop close emotional bonds with others. The authors review a body of work that has clearly identified callousness as a core feature of psychopathy.

Chapter 3 (Lilienfeld et al.) deals with *fearless dominance*, which is another facet of psychopathy. Fearless dominance includes characteristics such as interpersonal potency, physical fearlessness, risk taking, and calmness in the face of danger. The authors review evidence suggesting the intriguing possibility that fearless dominance, which seems like a positive quality on the surface, may be detrimental in daily life when it is paired with qualities such as poor impulse control.

Chapter 4 (Jones) is concerned with *Machiavellianism*, which reflects a tendency to use strategic behaviors for selfish gains (e.g., deceitfulness, manipulation). The author reviews research that suggests Machiavellianism is linked with characteristics and behaviors such as being calculating and strategic, cautious, and highly sensitive to rewards and punishments.

Chapter 5 (Paulhus & Dutton) reviews *sadism* (i.e., the enjoyment of other people's suffering) which may explain common behaviors such as humiliating others, bullying others, or enjoying depictions of violence in sports, films, or video games.

Chapter 6 (Marcus & Norris) concerns *spitefulness* which is the tendency for individuals to be willing to incur costs to themselves in order to inflict costs on others. The authors consider recent advancements in the study of spitefulness in psychology as well as the way that fields such as economics and evolutionary biology have included this intriguing construct.

Part II: Disinhibition

Part II (Chapters 7–9) examines specific aspects of disinhibition. Chapter 7 (Maples-Keller, Berke, Few, & Miller) concerns *sensation seeking*, which reflects the desire for varied, novel, and complex experiences as well as the willingness to take various risks (i.e., physical and social) to have these experiences. The authors explore the complex nomological network surrounding sensation seeking, which includes behaviors that are largely beneficial or neutral as well as those that are detrimental or antisocial.

Chapter 8 (Cyders, Coskunpinar, & VanderVeen) focuses on *urgency*, which reflects the tendency to engage in behaviors that may be detrimental to the self or others in response to extreme levels of affect. The authors suggest that urgency may be the most clinically relevant of the traits connected to impulsivity and that it serves as a common, transdiagnostic endophenotype for a wide array of negative outcomes and clinical disorders.

Chapter 9 (Barry et al.) reviews *distractibility*, which is an interruption in selective attention that is caused by an inability to ignore extraneous stimuli from both external and internal sources. Although it appears that there are some positive outcomes linked with distractibility (e.g., creativity), the existing evidence clearly indicates that distractibility is associated with a wide array of maladaptive outcomes.

Part III: Rigidity

Part III (Chapters 10–12) examines the broad domain of rigidity. Chapter 10 (Flett et al.) concerns a multidimensional view of *perfectionism* that includes self-oriented perfectionism (i.e., setting unrealistic self-standards), other-oriented perfectionism (i.e., setting exacting standards for other people), and socially prescribed perfectionism (i.e., the perception that others demand perfection from the self). Although the term *perfectionist* often has positive connotations linked to it, the authors provide compelling evidence that there is an important dark side to perfectionism.

Chapter 11 (Ludeke) reviews *authoritarianism*, which includes the tendency to submit to established authorities, a willingness to aggress against those condemned by those authorities, and a preference for traditional values. The author reviews evidence that the detrimental consequences of authoritarianism—especially for the lives of others—clearly outweighs its benefits as well as research concerning how to reduce authoritarianism or mitigate against its negative impact on others.

Chapter 12 (Ehrlinger & Eichenbaum) concerns *overconfidence*, which is defined as an overly positive perception of oneself relative to some comparison standard. The authors review research findings that suggest overconfidence is a ubiquitous feature of human judgment and decision making that stems from the desire to think well of oneself as well as how individuals organize information.

Part IV: Negative Affectivity

Part IV (Chapters 13–17) examines the broad domain of negative affectivity. Chapter 13 (Gratz, Dixon-Gordon, & Whalen) concerns *emotional lability*, which is concerned with intense, frequent, and reactive shifts in emotional states. The authors argue that a more complex model of emotional lability is needed because extreme levels of emotional lability—both high and low—are risk factors for some forms of psychopathology or other negative outcomes (e.g., an inability to respond appropriately to emotionally salient environmental cues).

Chapter 14 (Rosellini & Brown) focuses on *anxiousness*, which refers to a dispositional tendency to experience anxiety-related physiological reactions (e.g., increased heart rate), cognitions (e.g., worries), and behaviors (e.g., avoidance) when confronted with stressful events. The authors suggest that future research focusing on anxiousness, rather than higher order constructs such as negative affectivity, may shed additional light on the connections between personality and psychopathology.

Chapter 15 (Kessel & Klein) considers *depressive* personality features (i.e., a dispositional tendency to experience depression-related affect, cognitions, and behaviors) and *anhedonic* personality features (i.e., a dispositional inability to experience pleasure from activities that are usually found to be pleasurable). They argue that depressive and anhedonic personality features may have more in common than is generally recognized (e.g., both may stem from the same temperamental vulnerability) and that understanding the similarities and differences between these constructs will have broader benefits for our understanding of dark personality features.

Chapter 16 (Zeigler-Hill et al.) focuses on *self-esteem*, which is defined as the evaluative aspect of self-knowledge that reflects the extent that individuals like themselves and believe they are competent. The authors review the links that low self-esteem has with a range of outcomes as well as considering the role that fragile self-esteem plays in moderating the associations that self-esteem level has with important life outcomes.

Chapter 17 (Bornstein) concerns *interpersonal dependency*, which is often defined as the tendency to rely on others for help, nurturance, guidance, and protection even in those situations when autonomous functioning is possible. The author contends that the core of interpersonal dependency is a helpless self-schema in which individuals perceive themselves as weak and unable to survive without the guidance and support of others.

Part V: Current and Future Issues

Chapter 18 (Marcus & Zeigler-Hill) offers an integration of the chapters included in this volume as well as possible future directions for research concerning dark personality features.

CONCLUSION

We believe that the consideration of dark personality features has a great deal to offer to our understanding of human behavior. The Dark Triad traits of narcissism, psychopathy, and Machiavellianism have provided an excellent foundation for work in this area, but we believe that it is important for researchers to move beyond these traits and consider investigating other dark personality features. We contend that it is reasonable to use the term *dark* for socially aversive personality features that extend beyond those that are antagonistic or externalizing in nature. As a result, we believe that many of the personality features described in this volume (e.g., spitefulness, perfectionism) have the potential to be aversive or harmful to others—even when they are only present in modest levels—and so warrant consideration as part of an extended constellation of dark personality features. To be clear, we are not claiming that the personality features discussed in this volume represent a comprehensive list of dark personality features. Rather, we believe that our current efforts are merely an intermediate step in the process of developing a deeper and more complete understanding of dark personality features. The contributions of the authors included in this volume, as well as the many other researchers who are doing exciting work in this area of the literature, provide us with hope that there will be a bright future for research concerning dark personality features.

REFERENCES

American Psychiatric Association. (2013). *Diagnostic and statistical manual of mental disorders* (5th ed.). Arlington, VA: Author.

Arvan, M. (2013). Bad news for conservatives? Moral judgments and the Dark Triad personality traits: A correlational study. *Neuroethics, 6,* 307–318. http://dx.doi.org/10.1007/s12152-011-9140-6

Baughman, H. M., Jonason, P. K., Lyons, M., & Vernon, P. A. (2014). Liar liar pants on fire: Cheater strategies linked to the Dark Triad. *Personality and Individual Differences, 71,* 35–38. http://dx.doi.org/10.1016/j.paid.2014.07.019

Benning, S. D., Patrick, C. J., Hicks, B. M., Blonigen, D. M., & Krueger, R. F. (2003). Factor structure of the psychopathic personality inventory: Validity and implications for clinical assessment. *Psychological Assessment, 15,* 340–350.

Book, A., Visser, B. A., & Volk, A. A. (2015). Unpacking "evil": Claiming the core of the dark triad. *Personality and Individual Differences, 73,* 29–38. http://dx.doi.org/10.1016/j.paid.2014.09.016

Buckels, E. E., Jones, D. N., & Paulhus, D. L. (2013). Behavioral confirmation of everyday sadism. *Psychological Science, 24,* 2201–2209. http://dx.doi.org/10.1177/0956797613490749

Bushman, B. J., & Baumeister, R. F. (1998). Threatened egotism, narcissism, self-esteem, and direct and displaced aggression: Does self-love or self-hate lead to violence? *Journal of Personality and Social Psychology, 75,* 219–229. http://dx.doi.org/10.1037/0022-3514.75.1.219

Buss, D. M. (2009). How can evolutionary psychology successfully explain personality and individual differences? *Perspectives on Psychological Science, 4,* 359–366. http://dx.doi.org/10.1111/j.1745-6924.2009.01138.x

Carter, G. L., Campbell, A. C., & Muncer, S. (2014a). The dark triad: Beyond a "male" mating strategy. *Personality and Individual Differences, 56*, 159–164. http://dx.doi.org/10.1016/j.paid.2013.09.001

Carter, G. L., Campbell, A. C., & Muncer, S. (2014b). The Dark Triad personality: Attractiveness to women. *Personality and Individual Differences, 56*, 57–61. http://dx.doi.org/10.1016/j.paid.2013.08.021

Chabrol, H., Van Leeuwen, N., Rodgers, R., & Séjourné, N. (2009). Contributions of psychopathic, narcissistic, Machiavellian, and sadistic personality traits to juvenile delinquency. *Personality and Individual Differences, 47*, 734–739. http://dx.doi.org/10.1016/j.paid.2009.06.020

Crusio, W. E. (1995). The sociopathy of sociobiology. *Behavioral and Brain Sciences, 18*, 552. http://dx.doi.org/10.1017/S0140525X00039716

Crusio, W. E. (2004). The sociobiology of sociopathy: An alternative hypothesis. *Behavioral and Brain Sciences, 27*, 154–155. http://dx.doi.org/10.1017/S0140525X04220040

Figueredo, A. J., Wolf, P. S. A., Gladden, P. R., Olderbak, S. G., Andrzejczak, D. J., & Jacobs, W. J. (2009). Ecological approaches to personality. In D. M. Buss & P. H. Hawley (Eds.), *The evolution of personality and individual differences* (pp. 210–241). New York, NY: Oxford University Press.

Furnham, A., Richards, S. C., & Paulhus, D. L. (2013). The Dark Triad of personality: A 10-year review. *Social and Personality Psychology Compass, 7*, 199–216. http://dx.doi.org/10.1111/spc3.12018

Furnham, A., Richards, S., Rangel, L., & Jones, D. N. (2014). Measuring malevolence: Quantitative issues surrounding the Dark Triad. *Personality and Individual Differences, 67*, 114–121. http://dx.doi.org/10.1016/j.paid.2014.02.001

Glenn, A. L., Iyer, R., Graham, J., Koleva, S., & Haidt, J. (2009). Are all types of morality compromised in psychopathy? *Journal of Personality Disorders, 23*, 384–398. http://dx.doi.org/10.1521/pedi.2009.23.4.384

Glover, N., Miller, J. D., Lynam, D. R., Crego, C., & Widiger, T. A. (2012). The five-factor narcissism inventory: A five-factor measure of narcissistic personality traits. *Journal of Personality Assessment, 94*, 500–512. http://dx.doi.org/10.1080/00223891.2012.670680

Grant, A. M., & Schwartz, B. (2011). Too much of a good thing: The challenge and opportunity of the inverted U. *Perspectives on Psychological Science, 6*, 61–76. http://dx.doi.org/10.1177/1745691610393523

Hare, R. D. (1985). Comparison of procedures for the assessment of psychopathy. *Journal of Consulting and Clinical Psychology, 53*, 7–16. http://dx.doi.org/10.1037/0022-006X.53.1.7

Harpur, T. J., Hare, R. D., & Hakstian, R. A. (1989). Two-factor conceptualization of psychopathy: Construct validity and assessment implications. *Psychological Assessment: A Journal of Consulting and Clinical Psychology, 1*, 6–17. http://dx.doi.org/10.1037/1040-3590.1.1.6

Hart, S. D., & Dempster, R. J. (1997). Impulsivity and psychopathy. In C. D. Webster & M. A. Jackson (Eds.), *Impulsivity: Theory, assessment, and treatment* (pp. 212–232). New York, NY: Guilford Press.

Hodson, G., Hogg, S. M., & MacInnis, C. C. (2009). The role of "dark personalities" (narcissism, Machiavellianism, psychopathy), Big Five personality factors, and ideology in explaining prejudice. *Journal of Research in Personality, 43*, 686–690. http://dx.doi.org/10.1016/j.jrp.2009.02.005

Holtzman, N. S., & Strube, M. J. (2011). The intertwined evolution of narcissism and short-term mating: An emerging hypothesis. In W. K. Campbell & J. D. Miller (Eds.), *The handbook of narcissism and narcissistic personality disorder: Theoretical approaches, empirical findings, and treatments* (pp. 210–220). Hoboken, NJ: Wiley. http://dx.doi.org/10.1002/9781118093108.ch19

Holtzman, N. S., & Strube, M. J. (2013). Above and beyond short-term mating, long-term mating is uniquely tied to human personality. *Evolutionary Psychology, 11*, 1101–1129. http://dx.doi.org/10.1177/147470491301100514

Hopwood, C. J., Schade, N., Krueger, R. F., Wright, A. G. C., & Markon, K. E. (2013). Connecting *DSM–5* personality traits and pathological beliefs: Toward a unifying model. *Journal of Psychopathology and Behavioral Assessment, 35*, 162–172. http://dx.doi.org/10.1007/s10862-012-9332-3

Jonason, P. K. (2015). How "dark" personality traits and perceptions come together to predict racism in Australia. *Personality and Individual Differences, 72*, 47–51. http://dx.doi.org/10.1016/j.paid.2014.08.030

Jonason, P. K., & Buss, D. M. (2012). Avoiding entangling commitments: Tactics for implementing a short-term mating strategy. *Personality and Individual Differences, 52*, 606–610. http://dx.doi.org/10.1016/j.paid.2011.12.015

Jonason, P. K., Jones, A., & Lyons, M. (2013). Creatures of the night: Chronotypes and the Dark Triad traits. *Personality and Individual Differences, 55*, 538–541. http://dx.doi.org/10.1016/j.paid.2013.05.001

Jonason, P. K., & Krause, L. (2013). The emotional deficits associated with the Dark Triad traits: Cognitive empathy, affective empathy, and alexithymia. *Personality and Individual Differences, 55*, 532–537. http://dx.doi.org/10.1016/j.paid.2013.04.027

Jonason, P. K., Li, N. P., & Buss, D. M. (2010). The costs and benefits of the Dark Triad: Implications for mate poaching and mate retention tactics. *Personality and Individual Differences, 48*, 373–378. http://dx.doi.org/10.1016/j.paid.2009.11.003

Jonason, P. K., Li, N. P., Webster, G. D., & Schmitt, D. P. (2009). The Dark Triad: Facilitating a short-term mating strategy in men. *European Journal of Personality, 23*, 5–18. http://dx.doi.org/10.1002/per.698

Jonason, P. K., Luevano, V. X., & Adams, H. M. (2012). How the Dark Triad traits predict relationship choices. *Personality and Individual Differences, 53*, 180–184. http://dx.doi.org/10.1016/j.paid.2012.03.007

Jonason, P. K., Lyons, M., Bethell, E. J., & Ross, R. (2013). Different routes to limited empathy in the sexes: Examining the links between the Dark Triad and empathy.

Personality and Individual Differences, 54, 572–576. http://dx.doi.org/10.1016/j.paid.2012.11.009

Jonason, P. K., & McCain, J. (2012). Using the HEXACO model to test the validity of the Dirty Dozen measure of the Dark Triad. *Personality and Individual Differences, 53*, 935–938. http://dx.doi.org/10.1016/j.paid.2012.07.010

Jonason, P. K., & Webster, G. D. (2012). A protean approach to social influence: Dark Triad personalities and social influence tactics. *Personality and Individual Differences, 52*, 521–526. http://dx.doi.org/10.1016/j.paid.2011.11.023

Jones, D. N., & Paulhus, D. L. (2010). Different provocations trigger aggression in narcissists and psychopaths. *Social Psychological and Personality Science, 1*, 12–18. http://dx.doi.org/10.1177/1948550609347591

Jones, D. N., & Paulhus, D. L. (2011). Differentiating the Dark Triad within the interpersonal circumplex. In L. M. Horowitz & S. Strack (Eds.), *Handbook of interpersonal psychology: Theory, research, assessment, and therapeutic interventions* (pp. 249–269). New York, NY: Wiley.

Krueger, R. F., Derringer, J., Markon, K. E., Watson, D., & Skodol, A. E. (2012). Initial construction of a maladaptive personality trait model and inventory for *DSM–5*. *Psychological Medicine, 42*, 1879–1890. http://dx.doi.org/10.1017/S0033291711002674

Krueger, R. F., Eaton, N. R., Clark, L. A., Watson, D., Markon, K. E., Derringer, J., . . . Livesley, W. J. (2011). Deriving an empirical structure of personality pathology for *DSM–5*. *Journal of Personality Disorders, 25*, 170–191. http://dx.doi.org/10.1521/pedi.2011.25.2.170

Lee, K., & Ashton, M. C. (2014). The Dark Triad, the Big Five, and the HEXACO model. *Personality and Individual Differences, 67*, 2–5. http://dx.doi.org/10.1016/j.paid.2014.01.048

Lilienfeld, S. O. (2013). Is psychopathy a syndrome? Commentary on Marcus, Fulton, and Edens. *Personality Disorders: Theory, Research, and Treatment, 4*, 85–86. http://dx.doi.org/10.1037/a0027544

Lilienfeld, S. O., & Andrews, B. P. (1996). Development and preliminary validation of a self-report measure of psychopathic personality traits in noncriminal populations. *Journal of Personality Assessment, 66*, 488–524. http://dx.doi.org/10.1207/s15327752jpa6603_3

Marcus, D. K., Fulton, J. J., & Edens, J. F. (2013). The two-factor model of psychopathic personality: Evidence from the Psychopathic Personality Inventory. *Personality Disorders: Theory, Research, and Treatment, 4*, 67–76. http://dx.doi.org/10.1037/a0025282

Marcus, D. K., & Zeigler-Hill, V. (2015). A big tent of dark personality traits. *Social and Personality Psychology Compass, 9*, 434–446.

Marcus, D. K., Zeigler-Hill, V., Mercer, S. H., & Norris, A. L. (2014). The psychology of spite and the measurement of spitefulness. *Psychological Assessment, 26*, 563–574. http://dx.doi.org/10.1037/a0036039

McHoskey, J. W., Worzel, W., & Szyarto, C. (1998). Machiavellianism and psychopathy. *Journal of Personality and Social Psychology, 74*, 192–210. http://dx.doi.org/10.1037/0022-3514.74.1.192

Mealey, L. (1995). The sociobiology of sociopathy: An integrated evolutionary model. *Behavioral and Brain Sciences, 18*, 523–599. http://dx.doi.org/10.1017/S0140525X00039595

Miller, J. D., Dir, A., Gentile, B., Wilson, L., Pryor, L. R., & Campbell, W. K. (2010). Searching for a vulnerable dark triad: Comparing Factor 2 psychopathy, vulnerable narcissism, and borderline personality disorder. *Journal of Personality, 78*, 1529–1564. http://dx.doi.org/10.1111/j.1467-6494.2010.00660.x

Miller, J. D., & Lynam, D. R. (2012). An examination of the Psychopathic Personality Inventory's nomological network: A meta-analytic review. *Personality Disorders: Theory, Research, and Treatment, 3*, 305–326. http://dx.doi.org/10.1037/a0024567

Morf, C. C., & Rhodewalt, F. (2001). Expanding the dynamic self-regulatory processing model of narcissism: Research directions for the future. *Psychological Inquiry, 12*, 243–251. http://dx.doi.org/10.1207/S15327965PLI1204_3

Mouilso, E. R., & Calhoun, K. S. (2012). A mediation model of the role of sociosexuality in the associations between narcissism, psychopathy, and sexual aggression. *Psychology of Violence, 2*, 16–27. http://dx.doi.org/10.1037/a0026217

Noser, A. E., Zeigler-Hill, V., Vrabel, J. K., Besser, A., Ewing, T. D., & Southard, A. C. (2015). Dark and immoral: The links between pathological personality features and moral values. *Personality and Individual Differences, 75*, 30–35. http://dx.doi.org/10.1016/j.paid.2014.11.010

O'Connor, D. B., Conner, M., Jones, F., McMillan, B., & Ferguson, E. (2009). Exploring the benefits of conscientiousness: An investigation of the role of daily stressors and health behaviors. *Annals of Behavioral Medicine, 37*, 184–196. http://dx.doi.org/10.1007/s12160-009-9087-6

Patrick, C. J., Fowles, D. C., & Krueger, R. F. (2009). Triarchic conceptualization of psychopathy: Developmental origins of disinhibition, boldness, and meanness. *Development and Psychopathology, 21*, 913–938. http://dx.doi.org/10.1017/S0954579409000492

Paulhus, D. L. (2001). Normal narcissism: Two minimalist accounts. *Psychological Inquiry, 12*, 228–230.

Paulhus, D. L., & Williams, K. M. (2002). The Dark Triad of personality: Narcissism, Machiavellianism, and psychopathy. *Journal of Research in Personality, 36*, 556–563. http://dx.doi.org/10.1016/S0092-6566(02)00505-6

Rauthmann, J. F. (2012). The Dark Triad and interpersonal perception: Similarities and differences in the social consequences of narcissism, Machiavellianism, and psychopathy. *Social Psychological and Personality Science, 3*, 487–496. http://dx.doi.org/10.1177/1948550611427608

Rauthmann, J. F., & Kolar, G. P. (2012). How "dark" are the Dark Triad traits? Examining the perceived darkness of narcissism, Machiavellianism, and psychopathy.

Personality and Individual Differences, 53, 884–889. http://dx.doi.org/10.1016/j.paid.2012.06.020

Rauthmann, J. F., & Kolar, G. P. (2013a). The perceived attractiveness and traits of the dark triad: Narcissists are perceived as hot, Machiavellians and psychopaths not. *Personality and Individual Differences, 54,* 582–586. http://dx.doi.org/10.1016/j.paid.2012.11.005

Rauthmann, J. F., & Kolar, G. P. (2013b). Positioning the dark triad in the interpersonal circumplex: The friendly–dominant narcissist, hostile–submissive Machiavellian, and hostile–dominant psychopath? *Personality and Individual Differences, 54,* 622–627. http://dx.doi.org/10.1016/j.paid.2012.11.021

Ray, J. V., Poythress, N. G., Weir, J. M., & Rickelm, A. (2009). Relationships between psychopathy and impulsivity in the domain of self-reported personality features. *Personality and Individual Differences, 46,* 83–87. http://dx.doi.org/10.1016/j.paid.2008.09.005

Samuel, D. B., Simms, L. J., Clark, L. A., Livesley, W. J., & Widiger, T. A. (2010). An item response theory integration of normal and abnormal personality scales. *Personality Disorders: Theory, Research, and Treatment, 1,* 5–21. http://dx.doi.org/10.1037/a0018136

Southard, A. C., Noser, A. E., Pollock, N. C., Mercer, S. H., & Zeigler-Hill, V. (in press). The interpersonal nature of dark personality features. *Journal of Social and Clinical Psychology.*

Stoltenberg, S. F. (1997). Heritability estimates provide a crumbling foundation. *Behavioral and Brain Sciences, 20,* 525–532. http://dx.doi.org/10.1017/S0140525X97001519

Strickland, C. M., Drislane, L. E., Lucy, M., Krueger, R. F., & Patrick, C. J. (2013). Characterizing psychopathy using *DSM–5* personality traits. *Assessment, 20,* 327–338. http://dx.doi.org/10.1177/1073191113486691

Thomas, K. M., Yalch, M. M., Krueger, R. F., Wright, A. G. C., Markon, K. E., & Hopwood, C. J. (2013). The convergent structure of *DSM–5* personality trait facets and five-factor model trait domains. *Assessment, 20,* 308–311. http://dx.doi.org/10.1177/1073191112457589

Twenge, J. M., & Campbell, W. K. (2003). "Isn't it fun to get the respect that we're going to deserve?" Narcissism, social rejection, and aggression. *Personality and Social Psychology Bulletin, 29,* 261–272. http://dx.doi.org/10.1177/0146167202239051

Vazire, S., & Funder, D. C. (2006). Impulsivity and the self-defeating behavior of narcissists. *Personality and Social Psychology Review, 10,* 154–165. http://dx.doi.org/10.1207/s15327957pspr1002_4

Visser, B. A., Pozzebon, J. A., & Reina-Tamayo, A. (2014). Status-driven risk taking: Another "dark" personality? *Canadian Journal of Behavioural Science/Revue Canadienne Des Sciences Du Comportement, 46,* 485–496.

Whiteside, S. P., & Lynam, D. R. (2001). The five factor model and impulsivity: Using a structural model of personality to understand impulsivity. *Personality and Individual Differences, 30,* 669–689. http://dx.doi.org/10.1016/S0191-8869(00)00064-7

Zeigler-Hill, V., Enjaian, B., & Essa, L. (2013). The role of narcissistic personality features in sexual aggression. *Journal of Social and Clinical Psychology, 32,* 186–199. http://dx.doi.org/10.1521/jscp.2013.32.2.186

Zeigler-Hill, V., Southard, A. C., & Besser, A. (2014). Resource control strategies and personality traits. *Personality and Individual Differences, 66,* 118–123. http://dx.doi.org/10.1016/j.paid.2014.03.037

Zuroff, D. C., Fournier, M. A., Patall, E. A., & Leybman, M. J. (2010). Steps toward an evolutionary personality psychology: Individual differences in the social rank domain. *Canadian Psychology, 51,* 58–66. http://dx.doi.org/10.1037/a0018472

I

ANTAGONISM

1

THE DARK SIDE OF NARCISSISM

EMILY A. DOWGWILLO, SINDES DAWOOD, AND AARON L. PINCUS

DEFINITION AND BACKGROUND

The concept of narcissism can be traced to the Greek myth of Narcissus and its retelling in Homeric hymns. Psychology has considered narcissism a characteristic of personality pathology (i.e., a dark trait) for more than 100 years. Clinicians have been writing about narcissism since Freud's (1914/1957) initial discussion through today's contemporary clinical models (Kernberg, 2010; Ogrodniczuk, 2013; Pincus, Roche, & Good, 2015). Psychiatry classifies narcissism as narcissistic personality disorder (NPD) in the *Diagnostic and Statistical Manual of Mental Disorders* (5th ed.; *DSM–5*; American Psychiatric Association, 2013) and the *International Classification of Diseases* (10th rev.; *ICD–10*; World Health Organization, 1992). Social and personality psychologists have investigated the adaptive and maladaptive correlates of narcissism conceptualized as a normal personality trait dimension for decades (Tamborski & Brown, 2012).

http://dx.doi.org/10.1037/14854-002
The Dark Side of Personality: Science and Practice in Social, Personality, and Clinical Psychology, V. Zeigler-Hill and D. K. Marcus (Editors)

Although these disciplines often vary in their conceptualization and assessment of narcissism (Cain, Pincus, & Ansell, 2008; Miller & Campbell, 2008), these distinctions have been well discussed elsewhere (Pincus & Lukowitsky, 2010). There is also sufficient convergence across disciplines to effectively capture a contemporary, empirically supported, and clinically relevant general portrait of the dark narcissistic personality. In this chapter, we paint this portrait using an integrative contemporary model of pathological narcissism.

A Contemporary Model of Pathological Narcissism

Recent efforts to synthesize the corpus of description, theory, and research on pathological narcissism across the disciplines generated a contemporary model that conceptualizes pathological narcissism as a combination of maladaptive self-enhancement motivation (grandiosity) and impaired self, emotion, and interpersonal regulation in response to self-enhancement failures and lack of recognition and admiration from others (vulnerability; Pincus, 2013; Pincus, Cain, & Wright, 2014; Roche, Pincus, Lukowitsky, Ménard, & Conroy, 2013).

Self-Enhancement and Regulation

Narcissism can be defined as an individual's tendency to use a variety of self-regulation, affect regulation, and interpersonal processes to maintain a positive—and possibly inflated—self-image. Thus, it is necessarily a complex personality construct involving (a) needs for recognition and admiration; (b) motivations to seek out, overtly and covertly, self-enhancement experiences from the social environment; (c) strategies to satisfy these needs and motives; and (d) abilities to manage self-enhancement failures and social disappointments (Morf, Horvath, & Torchetti, 2011; Morf, Torchetti, & Schürch, 2012). Generally, such needs and motives are normal aspects of personality (i.e., normal narcissism). Normal narcissism underlies the tendencies for individuals to see themselves in a positive light and to seek out experiences of self-enhancement (Hepper, Gramzow, & Sedikides, 2010), such as successful achievements and competitive victories (Conroy, Elliot, & Thrash, 2009). Most individuals manage these normal narcissistic needs effectively, seek out their gratification in culturally and socially acceptable ways and contexts, and regulate self-esteem, negative emotions, and interpersonal behavior when disappointments are experienced. Narcissism becomes pathological, or dark, when the needs for a positive self-concept and self-enhancement dominate the personality and are coupled with impaired regulatory capacities.

Pathological narcissism involves impairment in the ability to regulate the self, emotions, and behavior in discharging impulses for self-enhancement and fulfilling needs for recognition and admiration. Put another way, the dark narcissistic personality has notable difficulties transforming narcissistic impulses (self-enhancement motivation) and needs (recognition and admiration) into mature and socially appropriate ambitions and conduct (Roche et al., 2013). In their dynamic self-regulatory processing model, Morf and colleagues (Morf, Horvath, & Torchetti, 2011; Morf & Rhodewalt, 2001; Morf, Torchetti, & Schürch, 2012) have provided a compelling argument for conceptualizing pathological narcissism through the strategies used to construct, maintain, and enhance one's view of the self. They suggested that early empathic failures by parental figures (see also Kohut, 1971) leave the child ill equipped to regulate the self, and instead self-regulation is played out in the social arena (Dickinson & Pincus, 2003; Kernberg, 2010). However, the early negative parenting experience also leaves the self with a mistrust and disdain for others, resulting in a tragic paradox in which other people are needed for the narcissist to self-enhance, but the devalued and skeptical view of others limits the narcissist's ability to experience others' admiration, praise, and validation as self-enhancing. This pattern leads to lingering self-doubt and increased vulnerability, reenergizing the self to continue seeking these self-enhancement experiences in increasingly maladaptive ways and inappropriate contexts (Morf, 2006; Morf & Rhodewalt, 2001). Thus, the fundamental dysfunction associated with dark narcissistic personalities involves "chronically unsatisfied needs for recognition and admiration that lead to an equally chronic preoccupation with the social status of the self and an unremitting prioritization of self-enhancement motivation" (Pincus, Roche, & Good, 2015, p. 798). These unsatisfied needs for recognition and admiration heighten narcissistic individuals' sensitivity to the daily ups and downs of life and relationships (e.g., Besser & Priel, 2010; Zeigler-Hill & Besser, 2013) and impair their regulation of self-esteem, emotion, and behavior (Roche et al., 2013). Importantly, conceptualizing narcissism from a regulatory perspective accounts for both narcissistic grandiosity and narcissistic vulnerability.

Narcissistic Grandiosity and Narcissistic Vulnerability

To the layperson, narcissism is most often associated with conceited, arrogant, and domineering attitudes and behaviors (Buss & Chiodo, 1991), which are captured by the term *narcissistic grandiosity*. This characterization accurately identifies some common expressions of maladaptive self-enhancement associated with pathological narcissism. However, our definition of narcissism combines maladaptive self-enhancement (e.g., grandiosity) with self, emotional, and behavioral dysregulation in response to ego threats or self-enhancement failures (e.g., vulnerability). This *narcissistic vulnerability* is reflected in experiences of anger, envy, aggression, helplessness, emptiness, low self-esteem,

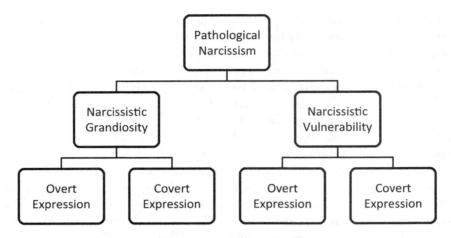

Figure 1.1. The hierarchical structure of pathological narcissism. Data from "Pathological Narcissism and Narcissistic Personality Disorder," by A. L. Pincus and M. R. Lukowitsky, 2010, *Annual Review of Clinical Psychology, 6*, p. 431. Copyright 2010 by Annual Reviews. Adapted with permission.

shame, avoidance of interpersonal relationships, and even suicidality (Kohut & Wolf, 1978; Krizan & Johar, 2012; Pincus & Roche, 2011; Ronningstam, 2005). A comprehensive hierarchical model of pathological narcissism is presented in Figure 1.1. Narcissistic grandiosity involves intensely felt needs for validation and admiration giving rise to urgent motives to seek out self-enhancement experiences. When these needs for validation and admiration dominate the personality, the individual is concomitantly vulnerable to increased sensitivity to ego threat and subsequent self, emotion, and behavioral dysregulation (i.e., narcissistic vulnerability). In recent years, recognition of both grandiose and vulnerable themes of narcissism has increasingly become the norm in clinical psychology (e.g., Pincus & Lukowitsky, 2010), psychiatry (e.g., Russ, Shedler, Bradley, & Westen, 2008), social work (e.g., Kealy & Ogrodniczuk, 2012), and social and personality psychology (e.g., Miller & Maples, 2012).

ADAPTIVE AND MALADAPTIVE FEATURES

The needs for recognition and admiration as well as motives for self-enhancement associated with narcissism are managed and expressed through various regulatory mechanisms (Roche et al., 2013). These mechanisms can be either mature or primitive in nature. The use of predominately mature regulatory strategies involves sublimating unmitigated needs for recognition and admiration into reasonable ambitions that are pursued through both agentic and communal experiences and results in the more adaptive features of narcissism that are explicated next. The use of predominantly primitive regulatory strategies involves the combination of an overly simplistic view of others and an inability to pursue one's own needs in socially appropriate ways resulting in the maladaptive features of narcissism that are discussed in the following section.

Adaptive Features

Most research linking narcissism with adaptive outcomes appears in the social and personality psychology literature. These studies typically assess narcissism using the Narcissistic Personality Inventory (NPI; Raskin & Hall, 1981), which measures a mix of adaptive (e.g., leadership/authority) and maladaptive (e.g., entitlement/exploitativeness) grandiose traits (Ackerman et al., 2011). This research suggests that the adaptive features of narcissism are mainly related to trait grandiosity, and there is currently no empirical evidence linking narcissistic vulnerability (or other more explicitly pathological conceptualizations of narcissism) to adaptive features. Therefore, we limit our discussion to trait grandiosity.

Broad and General Personality Traits

Trait grandiosity is positively related to extraversion and negatively related to neuroticism across numerous general trait models (e.g., five-factor model, HEXACO). In general, higher levels of extraversion and lower levels of neuroticism are associated with better mental health and physical health outcomes (Lahey, 2009; Turiano et al., 2012). These associations may help explain many similar findings linking trait grandiosity with health and well-being (Rhodewalt & Morf, 1995; Sedikides, Rudich, Gregg, Kumashiro, & Rusbult, 2004). Research consistently finds grandiosity to have inverse relationships with dispositional and daily depression, dispositional and daily loneliness, and dispositional and daily anxiety, as well as positive relationships with dispositional and daily subjective well-being and couple well-being (Sedikides et al., 2004). Additionally, grandiosity is negatively related to trait anxiousness, trait depressivity, and shame, and positively related to assertiveness (Pincus et al., 2009; Samuel & Widiger, 2008).

Leadership

Within organizations, individuals high in grandiosity are consistently selected as organizational leaders. Schnure (2010) found that in personnel selection interviews, experienced interviewers evaluated the applications of narcissists more favorably. Similarly, trained experts in managerial assessment favorably evaluate narcissists in leaderless group discussions (Brunell et al., 2008). In fact, those high in grandiosity emerge as leaders not only in business settings, but also in laboratory, military, and educational settings (Campbell, Hoffman, Campbell, & Marchisio, 2011), and narcissistic individuals appear to perform especially well on public tasks as they are motivated by the opportunity for recognition and glory (Wallace & Baumeister, 2002). Despite these results, research on the effectiveness of narcissists in leadership positions has been mixed at best (Grijalva, Harms, Newman, Gaddis, & Fraley, 2015).

Social Adaptation

Campbell and Campbell (2009) posited that many of the socially adaptive benefits associated with narcissism are short term in nature. Thus, narcissists are successful in the initial stages of dating, are rated as likable and attractive in initial meetings, and show emergent leadership potential in leaderless groups, although these same adaptive features do not appear to extend to longer term relationships (Brunell et al., 2008; Oltmanns, Friedman, Fiedler, & Turkheimer, 2004; Paulhus, 1998; Rhodewalt & Eddings, 2002).

Narcissistic grandiosity shows a significant negative association with general interpersonal sensitivity and is unrelated to subjective interpersonal distress (Hopwood, Pincus, DeMoor, & Koonce, 2008; Pincus et al., 2009). Thus individuals high in trait grandiosity are not particularly bothered by the interpersonal behaviors of others and do not report any distress regarding their own interpersonal behaviors. Individuals high in trait grandiosity also endorse believing there are people available who have positive opinions of them that they can turn to during stressful times (Rhodewalt & Morf, 1995).

Self-Esteem

Trait grandiosity is also positively related to self-esteem. Individuals high in grandiosity report holding positive illusions about themselves, resist feedback that disconfirms this positive view of self, and view themselves as successful, with relatively congruent actual and ideal selves (Morf & Rhodewalt, 2001; Rhodewalt & Morf, 1995; Sedikides et al., 2004). Importantly, self-esteem has been shown to mediate the relationship between grandiosity and psychological health (Sedikides et al., 2004).

Maladaptive Features

When pathological conceptualizations of narcissism are assessed via self-report, informant report, and diagnostic interviews, both grandiosity and vulnerability are associated with numerous maladaptive features. Therefore, in this section and throughout the remainder of the chapter, we review a much broader clinical literature than we did in the previous section.

Broad and General Personality Traits

Both narcissistic grandiosity and vulnerability exhibit negative associations with five-factor model agreeableness (Miller et al., 2010, 2011). Narcissistic vulnerability is also negatively correlated with extraversion and positively correlated with neuroticism, supporting prior associations between both high neuroticism and low agreeableness and personality pathology more generally (Saulsman & Page, 2004). The HEXACO[1] personality model shows similar associations and adds a negative relationship between the Honesty–Humility dimension and both grandiosity and vulnerability (Bresin & Gordon, 2011).

Impulsivity

Grandiosity and vulnerability are associated with impulsive traits (Miller et al., 2010). In particular, narcissistic grandiosity shows modest positive correlations with positive urgency and sensation seeking, indicating a tendency to pursue risky or novel activities and a difficulty resisting cravings and urges when in a positive affective state. Vulnerability, in contrast, is positively correlated with the both positive and negative urgency components of impulsivity, indicating a difficulty resisting cravings and urges when in both a positive or negative affective state.

Self-Conscious Emotions

Narcissistic grandiosity and vulnerability demonstrate distinct associations with affect and self-conscious emotions. For example, grandiosity is positively correlated with positive affectivity and unrelated to negative affectivity, whereas vulnerability is negatively correlated with positive affectivity and positively correlated with negative affectivity (Miller et al., 2010). Moreover, whereas grandiosity is positively associated with guilt, vulnerability is unrelated to guilt, but it is positively associated with shame, hubris, and envy, and negatively associated with authentic pride (Krizan & Johar, 2012; Pincus, Conroy, Hyde, & Ram, 2010).

---

[1]HEXACO's name is derived from its six major dimensions: Honesty–Humility, Emotionality, eXtraversion, Agreeableness (vs. Anger), Conscientiousness, and Openness to experience.

Externalizing Problems

Narcissistic grandiosity and narcissistic vulnerability show distinct relationships with a number of externalizing problems. Numerous laboratory-based and correlational studies (e.g., Lobbestael, Baumeister, Fiebig, & Eckel, 2014; Reidy, Foster, & Zeichner, 2010; Widman & McNulty, 2010) show that grandiosity is positively associated with all forms of aggression (e.g., reactive, proactive, unprovoked, sexual), as well as violent behavior and self-reported homicidal thoughts in psychotherapy inpatients and outpatients (Ellison, Levy, Cain, Ansell, & Pincus, 2013; Goldberg et al., 2007). Narcissistic grandiosity is also associated with increased criminal behavior and gambling (Miller et al., 2010). Narcissistic vulnerability, on the other hand, is associated with self-reported aggression but not with aggressive behavior assessed in the laboratory (Lobbestael et al., 2014). Additionally, narcissistic vulnerability interacted with self-reported childhood sexual abuse to predict the frequency of men's overt and cyber-stalking behaviors (Ménard & Pincus, 2012).

Self–Other Schemas and Interpersonal Characteristics

Narcissistic grandiosity and vulnerability are related to maladaptive views of the self and others (Zeigler-Hill, Green, Arnau, Sisemore, & Myers, 2011). These investigators found that grandiosity was positively correlated with entitlement schemas and negatively correlated with defectiveness schemas, indicating that these individuals perceive an idealized self that should be allowed to do or have whatever it wants (see also Kernberg, 2010). Narcissistic grandiosity also correlated with mistrust and abandonment schemas, reflecting the belief that others are manipulative and abusive and will likely leave them. Like grandiosity, vulnerability correlated positively with mistrust and abandonment schemas. Vulnerability was also positively correlated with subjugation, unrelenting standards, and emotional inhibition schemas and was negatively correlated with dependence schemas, reflecting belief in a world of important others that holds the self to unrealistically high standards and discourages emotional expression and interpersonal dependency (Zeigler-Hill et al., 2011).

In addition to maladaptive self and other schemas, researchers have found narcissistic grandiosity and vulnerability to be associated with specific types of interpersonal problems. In particular, narcissistic grandiosity is associated with predominately vindictive, domineering, and intrusive problematic behaviors (Ogrodniczuk, Piper, Joyce, Steinberg, & Duggal, 2009; Pincus et al., 2009). Narcissistic vulnerability is similarly associated with vindictive interpersonal problems but also shows positive associations with exploitable and avoidant problems (Pincus et al., 2009). Grandiosity and vulnerability also exhibit meaningful associations with interpersonal sensitivities, with grandiosity associated with sensitivity to remoteness, antagonism, and control, and vulnerability associated with sensitivity to remoteness, control, attention seeking, and affection (Dowgwillo, 2014; Hopwood et al., 2011).

Finally, grandiosity and vulnerability are both associated with a response to ego threat characterized by increases in anger and negative affect (Besser & Priel, 2010; Besser & Zeigler-Hill, 2010). These studies found that individuals high in narcissistic grandiosity respond most strongly to achievement failures and public ego threats, whereas individuals high in narcissistic vulnerability respond most strongly to interpersonal rejection and private ego threats.

Psychopathology

Narcissistic grandiosity and vulnerability show convergent and distinct associations with psychopathological symptoms and disorders in patient and student samples. In a sample of undergraduates (Tritt, Ryder, Ring, & Pincus, 2010), narcissistic grandiosity was positively correlated with a hyperthymic temperament, characterized by vivid extraversion and energy. In the same sample, narcissistic vulnerability was negatively associated with a hyperthymic temperament and showed positive associations with depressive and anxious temperaments, suggesting a predominate focus on avoiding narcissistic injury rather than fueling grandiose self-enhancement.

In patients presenting for outpatient psychotherapy, narcissistic grandiosity was associated with level of mania, and narcissistic vulnerability was significantly associated with level of sleep disturbance, psychosis, and depression (Ellison et al., 2013). Similarly, in student samples (Miller et al., 2010, 2011), narcissistic vulnerability was positively correlated with a history of emotional, verbal, physical, and sexual abuse; attachment anxiety and avoidance; anxiety; depression; hostility; interpersonal sensitivity; paranoid ideation; and global distress and negatively correlated with self-esteem. In contrast, narcissistic grandiosity was unrelated to these maladaptive etiological, developmental, and symptomatic variables. Although both grandiosity and vulnerability show positive associations with borderline personality pathology and suicide attempts, nonsuicidal self-injury is exclusively associated with narcissistic vulnerability (Pincus et al., 2009). Finally, in a sample of Israeli civilians under immediate missile threat, respondents' overall level of pathological narcissism moderated the association between severity of threat and both posttraumatic stress disorder and generalized anxiety disorder symptoms such that severity of threat and severity of symptoms were strongly linked for individuals high in pathological narcissism but were unrelated in individuals low in pathological narcissism (Besser, Zeigler-Hill, Pincus, & Neria, 2013).

DIRECTIONS FOR FUTURE RESEARCH

Although there is an abundant literature on pathological narcissism, the majority of research focuses on description. In this section, we highlight some key areas for future research.

Mechanisms

As this chapter demonstrates, narcissistic grandiosity and narcissistic vulnerability exhibit convergent and distinct associations with a variety of constructs, but underlying psychological mechanisms have not yet been articulated. Some efforts have been made to identify potential mechanisms. For instance, Marčinko and colleagues (Marčinko et al., 2014) found that dysfunctional perfectionistic attitudes partially mediated the relation between narcissistic vulnerability and depressive symptoms such that patients higher in narcissistic vulnerability were more likely to exhibit dysfunctional perfectionism, which in turn, might give rise to depressive symptoms. However, given the cross-sectional design of the study, it is unclear whether pathological narcissism or depression is a consequence of perfectionism. Additional longitudinal studies will be needed to clarify this association. It will also be important for researchers to investigate whether other mechanisms underlie the narcissism–depression association. These mechanisms may include self-criticism, shame, and anger, which are often seen in patients with narcissism and depression (e.g., Busch, 2009; Kealy, Tsai, & Ogrodniczuk, 2012). Beyond depression, research should also seek to identify the mechanisms linking narcissism with aggression, suicidality, and other important clinical phenomena (Pincus et al., 2015). Such findings could inform treatment planning and risk assessment for pathological narcissism.

Within-Person Dynamics of Pathological Narcissism

Although the contemporary clinical model of pathological narcissism recognizes both narcissistic grandiosity and narcissistic vulnerability, further research is needed to clarify their within-person temporal patterning. Several theorists have suggested that grandiose self-states vacillate with vulnerable self-states and dysregulation within the same person (e.g., Pincus et al., 2014; Ronningstam, 2009). Studies should examine these fluctuations in self-states at multiple time scales to detect whether changes in narcissistic self-states occur quickly within a short time frame (e.g., seconds, minutes, hours) or unfold slowly over time (e.g., days, weeks, months). Several emerging experience-sampling methodologies could be used to investigate this sequence (Lizdek, Sadler, Woody, Ethier, & Malet, 2012; Mehl & Conner, 2012; Ram et al., 2014; Roche, Pincus, Rebar, Conroy, & Ram, 2014).

Prospective research should not only examine the temporal patterning of narcissistic grandiosity and narcissistic vulnerability but also the predictive validity and diagnostic utility of these patterns. For instance, researchers could examine whether changes in these self-states predict dysregulation and its consequences such as suicidality, substance use, depression, anger, interpersonal conflicts, and aggression. Another area that could be explored is what role oscillations between grandiosity and vulnerability have in affecting a patient's clinical presentation, diagnosis, prognosis, and treatment (Pincus et al., 2014). Perhaps a better understanding of the within-person dynamics of narcissistic grandiosity and narcissistic vulnerability will lead to improved diagnostics, treatment approaches, and risk management.

CLINICAL IMPLICATIONS

Understanding the clinical phenomenology of pathological narcissism (i.e., narcissistic grandiosity and narcissistic vulnerability) and their links with depression, anxiety, suicidality, and other clinically relevant constructs is essential to accurately identify and treat highly narcissistic patients (Ogrodniczuk, 2013; Pincus et al., 2014). Below we touch on some of these areas and discuss their clinical importance in assessment and practice.

Depression

Clinicians should be familiar with certain depressive features that may signal pathological narcissism. Depressive symptoms in individuals with pathological narcissism are often characterized by anhedonia, feelings of emptiness, boredom, worthlessness, and agitation rather than melancholia or sadness (Pincus et al., 2014). These symptoms may also be exacerbated or accompanied by feelings of shame, anger, envy, resentment, and hostility. As noted previously, these are all maladaptive features associated with narcissistic vulnerability. It is therefore important for clinicians to use the contemporary clinical model of pathological narcissism and assess for both narcissistic grandiosity *and* narcissistic vulnerability (Pincus et al., 2015). This approach includes exploring the nature of depressive states and low self-esteem to distinguish mood disorder from personality pathology. We believe this distinction is important because narcissistic patients often present for psychotherapy in a vulnerable self-state (Ellison et al., 2013). Such early recognition is critical given depressive symptoms associated with pathological narcissism (and other personality disorders) are typically unresponsive to medications or electroconvulsive therapy, limiting effective treatment options.

Suicidality

Suicidality is also important to assess in patients with significant pathological narcissism; however, this assessment presents a significant clinical challenge. A primary problem faced by clinicians working with suicidal narcissistic patients is that their patients' suicidal behaviors may be lethal and unpredictable. There is evidence to suggest that narcissists are at a heightened risk for suicide even when not clinically depressed (e.g., Links, 2013), although they are more likely to attempt or complete suicide when feeling depressed (Maltsberger, 1998). Certain life stressors and changes may increase suicidal risk in narcissistic patients, such as arguing more with a spouse, being fired from work, foreclosure on a mortgage or loan, and serious personal injury or illness (Blasco-Fontecilla et al., 2010). Suicide attempters with narcissistic problems are also likely to minimize or deny any suicidal behavior or intent as well as minimize or dismiss obvious stressors/situations that lead to suicidality (Ronningstam & Maltsberger, 1998). These suicidal behaviors can reflect varying meanings, such as an attack to obliterate an imperfect self or a test of the grandiose fantasy of indestructibility. Although it may be difficult to easily recognize narcissistic suicidality, clinicians should regularly and closely monitor narcissistic patients for the early onset or co-occurrence of depressive symptoms (Links & Prakash, 2014) and also be aware that suicidal behaviors can occur in the absence of depression.

Perfectionism

Perfectionism also appears to play a clinically relevant role in narcissism and associated dysfunction. Narcissists strive to meet unrealistic standards of achievement, raising the bar higher after each accomplishment, which often results in a cycle of dissatisfaction (Dimaggio & Attinà, 2012). Individuals high in narcissism also impose perfectionistic standards on others and may disparage those who fail to live up to their expectations. Excessive perfectionism and entitlement may also diminish a patient's capacity to respond to positive reinforcement from work, social interactions, or recreation, which may, in turn, give rise to feelings of depression and/or social anxiety (Pincus et al., 2014). Other consequences associated with perfectionism may include social isolation or aggressiveness.

The relations among narcissism, depression, and perfectionism might also be important for understanding suicidality. Arie, Haruvi-Catalan, and Apter (2005) found that adolescent patients high in narcissism, self-oriented perfectionism (i.e., demanding perfection of oneself), and self-critical depression (i.e., the tendency to be critical of oneself, coupled with feelings of guilt, inferiority, and worthlessness) were prone to engage in severe suicidal behaviors. As such, clinicians should evaluate the role perfectionism plays in narcissistic patients' maladjustment and symptoms, including depression, suicidality, aggression, and social withdrawal.

Psychotherapy

There are several other challenges clinicians are likely to encounter when working with narcissistic patients, one of which is *narcissistic resistance*. According to Diamond, Yeomans, and Levy (2011), narcissistic patients often resent clinicians for "having the capacity for concern and caring, which bespeaks a level of wholeness and integration when the patient feels empty, fragmented, and worthless internally" (p. 427). A paradoxical situation is thereby created in which, to defend his or her self-esteem, the patient ignores, devalues, or denies any help or suggestion from the clinician because the person perceives the clinician as an ego threat. Thus, not only does the patient's narcissism make it difficult to build an alliance and move therapy forward (Ronningstam & Weinberg, 2013), it also increases the patient's likelihood of dropping out of therapy (Ellison et al., 2013). One way to help prevent early dropouts is for the clinician to avoid directly challenging or criticizing the patient's grandiosity too early in the treatment (Kealy & Ogrodniczuk, 2012; McWilliams, 2011).

Another difficult aspect of working with narcissistic patients is that they can arouse strong feelings of annoyance, anger, anxiety, resentment, and incompetence in the clinician, as well as feelings of being devalued, criticized, and unappreciated by the patient (Betan, Heim, Zittel Conklin, & Westen, 2005). Such experiences further interfere with the therapeutic alliance. However, these countertransference reactions may also be useful in identifying pathological narcissism (Gabbard, 2009). Such therapist reactions are particularly informative if they occur when a patient is presenting with depressed mood and anxiety, a clinical situation that more commonly evokes empathy and support (Pincus et al., 2014). These countertransference feelings may also provide the clinician with better insight into the feelings and thoughts that others may experience when interacting with the narcissistic patient.

CONCLUSIONS

Narcissism is a complex and broadly relevant dark personality trait that has been under study from multiple perspectives for more than a century. From Freud to the DSM–5 and ICD–10, from the bedroom to the boardroom, and from childhood through old age, narcissism has proven to be an important individual difference across disciplines. In the past decade, definitional conundrums and controversies have given way to a contemporary clinical model of pathological narcissism incorporating grandiosity and vulnerability that allows for a more unified approach to research (e.g., Miller et al., 2011; Pincus, 2013) and clinical practice (e.g., Ogrodniczuk, 2013). In contrast, NPD was first considered for deletion from the *DSM–5* and unfortunately its diagnostic criteria ultimately remain unchanged from the previous edition (American Psychiatric Association, 2013). We hope this chapter demonstrates that a contemporary clinical model of pathological narcissism should be prominently featured in future iterations of the *DSM* and *ICD*, dimensional conceptualizations of personality pathology, and interdisciplinary research in all domains where the dark side of personality is of interest.

REFERENCES

Ackerman, R. A., Witt, E. A., Donnellan, M. B., Trzesniewski, K. H., Robins, R. W., & Kashy, D. A. (2011). What does the narcissistic personality inventory really measure? *Assessment, 18*, 67–87. http://dx.doi.org/10.1177/1073191110382845

American Psychiatric Association. (2013). *Diagnostic and statistical manual of mental disorders* (5th ed.). Arlington, VA: Author.

Arie, M., Haruvi-Catalan, L., & Apter, A. (2005). Personality and suicidal behavior in adolescence. *Clinical Neuropsychiatry: Journal of Treatment Evaluation, 2*, 37–47.

Besser, A., & Priel, B. (2010). Grandiose narcissism versus vulnerable narcissism in threatening situations: Emotional reactions to achievement failure and interpersonal rejection. *Journal of Social and Clinical Psychology, 29*, 874–902. http://dx.doi.org/10.1521/jscp.2010.29.8.874

Besser, A., & Zeigler-Hill, V. (2010). The influence of pathological narcissism on emotional and motivational responses to negative events: The roles of visibility and concern about humiliation. *Journal of Research in Personality, 44*, 520–534. http://dx.doi.org/10.1016/j.jrp.2010.06.006

Besser, A., Zeigler-Hill, V., Pincus, A. L., & Neria, Y. (2013). Pathological narcissism and acute anxiety symptoms after trauma: A study of Israeli civilians exposed to war. *Psychiatry: Interpersonal and Biological Processes, 76*, 381–397. http://dx.doi.org/10.1521/psyc.2013.76.4.381

Betan, E., Heim, A. K., Zittel Conklin, C., & Westen, D. (2005). Countertransference phenomena and personality pathology in clinical practice: An empirical investigation. *The American Journal of Psychiatry, 162*, 890–898. http://dx.doi.org/10.1176/appi.ajp.162.5.890

Blasco-Fontecilla, H., Baca-Garcia, E., Duberstein, P., Perez-Rodriguez, M. M., Dervic, K., Saiz-Ruiz, J., . . . Oquendo, M. A. (2010). An exploratory study of the relationship between diverse life events and specific personality disorders in a sample of suicide attempters. *Journal of Personality Disorders, 24*, 773–784. http://dx.doi.org/10.1521/pedi.2010.24.6.773

Bresin, K., & Gordon, K. H. (2011). Characterizing pathological narcissism in terms of the HEXACO model of personality. *Journal of Psychopathology and Behavioral Assessment, 33,* 228–235. http://dx.doi.org/10.1007/s10862-010-9210-9

Brunell, A. B., Gentry, W. A., Campbell, W. K., Hoffman, B. J., Kuhnert, K. W., & Demarree, K. G. (2008). Leader emergence: The case of the narcissistic leader. *Personality and Social Psychology Bulletin, 34,* 1663–1676. http://dx.doi.org/10.1177/0146167208324101

Busch, F. N. (2009). Anger and depression. *Advances in Psychiatric Treatment, 15,* 271–278. http://dx.doi.org/10.1192/apt.bp.107.004937

Buss, D. M., & Chiodo, L. M. (1991). Narcissistic acts in everyday life. *Journal of Personality, 59,* 179–215. http://dx.doi.org/10.1111/j.1467-6494.1991.tb00773.x

Cain, N. M., Pincus, A. L., & Ansell, E. B. (2008). Narcissism at the crossroads: Phenotypic description of pathological narcissism across clinical theory, social/personality psychology, and psychiatric diagnosis. *Clinical Psychology Review, 28,* 638–656. http://dx.doi.org/10.1016/j.cpr.2007.09.006

Campbell, W. K., & Campbell, S. M. (2009). On the self-regulatory dynamics created by the peculiar benefits and costs of narcissism: A contextual reinforcement model and examination of leadership. *Self and Identity, 8,* 214–232. http://dx.doi.org/10.1080/15298860802505129

Campbell, W. K., Hoffman, B. J., Campbell, S. M., & Marchisio, G. (2011). Narcissism in organizational contexts. *Human Resource Management Review, 21,* 268–284.

Conroy, D. E., Elliot, A. J., & Thrash, T. M. (2009). Achievement motivation. In M. R. Leary & R. H. Hoyle (Eds.), *Handbook of individual differences in social behavior* (pp. 382–399). New York, NY: Guilford Press.

Diamond, D., Yeomans, F., & Levy, K. N. (2011). Psychodynamic psychotherapy for narcissistic personality. In W. K. Campbell & J. D. Miller (Eds.), *The handbook of narcissism and narcissistic personality disorder* (pp. 423–433). Hoboken, NJ: Wiley.

Dickinson, K. A., & Pincus, A. L. (2003). Interpersonal analysis of grandiose and vulnerable narcissism. *Journal of Personality Disorders, 17,* 188–207. http://dx.doi.org/10.1521/pedi.17.3.188.22146

Dimaggio, G., & Attinà, G. (2012). Metacognitive interpersonal therapy for narcissistic personality disorder and associated perfectionism. *Journal of Clinical Psychology, 68,* 922–934. http://dx.doi.org/10.1002/jclp.21896

Dowgwillo, E. A. (2014, June). *Dark Triad traits within and across interpersonal circumplex surfaces.* Paper presented at the annual meeting of the Society for Interpersonal Theory and Research, New Haven, CT.

Ellison, W. D., Levy, K. N., Cain, N. M., Ansell, E. B., & Pincus, A. L. (2013). The impact of pathological narcissism on psychotherapy utilization, initial symptom severity, and early-treatment symptom change: A naturalistic investigation. *Journal of Personality Assessment, 95,* 291–300. http://dx.doi.org/10.1080/00223891.2012.742904

Freud, S. (1957). On narcissism: An introduction. In J. Strachey (Ed. & Trans), *The standard edition of the complete psychological works of Sigmund Freud* (Vol. 7, pp. 66–102). London, England: Hogarth. (Original work published 1914)

Gabbard, G. O. (2009). Transference and countertransference: Developments in the treatment of narcissistic personality disorder. *Psychiatric Annals, 39,* 129–136. http://dx.doi.org/10.3928/00485713-20090301-03

Goldberg, B. R., Serper, M. R., Sheets, M., Beech, D., Dill, C., & Duffy, K. G. (2007). Predictors of aggression on the psychiatric inpatient service: Self-esteem, narcissism, and theory of mind deficits. *Journal of Nervous and Mental Disease, 195,* 436–442.

Grijalva, E., Harms, P. D., Newman, D. A., Gaddis, B. H., & Fraley, R. C. (2015). Narcissism and leadership: A meta-analytic review of linear and nonlinear relationships in personnel psychology. *Personnel Psychology, 68,* 1–47.

Hepper, E. G., Gramzow, R. H., & Sedikides, C. (2010). Individual differences in self-enhancement and self-protection strategies: An integrative analysis. *Journal of Personality, 78,* 781–814. http://dx.doi.org/10.1111/j.1467-6494.2010.00633.x

Hopwood, C. J., Ansell, E. B., Pincus, A. L., Wright, A. G. C., Lukowitsky, M. R., & Roche, M. J. (2011). The circumplex structure of interpersonal sensitivities. *Journal of Personality, 79,* 707–740. http://dx.doi.org/10.1111/j.1467-6494.2011.00696.x

Hopwood, C. J., Pincus, A. L., DeMoor, R. M., & Koonce, E. A. (2008). Psychometric characteristics of the Inventory of Interpersonal Problems—Short Circumplex (IIP–SC) with college students. *Journal of Personality Assessment, 90,* 615–618. http://dx.doi.org/10.1080/00223890802388665

Kealy, D., & Ogrodniczuk, J. S. (2012). Pathological narcissism: A front-line guide. *Practice: Social Work in Action, 24,* 161–174. http://dx.doi.org/10.1080/09503153.2012.679255

Kealy, D., Tsai, M., & Ogrodniczuk, J. S. (2012). Depressive tendencies and pathological narcissism among psychiatric outpatients. *Psychiatry Research, 196,* 157–159. http://dx.doi.org/10.1016/j.psychres.2011.08.023

Kernberg, O. F. (2010). Narcissistic personality disorder. In J. F. Clarkin, P. Fonagy, & G. O. Gabbard (Eds.), *Psychodynamic psychotherapy for personality disorders: A clinical handbook* (pp. 257–287). Washington, DC: American Psychiatric Press.

Kohut, H. (1971). *The analysis of the self.* New York, NY: International Universities Press.

Kohut, H., & Wolf, E. S. (1978). The disorders of the self and their treatment: An outline. *The International Journal of Psychoanalysis, 59,* 413–425.

Krizan, Z., & Johar, O. (2012). Envy divides the two faces of narcissism. *Journal of Personality, 80,* 1415–1451. http://dx.doi.org/10.1111/j.1467-6494.2012.00767.x

Lahey, B. B. (2009). Public health significance of neuroticism. *American Psychologist, 64,* 241–256. http://dx.doi.org/10.1037/a0015309

Links, P. S. (2013). Pathological narcissism and the risk of suicide. In J. S. Ogrodniczuk (Ed.), *Understanding and treating pathological narcissism* (pp. 167–182). Washington, DC: American Psychological Association. http://dx.doi.org/10.1037/14041-010

Links, P. S., & Prakash, A. (2014). Strategic issues in the psychotherapy of patients with narcissistic pathology. *Journal of Contemporary Psychotherapy, 44,* 97–107. http://dx.doi.org/10.1007/s10879-013-9258-4

Lizdek, I., Sadler, P., Woody, E., Ethier, N., & Malet, G. (2012). Capturing the stream of behavior: A computer-joystick method for coding interpersonal behavior continuously over time. *Social Science Computer Review, 30,* 513–521. http://dx.doi.org/10.1177/0894439312436487

Lobbestael, J., Baumeister, R. F., Fiebig, T., & Eckel, L. A. (2014). The role of grandiose and vulnerable narcissism in self-reported and laboratory aggression and testosterone reactivity. *Personality and Individual Differences, 69,* 22–27. http://dx.doi.org/10.1016/j.paid.2014.05.007

Maltsberger, J. T. (1998). Pathological narcissism and self-regulatory processes in suicidal states. In E. Ronningstam (Ed.), *Disorders of narcissism: Diagnostic, clinical, and empirical implications* (pp. 327–344). Washington, DC: American Psychiatric Press.

Marčinko, D., Jakšić, N., Ivezić, E., Skočić, M., Surányi, Z., Lončar, M., . . . Jakovljevič, M. (2014). Pathological narcissism and depressive symptoms in psychiatric outpatients: Mediating role of dysfunctional attitudes. *Journal of Clinical Psychology, 70,* 341–352. http://dx.doi.org/10.1002/jclp.22033

McWilliams, N. (2011). *Psychoanalytic diagnosis* (2nd ed.). New York, NY: Guilford Press.

Mehl, M., & Conner, T. (Eds.). (2012). *Handbook of research methods for studying daily life.* New York, NY: Guilford Press.

Ménard, K. S., & Pincus, A. L. (2012). Predicting overt and cyber stalking perpetration by male and female college students. *Journal of Interpersonal Violence, 27,* 2183–2207. http://dx.doi.org/10.1177/0886260511432144

Miller, J. D., & Campbell, W. K. (2008). Comparing clinical and social-personality conceptualizations of narcissism. *Journal of Personality, 76,* 449–476. http://dx.doi.org/10.1111/j.1467-6494.2008.00492.x

Miller, J. D., Dir, A., Gentile, B., Wilson, L., Pryor, L. R., & Campbell, W. K. (2010). Searching for a vulnerable Dark Triad: Comparing Factor 2 psychopathy, vulnerable narcissism, and borderline personality disorder. *Journal of Personality, 78,* 1529–1564. http://dx.doi.org/10.1111/j.1467-6494.2010.00660.x

Miller, J. D., Hoffman, B. J., Gaughan, E. T., Gentile, B., Maples, J., & Campbell, W. K. (2011). Grandiose and vulnerable narcissism: A nomological network analysis. *Journal of Personality, 79,* 1013–1042. http://dx.doi.org/10.1111/j.1467-6494.2010.00711.x

Miller, J. D., & Maples, J. (2012). Trait personality models of narcissistic personality disorder, grandiose narcissism, and vulnerable narcissism. In W. K. Campbell

& J. D. Miller (Eds.), *Handbook of narcissism and narcissistic personality disorders* (pp. 71–88). Hoboken, NJ: Wiley. http://dx.doi.org/10.1002/9781118093108.ch7

Morf, C. C. (2006). Personality reflected in a coherent idiosyncratic interplay of intra- and interpersonal self-regulatory processes. *Journal of Personality, 74*, 1527–1556. http://dx.doi.org/10.1111/j.1467-6494.2006.00419.x

Morf, C. C., Horvath, S., & Torchetti, T. (2011). Narcissistic self-enhancement: Tales of (successful?) self-portrayal. In M. D. Alicke & C. Sedikides (Eds.), *Handbook of self-enhancement and self-protection* (pp. 399–424). New York, NY: Guilford Press.

Morf, C. C., & Rhodewalt, F. (2001). Unraveling the paradoxes of narcissism: A dynamic self-regulatory processing model. *Psychological Inquiry, 12*, 177–196. http://dx.doi.org/10.1207/S15327965PLI1204_1

Morf, C. C., Torchetti, T., & Schürch, E. (2012). Narcissism from the perspective of the dynamic self-regulatory processing model. In W. K. Campbell & J. D. Miller (Eds.), *Handbook of narcissism and narcissistic personality disorder* (pp. 56–70). Hoboken, NJ: Wiley. http://dx.doi.org/10.1002/9781118093108.ch6

Ogrodniczuk, J. S. (Ed.). (2013). *Understanding and treating pathological narcissism*. Washington, DC: American Psychological Association. http://dx.doi.org/10.1037/14041-000

Ogrodniczuk, J. S., Piper, W. E., Joyce, A. S., Steinberg, P. I., & Duggal, S. (2009). Interpersonal problems associated with narcissism among psychiatric out-patients. *Journal of Psychiatric Research, 43*, 837–842. http://dx.doi.org/10.1016/j.jpsychires.2008.12.005

Oltmanns, T. F., Friedman, J. N. W., Fiedler, E. R., & Turkheimer, E. (2004). Perceptions of people with personality disorders based on thin slices of behavior. *Journal of Research in Personality, 38*, 216–229. http://dx.doi.org/10.1016/S0092-6566(03)00066-7

Paulhus, D. L. (1998). Interpersonal and intrapsychic adaptiveness of trait self-enhancement: A mixed blessing? *Journal of Personality and Social Psychology, 74*, 1197–1208. http://dx.doi.org/10.1037/0022-3514.74.5.1197

Pincus, A. L. (2013). The Pathological Narcissism Inventory. In J. Ogrodniczuk (Ed.), *Understanding and treating pathological narcissism* (pp. 93–110). Washington, DC: American Psychological Association. http://dx.doi.org/10.1037/14041-006

Pincus, A. L., Ansell, E. B., Pimentel, C. A., Cain, N. M., Wright, A. G., & Levy, K. N. (2009). Initial construction and validation of the Pathological Narcissism Inventory. *Psychological Assessment, 21*, 365–379. http://dx.doi.org/10.1037/a0016530

Pincus, A. L., Cain, N. M., & Wright, A. G. C. (2014). Narcissistic grandiosity and narcissistic vulnerability in psychotherapy. *Personality Disorders: Theory, Research, and Treatment, 5*, 439–443. http://dx.doi.org/10.1037/per0000031

Pincus, A. L., Conroy, D. E., Hyde, A. L., & Ram, N. (2010, May). *Pathological narcissism and the dynamics of self-conscious emotions*. Paper presented at the Association for Psychological Science Annual Convention, Boston, MA.

Pincus, A. L., & Lukowitsky, M. R. (2010). Pathological narcissism and narcissistic personality disorder. *Annual Review of Clinical Psychology, 6*, 421–446. http://dx.doi.org/10.1146/annurev.clinpsy.121208.131215

Pincus, A. L., & Roche, M. J. (2011). Narcissistic grandiosity and narcissistic vulnerability. In W. K. Campbell & J. D. Miller (Eds.), *Handbook of narcissism and narcissistic personality disorder* (pp. 31–40). Hoboken, NJ: Wiley.

Pincus, A. L., Roche, M. J., & Good, E. W. (2015). Narcissistic personality disorder and pathological narcissism. In P. H. Blaney, R. F. Krueger, & T. Millon (Eds.), *Oxford textbook of psychopathology* (3rd ed., pp. 791–814). New York, NY: Oxford University Press. http://dx.doi.org/10.1146/annurev.clinpsy.121208.131215

Ram, N., Conroy, D. E., Pincus, A. L., Lorek, A., Rebar, A. L., Roche, M. J., & Gerstorf, D. (2014). Examining the interplay of processes across multiple timescales: Illustration with the Intraindividual Study of Affect, Health, and Interpersonal Behavior (iSAHIB). *Research in Human Development, 11*, 142–160. http://dx.doi.org/10.1080/15427609.2014.906739

Raskin, R., & Hall, C. S. (1981). The Narcissistic Personality Inventory: Alternative form reliability and further evidence of construct validity. *Journal of Personality Assessment, 45*, 159–162. http://dx.doi.org/10.1207/s15327752jpa4502_10

Reidy, D. E., Foster, J. D., & Zeichner, A. (2010). Narcissism and unprovoked aggression. *Aggressive Behavior, 36*, 414–422. http://dx.doi.org/10.1002/ab.20356

Rhodewalt, F., & Eddings, S. K. (2002). Narcissus reflects: Memory distortion in response to ego-relevant feedback among high- and low-narcissistic men. *Journal of Research in Personality, 36*, 97–116. http://dx.doi.org/10.1006/jrpe.2002.2342

Rhodewalt, F., & Morf, C. (1995). Self and interpersonal correlates of the Narcissistic Personality Inventory: A review and new findings. *Journal of Research in Personality, 29*, 1–23. http://dx.doi.org/10.1006/jrpe.1995.1001

Roche, M. J., Pincus, A. L., Lukowitsky, M. R., Ménard, K. S., & Conroy, D. E. (2013). An integrative approach to the assessment of narcissism. *Journal of Personality Assessment, 95*, 237–248. http://dx.doi.org/10.1080/00223891.2013.770400

Roche, M. J., Pincus, A. L., Rebar, A. L., Conroy, D. E., & Ram, N. (2014). Enriching psychological assessment using a person-specific analysis of interpersonal processes in daily life. *Assessment, 21*, 515–528. http://dx.doi.org/10.1177/1073191114540320

Ronningstam, E. F. (2005). *Identifying and understanding the narcissistic personality.* New York, NY: Oxford University Press.

Ronningstam, E. F. (2009). Narcissistic personality disorder: Facing *DSM–5*. *Psychiatric Annals, 39*, 111–121. http://dx.doi.org/10.3928/00485713-20090301-09

Ronningstam, E. F., & Maltsberger, J. T. (1998). Pathological narcissism and sudden suicide-related collapse. *Suicide and Life-Threatening Behavior, 28*, 261–271.

Ronningstam, E. F., & Weinberg, I. (2013). Contributing factors to suicide in narcissistic personalities. *Directions in Psychiatry, 29*, 317–329.

Russ, E., Shedler, J., Bradley, R., & Westen, D. (2008). Refining the construct of narcissistic personality disorder: Diagnostic criteria and subtypes. *The*

American Journal of Psychiatry, 165, 1473–1481. http://dx.doi.org/10.1176/ appi.ajp.2008.07030376

Samuel, D. B., & Widiger, T. A. (2008). Convergence of narcissism measures from the perspective of general personality functioning. *Assessment, 15,* 364–374. http://dx.doi.org/10.1177/1073191108314278

Saulsman, L. M., & Page, A. C. (2004). The five-factor model and personality disorder empirical literature: A meta-analytic review. *Clinical Psychology Review, 23,* 1055–1085. http://dx.doi.org/10.1016/j.cpr.2002.09.001

Schnure, K. A. (2010, April). *Narcissism levels and ratings of executive leadership potential.* Paper presented at the Annual Conference of the Society for Industrial and Organizational Psychology, Atlanta, GA.

Sedikides, C., Rudich, E. A., Gregg, A. P., Kumashiro, M., & Rusbult, C. (2004). Are normal narcissists psychologically healthy? Self-esteem matters. *Journal of Personality and Social Psychology, 87,* 400–416. http://dx.doi.org/10.1037/ 0022-3514.87.3.400

Tamborski, M., & Brown, R. P. (2012). The measurement of trait narcissism in social-personality research. In W. K. Campbell & J. D. Miller (Eds.), *Handbook of narcissism and narcissistic personality disorder* (pp. 133–140). New York, NY: Guilford Press. http://dx.doi.org/10.1002/9781118093108.ch11

Tritt, S. M., Ryder, A. G., Ring, A. J., & Pincus, A. L. (2010). Pathological narcissism and the depressive temperament. *Journal of Affective Disorders, 122,* 280–284. http://dx.doi.org/10.1016/j.jad.2009.09.006

Turiano, N. A., Pitzer, L., Armour, C., Karlamangla, A., Ryff, C. D., & Mroczek, D. K. (2012). Personality trait level and change as predictors of health outcomes: Findings from a national study of Americans (MIDUS). *The Journals of Gerontology: Series B, Psychological Sciences and Social Sciences, 67,* 4–12. http:// dx.doi.org/10.1093/geronb/gbr072

Wallace, H. M., & Baumeister, R. F. (2002). The performance of narcissists rises and falls with perceived opportunity for glory. *Journal of Personality and Social Psychology, 82,* 819–834. http://dx.doi.org/10.1037/0022-3514.82.5.819

Widman, L., & McNulty, J. K. (2010). Sexual narcissism and the perpetration of sexual aggression. *Archives of Sexual Behavior, 39,* 926–939. http://dx.doi.org/ 10.1007/s10508-008-9461-7

World Health Organization. (1992). *International statistical classification of diseases and related health problems* (10th rev.). Geneva, Switzerland: Author.

Zeigler-Hill, V., & Besser, A. (2013). A glimpse behind the mask: Facets of narcissism and feelings of self-worth. *Journal of Personality Assessment, 95,* 249–260. http:// dx.doi.org/10.1080/00223891.2012.717150

Zeigler-Hill, V., Green, B. A., Arnau, R. C., Sisemore, T. B., & Myers, E. M. (2011). Trouble ahead, trouble behind: Narcissism and early maladaptive schemas. *Journal of Behavior Therapy and Experimental Psychiatry, 42,* 96–103. http://dx.doi.org/ 10.1016/j.jbtep.2010.07.004

2

CONTEMPORARY CONCEPTUALIZATIONS OF CALLOUS PERSONALITY FEATURES FROM CHILDHOOD TO ADULTHOOD

DUSTIN A. PARDINI AND JAMES V. RAY

Callous personality features are characterized by an indifference to the pain and suffering of others, a lack of remorse and guilt, blunted emotional responsivity, and a failure to develop close emotional bonds with others (Hare & Neumann, 2008). In antisocial populations, these features represent a core affective component of psychopathy, which is conceptualized as a multi-faceted personality disorder that also includes an interrelated set of inter-personal (e.g., superficial charm, manipulative) and behavioral (e.g., impulsive, irresponsible) features (Hare & Neumann, 2008; Skeem & Cooke, 2010). Although extensive research has been conducted on the higher order person-ality construct of psychopathy, much of the research on callousness is focused on children and youth, so the purpose of the current chapter is to provide a brief overview of the following: (a) contemporary research documenting the importance of callous features for delineating children and adults at high risk for engaging in chronic and severe criminal behavior, (b) studies examining

http://dx.doi.org/10.1037/14854-003
The Dark Side of Personality: Science and Practice in Social, Personality, and Clinical Psychology, V. Zeigler-Hill and D. K. Marcus (Editors)

the developmental continuity of callous features from childhood to adulthood, (c) select research concerning the etiological factors linked to the early emergence and change in callous features over time, and (d) studies examining the effectiveness of interventions with youth and adults exhibiting callous features. Future directions for research on callous personality features are discussed in the context of limitations within the existing literature.

DEFINITION AND BACKGROUND

Features of callousness in adults have been described as a core dimension of a higher order psychopathic personality construct in adults since Cleckley's foundational conceptualization of the disorder in the early 1940s (Cleckley, 1976). Factor analyses with various measures have consistently delineated callousness as a distinct facet of the disorder (Hawes, Mulvey, Schubert, & Pardini, 2014; Patrick, Fowles, & Krueger, 2009). Studies examining these features in adults have relied on a diverse array of scales, including the Affective subscale of the Psychopathy Checklist—Revised (Hare, 2003), the Coldheartedness subscale of the Psychopathic Personality Inventory (Lilienfeld & Widows, 2005), the Callous Affect subscale of the Self-Report Psychopathy Scale—III (Paulhus, Neumann, & Hare, in press), and the Meanness subscale of the Triarchic Personality Measure (Patrick, 2010). These measures differ in their coverage of the callousness construct and method of assessment, which may account for the fact that the measures tend to exhibit low to moderate intercorrelations in adults (Derefinko & Lynam, 2006; Neumann, Hare, & Pardini, 2014; Neumann & Pardini, 2014).

In children and adolescents, behaviors consistent with an emerging callous personality have also been recognized as important for understanding the development of severe conduct problems. More than three decades ago, an undersocialized subtype of conduct disorder (CD) was added to the third edition of the *Diagnostic and Statistical Manual of Mental Disorders* (*DSM–III*; American Psychiatric Association, 1980), which included "a lack of concern for the feelings, wishes and well-being of others, as shown by callous behavior" (p. 44). The subtype was believed to delineate youth whose conduct problems emerged in early childhood due to severe familial dysfunction who were at high risk for developing adult antisocial personality disorder (American Psychiatric Association, 1980). However, the evidence base supporting the clinical utility of the subtyping scheme was weak, leading to its eventual elimination during the transition to *DSM–IV* (Pardini, Frick, & Moffitt, 2010).

After the removal of the undersocialized subtyping scheme, the study of callous features in youth continued as investigators increasingly attempted to extend the concept of adult psychopathy downwardly to children. This effort included developing parent and teacher rating scales to reliably assess "callous-unemotional" (CU) traits in youth. One of the earliest and most widely used assessment tools developed for this purpose is the Antisocial Processes Screening Device (Frick & Hare, 2001). Modified versions of this instrument were subsequently developed for use in preschool-age children as young as age 3 (Dadds, Fraser, Frost, & Hawes, 2005). In addition, various measures containing scales measuring callous personality features were created for use with adolescence, such as the Youth Psychopathy Inventory (Andershed, Kerr, Stattin, & Levander, 2002) and the Psychopathy Checklist—Youth Version (PCL–YV; Forth, Kosson, & Hare, 2003). Similar to studies conducted with adults, factor analytic studies indicate that callous personality features assessed using these various methods can be reliably distinguished from symptoms of disruptive behavior disorders and other features of psychopathy (Dadds et al., 2005; Fite, Greening, Stoppelbein, & Fabiano, 2009; Frick, Bodin, & Barry, 2000).

REVIEW OF THE RELEVANT LITERATURE

Callousness and Normative Dimensions of Adult Personality

A growing number of studies within the adult literature have begun examining the extent to which callousness (and other pathological aspects of adult personality) can be seen as an extreme variant of normative personality features. Studies in this area have helped to clarify whether existing measures of normal personality dimensions capture key features of callousness, helping to place callousness research within the context of a broader literature on personality development (Lynam & Derefinko, 2006). Most of these studies have examined the association between psychopathic features and dimensions of the five-factor model of personality (Lynam & Derefinko, 2006), which includes agreeableness (e.g., compliant, altruistic, tender-mindedness), conscientiousness (e.g., competent, orderly, dutiful), neuroticism (e.g., anxious, angry, self-conscious), extraversion (e.g., warm, assertive, sociable), and openness to experience (e.g., imaginative, aesthetic). Across these studies, callousness has been consistently negatively associated with the higher order personality dimension of agreeableness and its constituent facets indexing trustfulness, straightforwardness, altruism, compliance, modesty, and tender-mindedness (Hall et al., 2014; Latzman, Vaidya, Malikina, Berg, & Lilienfeld, 2014; Poy, Segarra, Esteller, López, & Moltó, 2014; Sherman, Lynam, & Heyde, 2014). More nuanced associations have been found when examining associations between callousness and specific facets of the four other higher order personality dimensions. Specifically, callousness tends to be positively associated with anger/hostility (neuroticism) and negatively associated with interpersonal warmth (extraversion), positive emotions (extraversion), feelings (openness to experience), values (openness to experience), and dutifulness (conscientiousness) across various community samples (Hall et al., 2014; Latzman et al., 2014; Poy et al., 2014; Sherman et al., 2014).

Stability and Change in Callousness Across Development

The downward extension of adult psychopathic traits such as callousness to children has raised critical issues about the continuity of these features across development. These issues include examining to what extent features of callousness remain relatively stable during early childhood and adolescence, as well as determining whether these features delineate youth at risk for exhibiting the affective features of adult psychopathy. In terms of the former, most existing longitudinal studies indicate that the rank order stability of callous personality features is moderate to high across 1- to 4-year temporal lags in childhood and adolescence when assessed using parent- and teacher-report rating scales (for a review, see Andershed, 2010), and the magnitude of these stability estimates are similar to those reported for other measures of temperament and adult personality (Roberts & DelVecchio, 2000). However, one longitudinal study found relatively modest stability estimates for parent ($r = .32$) and teacher ($r = .27$) ratings of CU traits in a general population sample of twins followed from ages 7 to 12 (Viding, Fontaine, Oliver, & Plomin, 2009), with approximately half of those children initially high on CU exhibiting precipitous declines in these features over time (Fontaine, McCrory, Boivin, Moffitt, & Viding, 2011).

The few longitudinal studies that have examined the stability of callousness from adolescence into early adulthood suggest that these features also show low-moderate to moderate levels of rank-order stability (Andershed, 2010; Hawes, Mulvey, et al., 2014). The most comprehensive study conducted to date examined the stability of self-reported callousness among a large group of male adolescent offenders assessed annually from age 17 to 23. Self-reported callous personality ratings exhibited moderate stability across 1-year temporal lags ($rs = .38–.52$), and slightly lower stability from age 17 to 23 ($r = .34$). In comparison, longitudinal studies of normative personality have typically reported higher test–retest correlations ($\sim.40–.60$) across periods of up to 8 to 10 years (Roberts, Walton, & Viechtbauer, 2006). The lower stability of callousness may have arisen in part because some adolescents began desisting from serious offending into adulthood and increasingly adopted prosocial roles. These life changes may have been coupled with a shift in self-concept, particularly as it relates to deviant personality features.

There are currently no studies that have explicitly examined the stability of callous personality features across multiple years in middle or late adulthood. However, one longitudinal study reported that the interpersonal and affective features of psychopathy measured using the PCL–R were moderately stable (males intraclass correlation coefficient [ICC] = .43; females ICC = .63) among a group of middle-aged methadone patients followed over a 2-year period (Rutherford, Cacciola, Alterman, McKay, & Cook, 1999). This finding suggests that changes in callous personality features may continue into late adulthood or be difficult to assess reliably.

Developmental Origins of Callousness Personality Features

In conjunction with studies examining the stability of callousness, there has been an increased interest in identifying factors that lead to the early emergence and subsequent persistence of callousness over time. Evidence from twin studies indicates that there is a significant heritable component to callous personality features in children, adolescent, and adult samples (Blonigen, Carlson, Krueger, & Patrick, 2003; Frick, Ray, Thornton, & Kahn, 2014; Viding et al., 2013). There is also some developmental evidence indicating that the stability of callousness from childhood to adolescence may be highly heritable in boys but more strongly influenced by environmental factors in girls (Fontaine, Rijsdijk, McCrory, & Viding, 2010). Studies attempting to identify the specific genes responsible for the heritability of callousness have generally produced inconsistent findings, although emerging evidence suggests that genes regulating the hormone oxytocin may be important (Dadds, Moul, et al., 2014; Herpers, Scheepers, Bons, Buitelaar, & Rommelse, 2014; Viding et al., 2013).

A large number of studies have found evidence that the development of callous personality features may be influenced in part by neurobiological deficits in various aspects of social and affective processing (Blair, 2010; Herpers et al., 2014). Although numerous neurobiological abnormalities have been implicated in the emergence and persistence of callousness (Blair, 2010; Herpers et al., 2014), developmental studies have consistently indicated that infants and children with a relatively fearless temperament tend to have difficulties developing moral emotions such as empathy and guilt/remorse (see Pardini & Byrd, 2013, for a review). Children with low fearfulness are posited to experience a lack of autonomic arousal when punished for misbehavior, reducing the likelihood that they will internalize parental messages about rules for appropriate conduct (Kochanska, 1997). The repeated experience of fearful arousal in the context of disciplinary interactions is also believed to condition youth to experience affective discomfort when considering or engaging in misconduct even in the absence of an authority figure, which is a core feature of guilt and remorse (Pardini & Byrd, 2013). Consistent with this developmental model, children with early features of callousness tend to be less responsive to punishment while engaged in a goal-directed card-playing task (Blair, Colledge, & Mitchell, 2001; Frick, Cornell, et al., 2003; O'Brien & Frick, 1996) and report less concern about being punished for aggressive behavior (Jones, Happé, Gilbert, Burnett, & Viding, 2010; Pardini, Lochman, & Frick, 2003). In addition, cross-sectional evidence suggests that the association between low fearfulness and CU traits in incarcerated adolescents is mediated by a lack of concern about being punished (Pardini, 2006).

A distinct, yet related, set of studies has postulated that relatively fearless children have an impaired ability to recognize distress cues in others, which places them at risk for developing CU traits (Marsh & Blair, 2008). According to the violence inhibition model, humans possess a basic neural system that responds to cues of distress in others (particularly fearful and sad faces) by initiating increased attention, behavioral freezing, and aversive arousal (Blair, 2001). As a result, normally developing children learn to avoid initiating violent behavior because the fearful distress it produces in the victim is repeatedly paired with aversive arousal in the perpetrator. Children with CU traits are believed to have subtle neurological impairments in limbic brain regions (particularly the amygdala) that limit their ability to recognize and become aroused by fearful distress cues in others (Blair, 2005). Consistent with this conceptualization, children and adolescents exhibiting CU traits have difficulty recognizing fearful distress cues in others (Marsh & Blair, 2008), in part because of a failure to attend to the eye region of the face (Dadds et al., 2006). Functional neuroimaging studies with children, adolescents and adults have also found that callousness is associated with lower neural reactivity to fearful distress cues in others within the cortico-limbic network that includes the amygdala (for a review, see Blair, 2010).

Although many studies have stressed the importance of neurobiological deficits in the development of callous personality features, early parenting behaviors associated with a warm and nurturing parent–child relationship may also be important. For example, developmental studies have found that infants who are exposed to high levels of parental warmth and responsiveness show increased levels of empathic responding (Kiang, Moreno, & Robinson, 2004) and guilt (Kochanska, Forman, Aksan, & Dunbar, 2005) in childhood. Longitudinal evidence also indicates that children exposed to high levels of positive parental reinforcement and involvement tend to be more likely to exhibit reductions in CU traits over time (Frick, Kimonis, Dandreaux, & Farell, 2003). Similarly, there is evidence suggesting that a warm/involved parent–child relationship may protect aggressive children with low anxiety from developing CU traits (Pardini, Lochman, & Powell, 2007) and buffer children with high CU traits from developing serious conduct problems (Kroneman, Hipwell, Loeber, Koot, & Pardini, 2011; Pasalich, Dadds, Hawes,

& Brennan, 2011). However, parents may have difficulties developing a strong emotional bond with children exhibiting CU traits because these youth exhibit impaired eye contact during both free interactions and emotional discussions with attachment figures (Dadds, Allen, et al., 2014; Dadds et al., 2012).

ADAPTIVE AND MALADAPTIVE FEATURES

Callousness and Antisocial Behavior in Youth and Adults

A large number of longitudinal studies have found that callous personality features can help to distinguish a subgroup of children and adolescents who are at high risk for exhibiting persistent conduct problems, future violence, and repeated offending (Frick et al., 2014). Importantly, callous personality features remain associated with these outcomes after controlling for co-occurring behaviors consistent with conduct disorder, which indicates that these features provide unique prognostic information about the developmental course of antisocial behavior in youth. However, it is important to note that studies examining self-report and interviewer-rated measures of callousness in adolescents (as opposed to parent and teacher report) have found less consistent evidence that these features predict future offending, particularly after controlling for the other facets of psychopathy (Cauffman, Kimonis, Dmitrieva, & Monahan, 2009; Spain, Douglas, Poythress, & Epstein, 2004).

As a result of this body of work, a "with limited prosocial emotions" specifier for CD was included in the fifth edition of the DSM (DSM–5; American Psychiatric Association, 2013), and these features will likely be added as a qualifier for oppositional defiant disorder, conduct-dissocial disorder, and intermittent explosive disorder in the eleventh revision of the International Classification of Diseases (ICD; Lochman, Burke, & Pardini, in press). In the DSM–5, symptoms for the specifier include the following: (a) a lack of remorse or guilt, (b) a lack of empathy, (c) a lack of concern about performance, and (d) shallow or deficient affect. To meet criteria for the specifier, youth with CD must exhibit two of four symptoms for at least 12 months and in more than one relationship or setting. This specific symptom threshold was supported by analyses indicating that it consistently identified a subgroup of CD youth in community and clinic samples with high levels of aggressive and cruel behaviors (Kahn, Frick, Youngstrom, Findling, & Youngstrom, 2012). However, the few longitudinal studies that have examined the predictive utility of the categorical specifier have found mixed results. Specifically, one longitudinal study found that girls ages 6 to 8 who met criteria for childhood-onset CD and the CU specifier exhibited more bullying behaviors and more severe CD symptoms at a 6-year follow-up than girls with childhood-onset CD alone

(Pardini, Stepp, Hipwell, Stouthamer-Loeber, & Loeber, 2012). However, another study with adolescents indicated that 89% of those youth who met criteria for CD and the CU specifier (8 out of 9) went on to exhibit antisocial behavior into adulthood compared with 82% of adolescents with CD only (65 of 79), which is a nonsignificant difference (McMahon, Witkiewitz, Kotler, & the Conduct Problems Prevention Research Group, 2010).

A callous lack of remorse for mistreating others is included as a symptom of antisocial personality disorder in *DSM–5* (American Psychiatric Association, 2013), and callousness toward others and an incapacity to feel guilt are included as two symptoms of dissocial personality disorder in the 10th revision of the *ICD* (World Health Organization, 1992). Although several studies have linked callous personality features with severe and persistent antisocial behavior in adults, it is less clear whether these features help to delineate adult offenders who are at increased risk for committing future crime after controlling other antisocial and psychopathic personality features. Meta-analytic evidence from studies on the PCL–R have found that the behavioral features of psychopathy tend to be stronger predictors of future institutional misconduct, violent offending, and recidivism compared with the interpersonal/affective dimensions (Leistico, Salekin, DeCoster, & Rogers, 2008). For example, a recent study of convicted male offenders found that the callous and unemotional dimension of psychopathy was not significantly associated with a risk for recidivism after controlling for the other psychopathy dimensions (Olver, Neumann, Wong, & Hare, 2013). Others have found that the affective features of psychopathy did not incrementally contribute to the prediction of future aggression among adults in an impatient forensic facility (Vitacco et al., 2009). Evidence from a longitudinal community sample of men indicated that callousness was associated with an increased likelihood of being charged with a serious criminal offense across a 3-year follow-up, even after controlling for a prior history of criminal behavior and several other indicators of offending risk (Kahn, Byrd, & Pardini, 2013; Vitacco, Neumann, & Pardini, 2014). However, this association was reduced to marginal significance after controlling for the other dimensions of psychopathy (Vitacco et al., 2014). In contrast to these findings, one longitudinal study reported that callous personality features were associated with future aggressive and violent behavior among discharged civil psychiatric inpatients even after controlling for the other facets of psychopathy (Vitacco, Neumann, & Jackson, 2005). Although these studies collectively suggest that callous personality features may provide little incremental predictive utility beyond other features of psychopathy in adulthood, many have assessed future criminal offending using official records. Given that a large portion of criminal behavior goes undetected by the police, it remains unclear whether callous personality features may help to delineate chronic offenders who are able to avoid detection.

Callousness As a Protective Factor Against Stress and Anxiety

Some have suggested that callousness may be an adaptive response to harsh environmental conditions including exposure to violence and victimization (Kimonis, Frick, Munoz, & Aucoin, 2008). That is, individuals may develop a blunted emotional response to traumatic events as a coping mechanism to deal with the harsh realities of their environment. Similarly, both youth and adults who engage in antisocial behavior often encounter and produce adverse life events (e.g., conflicted relationships, criminal justice involvement, occupational/financial instability), which can lead to increased levels of stress and anxiety (Frick et al., 2014). Some evidence suggests that callousness might actually insulate individuals from experiencing emotional distress in response to these life experiences. For example, one study found that young girls with conduct disorder and high callousness did not tend to have comorbid anxiety problems, unlike girls with conduct disorder alone (Pardini et al., 2012). Moreover, longitudinal evidence suggests that boys with callous personality features may be protected from developing internalizing problems over time (Pardini & Fite, 2010), and some studies have reported an inverse relationship between callousness and suicidality in male and female offenders (Douglas et al., 2008; Verona, Hicks, & Patrick, 2005).

DIRECTIONS FOR FUTURE RESEARCH

In light of the foregoing review, there are several notable gaps in the research that warrant future consideration. To start, few studies have examined race/ethnic or gender differences in callousness. For instance, research has been somewhat inconclusive regarding the ethnic differences in emotional processing deficits underlying callousness (Kimonis, Frick, Fazekas, & Loney, 2006; Kimonis et al., 2008; Kosson, Smith, & Newman, 1990). In terms of gender, some evidence suggests that environmental factors may be more important in the development of callousness in girls (Fontaine et al., 2010), and the association between callousness and antisocial outcomes may vary by gender (Rogstad & Rogers, 2008). There is also a need to better delineate the core neural deficits that may be driving the emergence and persistence of callous personality features across development, particularly because an extensive array of functional and structural abnormalities have been reported in the literature. It is likely that there are multiple neurobiological and environmental pathways to the development of callous features, and longitudinal studies are essential for understanding how these factors interact to influence stability and change in callousness at different points in development. Several issues regarding the measurement of callousness must also be addressed, including the relatively modest correlations across divergent measures of callousness and the relatively low agreement across multiple informants.

CLINICAL IMPLICATIONS

There has been long-standing speculation that existing treatments may not be effective for children and adults exhibiting high levels of antisocial behavior and callous personality features (Hawes, Price, & Dadds, 2014; Salekin, 2002). This hypothesis has led to a growing number of studies examining whether children with CU traits exhibit poorer responsiveness to empirically supported psychosocial treatments, as well as whether these treatments can facilitate enduring reductions in callous features over time. In terms of the former, some studies have found that children and adolescents with high CU traits exhibit more disruptive behaviors both during and after treatments involving parent management training/behavioral therapy relative to youth without these traits (for a review, see Kimonis, Pardini, Pasalich, & McMahon, 2014). These studies also suggest that intervention components focused on using "time-out" to reduce problem behavior may not be effective for children exhibiting CU traits (Haas et al., 2011; Hawes & Dadds, 2005). However, children with CU traits are by no means "untreatable." Other studies have found that youth with these features experience positive behavioral improvements when exposed to intensive interventions that involve parent management training as well as other treatment components, and these improvements are equivalent to those observed in youth without CU traits (Kimonis et al., 2014; Kolko & Pardini, 2010). More important, there are now several studies indicating that some psychosocial interventions involving parent management training of young children with conduct problems can lead to reductions in the CU traits over time, with medium to large effect sizes being reported (for a review, see Kimonis et al., 2014). Furthermore, some evidence suggests that reductions in mothers' harsh and inconsistent parenting partly accounts for the reductions in levels of CU traits (McDonald, Dodson, Rosenfield, & Jouriles, 2011).

Fewer studies have been conducted investigating the impact of interventions on serious adolescent offenders with high levels of callous personality features. One recent study found that juvenile justice involved adolescents with high CU traits more likely exhibit violence during the course of functional family therapy, although they did exhibit significant reductions in their pretreatment levels of antisocial behavior by the end of treatment (White, Frick, Lawing, & Bauer, 2013). Another study conducted with incarcerated adolescents found that an intervention consisting of group-based positive psychology sessions and staff training on the use of effective behavioral reinforcement principles did not significantly reduce adolescents' CU traits (Salekin, Tippey, & Allen, 2012). However, there is some evidence that intensive multimodal interventions (e.g., psychiatric services, group therapy, individual therapy) can reduce recidivism rates among incarcerated adolescents with high psychopathic traits, including callousness (Caldwell, Skeem, Salekin, & Van Rybroek, 2006).

The few randomized outcome studies that have examined the effectiveness of various treatments for adults with antisocial personality disorders and callous features have shown nonsignificant effects on overt criminal behavior (Gibbon et al., 2010). Given research documenting the high risk for recidivism among individuals with elevated psychopathic features, effective treatments designed to reduce antisocial behavior in these offenders are desperately needed. Service delivery may be particularly challenging with offenders who exhibit high levels of callousness (Olver, Lewis, & Wong, 2013) as they may have little motivation to change and fail to develop a therapeutic alliance with mental health professionals (Skeem, Polaschek, Patrick, & Lilienfeld, 2011). For example, high levels of callousness have been associated with an increased risk for treatment dropout (Olver & Wong, 2011) and lower levels of positive behavioral change after treatment (Olver, Lewis, et al., 2013). To address this resistance, incorporating motivational interviewing techniques into treatment may prove useful because these techniques are designed to increase motivation to change among difficult clients (McMurran, 2009).

SUMMARY AND CONCLUSIONS

Decades of research has consistently delineated callousness as a core feature of a psychopathic personality. Early features of callousness can be assessed reliably beginning in early childhood, show levels of stability similar to other dimensions of adult personality, and appear to delineate youth and adults with unique etiological factors driving their antisocial behavior. Moving forward, it will be important to better tailor targeted interventions to the unique developmental mechanisms believed to underlie the antisocial behavior of individuals with callous personality features to achieve more pronounced and sustained treatment effects. Continued developmental research aimed at uncovering the unique etiological factors underlying the antisocial behavior of individuals exhibiting callous personality features will help to facilitate future innovations in these comprehensive and individualized approaches to prevention and treatment.

REFERENCES

American Psychiatric Association. (1980). *Diagnostic and statistical manual of mental disorders* (3rd ed.). Washington, DC: Author.

American Psychiatric Association. (2013). *Diagnostic and statistical manual of mental disorders* (5th ed.). Arlington, VA: Author.

Andershed, H. (2010). Stability and change of psychopathic traits: What do we know? In R. T. Salekin & D. R. Lynam (Eds.), *Handbook of child and adolescent psychopathy* (pp. 233–250). New York, NY: Guilford Press.

Andershed, H., Kerr, M., Stattin, H., & Levander, S. (2002). Psychopathic traits in non-referred youths: A new assessment tool. In E. Blaauw & L. Sheridan (Eds.), *Psychopaths: Current international perspectives* (pp. 131–158). The Hague, The Netherlands: Elsevier.

Blair, R. J. R. (2001). Neurocognitive models of aggression, the antisocial personality disorders, and psychopathy. *Journal of Neurology, Neurosurgery, & Psychiatry, 71,* 727–731. http://dx.doi.org/10.1136/jnnp.71.6.727

Blair, R. J. R. (2005). Applying a cognitive neuroscience perspective to the disorder of psychopathy. *Development and Psychopathology, 17,* 865–891. http://dx.doi.org/10.1017/S0954579405050418

Blair, R. J. R. (2010). Neuroimaging of psychopathy and antisocial behavior: A targeted review. *Current Psychiatry Reports, 12,* 76–82. http://dx.doi.org/10.1007/s11920-009-0086-x

Blair, R. J. R., Colledge, E., & Mitchell, D. G. V. (2001). Somatic markers and response reversal: Is there orbitofrontal cortex dysfunction in boys with psychopathic tendencies? *Journal of Abnormal Child Psychology, 29,* 499–511. http://dx.doi.org/10.1023/A:1012277125119

Blonigen, D. M., Carlson, S. R., Krueger, R. F., & Patrick, C. J. (2003). A twin study of self-reported psychopathic personality traits. *Personality and Individual Differences, 35,* 179–197. http://dx.doi.org/10.1016/S0191-8869(02)00184-8

Caldwell, M., Skeem, J., Salekin, R., & Van Rybroek, G. (2006). Treatment response of adolescent offenders with psychopathy features: A 2-year follow-up. *Criminal Justice and Behavior, 33,* 571–596. http://dx.doi.org/10.1177/0093854806288176

Cauffman, E., Kimonis, E. R., Dmitrieva, J., & Monahan, K. C. (2009). A multi-method assessment of juvenile psychopathy: Comparing the predictive utility of the PCL:YV, YPI, and NEO PRI. *Psychological Assessment, 21,* 528–542. http://dx.doi.org/10.1037/a0017367

Cleckley, H. (1976). *The mask of sanity* (5th ed.). St. Louis, MO: Mosby.

Dadds, M. R., Allen, J. L., McGregor, K., Woolgar, M., Viding, E., & Scott, S. (2014). Callous-unemotional traits in children and mechanisms of impaired eye contact during expressions of love: A treatment target? *Journal of Child Psychology and Psychiatry, 55,* 771–780. http://dx.doi.org/10.1111/jcpp.12155

Dadds, M. R., Allen, J. L., Oliver, B. R., Faulkner, N., Legge, K., Moul, C., . . . Scott, S. (2012). Love, eye contact and the developmental origins of empathy v. psychopathy. *The British Journal of Psychiatry, 200,* 191–196. http://dx.doi.org/10.1192/bjp.bp.110.085720

Dadds, M. R., Fraser, J., Frost, A., & Hawes, D. J. (2005). Disentangling the underlying dimensions of psychopathy and conduct problems in childhood: A community study. *Journal of Consulting and Clinical Psychology, 73,* 400–410. http://dx.doi.org/10.1037/0022-006X.73.3.400

Dadds, M. R., Moul, C., Cauchi, A., Dobson-Stone, C., Hawes, D. J., Brennan, J., . . . Ebstein, R. E. (2014). Polymorphisms in the oxytocin receptor gene are associated with the development of psychopathy. *Development and Psychopathology, 26,* 21–31. http://dx.doi.org/10.1017/S0954579413000485

Dadds, M. R., Perry, Y., Hawes, D. J., Merz, S., Riddell, A. C., Haines, D. J., . . . Abeygunawardane, A. I. (2006). Attention to the eyes and fear-recognition deficits in child psychopathy. *The British Journal of Psychiatry, 189,* 280–281. http://dx.doi.org/10.1192/bjp.bp.105.018150

Derefinko, K. J., & Lynam, D. R. (2006). Convergence and divergence among self-report psychopathy measures: A personality-based approach. *Journal of Personality Disorders, 20,* 261–280. http://dx.doi.org/10.1521/pedi.2006.20.3.261

Douglas, K. S., Lilienfeld, S. O., Skeem, J. L., Poythress, N. G., Edens, J. F., & Patrick, C. J. (2008). Relation of antisocial and psychopathic traits to suicide-related behavior among offenders. *Law and Human Behavior, 32,* 511–525. http://dx.doi.org/10.1007/s10979-007-9122-8

Fite, P. J., Greening, L., Stoppelbein, L., & Fabiano, G. A. (2009). Confirmatory factor analysis of the antisocial process screening device with a clinical inpatient population. *Assessment, 16,* 103–114. http://dx.doi.org/10.1177/1073191108319893

Fontaine, N. M. G., McCrory, E. J. P., Boivin, M., Moffitt, T. E., & Viding, E. (2011). Predictors and outcomes of joint trajectories of callous–unemotional traits and conduct problems in childhood. *Journal of Abnormal Psychology, 120,* 730–742. http://dx.doi.org/10.1037/a0022620

Fontaine, N. M. G., Rijsdijk, F. V., McCrory, E. J. P., & Viding, E. (2010). Etiology of different developmental trajectories of callous-unemotional traits. *Journal of the American Academy of Child & Adolescent Psychiatry, 49,* 656–664.

Forth, A., Kosson, D., & Hare, R. (2003). *The Hare Psychopathy Checklist: Youth Version, Technical Manual.* New York, NY: Multi-Health Systems.

Frick, P. J., Bodin, S. D., & Barry, C. T. (2000). Psychopathic traits and conduct problems in community and clinic-referred samples of children: Further development of the psychopathy screening device. *Psychological Assessment, 12,* 382–393. http://dx.doi.org/10.1037/1040-3590.12.4.382

Frick, P. J., Cornell, A. H., Bodin, S. D., Dane, H. E., Barry, C. T., & Loney, B. R. (2003). Callous-unemotional traits and developmental pathways to severe conduct problems. *Developmental Psychology, 39,* 246–260.

Frick, P. J., & Hare, R. D. (2001). *Antisocial process screening device technical manual.* Toronto, Ontario, Canada: Multi-Health Systems.

Frick, P. J., Kimonis, E. R., Dandreaux, D. M., & Farell, J. M. (2003). The 4-year stability of psychopathic traits in non-referred youth. *Behavioral Sciences & the Law, 21,* 713–736. http://dx.doi.org/10.1002/bsl.568

Frick, P. J., Ray, J. V., Thornton, L. C., & Kahn, R. E. (2014). Can callous–unemotional traits enhance the understanding, diagnosis, and treatment of serious conduct problems in children and adolescents? A comprehensive review. *Psychological Bulletin, 140,* 1–57. http://dx.doi.org/10.1037/a0033076

Gibbon, S., Duggan, C., Stoffers, J., Huband, N., Völlm, B. A., Ferriter, M., & Lieb, K. (2010). Psychological interventions for antisocial personality disorder. *Cochrane Database of Systematic Reviews, 16,* CD007668.

Haas, S. M., Waschbusch, D. A., Pelham, W. E., Jr., King, S., Andrade, B. F., & Carrey, N. J. (2011). Treatment response in CP/ADHD children with callous/unemotional traits. *Journal of Abnormal Child Psychology, 39,* 541–552. http://dx.doi.org/10.1007/s10802-010-9480-4

Hall, J. R., Drislane, L. E., Patrick, C. J., Morano, M., Lilienfeld, S. O., & Poythress, N. G. (2014). Development and validation of Triarchic construct scales from the psychopathic personality inventory. *Psychological Assessment, 26,* 447–461. http://dx.doi.org/10.1037/a0035665

Hare, R. D. (2003). *Hare Psychopathy Checklist—Revised (PCL–R; 2nd ed.).* North Tonawanda, NY: Multi-Health Systems, Inc.

Hare, R. D., & Neumann, C. S. (2008). Psychopathy as a clinical and empirical construct. *Annual Review of Clinical Psychology, 4,* 217–246. http://dx.doi.org/10.1146/annurev.clinpsy.3.022806.091452

Hawes, D. J., & Dadds, M. R. (2005). The treatment of conduct problems in children with callous–unemotional traits. *Journal of Consulting and Clinical Psychology, 73,* 737–741. http://dx.doi.org/10.1037/0022-006X.73.4.737

Hawes, D. J., Price, M. J., & Dadds, M. R. (2014). Callous-unemotional traits and the treatment of conduct problems in childhood and adolescence: A comprehensive review. *Clinical Child and Family Psychology Review, 17,* 248–267. http://dx.doi.org/10.1007/s10567-014-0167-1

Hawes, S. W., Mulvey, E. P., Schubert, C. A., & Pardini, D. A. (2014). Structural coherence and temporal stability of psychopathic personality features during emerging adulthood. *Journal of Abnormal Psychology, 123,* 623–633. http://dx.doi.org/10.1037/a0037078

Herpers, P. C., Scheepers, F. E., Bons, D. M., Buitelaar, J. K., & Rommelse, N. N. (2014). The cognitive and neural correlates of psychopathy and especially callous-unemotional traits in youths: A systematic review of the evidence. *Development and Psychopathology, 26,* 245–273. http://dx.doi.org/10.1017/S0954579413000527

Jones, A. P., Happé, F. G. E., Gilbert, F., Burnett, S., & Viding, E. (2010). Feeling, caring, knowing: Different types of empathy deficit in boys with psychopathic tendencies and autism spectrum disorder. *Journal of Child Psychology and Psychiatry, 51,* 1188–1197. http://dx.doi.org/10.1111/j.1469-7610.2010.02280.x

Kahn, R. E., Byrd, A. L., & Pardini, D. A. (2013). Callous–unemotional traits robustly predict future criminal offending in young men. *Law and Human Behavior, 37,* 87–97. http://dx.doi.org/10.1037/b0000003

Kahn, R. E., Frick, P. J., Youngstrom, E., Findling, R. L., & Youngstrom, J. K. (2012). The effects of including a callous-unemotional specifier for the diagnosis of conduct disorder. *Journal of Child Psychology and Psychiatry, 53,* 271–282. http://dx.doi.org/10.1111/j.1469-7610.2011.02463.x

Kiang, L., Moreno, A. J., & Robinson, J. L. (2004). Maternal preconceptions about parenting predict child temperament, maternal sensitivity, and children's empathy. *Developmental Psychology, 40,* 1081–1092. http://dx.doi.org/10.1037/0012-1649.40.6.1081

Kimonis, E. R., Frick, P. J., Fazekas, H., & Loney, B. R. (2006). Psychopathy, aggression, and the processing of emotional stimuli in non-referred girls and boys. *Behavioral Sciences & the Law, 24,* 21–37. http://dx.doi.org/10.1002/bsl.668

Kimonis, E. R., Frick, P. J., Munoz, L. C., & Aucoin, K. J. (2008). Callous-unemotional traits and the emotional processing of distress cues in detained boys: Testing the moderating role of aggression, exposure to community violence, and histories of abuse. *Development and Psychopathology, 20,* 569–589. http://dx.doi.org/10.1017/S095457940800028X

Kimonis, E. R., Pardini, D., Pasalich, D., & McMahon, R. J. (2014). With limited prosocial emotions specifier for conduct disorder. In G. O. Gabbard (Ed.), *Gabbard's treatments of psychiatric disorders* (5th ed., pp. 747–754). Arlington, VA: American Psychiatric Publishing. http://dx.doi.org/10.1176/appi.books.9781585625048.gg43

Kochanska, G. (1997). Multiple pathways to conscience for children with different temperaments: From toddlerhood to age 5. *Developmental Psychology, 33,* 228–240. http://dx.doi.org/10.1037/0012-1649.33.2.228

Kochanska, G., Forman, D. R., Aksan, N., & Dunbar, S. B. (2005). Pathways to conscience: Early mother–child mutually responsive orientation and children's moral emotion, conduct, and cognition. *Journal of Child Psychology and Psychiatry, 46,* 19–34. http://dx.doi.org/10.1111/j.1469-7610.2004.00348.x

Kolko, D. J., & Pardini, D. A. (2010). ODD dimensions, ADHD, and callous–unemotional traits as predictors of treatment response in children with disruptive behavior disorders. *Journal of Abnormal Psychology, 119,* 713–725. http://dx.doi.org/10.1037/a0020910

Kosson, D. S., Smith, S. S., & Newman, J. P. (1990). Evaluating the construct validity of psychopathy in Black and White male inmates: Three preliminary studies. *Journal of Abnormal Psychology, 99,* 250–259. http://dx.doi.org/10.1037/0021-843X.99.3.250

Kroneman, L. M., Hipwell, A. E., Loeber, R., Koot, H. M., & Pardini, D. A. (2011). Contextual risk factors as predictors of disruptive behavior disorder trajectories in girls:

The moderating effect of callous-unemotional features. *Journal of Child Psychology and Psychiatry, 52,* 167–175. http://dx.doi.org/10.1111/j.1469-7610.2010.02300.x

Latzman, R. D., Vaidya, J. G., Malikina, M. V., Berg, J. M., & Lilienfeld, S. O. (2014). Exploring associations between psychopathic personality and components of disinhibition vs. constraint. *Journal of Psychopathology and Behavioral Assessment, 36,* 497–509.

Leistico, A.-M. R., Salekin, R. T., DeCoster, J., & Rogers, R. (2008). A large-scale meta-analysis relating the hare measures of psychopathy to antisocial conduct. *Law and Human Behavior, 32,* 28–45. http://dx.doi.org/10.1007/s10979-007-9096-6

Lilienfeld, S. O., & Widows, M. R. (2005). *Psychopathic Personality Inventory—Revised (PPI–R) professional manual.* Lutz, FL: Psychological Assessment Resources.

Lochman, J. E., Burke, J. D., & Pardini, D. A. (in press). Disruptive behavior and dissocial disorders. In M. Roberts (Ed.), *The evidence base for* ICD–11. Washington, DC: American Psychiatric Association.

Lynam, D. R., & Derefinko, K. J. (2006). Psychopathy and personality. In C. J. Patrick (Ed.), *Handbook of Psychopathy* (pp. 133–155). New York, NY: Guilford Press.

Marsh, A. A., & Blair, R. J. R. (2008). Deficits in facial affect recognition among antisocial populations: A meta-analysis. *Neuroscience and Biobehavioral Reviews, 32,* 454–465. http://dx.doi.org/10.1016/j.neubiorev.2007.08.003

McDonald, R., Dodson, M. C., Rosenfield, D., & Jouriles, E. N. (2011). Effects of a parenting intervention on features of psychopathy in children. *Journal of Abnormal Child Psychology, 39,* 1013–1023. http://dx.doi.org/10.1007/s10802-011-9512-8

McMahon, R. J., Witkiewitz, K., Kotler, J. S., & the Conduct Problems Prevention Research Group. (2010). Predictive validity of callous–unemotional traits measured in early adolescence with respect to multiple antisocial outcomes. *Journal of Abnormal Psychology, 119,* 752–763. http://dx.doi.org/10.1037/a0020796

McMurran, M. (2009). Motivational interviewing with offenders: A systematic review. *Legal and Criminological Psychology, 14,* 83–100. http://dx.doi.org/10.1348/135532508X278326

Neumann, C. S., Hare, R. D., & Pardini, D. A. (2014). Antisociality and the construct of psychopathy: Data from across the globe. *Journal of Personality.* Advance online publication. http://dx.doi.org/10.1111/jopy.12127

Neumann, C. S., & Pardini, D. A. (2014). Factor structure and construct validity of the Self-Report Psychopathy (SRP) scale and the Youth Psychopathic Traits Inventory (YPI) in young men. *Journal of Personality Disorders, 28,* 419–433. http://dx.doi.org/10.1521/pedi_2012_26_063

O'Brien, B. S., & Frick, P. J. (1996). Reward dominance: Associations with anxiety, conduct problems, and psychopathy in children. *Journal of Abnormal Child Psychology, 24,* 223–240. http://dx.doi.org/10.1007/BF01441486

Olver, M. E., Lewis, K., & Wong, S. C. P. (2013). Risk reduction treatment of high-risk psychopathic offenders: The relationship of psychopathy and treatment change to violent recidivism. *Personality Disorders: Theory, Research, and Treatment, 4,* 160–167. http://dx.doi.org/10.1037/a0029769

Olver, M. E., Neumann, C. S., Wong, S. C., & Hare, R. D. (2013). The structural and predictive properties of the Psychopathy Checklist—Revised in Canadian aboriginal and non-aboriginal offenders. *Psychological Assessment, 25,* 167–179. http://dx.doi.org/10.1037/a0029840

Olver, M. E., & Wong, S. (2011). Predictors of sex offender treatment dropout: Psychopathy, sex offender risk, and responsivity implications. *Psychology, Crime & Law, 17,* 457–471. http://dx.doi.org/10.1080/10683160903318876

Pardini, D. A. (2006). The callousness pathway to severe violent delinquency. *Aggressive Behavior, 32,* 590–598. http://dx.doi.org/10.1002/ab.20158

Pardini, D. A., & Byrd, A. L. (2013). Developmental conceptualizations of psychopathic features. In K. A. Kiehl & W. P. Sinnott-Armstrong (Eds.), *Handbook on psychopathy and law* (pp. 61–77). New York, NY: Oxford University Press.

Pardini, D. A., & Fite, P. J. (2010). Symptoms of conduct disorder, oppositional defiant disorder, attention-deficit/hyperactivity disorder, and callous-unemotional traits as unique predictors of psychosocial maladjustment in boys: Advancing an evidence base for *DSM–5. Journal of the American Academy of Child & Adolescent Psychiatry, 49,* 1134–1144.

Pardini, D. A., Frick, P. J., & Moffitt, T. E. (2010). Building an evidence base for *DSM–5* conceptualizations of oppositional defiant disorder and conduct disorder: Introduction to the special section. *Journal of Abnormal Psychology, 119,* 683–688. http://dx.doi.org/10.1037/a0021441

Pardini, D. A., Lochman, J. E., & Frick, P. J. (2003). Callous/unemotional traits and social-cognitive processes in adjudicated youths. *Journal of the American Academy of Child & Adolescent Psychiatry, 42,* 364–371. http://dx.doi.org/10.1097/00004583-200303000-00018

Pardini, D. A., Lochman, J. E., & Powell, N. (2007). The development of callous-unemotional traits and antisocial behavior in children: Are there shared and/or unique predictors? *Journal of Clinical Child and Adolescent Psychology, 36,* 319–333. http://dx.doi.org/10.1080/15374410701444215

Pardini, D. A., Stepp, S., Hipwell, A., Stouthamer-Loeber, M., & Loeber, R. (2012). The clinical utility of the proposed *DSM–5* callous-unemotional subtype of conduct disorder in young girls. *Journal of the American Academy of Child & Adolescent Psychiatry, 51,* 62–73.e4. http://dx.doi.org/10.1016/j.jaac.2011.10.005

Pasalich, D. S., Dadds, M. R., Hawes, D. J., & Brennan, J. (2011). Do callous-unemotional traits moderate the relative importance of parental coercion versus warmth in child conduct problems? An observational study. *Journal of Child Psychology and Psychiatry, 52,* 1308–1315. http://dx.doi.org/10.1111/j.1469-7610.2011.02435.x

Patrick, C. J. (2010). *Operationalizing the triarchic conceptualization of psychopathy: Preliminary description of brief scales for assessment of boldness, meanness, and disinhibition.* Unpublished manual, Florida State University, Tallahassee. Retrieved from https://www.phenxtoolkit.org/toolkit_content/supplemental_info/psychiatric/measures/Triarchic_Psychopathy_Measure_Manual.pdf

Patrick, C. J., Fowles, D. C., & Krueger, R. F. (2009). Triarchic conceptualization of psychopathy: Developmental origins of disinhibition, boldness, and meanness. *Development and Psychopathology, 21,* 913–938. http://dx.doi.org/10.1017/S0954579409000492

Paulhus, D., Neumann, C. S., & Hare, R. D. (in press). *Manual for the Self-Report of Psychopathy (SRP–III) scale.* Multi-Health Systems: Toronto, Ontario, Canada.

Poy, R., Segarra, P., Esteller, À., López, R., & Moltó, J. (2014). FFM description of the triarchic conceptualization of psychopathy in men and women. *Psychological Assessment, 26,* 69–76. http://dx.doi.org/10.1037/a0034642

Roberts, B. W., & DelVecchio, W. F. (2000). The rank-order consistency of personality traits from childhood to old age: A quantitative review of longitudinal studies. *Psychological Bulletin, 126,* 3–25. http://dx.doi.org/10.1037/0033-2909.126.1.3

Roberts, B. W., Walton, K. E., & Viechtbauer, W. (2006). Patterns of mean-level change in personality traits across the life course: A meta-analysis of longitudinal studies. *Psychological Bulletin, 132,* 1–25.

Rogstad, J. E., & Rogers, R. (2008). Gender differences in contributions of emotion to psychopathy and antisocial personality disorder. *Clinical Psychology Review, 28,* 1472–1484. http://dx.doi.org/10.1016/j.cpr.2008.09.004

Rutherford, M., Cacciola, J. S., Alterman, A. I., McKay, J. R., & Cook, T. G. (1999). The 2-year test–retest reliability of the Psychopathy Checklist Revised in methadone patients. *Assessment, 6,* 285–292. http://dx.doi.org/10.1177/107319119900600308

Salekin, R. T. (2002). Psychopathy and therapeutic pessimism. Clinical lore or clinical reality? *Clinical Psychology Review, 22,* 79–112. http://dx.doi.org/10.1016/S0272-7358(01)00083-6

Salekin, R. T., Tippey, J. G., & Allen, A. D. (2012). Treatment of conduct problem youth with interpersonal callous traits using mental models: Measurement of risk and change. *Behavioral Sciences & the Law, 30,* 470–486. http://dx.doi.org/10.1002/bsl.2025

Sherman, E. D., Lynam, D. R., & Heyde, B. (2014). Agreeableness accounts for the factor structure of the youth psychopathic traits inventory. *Journal of Personality Disorders, 28,* 262–280. http://dx.doi.org/10.1521/pedi_2013_27_124

Skeem, J. L., & Cooke, D. J. (2010). Is criminal behavior a central component of psychopathy? Conceptual directions for resolving the debate. *Psychological Assessment, 22,* 433–445. http://dx.doi.org/10.1037/a0008512

Skeem, J. L., Polaschek, D. L. L., Patrick, C. J., & Lilienfeld, S. O. (2011). Psychopathic personality: Bridging the gap between scientific evidence and public policy. *Psychological Science in the Public Interest, 12,* 95–162. http://dx.doi.org/10.1177/1529100611426706

Spain, S. E., Douglas, K. S., Poythress, N. G., & Epstein, M. (2004). The relationship between psychopathic features, violence and treatment outcome: The comparison of three youth measures of psychopathic features. *Behavioral Sciences & the Law, 22,* 85–102. http://dx.doi.org/10.1002/bsl.576

Verona, E., Hicks, B. M., & Patrick, C. J. (2005). Psychopathy and suicidality in female offenders: Mediating influences of personality and abuse. *Journal of Consulting and Clinical Psychology, 73*, 1065–1073. http://dx.doi.org/10.1037/0022-006X.73.6.1065

Viding, E., Fontaine, N. M., Oliver, B. R., & Plomin, R. (2009). Negative parental discipline, conduct problems and callous-unemotional traits: Monozygotic twin differences study. *The British Journal of Psychiatry, 195*, 414–419. http://dx.doi.org/10.1192/bjp.bp.108.061192

Viding, E., Price, T. S., Jaffee, S. R., Trzaskowski, M., Davis, O. S., Meaburn, E. L., . . . Plomin, R. (2013). Genetics of callous-unemotional behavior in children. *PLoS ONE, 8*, e65789. http://dx.doi.org/10.1371/journal.pone.0065789

Vitacco, M. J., Neumann, C. S., & Jackson, R. L. (2005). Testing a four-factor model of psychopathy and its association with ethnicity, gender, intelligence, and violence. *Journal of Consulting and Clinical Psychology, 73*, 466–476. http://dx.doi.org/10.1037/0022-006X.73.3.466

Vitacco, M. J., Neumann, C. S., & Pardini, D. A. (2014). Predicting future criminal offending in a community-based sample of males using self-reported psychopathy. *Criminal Justice and Behavior, 41*, 345–363. http://dx.doi.org/10.1177/0093854813500488

Vitacco, M. J., Van Rybroek, G. J., Rogstad, J. E., Yahr, L. E., Tomony, J. D., & Saewert, E. (2009). Predicting short-term institutional aggression in forensic patients: A multitrait method for understanding subtypes of aggression. *Law and Human Behavior, 33*, 308–319. http://dx.doi.org/10.1007/s10979-008-9155-7

White, S. F., Frick, P. J., Lawing, K., & Bauer, D. (2013). Callous-unemotional traits and response to functional family therapy in adolescent offenders. *Behavioral Sciences & the Law, 31*, 271–285. http://dx.doi.org/10.1002/bsl.2041

World Health Organization. (1992). *The ICD–10 classification of mental and behavioural disorders: Clinical descriptions and diagnostic guidelines*. Geneva, Switzerland: Author.

3

FEARLESS DOMINANCE AND ITS IMPLICATIONS FOR PSYCHOPATHY: ARE THE RIGHT STUFF AND THE WRONG STUFF FLIP SIDES OF THE SAME COIN?

SCOTT O. LILIENFELD, SARAH FRANCIS SMITH, AND ASHLEY L. WATTS

Charles Elwood Yeager, better known to the world as Chuck Yeager, was already a flying legend by his early 20s. During his stint as an American fighter pilot in World War II, Yeager shot down over a dozen German planes. In 1944, he twice took out four enemy planes on a single day. Shot down over German-occupied France on his ninth mission, Yeager managed to disguise himself as a peasant and avoid detection by the Nazis while escaping across the Pyrenees Mountains into Spain. Although Yeager could then have returned to the United States to find other employment, he formally appealed to then-General Dwight Eisenhower to rejoin the war effort. Eisenhower granted his wish, allowing him to strike terror in the hearts of more German pilots.

We dedicate this chapter to the memory of Lawrence (Larry) James (1943–2014), Professor of Psychology at the Georgia Institute of Psychology, whose remarkable friendship and mentorship were invaluable in shaping many of the ideas in this chapter.

http://dx.doi.org/10.1037/14854-004
The Dark Side of Personality: Science and Practice in Social, Personality, and Clinical Psychology, V. Zeigler-Hill and D. K. Marcus (Editors)

In light of his storied flying prowess, Yeager was handpicked by the U.S. Air Force to become the first human to surpass the speed of sound. A previous effort by a British pilot had ended tragically, with the plane careening wildly out of control and crashing. At the time, some prominent engineers confidently predicted that any vehicle that attained Mach 1—often dubbed the *sound barrier* because it was presumably unbreakable—would become aeronautically unstable and immediately disintegrate. Yeager scoffed at the suggestion.

On October 14, 1947, in the Mohave Desert, Chuck Yeager climbed into a tiny Bell X-I experimental plane, hitched to the bottom of a much larger B-29 plane. The B-29 brought Yeager's bullet-shaped X-I up to 26,000 feet, and promptly jettisoned it like a bomb. Yeager's plane at first plummeted, and then soared to 45,000 feet, accelerating to 670 miles per hour. The small top-secret military crowd that had gathered on the ground in anxious anticipation saw Yeager's climbing plane disappear into the stratosphere and waited . . . and waited. As his plane approached Mach 1, Yeager casually informed the ground engineers about a jolt of turbulence: "Had a mild buffet there—jes [sic] the usual instability" (Wolfe, 1979, p. 44). Eventually, the onlookers below heard an enormous thunderclap ripple across the vast California desert.

It was the first sonic boom generated by a human-made vehicle. Chuck Yeager had shattered the sound barrier. Yeager's plane soon reappeared from out of the clouds, and on his 7-minute trip back to terra firma, Yeager punctuated his achievement by performing several wing-over-wing acrobatic maneuvers before landing safely. Six years later, Yeager broke another world record, reaching Mach 2.44 (1,650 miles per hour) in an X-1A. In the 1950s and 1960s, Yeager flew combat missions in the Korean and Vietnam Wars and, along the way, helped to train many of the first astronauts. Yeager last broke the sound barrier in 2002, at the age of 79 (CNN Wire Staff, 2012).

DEFINITION AND BACKGROUND

In essentially all respects, Chuck Yeager is the embodiment of a set of personality traits that comprise the higher order dimension of *fearless dominance* (FD; Lykken, 1982, 1995; Patrick, 2006). These traits include interpersonal potency, physical fearlessness, risk taking, and calmness in the face of danger. As described by American writer Tom Wolfe, who immortalized Yeager in his nonfiction book *The Right Stuff* (Wolfe, 1979), the "right stuff" is a potent cocktail of fearlessness, machismo, and sangfroid under intense pressure. Indeed, Yeager now looks back on his multiple near-death experiences with astonishing equanimity. As a *USA Today* reporter observed during a 2011 interview with him, "Even today, he describes the day he almost died when the X-1A spun out in 1953 as if it were just a bad day at the office" (Cava, 2012). Although Yeager never made it into outer space (he never attended college and because of NASA regulations was expressly forbidden from joining the space program), nearly all of the early astronauts who followed in his wake strove to emulate his inimitable flying technique, coolness in the face of imminent disaster, and even his folksy, nonchalant West Virginia drawl ("Well, folks, it looks like we may have a little problem on or our hands here. No worries, I'll just eject from this baby").

Yeager's remarkable life story provides an apt segue for many of the themes we explore in this chapter, including the potential fine line between the right stuff and the wrong stuff. Although Yeager has been justifiably hailed as a hero—in 1985, President Ronald Reagan presented him with the Presidential Medal of Freedom—he was hardly a choirboy in his personal life. For example, 2 days before his record-breaking flight in 1947, Yeager foolishly went drinking at a local bar and then horseback riding by moonlight, falling off his horse and cracking two ribs in the process. He concealed the information about his medical condition—and the excruciating pain that made it difficult for him to maneuver his plane—from his superiors. The following year, during a regatta in West Virginia, Yeager blatantly violated Air Force and Federal Aviation Administration regulations by flying under a city bridge at more than 600 miles an hour, buzzing the boats on the water, and performing three victory rolls before heading all the way to California. When asked to explain Yeager's notorious rabble-rousing behavior over the years, retired General J. Kemp McLaughlin and ex-commander of the West Virginia National Guard told a reporter, "He broke every rule in the book. Chuck was a maverick all his life. That guy would do anything" (Wells, 2008).

Fearless Dominance and Psychopathy

Yeager's life story raises a set of fascinating questions that bear broader implications for the construct of FD. For example, was Yeager's FD the wellspring of both his success and his hell raising? Had Yeager been born to neglectful parents or had he lacked remarkable physical talent and high levels of innate intelligence, might he have acquired more marked psychopathic traits? Was Yeager's success the product of his FD per se, or was it instead the conjoint product of FD and other personality traits, such as high levels of impulse control? In this chapter, we address these and other issues with an eye toward their eventual resolution.

In his classic book *The Mask of Sanity*, psychiatrist Hervey Cleckley (1941/1988) was the first scholar to systematically delineate the core features of psychopathy, which he described as a condition marked by 16 criteria, including superficial charm and poise, absence of anxiety, guiltlessness, dishonesty, unreliability, self-centeredness, failure to form intimate personal attachments, and poor impulse control. According to Cleckley, psychopaths present with a veneer of healthy functioning, rendering them especially dangerous interpersonally and, more rarely, physically. Perhaps the prototypical psychopath is Theodore (Ted) Bundy (1946–1989), a notorious American serial killer renowned for his charisma, gift-of-gab, outrageous risk taking, ruthlessness, and extraordinary callousness. More than 60 years after Cleckley's seminal writings, Patrick (2006) proposed that FD captures much of what Cleckley referred to as the "mask" of superficially healthy functioning displayed by most psychopathic individuals. In particular, Patrick maintained that four of Cleckley's 16 criteria map on well to the FD construct, namely, superficial charm and good "intelligence" (the latter of which is probably better conceptualized as "gift of gab" than genuine high verbal intelligence), absence of anxiety and other neurotic manifestations, relative immunity to suicide attempts or completions, and failure to learn from experience, which is better described as a failure to learn from punishment.

In their classic writings on the development of the Minnesota Multiphasic Personality Inventory Psychopathic deviate scale, McKinley and Hathaway (1944) similarly remarked that individuals with elevated scores on this scale "are so often characterized by a relatively appealing personality," and that the superficial psychological health of such individuals "are misleading to clinicians so that a halo effect operates toward too lenient a view of the clinical problem" (p. 173). Further anticipating the concept of FD are (a) the classic theoretical writings of Karpman (1941), which distinguish "primary" (genuine) psychopaths, who are characterized by low levels of anxiety and a failure to alter behavior following punishing experiences, from "secondary" psychopaths (pseudo-psychopaths), who are marked by high levels of anxiety and neurotic conflict; (b) the theoretical and empirical writings of Lykken (1957, 1982) on fearlessness, as noted earlier; (c) the theoretical writings of Quay (1965) on psychopaths' low levels of tonic physiological arousal and propensities toward excitement seeking; and (d) the work of Gray (1982) and Fowles (1980) linking low levels of activity of the behavioral inhibition system (a brain-based system comprising the septum, hippocampus, orbitofrontal cortex, and amygdala, among other structures) to primary psychopathy (for a discussion, see Patrick & Drislane, 2014).

Unresolved Questions

It remains unclear, however, whether FD is part-and-parcel of psychopathy or is irrelevant or at best peripheral to it. For example, although Chuck Yeager is hardly a prototypical psychopath, some authors have suggested that he possesses the "genetic talent" for this condition (e.g., Lykken, 1982, 1995). Alternatively, perhaps FD is not part of psychopathy per se but only moderates its behavioral expression, predisposing individuals to what has been termed *successful* or *adaptive* psychopathy (Hall & Benning, 2006; Widom, 1977). It is also unclear whether FD is entirely psychologically adaptive or whether, like most features of psychopathy (Paulhus & Williams, 2002), it has a dark side as well. Perhaps when FD becomes too extreme or when it is coupled with certain unsavory personality traits, such as poor impulse control or antagonism, the right stuff can transmogrify into the wrong stuff, crossing the murky line from fearlessness to recklessness.

Psychometric Emergence of FD

The FD construct originated in research on the Psychopathic Personality Inventory (PPI), now a widely used self-report measure of psychopathy along with its revised version, the PPI—Revised (PPI–R; Lilienfeld & Widows, 2005). To develop the PPI, Lilienfeld (1990; Lilienfeld & Andrews, 1996) used a hybrid inductive–deductive approach (see Tellegen & Waller, 2008) to identify salient constructs relevant to psychopathy, as well as several candidate items for each construct. Specifically, Lilienfeld began by surveying the broad historical clinical and research literatures on psychopathy and identified more than 30 focal constructs that had been deemed relevant to this condition by influential authors over the years (Lilienfeld & Andrews, 1996). He then wrote multiple items to assess each construct.

Exploratory factor analyses across three rounds of test development in undergraduate samples ($N = 1,156$) yielded eight lower order subscales: (a) *Machiavellian Egocentricity* (a ruthless and self-centered willingness to exploit others); (b) *Social Potency*, renamed *Social Influence* in the PPI–R (a propensity to enjoy influencing others and to relish being in the spotlight); (c) *Fearlessness* (a paucity of fear in anticipation of impending danger); (d) *Impulsive Nonconformity*, renamed *Rebellious Nonconformity* in the PPI–R (a tendency to flout traditions and defy authority); (e) *Carefree Nonplanfulness* (an insouciant disregard for the future); (f) *Blame Externalization* (a propensity to adopt the victim role and to blame others for one's life circumstances); (g) *Stress Immunity* (a relative absence of manifest anxiety in the face of harrowing circumstances); and (h) *Coldheartedness* (affective detachment from others, manifested in the absence of deep guilt, empathy, love, or loyalty).

In his initial exploratory higher order factor analyses of these eight subscales in undergraduates, Lilienfeld (1990) observed that four of the subscales, namely, Fearlessness, Social Potency, Stress Immunity, and Impulsive Nonconformity, loaded on a higher order dimension in both two and three factor solutions. Lilienfeld provisionally christened this higher order dimension

Low Anxiety but did not pursue it in further research. In later exploratory factor analyses of the PPI subscales in a community twin sample, Benning, Patrick, Hicks, Blonigen, and Krueger (2003) identified a two-factor structure for the PPI. The first higher order dimension, which they termed *Fearless Dominance*, was marked by high loadings on the Social Potency, Fearlessness, and Stress Immunity subscales; in contrast to Lilienfeld (1990), they did not find that Impulsive Nonconformity loaded substantially on this dimension. The second higher order dimension, which they termed *Impulsive Antisociality*, was marked by high loadings on the Machiavellian Egocentricity, Impulsive Nonconformity, Carefree Nonplanfulness, and Blame Externalization scales; Lilienfeld and Widows (2005) later christened this dimension *Self-Centered Impulsivity* (SCI), the appellation we use for the remainder of this chapter. Coldheartedness did not load highly on either dimension and was excluded from computation of the higher order factors. Today, Coldheartedness is frequently treated as a stand-alone dimension in analyses.

Strikingly, in contrast to the two higher order dimensions of most other psychopathy measures, including the widely used Psychopathy Checklist—Revised (PCL–R; Hare, 2003), Benning et al. (2003) found that FD and SCI were largely orthogonal (uncorrelated), a finding buttressed by subsequent meta-analyses (Marcus, Fulton, & Edens, 2013; see also Malterer, Lilienfeld, Neumann, & Newman, 2010). This finding raises intriguing questions regarding the construct validity of FD and, perhaps more provocatively, the nature of psychopathy itself.

The Etiology of Fearless Dominance

Although the etiology of FD is unknown, Patrick, Fowles, and Krueger (2009), who termed this dimension *boldness*, conjectured that it stems from individual differences in the sensitivity of the brain's defensive systems, including those rooted in the amygdala and other structures involved in threat processing. Indeed, compared with other individuals, individuals with elevated levels of FD display low levels of fear-potentiated startle responses (Benning, Patrick, & Iacono, 2005; Vaidyanathan, Hall, Patrick, & Bernat, 2011; see also Lilienfeld, Patrick, et al., 2012) as well as low electrodermal (skin conductance) activity in anticipation of loud, aversive noises (Dindo & Fowles, 2011; see also López, Poy, Patrick, & Moltó, 2013). Both of these findings point to a low level of responding in the defensive system among fearless dominant participants. According to Patrick et al.'s defensive processing model of boldness, individuals with a low sensitivity for responding to threat are prone to a fearless temperament in childhood that tends to develop into social confidence, venturesomeness, and emotional resilience in adolescence and adulthood.

Patrick et al.'s (2009) hypothesis regarding the etiology of FD harkens back to Lykken's (1957, 1982) claims that psychopathy is associated with a "low fear IQ," that is, a heightened threshold for responding to fear-provoking stimuli. In a classic study, Lykken (1957) showed that, compared with nonpsychopathic prisoners, psychopathic prisoners (a) scored lower on a self-report index of harm avoidance; (b) displayed lower skin conductance activity in response to conditioned stimuli (buzzers) that had been paired with electric shocks; and (c) exhibited poor passive avoidance learning on a "mental maze" task that required participants to learn a complicated series of lever presses, some of which were "baited" with electric shock. These seminal psychometric and laboratory findings were replicated and extended by a number of later investigators (for reviews, see Hare, 1978; Lorber, 2004). In his later writings, Lykken (1995) argued that fearlessness gives rise to all the other core features of psychopathy, including lack of guilt, dishonesty, poor impulse control, and failure to learn from punishment.

REVIEW OF THE RELEVANT LITERATURE

The past decade has witnessed a proliferation of research on the correlates of FD. This work has clarified the nomological network surrounding FD while raising provocative questions regarding the nature and relations with psychopathy of FD.

FD and Relations with Psychopathology

In their original article on the factor-analytic derivation of the PPI higher order dimensions, Benning et al. (2003) reported that FD and SCI displayed strikingly different correlates. Specifically, they found that only SCI was associated significantly with various indices of substance and drug abuse; this dimension was also significantly associated with a host of measures of childhood and adult antisocial behavior. In contrast, FD was essentially unrelated to childhood antisocial behavior, although it was slightly but significantly associated with interview-based adult antisocial behavior ($r = .15$). In a later series of studies of community twin, student, and inmate samples, Benning, Patrick, Blonigen, Hicks, and Iacono (2005) reported that FD, as estimated by scores on the lower order trait scales of the Multidimensional Personality Questionnaire (Tellegen & Waller, 2008), a well-validated measure of normal-range personality traits, was significantly and negatively associated with measures of social phobia, other phobic fears, and depression, and positively associated with measures of narcissism.

A meta-analysis of 61 studies by Miller and Lynam (2012) clarified the psychopathological correlates of FD. They found that FD was moderately and negatively associated with conditions marked by internalizing symptoms (mean weighted $r = -.34$), including anxiety and mood symptoms. Corroborating the findings of Benning et al. (2003), FD was largely or entirely unassociated with externalizing symptoms, including aggression, antisocial behavior, and substance use, although the associations with antisocial behavior and substance abuse were statistically significant ($r = .12$ and $r = .07$, respectively). With respect to Cluster B (dramatic, emotional) personality disorders, FD was significantly correlated with symptoms of antisocial personality disorder (ASPD), although this relation was at best small in magnitude ($r = .07$); FD was significantly and moderately correlated with symptoms of narcissistic personality disorder (NPD; $r = .37$) and significantly and negatively correlated with symptoms of borderline personality disorder (BPD; $r = -.17$).

FD: Relations With Psychopathy and ASPD

The relation of FD with other psychopathy constructs is complex and inconsistent across measures. On one hand, FD is only weakly related to total scores on the PCL–R (Hare, 2003), a largely interview-based measure that is arguably the best validated measure of psychopathy. FD is modestly associated with scores on PCL–R Factor I (mean weighted average $r = .23$), which assesses the core interpersonal and affective features of psychopathy but is largely unassociated with scores on PCL–R Factor II (mean weighted average $r = .07$), which assesses the antisocial lifestyle features of psychopathy (Miller & Lynam, 2012; see also Marcus et al., 2013). When one burrows down more deeply to the four-facet level of the PCL–R, a more nuanced picture emerges. Specifically, FD is largely unassociated with three of the four facets of the PCL–R but moderately associated with the Interpersonal facet, which assesses the superficial charm and glibness of psychopathy along with a grandiose sense of self-worth (Wall, Wygant, & Sellbom, 2015).

A meta-analysis by Marcus et al. (2013) revealed that, across 10 studies, FD displayed a similar pattern and magnitude of associations with the two factors of the Levenson Self-Report Psychopathy Scale (LSRP; Levenson, Kiehl, & Fitzpatrick, 1995), a widely used self-report measure of psychopathy modeled largely after the PCL–R. In contrast, Marcus et al. found that across five studies, FD was highly associated with Factor I (mean weighted $r = .53$) and moderately to highly associated with Factor II (mean weighted $r = .40$) of the Self-Report Psychopathy Scale—III (SRP; Paulhus, Neumann, & Hare, 2014), another self-report measure modeled after the PCL–R. The most parsimonious explanation for these discrepancies is that whereas the PCL–R and LSRP are only weakly or at best moderately saturated with boldness, the

SRP is substantially saturated with boldness (Drislane, Patrick, & Arsal, 2014; Lilienfeld, Watts, Smith, Berg, & Latzman, 2014), thereby engendering substantial correlations with FD. Moreover, several other self-report measures of psychopathy, including the Elemental Psychopathy Assessment (Lynam et al., 2011), are also substantially saturated with boldness (Lilienfeld et al., 2014).

As Miller and Lynam (2012) demonstrated in their meta-analysis, FD is at best weakly associated with ASPD features. This finding is perhaps not surprising given that ASPD is associated with a long-standing history of antisocial and criminal behavior and is therefore almost invariably maladaptive. The results of two recent studies (Patrick, Venables, & Drislane, 2013; Wall et al., 2015) demonstrate that FD/boldness differentiates psychopathy, as measured by the PCL–R, from ASPD. These findings are consistent with the long-standing view that psychopathy is more associated with adaptive functioning than is ASPD (Lilienfeld et al., 2014). These findings also dovetail with the inclusion of the new psychopathy specifier for ASPD in Section III of the *Diagnostic and Statistical Manual of Mental Disorders* (5th ed.; *DSM–5*; American Psychiatric Association, 2013). This specifier, which consists of criteria assessing low anxiousness, low withdrawal, and high attention seeking, appears to assess many of the key features of FD/boldness. Indeed, data from undergraduate and community samples demonstrate the scores on the psychopathy specifier are highly associated with FD/boldness (Anderson, Sellbom, Wygant, Salekin, & Krueger, 2014). In contrast, FD/boldness is not explicitly represented in the diagnostic criteria for dissocial personality disorder in the *International Statistical Classification of Diseases and Related Health Problems* (World Health Organization, 1992), which, like *DSM–5*, remains focused on impulsivity, callousness, and chronic antisocial behavior.

ADAPTIVE FEATURES

FD and Normal-Range Personality

In the two meta-analyses already discussed, Miller and Lynam (2012) examined the correlates of PPI FD within the prism of the five-factor model (FFM) of personality (Costa & McCrae, 2008), and Marcus et al. (2013) examined the correlates of PPI FD within the prism of the three-factor model of personality (Tellegen & Waller, 2008). Miller and Lynam reported that FD was primarily negatively associated with FFM Neuroticism (mean weighted $r = -.50$), FFM Extraversion (mean weighted $r = .50$), and, to a lesser extent, FFM Openness to Experience (mean weighted $r = .25$); associations with FFM Agreeableness and Conscientiousness were negligible. Broadly corroborating Miller and Lynam's results, Marcus et al. reported that FD was correlated with Positive Emotionality (mean weighted $r = .39$) and negatively correlated with Negative Emotionality (mean weighted $r = -.35$), but essentially uncorrelated with Constraint (mean weighted $r = -.04$). Marcus et al. also found that FD was highly associated with sensation seeking (mean weighted $r = .51$; for similar findings, see Lynam & Miller, 2013).

In aggregate, data on the relation between FD and normal-range personality traits indicate that this construct is associated with high levels of extraversion and positive emotionality and low levels of neuroticism and negative emotionality (Lynam & Miller, 2013). In addition, FD is consistently, although only moderately, associated with Openness to Experience, which is most likely attributable primarily to the inclusion of content assessing novelty seeking within the openness construct (Lilienfeld, Patrick, et al., 2012). These findings again suggest that FD is tied largely to psychologically adaptive functioning.

FD and Interpersonal Behavior

Several investigative teams have begun to explore the implications of FD for interpersonal behavior that is often associated with adaptive qualities, including leadership and heroism. To examine the relations between FD and political leadership, Lilienfeld, Waldman, et al. (2012) asked 121 presidential biographers and other experts to rate the 42 U.S. presidents, up to and including George W. Bush, on their preoffice personality traits using the revised NEO Personality Inventory (Costa & McCrae, 2008), which is a widely used measure of the FFM. They then obtained estimates of presidents' PPI-related psychopathic traits by using previously validated formulas for predicting these traits from normal-range personality dimensions (see Ross, Benning, Patrick, Thompson, & Thurston, 2009). The experts' ratings of the president's FD displayed moderate to high interrater agreement. Using generalized estimated equations, Lilienfeld, Waldman, et al. then compared these presidential personality ratings with the results of several large-scale polls of presidential performance by well-known historians (e.g., the 2009 C-SPAN Poll of Presidential Performance; the 2010 Siena College Poll) and objective indicators of presidential performance (see C-SPAN.org, 2009, and Siena College, 2010). FD was positively associated not only with historians' ratings of overall presidential performance but with independently rated leadership, public persuasiveness, communication ability, and willingness to take risks. FD was also associated with initiating new legislation, winning elections by a landslide, and being viewed as a world figure. Interestingly, FD was positively associated with assassination attempts, perhaps because bolder presidents tend to be willing to make enemies if necessary.

Following up on Lykken's (1982) conjecture that "the hero and the psychopath are twigs from the same branch" (p. 22) and are linked by high levels of dispositional fearlessness, Smith, Lilienfeld, Coffey, and Dabbs (2013) examined the relation between PPI-assessed psychopathy and what they termed *everyday heroism*. To assess heroism, which they operationalized as altruism associated with social or physical risk, they administered a questionnaire to assess the frequency with which individuals engaged in a variety of heroic behaviors that are reasonably common in real-world settings, such as assisting a stranded motorist, administering cardiopulmonary resuscitation to a collapsed individual, and attempting to break up a fight in public. Participants also completed a measure of altruistic behavior subdivided into two subscales, altruism toward charities and altruism toward strangers. Across several undergraduate and community samples, Smith, Lilienfeld, et al. found that FD was in general positively, albeit weakly to moderately, associated with heroism and altruism toward strangers, suggesting that a predisposition toward fearlessness and a willingness to take risks may contribute to heroism. In a second part of the study, Smith, Lilienfeld, et al. examined the relation between psychopathy and an ostensibly more objective indicator of heroism— war heroism among the 42 U.S. presidents using the same methodology described earlier. As predicted, they found that estimated FD scores were positively associated with presidential war heroism; in contrast, these scores were unassociated with whether presidents had led the country through war, making it unlikely that historians' ratings of FD were influenced merely by a history of presidential risk taking. These preliminary findings need to be extended to other samples, especially those marked by high levels of occupational heroism.

POTENTIALLY MALADAPTIVE FEATURES

The life story of Chuck Yeager brings us back full circle to the question of whether FD is purely adaptive or whether it is also associated with maladaptive correlates, either alone or in conjunction with other variables (Miller & Lynam, 2012). Although extant data do not permit a clear-cut answer to this question, they offer a number of tantalizing hints.

Zero-Order Associations Between FD and Maladaptive Correlates

As noted earlier, FD tends to be positively associated with measures of antisocial behavior, although the magnitude of this association is at best modest (Lynam & Miller, 2013). To further examine the possibility that FD has a "dark side," we conducted a small meta-analysis of the relation between FD and sexual risk taking. We selected sexual risk taking as a target variable given that the ability to initiate sexual interactions presumably often requires a modicum of social boldness, novelty seeking, and a devil-may-care attitude (Hoyle, Fejfar, & Miller, 2000), propensities that are especially marked among individuals with elevated FD. For the sake of completeness, we also examined the relations between the other two major PPI dimensions, SCI and Coldheartedness, and sexual risk taking. We identified four studies (Fulton, Marcus, & Payne, 2010; Fulton, Marcus, & Zeigler-Hill, 2014; Kastner & Sellbom, 2012; Marcus & Norris, 2014) of undergraduates or community members who received either the Sexual Risk Survey (Turchik & Garske, 2009) or the Sociosexual Orientation Inventory (Simpson & Gangestad, 1991), two well-validated self-report indices of sexual risk taking. Additionally, we used two existing data sets collected by our laboratory and the laboratory of Robert Latzman of Georgia State University.

As can be seen in Table 3.1, all three PPI higher order dimensions are associated with sexual risk taking, with the relation for FD being small to medium in magnitude, using Cohen's (1988) provisional metrics, and the relation with SCI being medium in magnitude. Although these findings raise the possibility that FD is tied modestly to risky and potentially maladaptive outcomes in the sexual domain, they should be interpreted in light of two caveats. First, the number of studies is small, and replication in other samples, especially more severely affected samples (e.g., prison samples) that may be marked by high levels of sexual risk taking, will be necessary. Second, the small to medium correlation between FD and risky sexual behavior could be attributable at least partly to the small amount of shared variance between FD and SCI. Indeed, Fulton et al. (2014) found that controlling statistically for SCI scores reduced the association between FD and sexual risk taking to nonsignificance. Hence, further studies will

TABLE 3.1
Correlations Between Psychopathy Dimensions
and Risky Sexual Behavior

	Zero-order r	N	k
PPI Total	.35**	3,594	5
PPI FD	.21**	3,679	6
PPI SCI	.31**	3,679	6
PPI C	.14*	611	3

Note. C = Coldheartedness; FD = fearless dominance; PPI = Psychopathic Personality Inventory; SCI = Self-Centered Impulsivity.
*$p < .01$. **$p < .001$.

be needed to exclude the possibility that the association between FD and sexual risk taking reflects the "hitchhiking" of this psychopathy dimension on top of other psychopathy dimensions, especially those assessing impulsivity.

Statistical Interactions Between FD and Self-Centered Impulsivity

One intriguing possibility is that FD is rarely malignant by itself but becomes so in the presence of other traits, especially SCI. Indeed, what Tom Wolfe (1979) described as the "right stuff" may be the conjunction of FD with largely intact executive functioning. In contrast, when FD is conjoined with poor executive functioning, it may be channeled (for a broader discussion of the channeling of motives, see Frost, Ko, & James, 2007, and James, 2008) into poorly planned risk taking, giving rise to the "poor judgment" (p. 345) that Cleckley (1941/1988) described as emblematic of psychopathy. In this vein, some authors have reported significant statistical interactions, usually but not always of a potentiating form, between FD and SCI on clinically relevant outcomes, such as predatory aggression (Smith, Edens, & McDermott, 2013) and sexual risk taking (Fulton et al., 2010; Kastner & Sellbom, 2012).

In contrast, Maples et al. (2014) found little evidence for statistical interactions between FD and SCI in predicting scores on more than 20 external correlates, including indices of antisocial behavior, substance use, or pathological gambling. This interaction did account for a statistically significant, but small (2%), amount of the variance in narcissism scores, although replication of this finding will be necessary. The evidence at present is too preliminary and susceptible to potential "file-drawer effects" to draw confident conclusions regarding the interactional hypothesis. Hence, further investigation of potential statistical interactions between FD and other dimensions of psychopathy is clearly warranted.

It will also be important to investigate the intriguing hypothesis that FD can be channeled into either adaptive (e.g., heroism) or maladaptive (e.g., criminal behavior) outcomes depending on executive functioning, impulsivity, and allied individual differences. In addition, further research should examine the possibility of curvilinear relations between FD and maladaptive outcomes, whereby FD is adaptive at intermediate levels but maladaptive at extremely high levels (for preliminary negative data for this proposition among the U.S. presidents, see Lilienfeld, Waldman, et al., 2012). As Grant and Schwartz (2011) argued, many psychological variables (e.g., happiness, self-esteem) bear curvilinear relations with important real-world outcomes, whereby intermediate levels tend to be psychologically healthy and extreme levels tend to be psychologically unhealthy.

CRITICISMS AND DIRECTIONS FOR FUTURE RESEARCH

Despite the accumulating evidence for its construct validity, the FD construct has not been immune from criticism. The principal criticisms have taken two major forms and raise important directions for research on the nature of this construct.

Factorial Coherence of FD

First, some authors have argued that the higher order dimension of FD, at least as derived from the PPI and PPI–R, lacks clear-cut factorial coherence. Specifically, some factor analyses of the PPI subscales have failed to replicate Benning et al.'s (2003) findings and have not obtained satisfactory model fit for the FD factor (e.g., Neumann, Malterer, & Newman, 2008; Smith, Edens, & Vaughn, 2011). This suboptimal fit derives largely from the fact that two of the three subscales loading onto FD, Fearlessness and Stress Immunity, frequently exhibit substantial positive cross-loadings on the SCI higher order dimension. This lack of stringent factor analytic fit is unsurprising given that the PPI was not developed to yield a higher order factor structure, which emerged only in post hoc analyses of the PPI subscales (Benning et al., 2003; Lilienfeld, 1990).

In part to allay concerns regarding the questionable factorial coherence of PPI-derived FD, Patrick (2010) developed the Triarchic Psychopathy Measure (TriPM), which operationalizes the three constructs of their "triarchic model" of psychopathy: boldness, disinhibition, and meanness. As noted earlier, the construct of boldness is essentially isomorphic with FD. The TriPM is an effort to assess the same higher order constructs as assessed by the PPI and PPI–R but using factorially "purer" (more homogeneous) indices. Preliminary work suggests that the TriPM boldness is correlated highly with PPI/PPI–R FD and displays an extremely similar set of external correlates to FD (Sellbom & Phillips, 2013; Stanley, Wygant, & Sellbom, 2013). Nevertheless, further research will be needed to clarify both the adaptive and maladaptive correlates of TriPM boldness.

Clinical Implications: Relevance of FD to Psychopathy

Second, some authors have contended that FD is of questionable relevance to psychopathy (Lynam & Miller, 2013; Neumann, Uzieblo, Crombez, & Hare, 2013). Specifically, they have argued that findings, including those reviewed earlier, demonstrating that PPI FD is (a) only weakly associated with scores on the two major PCL–R factors; (b) negligibly associated with externalizing (e.g., antisocial) behavior; and (c) associated largely or entirely with adaptive functioning, suggest that this dimension is of dubious importance to personality pathology, including psychopathy. According to these authors, FD is perhaps best regarded as a "specifier" for psychopathy, one that distinguishes more successful from less successful individuals with this condition. Nevertheless, they contend that it is not inherently part of psychopathy.

In response, Lilienfeld, Patrick, et al. (2012) pointed out that key elements of FD, including social poise, charm, venturesomeness, fearlessness, and immunity to anxiety, can be found in numerous classic writings on psychopathy (e.g., Cleckley, 1941/1988; Henderson, 1939; Lykken, 1957; McKinley & Hathaway, 1944). They also noted that PPI-assessed FD (a) distinguishes primary from secondary psychopathy in cluster analytic studies (Hicks, Markon, Patrick, Krueger, & Newman, 2004) and (b) is moderately to highly associated (rs in the .4–.6 range) with total scores on several well-validated self-report psychopathy measures, including the Elemental Psychopathy Assessment (EPA; Few, Miller, & Lynam, 2013), Psychopathy Resemblance Index (PRI; Ross et al., 2009) and, as noted earlier, the SRP (Marcus et al., 2013). Nevertheless, the precise role of FD within the broader construct of psychopathy remains to be resolved. As noted earlier, future research should focus in particular on potential statistical interactions between FD and other psychopathy components in predicting important outcomes.

We are unaware of any systematic research on the implications of FD for intervention in forensic or clinical settings. We suspect, however, that FD could be something of both a blessing and a curse among individuals with psychopathy. On one hand, we speculate that psychopathic individuals with high levels of FD might be more willing to attempt and master novel behaviors in therapy (e.g., acquiring assertiveness skills with friends or coworkers), many of which may be anxiety-provoking to their low-FD counterparts. Moreover, high-FD individuals' levels of emotional resilience during stressful periods of treatment may buffer them against feelings of disappointment and hopelessness. Furthermore, their low levels of social anxiety might foster their ability to establish rapport with therapists, at least in the short run.

On the other hand, we anticipate that psychopathic individuals with high levels of FD may be largely nonresponsive to aversive outcomes, such as relationship dissolution or job loss, given their relative immunity toward distress. Such nonresponsiveness could hinder their ability to learn from mistakes in their romantic or occupational lives. Moreover, their heightened social potency may allow them to be especially persuasive with mental health professionals and influential over their fellow patients or inmates. Thus, such individuals could be especially problematic within therapeutic community or group therapy contexts. Finally, as we noted earlier (see McKinley & Hathaway, 1944), their facade of seeming normality may sometimes lead clinicians to underestimate the severity of their impairment. We encourage researchers to investigate these conjectures.

SUMMARY AND CONCLUSIONS

The inclusion of the construct of fearless dominance may appear anomalous in a book on the dark side of personality. Superficially, at least, there would seem to be few or no downsides to being bold, especially in the social realm. Certainly, few of us would turn down the opportunity to be more charming, interpersonally poised, adventurous, and free of disabling anxiety than we are.

Nevertheless, preliminary but still mixed evidence from several sources raises the intriguing possibility that the construct of FD may carry not only adaptive but maladaptive implications for everyday life, especially when conjoined with high levels of poor impulse control and allied traits. Moreover, although charisma may initially strike us as an unalloyed blessing, this trait may predispose to a heightened propensity for chronic deceptiveness in the presence of a callous, coldhearted disposition (Lilienfeld, Patrick, et al., 2012).

To fully grasp the multifaceted and protean nature of psychopathy, we also need to understand its "mask" of superficial normality (Cleckley, 1941/1988; Patrick, 2006). This misleading veneer of psychological health may allow psychopathic individuals to flourish in a host of challenging interpersonal settings, including business and politics, but in some cases, it also may lead them down the slow but steady path to destruction. Still, as a field, we have made scant progress toward elucidating the nature of this potential double-edged sword. Examining not only the Ted Bundys of the world but also its Chuck Yeagers will be a crucial step in this direction.

REFERENCES

American Psychiatric Association. (2013). *Diagnostic and statistical manual of mental disorders* (5th ed.). Arlington, VA: Author.

Anderson, J. L., Sellbom, M., Wygant, D. B., Salekin, R. T., & Krueger, R. F. (2014). Examining the associations between *DSM–5* section III antisocial personality disorder traits and psychopathy in community and university samples. *Journal of Personality Disorders, 28,* 675–697. http://dx.doi.org/10.1521/pedi_2014_28_134

Benning, S. D., Patrick, C. J., Blonigen, D. M., Hicks, B. M., & Iacono, W. G. (2005). Estimating facets of psychopathy from normal personality traits: A step toward community epidemiological investigations. *Assessment, 12,* 3–18. http://dx.doi.org/10.1177/1073191104271223

Benning, S. D., Patrick, C. J., Hicks, B. M., Blonigen, D. M., & Krueger, R. F. (2003). Factor structure of the psychopathic personality inventory: Validity and implications for clinical assessment. *Psychological Assessment, 15,* 340–350. http://dx.doi.org/10.1037/1040-3590.15.3.340

Benning, S. D., Patrick, C. J., & Iacono, W. G. (2005). Psychopathy, startle blink modulation, and electrodermal reactivity in twin men. *Psychophysiology, 42,* 753–762. http://dx.doi.org/10.1111/j.1469-8986.2005.00353.x

Cava, M. (2012, December 6). Chuck Yeager, still soaring at 89. *USA Today.* Retrieved from http://www.usatoday.com/story/life/tv/2012/12/05/chuck-yeager-intervew/1695301

Cleckley, H. (1988). *The mask of sanity.* St. Louis, MO: Mosby. (Original work published 1941)

CNN Wire Staff. (2012, October 15). *Chuck Yeager retraces history in the sky, breaking the sound barrier—again.* Retrieved from http://www.cnn.com/2012/10/15/us/nevada-yeager-anniversary-flight

Cohen, J. (1988). *Statistical power for the behavioral sciences.* Hillside, NJ: Erlbaum.

Costa, P. T., & McCrae, R. R. (2008). The revised NEO Personality Inventory (NEO–PI–R). In G. J. Boyle, G. Matthews, & D. H. Saklofske (Eds.), *The SAGE handbook of personality theory and assessment: Vol. II. Personality measurement and assessment* (pp. 179–198). Thousand Oaks, CA: Sage.

C-SPAN.org. (2009). *C-SPAN 2009 historians presidential leadership survey.* Retrieved from http://legacy.c-span.org/PresidentialSurvey/Overall-Ranking.aspx

Dindo, L., & Fowles, D. (2011). Dual temperamental risk factors for psychopathic personality: Evidence from self-report and skin conductance. *Journal of Personality and Social Psychology, 100,* 557–566. http://dx.doi.org/10.1037/a0021848

Drislane, L. E., Patrick, C. J., & Arsal, G. (2014). Clarifying the content coverage of differing psychopathy inventories through reference to the Triarchic Psychopathy Measure. *Psychological Assessment, 26,* 350–362.

Few, L. R., Miller, J. D., & Lynam, D. R. (2013). An examination of the factor structure of the Elemental Psychopathy Assessment. *Personality Disorders: Theory, Research, and Treatment, 4,* 247–253. http://dx.doi.org/10.1037/per0000016

Fowles, D. C. (1980). The three arousal model: Implications of Gray's two-factor learning theory for heart rate, electrodermal activity, and psychopathy. *Psychophysiology, 17,* 87–104. http://dx.doi.org/10.1111/j.1469-8986.1980.tb00117.x

Frost, B. C., Ko, C. H. E., & James, L. R. (2007). Implicit and explicit personality: A test of a channeling hypothesis for aggressive behavior. *Journal of Applied Psychology, 92,* 1299–1319. http://dx.doi.org/10.1037/0021-9010.92.5.1299

Fulton, J. J., Marcus, D. K., & Payne, K. T. (2010). Psychopathic personality traits and risky sexual behavior in college students. *Personality and Individual Differences, 49,* 29–33. http://dx.doi.org/10.1016/j.paid.2010.02.035

Fulton, J. J., Marcus, D. K., & Zeigler-Hill, V. (2014). Psychopathic personality traits, risky sexual behavior, and psychological adjustment among college-age women. *Journal of Social and Clinical Psychology, 33,* 143–168.

Grant, A. M., & Schwartz, B. (2011). Too much of a good thing: The challenge and opportunity of the inverted U. *Perspectives on Psychological Science, 6,* 61–76. http://dx.doi.org/10.1177/1745691610393523

Gray, J. A. (1982). *The neuropsychology of anxiety: An enquiry into the function of the septo-hippocampal system*. Oxford, England: Oxford University Press.

Hall, J. R., & Benning, S. D. (2006). The "successful" psychopath: Adaptive and subclinical manifestations of psychopathy in the general population. In C. J. Patrick (Ed.), *Handbook of psychopathy* (pp. 459–478). New York, NY: Guilford Press.

Hare, R. D. (1978). Electrodermal and cardiovascular correlates of psychopathy. In R. D. Hare & D. Schalling (Eds.), *Psychopathic behavior: Approaches to research* (pp. 107–144). New York, NY: Wiley.

Hare, R. D. (2003). *Manual for the Revised Psychopathy Checklist* (2nd ed.). Toronto, Ontario, Canada: Multi-Health Systems.

Henderson, D. K. (1939). *Psychopathic states*. New York, NY: Norton.

Hicks, B. M., Markon, K. E., Patrick, C. J., Krueger, R. F., & Newman, J. P. (2004). Identifying psychopathy subtypes on the basis of personality structure. *Psychological Assessment, 16*, 276–288. http://dx.doi.org/10.1037/1040-3590.16.3.276

Hoyle, R. H., Fejfar, M. C., & Miller, J. D. (2000). Personality and sexual risk taking: A quantitative review. *Journal of Personality, 68*, 1203–1231. http://dx.doi.org/10.1111/1467-6494.00132

James, L. R. (2008). On the path to mediation. *Organizational Research Methods, 11*, 359–363. http://dx.doi.org/10.1177/1094428107308016

Karpman, B. (1941). On the need of separating psychopathy into two distinct clinical types: The symptomatic and the idiopathic. *Journal of Criminal Psychopathology, 3*, 112–137.

Kastner, R. M., & Sellbom, M. (2012). Hypersexuality in college students: The role of psychopathy. *Personality and Individual Differences, 53*, 644–649. http://dx.doi.org/10.1016/j.paid.2012.05.005

Levenson, M. R., Kiehl, K. A., & Fitzpatrick, C. M. (1995). Assessing psychopathic attributes in a noninstitutionalized population. *Journal of Personality and Social Psychology, 68*, 151–158. http://dx.doi.org/10.1037/0022-3514.68.1.151

Lilienfeld, S. O. (1990). *Development and preliminary validation of a self-report measure of psychopathic traits in noncriminal populations* (Unpublished doctoral dissertation). Minneapolis: University of Minnesota.

Lilienfeld, S. O., & Andrews, B. P. (1996). Development and preliminary validation of a self-report measure of psychopathic personality traits in noncriminal populations. *Journal of Personality Assessment, 66*, 488–524. http://dx.doi.org/10.1207/s15327752jpa6603_3

Lilienfeld, S. O., Patrick, C. J., Benning, S. D., Berg, J., Sellbom, M., & Edens, J. F. (2012). The role of fearless dominance in psychopathy: Confusions, controversies, and clarifications. *Personality Disorders: Theory, Practice, and Research, 3*, 327–340. http://dx.doi.org/10.1037/a0026987

Lilienfeld, S. O., Waldman, I. D., Landfield, K., Watts, A. L., Rubenzer, S., & Faschingbauer, T. R. (2012). Fearless dominance and the U.S. presidency:

Implications of psychopathic personality traits for successful and unsuccessful political leadership. *Journal of Personality and Social Psychology, 103*, 489–505. http://dx.doi.org/10.1037/a0029392

Lilienfeld, S. O., Watts, A. L., Smith, S. F., Berg, J., & Latzman, R. D. (2014). Psychopathy deconstructed and reconstructed: Identifying and assembling the building blocks of Cleckley's chimera. *Journal of Personality Disorders*. Advance online publication. http://dx.doi.org/10.1111/jopy.12118.

Lilienfeld, S. O., & Widows, M. R. (2005). *The Psychopathic Personality Inventory— Revised (PPI–R)*. Lutz, FL: Psychological Assessment Resources.

López, R., Poy, R., Patrick, C. J., & Moltó, J. (2013). Deficient fear conditioning and self-reported psychopathy: The role of fearless dominance. *Psychophysiology, 50*, 210–218. http://dx.doi.org/10.1111/j.1469-8986.2012.01493.x

Lorber, M. F. (2004). Psychophysiology of aggression, psychopathy, and conduct problems: A meta-analysis. *Psychological Bulletin, 130*, 531–552. http://dx.doi.org/10.1037/0033-2909.130.4.531

Lykken, D. T. (1957). A study of anxiety in the sociopathic personality. *The Journal of Abnormal and Social Psychology, 55*, 6–10. http://dx.doi.org/10.1037/h0047232

Lykken, D. T. (1982). Fearlessness: Its carefree charm and deadly risks. *Psychology Today, 16*, 20–28.

Lykken, D. T. (1995). *The antisocial personalities*. Hillsdale, NJ: Erlbaum.

Lynam, D. R., Gaughan, E. T., Miller, J. D., Miller, D. J., Mullins-Sweatt, S., & Widiger, T. A. (2011). Assessing the basic traits associated with psychopathy: Development and validation of the Elemental Psychopathy Assessment. *Psychological Assessment, 23*, 108–124. http://dx.doi.org/10.1037/a0021146

Lynam, D. R., & Miller, J. D. (2013). Fearless dominance and psychopathy: A response to Lilienfeld et al. *Personality Disorders: Theory, Research, and Treatment, 3*, 341–353. http://dx.doi.org/10.1037/a0028296

Malterer, M. B., Lilienfeld, S. O., Neumann, C. S., & Newman, J. P. (2010). Concurrent validity of the psychopathic personality inventory with offender and community samples. *Assessment, 17*, 3–15. http://dx.doi.org/10.1177/1073191109349743

Maples, J. L., Miller, J. D., Fortune, E., MacKillop, J., Campbell, W. K., Lynam, D. R., . . . Goodie, A. S. (2014). An examination of the correlates of fearless dominance and self-centered impulsivity among high-frequency gamblers. *Journal of Personality Disorders, 28*, 379–393. http://dx.doi.org/10.1521/pedi_2013_27_125

Marcus, D. K., Fulton, J. J., & Edens, J. F. (2013). The two-factor model of psychopathic personality: Evidence from the psychopathic personality inventory. *Personality Disorders: Theory, Research, and Treatment, 4*, 67–76. http://dx.doi.org/10.1037/a0025282

Marcus, D. K., & Norris, A. L. (2014). A new measure of attitudes toward sexually predatory tactics and its relation to the triarchic model of psychopathy. *Journal of Personality Disorders, 28*, 247–261. http://dx.doi.org/10.1521/pedi_2013_27_118

McKinley, J. C., & Hathaway, S. R. (1944). The Minnesota Multiphasic Personality Inventory. V. Hysteria, hypomania, and psychopathic deviate. *Journal of Applied Psychology, 28,* 153–174. http://dx.doi.org/10.1037/h0059245

Miller, J. D., & Lynam, D. R. (2012). An examination of the Psychopathic Personality Inventory's nomological network: A meta-analytic review. *Personality Disorders: Theory, Research, and Treatment, 3,* 305–326. http://dx.doi.org/10.1037/a0024567

Neumann, C. S., Malterer, M. B., & Newman, J. P. (2008). Factor structure of the Psychopathic Personality Inventory (PPI): Findings from a large incarcerated sample. *Psychological Assessment, 20,* 169–174. http://dx.doi.org/10.1037/1040-3590.20.2.169

Neumann, C. S., Uzieblo, K., Crombez, G., & Hare, R. D. (2013). Understanding the Psychopathic Personality Inventory (PPI) in terms of the unidimensionality, orthogonality, and construct validity of PPI–I and–II. *Personality Disorders: Theory, Research, and Treatment, 4,* 77–79. http://dx.doi.org/10.1037/a0027196

Patrick, C. J. (2006). Back to the future: Cleckley as a guide to the next generation of psychopathy research. In C. J. Patrick (Ed.), *Handbook of psychopathy* (pp. 605–617). New York, NY: Guilford Press.

Patrick, C. J. (2010). *Operationalizing the triarchic conceptualization of psychopathy: Description of brief scales for assessment of boldness, meanness, and disinhibition.* Unpublished manual, University of Minnesota, Minneapolis. Retrieved from https://www.phenxtoolkit.org/toolkit_content/supplemental_info/psychiatric/measures/Triarchic_Psychopathy_Measure_Manual.pdf

Patrick, C. J., & Drislane, L. E. (2014). Triarchic model of psychopathy: Origins, operationalizations, and observed linkages with personality and general psychopathology. *Journal of Personality.* Advance online publication. http://dx.doi.org/10.1111/jopy.12119.

Patrick, C. J., Fowles, D. C., & Krueger, R. F. (2009). Triarchic conceptualization of psychopathy: Developmental origins of disinhibition, boldness, and meanness. *Development and Psychopathology, 21,* 913–938. http://dx.doi.org/10.1017/S0954579409000492

Patrick, C. J., Venables, N. C., & Drislane, L. E. (2013). The role of fearless dominance in differentiating psychopathy from antisocial personality disorder: Comment on Marcus, Fulton, and Edens. *Personality Disorders: Theory, Research, and Treatment, 4,* 80–82. http://dx.doi.org/10.1037/a0027173

Paulhus, D. L., Neumann, C. S., & Hare, R. D. (2014). *The SRP–III.* Toronto, Ontario, Canada: Multi-Health Systems.

Paulhus, D. L., & Williams, K. M. (2002). The dark triad of personality: Narcissism, Machiavellianism, and psychopathy. *Journal of Research in Personality, 36,* 556–563. http://dx.doi.org/10.1016/S0092-6566(02)00505-6

Quay, H. C. (1965). Psychopathic personality as pathological stimulation-seeking. *The American Journal of Psychiatry, 122,* 180–183. http://dx.doi.org/10.1176/ajp.122.2.180

Ross, S. R., Benning, S. D., Patrick, C. J., Thompson, A., & Thurston, A. (2009). Factors of the psychopathic personality inventory: Criterion-related validity and relationship to the BIS/BAS and five-factor models of personality. *Assessment, 16*, 71–87. http://dx.doi.org/10.1177/1073191108322207

Sellbom, M., & Phillips, T. R. (2013). An examination of the triarchic conceptualization of psychopathy in incarcerated and nonincarcerated samples. *Journal of Abnormal Psychology, 122*, 208–214. http://dx.doi.org/10.1037/a0029306

Siena College. (2010, July 1). *Siena's 5th presidential expert poll 1982–2010.* Retrieved from http://www2.siena.edu/pages/179.asp?item=2566

Simpson, J. A., & Gangestad, S. W. (1991). Individual differences in sociosexuality: Evidence for convergent and discriminant validity. *Journal of Personality and Social Psychology, 60*, 870–883. http://dx.doi.org/10.1037/0022-3514.60.6.870

Smith, S. F., Lilienfeld, S. O., Coffey, K., & Dabbs, J. M. (2013). Are psychopaths and heroes twigs off the same branch? Evidence from college, community, and presidential samples. *Journal of Research in Personality, 47*, 634–646. http://dx.doi.org/10.1016/j.jrp.2013.05.006

Smith, S. T., Edens, J. F., & McDermott, B. E. (2013). Fearless dominance and self-centered impulsivity interact to predict predatory aggression among forensic psychiatric inpatients. *The International Journal of Forensic Mental Health, 12*, 33–41. http://dx.doi.org/10.1080/14999013.2012.760186

Smith, S. T., Edens, J. F., & Vaughn, M. G. (2011). Assessing the external correlates of alternative factor models of the Psychopathic Personality Inventory—Short Form across three samples. *Journal of Personality Assessment, 93*, 244–256. http://dx.doi.org/10.1080/00223891.2011.558876

Stanley, J. H., Wygant, D. B., & Sellbom, M. (2013). Elaborating on the construct validity of the Triarchic Psychopathy Measure in a criminal offender sample. *Journal of Personality Assessment, 95*, 343–350. http://dx.doi.org/10.1080/00223891.2012.735302

Tellegen, A., & Waller, N. G. (2008). Exploring personality through test construction: Development of the Multidimensional Personality Questionnaire. In G. J. Boyle, G. Matthews, & D. H. Saklofske (Eds.), *Handbook of personality theory and testing: Vol. II. Personality measurement and assessment* (pp. 261–292). Thousand Oaks, CA: Sage. http://dx.doi.org/10.4135/9781849200479.n13

Turchik, J. A., & Garske, J. P. (2009). Measurement of sexual risk taking among college students. *Archives of Sexual Behavior, 38*, 936–948. http://dx.doi.org/10.1007/s10508-008-9388-z

Vaidyanathan, U., Hall, J. R., Patrick, C. J., & Bernat, E. M. (2011). Clarifying the role of defensive reactivity deficits in psychopathy and antisocial personality using startle reflex methodology. *Journal of Abnormal Psychology, 120*, 253–258. http://dx.doi.org/10.1037/a0021224

Wall, T. D., Wygant, D. B., & Sellbom, M. (2015). Boldness explains a key difference between psychopathy and antisocial personality disorder. *Psychiatry, Psychology and Law, 22*, 94–105.

Wells, S. (2008). Did Yeager really fly under WV bridge? *The Charleston Gazette*. Retrieved from http://www.ar15.com/archive/topic.html?b=1&f=5&t=767739

Widom, C. S. (1977). A methodology for studying noninstitutionalized psychopaths. *Journal of Consulting and Clinical Psychology, 45*, 674–683. http://dx.doi.org/10.1037/0022-006X.45.4.674

Wolfe, T. (1979). *The right stuff*. New York, NY: Random House.

World Health Organization. (1992). *International statistical classification of diseases and related health problems* (10th rev.). Geneva, Switzerland: Author.

4

THE NATURE OF MACHIAVELLIANISM: DISTINCT PATTERNS OF MISBEHAVIOR

DANIEL N. JONES

DEFINITION AND BACKGROUND

Machiavellianism is a personality trait designed to assess dispositional agreement with the influential philosopher Niccolò Machiavelli. Christie and Geis (1970) noticed that there were stable individual differences among individuals who agreed versus disagreed with Machiavelli's ideas. These observations were developed into formal theoretical arguments, assessments, and research on the construct that came to be known as Machiavellianism. Machiavellianism has traditionally been associated with the "darker side" of human nature (Paulhus & Williams, 2002). Machiavelli's philosophy—and the dispositional tendencies with which it aligns—facilitates antisocial methods of goal attainment. Often, these tendencies are also associated with greed and selfishness, which are justified through rationalizations surrounding expediency and bottom-line goals.

http://dx.doi.org/10.1037/14854-005
The Dark Side of Personality: Science and Practice in Social, Personality, and Clinical Psychology, V. Zeigler-Hill and D. K. Marcus (Editors)
Copyright © 2016 by the American Psychological Association. All rights reserved.

Empirical research has supported the link between Machiavellianism and antisocial strategies. Machiavellianism is associated with low levels of agreeableness and conscientiousness (Jakobwitz & Egan, 2006), empathy (Wai & Tiliopoulos, 2012), and cooperation (Paal & Bereczkei, 2007). Individuals higher in Machiavellianism surrender interpersonal connections in the service of tangible goals (Hawley & Geldhof, 2012; Jonason & Schmitt, 2012; Lyons & Aitken, 2010; Wei & Chen, 2012). Callousness and manipulation make up the core of many dark personality traits, including Machiavellianism (Jones & Figueredo, 2013).

Some researchers disagree with the idea that Machiavellianism is a destructive trait (e.g., Rauthmann & Kolar, 2012). Research on leadership dispositions suggests that Machiavellianism can lead to pragmatic and effective leadership (e.g., Deluga, 2001). Furthermore, some popular press authors have rejected the notion that Machiavelli espoused antisocial ideas (Evans, 2013). Evans (2013) argued that Machiavelli was a role model and that his ideas are beneficial in many endeavors, ranging from business to parenting. Research has also found that too little Machiavellianism is associated with poor business performance (Zettler & Solga, 2013). There is also theoretical and empirical support for the idea that Machiavellianism leads to greater resource control and adjustment in children (Hawley, 2003). Hawley, Little, and Card (2007) showed that although Machiavellian individuals are likely to control resources in a way that is self-serving, they may also serve the interests of others when doing so is mutually beneficial. Indeed, Machiavellianism is a key variable in examining resource control, which is related to a variety of strategies including bistrategic, prosocial, and coercive strategies (Zeigler-Hill, Southard, & Besser, 2014). Christie and Geis (1970) referred to Machiavellian individuals as "amoral." It is not that they are immoral or innately antisocial, they simply appear willing to turn a blind eye to the morality of their decisions. In other words, Machiavellian individuals simply do what they think will work for selfish gain. Thus, Machiavellianism appears to pose a trade-off rather than an unequivocal deficit.

In sum, Machiavellian individuals may be useful under the right circumstances. Although they may find ways to get a job done where others could not, Machiavellian individuals are ultimately self-interested and open to unethical behavior. Thus, allegiance with a Machiavellian individual may be a risky trade-off.

REVIEW OF THE RELEVANT LITERATURE

What Is Machiavellianism? Unique Aspects of the Trait

In defining Machiavellianism, it is critical to understand Machiavelli's ideas. Jones and Paulhus (2011a) reviewed the elemental components of the political strategist Machiavelli, as well as those of military strategist Sun Tzu. They concluded that the philosophical, strategic, and tactical rhetoric of these authors suggested that ideal leaders are strategically manipulative. These classic writings greatly emphasized preparation, planning, forethought, expedience, rationality, logic, opportunism, reputation cultivation, and decision-making tendencies that are divorced from personal bias and sympathies.

Thus, any assessment of Machiavellianism should contain or relate to aspects of selfish planning and strategy, caution, expedience, self-interest, cynical perspectives, callousness, manipulative tactics, and deceit. Individuals higher in Machiavellianism use strategic behaviors for selfish gain (Czibor & Bereczkei, 2012), which is unlike those high in psychopathy and narcissism. Moreover, Machiavellianism is associated with sensitivity to social situations (Bereczkei, Deak, Papp, Perlaki, & Orsi, 2013; Spitzer, Fischbacher, Herrnberger, Grön, & Fehr, 2007), and with a dark view of humanity (Burris, Rempel, Munteanu, & Therrien, 2013). Finally, Machiavellianism is associated with a lack of guilt or remorse when misbehaving selfishly (Murphy, 2012), manipulating others (e.g., Jonason, Slomski, & Partyka, 2012), and being dishonest (Lee & Ashton, 2005). It should be noted that these last three characteristics are also associated with psychopathy, which sometimes leads to confusion between the two constructs.

Construct Confusion—What Is Not Machiavellianism

McHoskey, Worzel, and Szyarto (1998) pointed out that there is substantial overlap between Machiavellianism and subclinical psychopathy. The two constructs predicted similar outcomes and traits and were highly correlated with one another. They noted that these two traits developed in different areas of psychology and were therefore examined in isolation from one another. Thus, the construct overlap may be because authors were discussing similar ideas with different names.

Paulhus and Williams (2002) examined this idea more closely in their seminal research on the *Dark Triad*. They found that three of the most commonly researched traits predicting interpersonal harm (Machiavellianism, psychopathy, and narcissism) were indeed distinct. Paulhus and Williams urged researchers to examine all three traits when conducting research on misbehavior. In this way, the field may begin to clarify which outcomes are best predicted by which trait. Despite the body of literature describing differences between Machiavellianism and the other two Dark Triad traits, some have resurrected a unificationist perspective (Jonason, Li, Webster, & Schmitt, 2009; Jonason, Webster, Schmitt, Li, & Crysel, 2012).

Glenn and Sellbom (2015) articulated the problems with treating the Dark Triad as a construct, finding that psychopathy usually accounts for most of the predictive variance. There are at least two additional reasons why merging Machiavellianism with other dark personality traits—and discussing them as being interchangeable or as a Dark Triad construct—is an inappropriate oversimplification. First, there are conceptual nuances among the traits that are lost. Machiavellianism, which is associated with caution and expedience, represents manipulation and callousness in a strategic form. By contrast, psychopathy and narcissism are manipulation and callousness in reckless and grandiose forms, respectively (for reviews, see Chapters 1 and 2, this volume). Unlike psychopathy, Machiavellianism has no association with short-term thinking when properly assessed (Jonason & Tost, 2010, Study 1). Furthermore, although psychopathy and narcissism have unique links with impulsivity, Machiavellianism does not (Jones & Paulhus, 2011b). It should be noted that both Machiavellianism and psychopathy predict stealing (Jones, 2013), sexual infidelity (McHoskey, 2001), and academic dishonesty (Williams, Nathanson, & Paulhus, 2010). However, unlike psychopathic individuals (e.g., Hare, 1996), Machiavellian individuals use caution when stealing (e.g., Cooper & Peterson, 1980; Jones, 2014), maintain relationships in the face of infidelity (Jones & Weiser, 2014), and do not engage in impulsive forms of academic dishonesty (Williams et al., 2010).

Similar confusion exists with respect to overconfidence and self-deception, which are associated with grandiose narcissism (Paulhus, Harms, Bruce, & Lysy, 2003) but not associated with Machiavellianism. For example, narcissism, but not Machiavellianism, correlates with overclaiming knowledge and overestimating one's intelligence (Paulhus & Williams, 2002). Machiavellian individuals, given their interest in the instrumental bottom line, chart a realistic (albeit cynical and selfish) course to attain their goals.

The second reason for considering the Dark Triad as distinct constructs is that the majority of research arguing for their interchangeability relies on self-reported behavior in hypothetical situations. It is likely that most callous-manipulative individuals would endorse a willingness to engage in hypothetical antisocial behaviors in a consequence-free anonymous survey. Thus, behavioral outcomes (or at least past behaviors) are needed to reveal differences among these traits. Moreover, research concerning the Dark Triad has found important trait differences in behavioral genetics (Vernon, Villani, Vickers, & Harris, 2008) and laboratory aggression (Jones & Paulhus, 2010). Finally, meta-analytic evidence has supported the assertion that it is critical to differentiate the traits when examining important outcomes (O'Boyle, Forsyth, Banks, & McDaniel, 2012).

In sum, characteristics such as recklessness, impulsivity, overconfidence, and self-deception are not part of the original conceptualization of Machiavellianism, and empirical research does not support associations between these characteristics and Machiavellianism. Thus, Machiavellianism is unlikely to predict behaviors, crimes, or malevolence associated with (a) recklessness or impulsivity (e.g., petty theft, street crimes, drug-related crimes); (b) reactivity/emotionality (e.g., domestic violence, physical abuse); (c) social pressure (e.g., drug use, vandalism); (d) ego threat (e.g., responses to insults, anger); (e) sadistic desires (e.g., Internet trolling; Buckels, Trapnell, & Paulhus, 2014); (f) deficits in impulse control (e.g., sexual coaxing or coercion; Jones & Olderbak, 2014); or (g) low socioeconomic status, poverty, or desperation (e.g., robbery). It is not the case that Machiavellianism would predict moral objection to these behaviors, they just simply fail to yield sufficient material reward or pose too much direct risk to be predicted by Machiavellianism.

Theory of Mind and Machiavellianism

Many researchers have searched for a connection between *theory of mind* (ToM) and Machiavellianism. It seemed plausible that individuals who manipulate others must have some aptitude at, or at least predilection for, taking another's perspective for the purposes of successful manipulation (e.g., McIlwain, 2003). However, repeated attempts have failed to find any positive association between Machiavellianism and ToM (Jonason & Krause, 2013; Lyons, Caldwell, & Shultz, 2010; Paal & Bereczkei, 2007). Instead, almost all of these studies found a negative correlation between the two.

The exception to the pattern that Machiavellianism is associated with deficits in ToM is that individuals higher in Machiavellianism are actually better at recognizing negative emotional states (Ali & Chamorro-Premuzic, 2010; Bagozzi et al., 2013). Following these conflicting findings, neurological research by Bagozzi and colleagues (2013) discovered that Machiavellian individuals are more attuned to others with respect to the detection of negative emotions but less likely to take another's perspective. This negative association suggests an ability trade-off in Machiavellianism.

Neurological Research

In most studies dealing with financial decision making, individuals higher in Machiavellianism gain more money (e.g., Bereczkei et al., 2013; Nestor et al., 2013; Spitzer et al., 2007). To understand why, neurological research (i.e., structural and functional magnetic resonance imaging [MRI]) has explored the Machiavellian brain. Region volume and activation associated with Machiavellianism points to a focus on bottom-line goals, situational flexibility, sensitivity to environmental cues, and cautious/strategic dispositions.

For example, Verbeke et al. (2011) found that Machiavellianism was associated with thicker brain regions associated with reward seeking (e.g., the caudate, pallidum, and putamen), emotion suppression (e.g., insula), social strategizing (e.g., orbital frontal gyrus, superior medial frontal gyrus, middle and superior frontal gyrus), and social learning (e.g., right hippocampus and left parahippocampal gyrus). Spitzer and colleagues (2007) also found evidence for Machiavellian reward (and punishment) sensitivity. In a series of financial decision tasks, they found that individuals higher in Machiavellianism were opportunistically selfish when no punishment could befall them. However, when a partner could punish them, individuals higher in Machiavellianism behaved fairly. Additionally, Spitzer and colleagues (2007) found that individuals higher in Machiavellianism showed greater activation in the lateral orbitofrontal cortex (OFC) and the right insula while making financial decisions. They argued that because the lateral OFC is responsive to reward and punishment, and the right insula shows awareness of impending harm, Machiavellian individuals are honed in on maximizing their profits given a particular situation. It is interesting to note that the Machiavellian brain only shows sensitivity to social norms in punishment context. By contrast, whether punishment was possible or not, individuals lower in Machiavellianism showed sensitivity to social norms both behaviorally and neurologically.

Nestor and colleagues (2013) explored structural differences in the Machiavellian brain. Complementing the work of Spitzer and colleagues (2007), they found that Machiavellianism was associated with increased volume in the left lateral orbital gyrus and left middle orbital gyrus. Not only was the volume of these regions associated with self-reported Machiavellianism, but the associations could not be explained through any index of intelligence. In fact, the authors found evidence of a double dissociation in OFC regions with respect to intelligence and Machiavellianism, which may explain why high intelligence may interact with Machiavellianism to determine financial success (Turner & Martinez, 1977).

Finally, Bereczkei and colleagues (2013) had individuals play an investment game for money under functional MRI observation. Player A could invest a certain amount of money in Player B. That money would then be tripled by the experimenter, and Player B would have the option to return some, all, or none of the money to Player A. They found that individuals higher in Machiavellianism invested less money in others and reciprocated less money than others. They also examined the neurological activity of individuals higher versus lower in Machiavellianism during this financial trust game. They found that individuals higher in Machiavellianism experienced greater activation in regions of the brain that are indicative of risk aversion (inferior frontal gyrus) as well as executive control, anticipation of benefits, and mental flexibility (bilateral middle frontal gyrus). There was also greater activation in the right thalamus, which is essential in processing monetary rewards and reward anticipation. Finally, Machiavellianism was associated with greater activation in the anterior cingulate cortex. In particular, this activation was related to deliberation over response times, suggesting that Machiavellian individuals are carefully processing the long- versus short-term consequences of their decisions.

These findings further support the idea that Machiavellianism is a trait that leads individuals to focus on reward-based outcomes, caution, flexibility, and context sensitivity. Spitzer and colleagues (2007) noted that although individuals higher in both psychopathy and Machiavellianism are insensitive to social norms, only Machiavellian individuals are sensitive to reward and punishment. In fact, such sensitivity to punishment may help explain why Machiavellianism is associated (albeit slightly) with higher levels of neuroticism (Jakobwitz & Egan, 2006; Paulhus & Williams, 2002). In sum, although individuals higher in Machiavellianism have poor ToM (Bagozzi et al., 2013), they are sensitive to social context, cautious and controlled in their misbehavior, unconcerned about social norms, and focused on bottom-line tangible rewards.

Context and Decision Making

Bagozzi and colleagues (2013) found that Machiavellian individuals are sensitive to their social environment in business settings and act to maximize selfish benefits. Machiavellianism is associated with engaging in visible types of prosocial behaviors (referred to as *organizational citizenship behaviors*, or OCBs) such as attending meetings in work settings. In particular, Machiavellianism is also associated with increases in these prosocial tendencies under high levels of management control. By contrast, individuals higher in Machiavellianism are less likely to engage in *individual-directed* OCBs, such as privately helping others and engage in these behaviors even less often when under increased management control. Bagozzi and colleagues also found that in addition to helping other coworkers, increased supervisor control increased sales performance and coworker aid among individuals lower (but not higher) in Machiavellianism. This latter finding replicates previous research about the Machiavellian desire for improvisation and relaxed ethical constraints (Sparks, 1994).

Using behavioral economics games and social dilemma research, Czibor and Bereczkei (2012) found Machiavellianism to be associated with a tendency to focus on the potential thoughts and moves of others before acting. This attention paid to the deliberations of others, and the monitoring of their potential future decisions, provides Machiavellian individuals with potential advantages in manipulation. Similarly, Esperger and Bereczkei (2012) found that Machiavellian individuals spontaneously generate future predictions about others' behaviors, thereby demonstrating some of the processes that make them strategic manipulators. In sum, Machiavellian individuals are cautious and calculating and adjust their behavior to a given situation to maximize their profit.

Context is a critical factor in Machiavellian decision making. Machiavellian individuals do not volunteer their time under anonymous conditions (Bereczkei, Birkas, & Kerekes, 2007) but do so when their public efforts might bring social benefits (Bereczkei, Birkas, & Kerekes, 2010). They are also responsive to social situations with financial consequences. For example Bereczkei and Czibor (2014) assessed temperament and Machiavellianism among five participants who engaged in a public goods game, which involves making decisions about individual contributions to the larger group. Individuals higher in Machiavellianism contributed less money to the group but earned significantly more. They also engaged in financial investing suggestive of sensitivity to context. Specifically, the behavior of individuals higher in Machiavellianism depended greatly on the emergent number of "free-riders" (i.e., individuals who did not contribute to, but benefited from, the group) versus "cooperators" (i.e., individuals who contributed to the group) in a given pool of participants. In essence, when others contributed less, so did Machiavellian individuals.

Research on Machiavellian selfishness in a consequence-free environment found that individuals higher in Machiavellianism took from others for selfish gain (Jones, 2013) or selfishly withheld funds from others (Bereczkei et al., 2013). These results replicate previous research findings that when individuals higher in Machiavellianism have a single interaction (i.e., there are no repercussions), they behave selfishly (Gunnthorsdottir, McCabe, & Smith, 2002). Spitzer and colleagues (2007) replicated this effect as well, finding that in a "no punishment" condition, individuals higher in Machiavellianism were selfishly unfair with money. However, when punishment was possible, individuals higher in Machiavellianism were quite fair (see also Jones, 2014).

ADAPTIVE AND MALADAPTIVE FEATURES

Machiavellianism has unique implications for financially based crimes and other misbehaviors related to modern business. In a review, Jones and Paulhus (2009) found that individuals higher in Machiavellianism were generally unethical and primarily focused on personal gain. More recent research continues to find associations between Machiavellianism and unethical business-related behaviors. Machiavellianism is associated with increases in counterproductive and unethical work behaviors, such as prolonging work to gain overtime compensation (O'Boyle et al., 2012). One recent program of research found that individuals higher in Machiavellianism make fewer overall contributions and inflict more harm on their organization by engaging in behaviors such as contract breaches, especially when not personally affected (Zagenczyk et al., 2013; Zagenczyk, Restubog, Kiewitz, Kiazad, & Tang, 2014). Possibly because of their cynical and bottom-line nature, individuals higher in Machiavellianism viewed work relationships as financial contracts of gain and loss (i.e., transactional psychological contracts). Machiavellianism was associated with fewer private citizenship behaviors (e.g., helping others in the company who may need it) and more deviant work behaviors such as ridiculing colleagues (O'Boyle et al., 2012). Zagenczyk and colleagues (2014) found that these associations were mediated by transactional psychological contracts, which are defined by keeping close tabs on give/reward and take/ punishment in social exchanges. Finally, although Machiavellianism was unrelated to actual task performance (i.e., productivity), it was a strong predictor of contextual performance (i.e., performing well when it is beneficial to the individual). In general, employees who are higher in Machiavellianism may be a liability to a business or organization. They may bring benefits under certain conditions (such as when their personal goals align with that of the company) but are unlikely to sacrifice for the good of the company or fellow coworkers. These tendencies may produce unethical behavior, counterproductive behaviors, deviant behaviors, and a poor work environment (e.g., Kiazad, Restubog, Zagenczyk, Kiewitz, & Tang, 2010). These findings are also consistent with research arguing that moderate-level endorsement of darker traits can be effective in business contexts (Kaiser, LeBreton, & Hogan, 2015; Zettler & Solga, 2013).

Machiavellian leadership can also have a negative effect on subordinates by creating a propensity for unethical and counterproductive behaviors. Machiavellian leaders are perceived by subordinates as disingenuous when modeling ethical behavior, despite attempts to portray an outward veneer of ethics (Den Hartog & Belschak, 2012). Machiavellian leadership also has a profound negative impact on subordinates with respect to how they see themselves. For example, individuals low in organizationally based self-esteem (which is a domain of self-worth predicated on one's work environment) responded most negatively to Machiavellian leadership (Kiazad et al., 2010). Thus, Machiavellian leaders producing a harsh "bottom-line"-driven work environment may not provide the encouragement or reinforcement needed by subordinates, and this environment may be especially toxic for those insecure about their own abilities.

In addition to a toxic and bottom-line driven atmosphere, individuals higher in Machiavellianism also endorse a lax ethical environment for their subordinates (Vladu, 2013). This combination of pushing the bottom line and few ethical constraints produces environments that encourage unethical business behaviors. Furthermore, individuals most likely to thrive in such environments are those who are also higher in Machiavellianism. This assertion is consistent with the finding that when individuals higher in Machiavellianism are part of a deal, they are easily persuaded to create "slack" in a budget, allowing for misappropriation of funds (Hartmann & Maas, 2010).

Individuals higher in Machiavellianism rationalize financial misbehaviors such as misreporting (Murphy, 2012). Murphy found that individuals higher in Machiavellianism were likely to misreport their financial earnings in a laboratory experiment and felt little guilt in doing so. Furthermore, unlike those lower in Machiavellianism who selfishly misreported funds and felt guilty later, guilt was not a motivating force behind the production of rationalizations among individuals higher in Machiavellianism who misreported for selfish gain. Thus, individuals higher in Machiavellianism were undisturbed by their selfish behavior, and rationalizations came quite automatically and naturally (rather than reactively and viscerally).

In addition to a lack of guilt, individuals higher in Machiavellianism appear to be responsive to ethical violations only when it suits them. For example, they are unlikely to report unethical behaviors by coworkers unless there is an opportunity for personal gain (Dalton & Radtke, 2013). Such individuals explore a given situation and turn others in rather than suffer punishment. These findings are consistent with previous literature that found Machiavellian individuals would spy on coworkers to gain a competitive company advantage (Macrosson & Hemphill, 2001). Individuals higher in Machiavellianism are similarly unconcerned with information technology violations of ethics when they have the skills to perpetrate such crimes, but are highly concerned with Internet privacy and related ethical concerns when they lack the skills to commit those crimes (Stylianou, Winter, Niu, Giacalone, & Campbell, 2013).

Individuals higher in Machiavellianism engage in crimes of opportunity (Christie & Geis, 1970) that present maximum benefits and require minimal cost or risk (Spitzer et al., 2007). Machiavellian individuals endorse attitudes that are convenient and coincide with opportunities (Mudrack, 1993) or skills available to them (Stylianou et al., 2013). They endorse breaches in ethical standards or contractual agreements when they personally stand to gain (Dalton & Radtke, 2013) or have no stake in the company (Zagenczyk et al., 2013), and selfishly misreport information for gain (Murphy, 2012). Whether cheating financially or academically (Williams et al., 2010), individuals higher in Machiavellianism only engage in these behaviors when they are unlikely to be detected.

In sum, Machiavellianism would be expected to be related to a range of misbehaviors that bring about financial, social, or political benefits. Individuals higher in Machiavellianism are well suited for crimes in the financial world, especially crimes that skirt the legal boundaries and are difficult to prosecute

(Ivancevich, Duening, Gilbert, & Konopaske, 2003). In particular, white-collar crimes (Benson & Simpson, 2009) such as antitrust violations, embezzlement, financial misreporting (e.g., "book cooking"), labor violations securities fraud, and other related crimes of a long-term nature seem as though they would be especially tempting and attractive to an individual higher in Machiavellianism. Furthermore, individuals higher in Machiavellianism (especially those with higher intelligence; Turner & Martinez, 1977; see also Nestor et al., 2013) may be especially well suited and predisposed to committing such crimes.

DIRECTIONS FOR FUTURE RESEARCH

Dark Triad Assessments

Research on Machiavellianism should continue to include other dark personality covariates to ensure that Machiavellianism, in particular, is predicting unique variance in outcome variables (Paulhus & Williams, 2002). It is understandable that, until recently, this was a daunting task because of the length of the assessments that were available for other overlapping traits. However, two brief assessments of the Dark Triad have emerged. The first was the *Dirty Dozen* (Jonason & Webster, 2010), which attempted to assess the Dark Triad traits using four items for each construct. This assessment was developed with an agenda of uniting the Dark Triad traits into a single composite (e.g., Jonason et al., 2009). Unfortunately, this approach is limited and the Dirty Dozen has been regarded as a "cautionary tale" (Miller et al., 2012) for assessments that are too brief to capture critical construct variance (see also Carter, Campbell, Muncer, & Carter, 2015). Another assessment, the Short Dark Triad (SD3; Jones & Paulhus, 2014), has emerged, which attempted to assess Dark Triad traits using nine items per trait. In head-to-head comparisons, the SD3 has been recommended as the brief assessment of choice for the Dark Triad (Lee et al., 2013; Maples, Lamkin, & Miller, 2014).

New Methods of Assessment

Paulhus and Jones (2015) surveyed the current assessments across a host of dark personality features, including Machiavellianism. There are several highlights to note. First, the Mach–IV (Christie & Geis, 1970) is still the most widely used instrument to assess Machiavellianism, although it is more than 40 years old. Importantly, there are outdated items that no longer assess Machiavellianism, such as questions pertaining to euthanasia (see Bagozzi et al., 2013). In addition, the Mach–IV was designed without much knowledge with respect to surrounding constructs (Paulhus & Williams, 2002). As a consequence, efforts to revise the Mach scales are needed (Jones & Paulhus, 2009; Rauthmann, 2012).

Self-report notwithstanding, the future of Machiavellianism assessment is likely to be in surreptitious measures, observational accounts, or peer assessment (see Zagenczyk et al., 2014). Machiavellianism is critical (albeit difficult) to detect in certain populations (e.g., business professionals, politicians) given the deceptive nature of these individuals. As such, individuals higher in Machiavellianism may be reluctant to provide accurate assessments of their own personality features. One solution may be peer assessment. I have made several attempts to create a "Dark Triad Peer Assessment." Most of the latent variable procedures resulted in a large single factor explaining most of the variance. This "scoundrel factor" seems to consume all the peer-report items into a common factor driven by disliking a person. A peer-report driven solution for Machiavellianism may present unique challenges because these individuals (by definition) prefer to maintain a shroud of secrecy over their misbehavior due to caution or expedience.

There may be ways of overcoming these limitations. For example, one might approach changes in behavior across different contexts and individuals. Because individuals higher in Machiavellianism are sensitive to social contexts, they are likely to change their behavior more efficiently across different social situations. Thus, the total "scoundrel" score combined with the variance across situations may be a fruitful avenue to pursue. Similarly, there may be pronounced differences in personality assessment across individuals who have known those higher in Machiavellianism for a long versus short period of time. Given that Machiavellianism is a trait associated with secrecy, it might take substantial periods of time for "Machiavellian secrets" to be revealed. Whatever the assessment, researchers need to find better ways of detecting Machiavellianism without relying exclusively on self-report. This task should be met with urgency given the critical nature of the trait and its implications for predicting unique misbehavior.

CLINICAL IMPLICATIONS

There are several ways in which Machiavellianism may inform clinical practice. Although Christie and Geis (1970) originally conceptualized Machiavellianism as free of psychopathology, research has shown that Machiavellianism is associated with mental health issues (Latorre & McLeod, 1978) and has moderate correlations with neuroticism (Jakobwitz & Egan, 2006; Paulhus & Williams, 2002; Vernon et al., 2008). In some cases, Machiavellianism may be derived from, and be reflective of, other forms of psychopathology. Thus, it is difficult to determine whether Machiavellianism is the cause or consequence of mental health issues.

At the very least, given the cynical worldview that is inherent to Machiavellianism, such individuals have a perceived necessity to look out for one's self (e.g., "He must stick to the good for as long as he can, but, being compelled by necessity, be prepared to take the path of evil"; Machiavelli, 1513/1981, p. 69). However, there are two ways in which one may perceive the need to manipulate others: *real* and *imagined*, which roughly correspond to *alpha* and *beta* press (Murray, 1938). Briefly, alpha press corresponds to real pressures pushing an individual toward a particular behavior, whereas beta press constitutes perceived pressures. Individuals who are dispositionally selfish, greedy, and callous may perceive what they have to never be enough. Furthermore, their cynicism may contribute to the perception that others are a constant threat and deserve to be manipulated. These individuals are compelled by perceptions of need, or beta press, such that they are driven by a selfish and callous dispositional approach to the world.

In contrast, there are individuals who have actually struggled with unfair situations or abusive environments, have been made to feel helpless or hopeless due to unfair treatment, and may develop a manipulative nature and cynical worldview as defense mechanisms against further interpersonal harm. In this case, Machiavellianism would be a downstream correlate or consequence of psychopathology or environmental struggles. Naturally, in this case, psychopathology and Machiavellianism would be highly correlated. Furthermore, any Machiavellianism assessment would pick up on individuals who feel "compelled by necessity" to manipulate others, due to either real or imagined injustice.

This argument is further bolstered by the fact that, among the three Dark Triad traits, Machiavellianism is predicted as much by shared environment as it is by genetics (Vernon et al., 2008). Thus, it may be that life experiences (especially those during the early years of life) may create environmental risks for developing (among other issues) high levels of Machiavellianism. Indeed, research has begun examining how childhood environments may contribute to the development of Machiavellianism (Láng, & Lénárd, 2015). In particular, neglect may contribute to a perceived need for exaggerated self-reliance, which may compromise secure attachment and empathy (Jonason, Lyons, & Bethell, 2014).

In some cases, clinicians may be treating the manipulative tendencies of an individual without realizing that they are serving ego-defensive functions. Thus, for some individuals presenting with Machiavellian tendencies, dealing with insecure attachment, mistrust of others, and perceptions of helplessness and hopelessness may also attenuate the client's Machiavellian approach toward others. In other cases, the Machiavellianism displayed by the individual may not be a result of pathology but may be more of a core feature of the individual's personality. Given that rationalization is a key feature of the Machiavellianism construct (Murphy, 2012), dealing directly with Machiavellianism in treatment settings may require restructuring those rationalizations in an effort to short-circuit them.

SUMMARY AND CONCLUSIONS

Machiavellianism is perhaps the most well-studied but misunderstood trait in the psychological literature. The overlap it shares with similar dark personality features has led to confusion and misinterpretation of research findings. From a review of the current literature, it appears that the most accurate conceptualization of Machiavellianism is one of strategic selfishness. Individuals higher in Machiavellianism are calculating, strategic, long-term, flexible, bottom–line-focused, cautious, and sensitive to rewards and punishments. These assertions are supported by behavioral and neurological research. Machiavellian individuals are significantly more likely to be found committing long-term and high-payoff crimes. For example, future research may wish to further examine links between white-collar crimes and Machiavellianism. In addition, research should also explore ways of finding unobtrusive (but valid and reliable) measures of Machiavellianism that are also ecologically valid for use in applied settings. In sum, Machiavellianism is a critical variable in the psychology literature that has unique ties with destructive human behaviors.

REFERENCES

Ali, F., & Chamorro-Premuzic, T. (2010). Investigating theory of mind deficits in nonclinical psychopathy and Machiavellianism. *Personality and Individual Differences, 49*, 169–174. http://dx.doi.org/10.1016/j.paid.2010.03.027

Bagozzi, R. P., Verbeke, W. J., Dietvorst, R. C., Belschak, F. D., van den Berg, W. E., & Rietdijk, W. J. (2013). Theory of mind and empathic explanations of Machiavellianism: A neuroscience perspective. *Journal of Management, 39*, 1760–1798. http://dx.doi.org/10.1177/0149206312471393

Benson, M. L., & Simpson, S. S. (2009). *White-collar crime: An opportunity perspective.* New York, NY: Routledge. http://dx.doi.org/10.4135/9781412971997.n64

Bereczkei, T., Birkas, B., & Kerekes, Z. (2007). Public charity offer as a proximate factor of evolved reputation-building strategy: An experimental analysis of a real-life situation. *Evolution and Human Behavior, 28*, 277–284. http://dx.doi.org/10.1016/j.evolhumbehav.2007.04.002

Bereczkei, T., Birkas, B., & Kerekes, Z. (2010). The presence of others, prosocial traits, Machiavellianism: A personality × situation approach. *Social Psychology, 41*, 238–245. http://dx.doi.org/10.1027/1864-9335/a000032

Bereczkei, T., & Czibor, A. (2014). Personality and situational factors differentially influence high Mach and low Mach persons' decisions in a social dilemma game. *Personality and Individual Differences, 65*, 168–173. http://dx.doi.org/10.1016/j.paid.2014.02.035

Bereczkei, T., Deak, A., Papp, P., Perlaki, G., & Orsi, G. (2013). Neural correlates of Machiavellian strategies in a social dilemma task. *Brain and Cognition, 82*, 108–116. http://dx.doi.org/10.1016/j.bandc.2013.02.012

Buckels, E. E., Trapnell, P., & Paulhus, D. L. (2014). Trolls just want to have fun. *Personality and Individual Differences, 67*, 97–102. http://dx.doi.org/10.1016/j.paid.2014.01.016

Burris, C. T., Rempel, J. K., Munteanu, A. R., & Therrien, P. A. (2013). More, more, more: The dark side of self-expansion motivation. *Personality and Social Psychology Bulletin, 39*, 578–595. http://dx.doi.org/10.1177/0146167213479134

Carter, G. L., Campbell, A. C., Muncer, S., & Carter, K. A. (2015). A Mokken analysis of the Dark Triad "Dirty Dozen": Sex and age differences in scale structures, and issues with individual items. *Personality and Individual Differences, 83*, 185–191. http://dx.doi.org/10.1016/j.paid.2015.04.012

Christie, R., & Geis, F. (1970). *Studies in Machiavellianism*. New York, NY: Academic Press.

Cooper, S., & Peterson, C. (1980). Machiavellianism and spontaneous cheating in competition. *Journal of Research in Personality, 14*, 70–75. http://dx.doi.org/10.1016/0092-6566(80)90041-0

Czibor, A., & Bereczkei, T. (2012). Machiavellian people's success results from monitoring their peers. *Personality and Individual Differences, 53*, 202–206. http://dx.doi.org/10.1016/j.paid.2012.03.005

Dalton, D., & Radtke, R. R. (2013). The joint effects of Machiavellianism and ethical environment on whistle-blowing. *Journal of Business Ethics, 117*, 153–172. http://dx.doi.org/10.1007/s10551-012-1517-x

Deluga, R. J. (2001). American presidential Machiavellianism: Implications for charismatic leadership and rated performance. *The Leadership Quarterly, 12*, 339–363. http://dx.doi.org/10.1016/S1048-9843(01)00082-0

Den Hartog, D. N., & Belschak, F. D. (2012). Work engagement and Machiavellianism in the ethical leadership process. *Journal of Business Ethics, 107*, 35–47. http://dx.doi.org/10.1007/s10551-012-1296-4

Esperger, Z., & Bereczkei, T. (2012). Machiavellianism and spontaneous mentalization: One step ahead of others. *European Journal of Personality, 26*, 580–587. http://dx.doi.org/10.1002/per.859

Evans, S. (2013). *Machiavelli for moms: Maxims on the effective governance of children*. New York, NY: Simon & Schuster.

Glenn, A. L., & Sellbom, M. (2015). Theoretical and empirical concerns regarding the Dark Triad as a construct. *Journal of Personality Disorders, 29*, 360–377. http://dx.doi.org/10.1521/pedi_2014_28_162

Gunnthorsdottir, A., McCabe, K., & Smith, V. (2002). Using the Machiavellianism instrument to predict trustworthiness in a bargaining game. *Journal of Economic Psychology, 23*, 49–66. http://dx.doi.org/10.1016/S0167-4870(01)00067-8

Hare, R. D. (1996). Psychopathy: A clinical construct whose time has come. *Criminal Justice and Behavior, 23*, 25–54. http://dx.doi.org/10.1177/0093854896023001004

Hartmann, F. G. H., & Maas, V. S. (2010). Why business unit controllers create budget slack: Involvement in management, social pressure, and Machiavellianism. *Behavioral Research in Accounting, 22*, 27–49. http://dx.doi.org/10.2308/bria.2010.22.2.27

Hawley, P. H. (2003). Prosocial and coercive configurations of resource control in early adolescence: A case for the well-adapted Machiavellian. *Merrill-Palmer Quarterly, 49*, 279–309. http://dx.doi.org/10.1353/mpq.2003.0013

Hawley, P. H., & Geldhof, G. J. (2012). Preschoolers' social dominance, moral cognition, and moral behavior: An evolutionary perspective. *Journal of Experimental Child Psychology, 112*, 18–35. http://dx.doi.org/10.1016/j.jecp.2011.10.004

Hawley, P. H., Little, T. D., & Card, N. E. (2007). The allure of a mean friend: Relationship quality and processes of aggressive adolescents with prosocial skills. *International Journal of Behavioral Development, 31*, 170–180. http://dx.doi.org/10.1177/0165025407074630

Ivancevich, J. M., Duening, T. N., Gilbert, J. A., & Konopaske, R. (2003). Deterring white-collar crime. *The Academy of Management Perspectives, 17*, 114–127.

Jakobwitz, S., & Egan, V. (2006). The dark triad and normal personality traits. *Personality and Individual Differences, 40*, 331–339. http://dx.doi.org/10.1016/j.paid.2005.07.006

Jonason, P. K., & Krause, L. (2013). The emotional deficits associated with the Dark Triad traits: Cognitive empathy, affective empathy, and alexithymia. *Personality and Individual Differences, 55*, 532–537. http://dx.doi.org/10.1016/j.paid.2013.04.027

Jonason, P. K., Li, N. P., Webster, G. W., & Schmitt, D. P. (2009). The Dark Triad: Facilitating a short-term mating strategy in men. *European Journal of Personality, 23*, 5–18. http://dx.doi.org/10.1002/per.698

Jonason, P. K., Lyons, M., & Bethell, E. (2014). The making of Darth Vader: Parent–child care and the Dark Triad. *Personality and Individual Differences, 67*, 30–34. http://dx.doi.org/10.1016/j.paid.2013.10.006

Jonason, P. K., & Schmitt, D. P. (2012). What have you done for me lately? Friendship-selection in the shadow of the Dark Triad traits. *Evolutionary Psychology, 10*, 400–421. http://dx.doi.org/10.1177/147470491201000303

Jonason, P. K., Slomski, S., & Partyka, J. (2012). The Dark Triad at work: How toxic employees get their way. *Personality and Individual Differences, 52*, 449–453. http://dx.doi.org/10.1016/j.paid.2011.11.008

Jonason, P. K., & Tost, J. (2010). I just cannot control myself: The Dark Triad and self-control. *Personality and Individual Differences, 49,* 611–615. http://dx.doi.org/10.1016/j.paid.2010.05.031

Jonason, P. K., & Webster, G. D. (2010). The dirty dozen: A concise measure of the Dark Triad. *Psychological Assessment, 22,* 420–432. http://dx.doi.org/10.1037/a0019265

Jonason, P. K., Webster, G. D., Schmitt, D. P., Li, N. P., & Crysel, L. (2012). The antihero in popular culture: Life history theory and the Dark Triad personality traits. *Review of General Psychology, 16,* 192–199. http://dx.doi.org/10.1037/a0027914

Jones, D. N. (2013). What's mine is mine and what's yours is mine: The Dark Triad and gambling with your neighbor's money. *Journal of Research in Personality, 47,* 563–571. http://dx.doi.org/10.1016/j.jrp.2013.04.005

Jones, D. N. (2014). Risk in the face of retribution: Psychopathic individuals persist in financial misbehavior among the Dark Triad. *Personality and Individual Differences, 67,* 109–113. http://dx.doi.org/10.1016/j.paid.2014.01.030

Jones, D. N., & Figueredo, A. J. (2013). The core of darkness: Uncovering the heart of the Dark Triad. *European Journal of Personality, 27,* 521–531. http://dx.doi.org/10.1002/per.1893

Jones, D. N., & Olderbak, S. G. (2014). The associations among dark personalities and sexual tactics across different scenarios. *Journal of Interpersonal Violence, 29,* 1050–1070. http://dx.doi.org/10.1177/0886260513506053

Jones, D. N., & Paulhus, D. L. (2009). Machiavellianism. In M. R. Leary & R. H. Hoyle (Eds.), *Handbook of individual differences in social behavior* (pp. 93–108). New York, NY: Guilford Press.

Jones, D. N., & Paulhus, D. L. (2010). Different provocations trigger aggression in narcissists and psychopaths. *Social Psychological and Personality Science, 1,* 12–18. http://dx.doi.org/10.1177/1948550609347591

Jones, D. N., & Paulhus, D. L. (2011a). Differentiating the dark triad within the interpersonal circumplex. In L. M. Horowitz & S. N. Strack (Eds.), *Handbook of interpersonal theory and research* (pp. 249–267). New York, NY: Guilford Press.

Jones, D. N., & Paulhus, D. L. (2011b). The role of impulsivity in the Dark Triad of personality. *Personality and Individual Differences, 51,* 679–682. http://dx.doi.org/10.1016/j.paid.2011.04.011

Jones, D. N., & Paulhus, D. L. (2014). Introducing the short Dark Triad (SD3): A brief measure of dark personality traits. *Assessment, 21,* 28–41. http://dx.doi.org/10.1177/1073191113514105

Jones, D. N., & Weiser, D. A. (2014). Differential infidelity patterns among the Dark Triad. *Personality and Individual Differences, 57,* 20–24. http://dx.doi.org/10.1016/j.paid.2013.09.007

Kaiser, R. B., LeBreton, J. M., & Hogan, J. (2015). The dark side of personality and extreme leader behavior. *Applied Psychology: An International Review, 64,* 55–92.

Kiazad, K., Restubog, S. L. D., Zagenczyk, T. J., Kiewitz, C., & Tang, R. L. (2010). In pursuit of power: The role of authoritarian leadership in the relationship between supervisors' Machiavellianism and subordinates' perceptions of abusive supervisory behavior. *Journal of Research in Personality, 44,* 512–519. http://dx.doi.org/10.1016/j.jrp.2010.06.004

Láng, A., & Lénárd, K. (2015). The relation between memories of childhood psychological maltreatment and Machiavellianism. *Personality and Individual Differences, 77,* 81–85. http://dx.doi.org/10.1016/j.paid.2014.12.054

Latorre, R. A., & McLeoad, E. (1978). Machiavellianism and clinical depression in a geriatric sample. *Journal of Clinical Psychology, 34,* 659–660. http://dx.doi.org/10.1002/1097-4679(197807)34:3<659::AID-JCLP2270340315>3.0.CO;2-B

Lee, K., & Ashton, M. C. (2005). Psychopathy, Machiavellianism, and narcissism in the five-factor model and the HEXACO model of personality structure. *Personality and Individual Differences, 38,* 1571–1582. http://dx.doi.org/10.1016/j.paid.2004.09.016

Lee, K., Ashton, M. C., Wiltshire, J., Bourdage, J. S., Visser, B. A., & Gallucci, A. (2013). Sex, power, and money: Prediction from the Dark Triad and Honesty–Humility. *European Journal of Personality, 27,* 169–184. http://dx.doi.org/10.1002/per.1860

Lyons, M., & Aitken, S. (2010). Machiavellian friends? The role of Machiavellianism in friendship formation and maintenance. *Journal of Social, Evolutionary, and Cultural Psychology, 4,* 194–202. http://dx.doi.org/10.1037/h0099290

Lyons, M., Caldwell, T., & Shultz, S. (2010). Mind-reading and manipulation—Is Machiavellianism related to theory of mind? *Journal of Evolutionary Psychology, 8,* 261–274. http://dx.doi.org/10.1556/JEP.8.2010.3.7

Machiavelli, N. (1981). *The prince.* New York, NY: Bantam Classics. (Original work published 1513)

Macrosson, W. D. K., & Hemphill, D. J. (2001). Machiavellianism in Belbin team roles. *Journal of Managerial Psychology, 16,* 355–363. http://dx.doi.org/10.1108/EUM0000000005524

Maples, J. L., Lamkin, J., & Miller, J. D. (2014). A test of two brief measures of the dark triad: The dirty dozen and short dark triad. *Psychological Assessment, 26,* 326–331. http://dx.doi.org/10.1037/a0035084

McHoskey, J. W. (2001). Machiavellianism and sexuality: On the moderating role of biological sex. *Personality and Individual Differences, 31,* 779–789. http://dx.doi.org/10.1016/S0191-8869(00)00180-X

McHoskey, J. W., Worzel, W., & Szyarto, C. (1998). Machiavellianism and psychopathy. *Journal of Personality and Social Psychology, 74,* 192–210. http://dx.doi.org/10.1037/0022-3514.74.1.192

McIlwain, D. (2003). Bypassing empathy: A Machiavellian theory of mind and sneaky power. In B. Repacholi & V. Slaughter (Eds.), *Individual differences in theory of mind: Implications for typical and atypical development* (pp. 39–67). Hove, England: Psychology Press.

Miller, J. D., Few, L. R., Seibert, L. A., Watts, A., Zeichner, A., & Lynam, D. R. (2012). An examination of the Dirty Dozen measure of psychopathy: A cautionary tale about the costs of brief measures. *Psychological Assessment, 24,* 1048–1053. http://dx.doi.org/10.1037/a0028583

Mudrack, P. E. (1993). An investigation into the acceptability of workplace behaviors of a dubious ethical nature. *Journal of Business Ethics, 12,* 517–524. http://dx.doi.org/10.1007/BF00872373

Murphy, P. R. (2012). Attitude, Machiavellianism, and the rationalization of misreporting. *Accounting, Organizations and Society, 37,* 242–259. http://dx.doi.org/10.1016/j.aos.2012.04.002

Murray, H. A. (1938). *Explorations in personality: A clinical study of 50 men of college age.* New York, NY: Oxford University Press.

Nestor, P. G., Nakamura, M., Niznikiewicz, M., Thompson, E., Levitt, J. J., Choate, V., . . . McCarley, R. W. (2013). In search of the functional neuroanatomy of sociality: MRI subdivisions of orbital frontal cortex and social cognition. *Social Cognitive and Affective Neuroscience, 8,* 460–467. http://dx.doi.org/10.1093/scan/nss018

O'Boyle, E. H., Forsyth, D. R., Banks, G. C., & McDaniel, M. A. (2012). A meta-analysis of the Dark Triad and work behavior: A social exchange perspective. *Journal of Applied Psychology, 97,* 557–579. http://dx.doi.org/10.1037/a0025679

Paal, T., & Bereczkei, T. (2007). Adult theory of mind, cooperation, Machiavellianism: The effect of mindreading on social relations. *Personality and Individual Differences, 43,* 541–551. http://dx.doi.org/10.1016/j.paid.2006.12.021

Paulhus, D. L., Harms, P. D., Bruce, M. N., & Lysy, D. C. (2003). The over-claiming technique: Measuring self-enhancement independent of ability. *Journal of Personality and Social Psychology, 84,* 890–904. http://dx.doi.org/10.1037/0022-3514.84.4.890

Paulhus, D. L., & Jones, D. N. (2015). Measures of dark personalities. In G. J. Boyle, D. H. Saklofske, & G. Matthews (Eds.), *Measures of personality and social psychological constructs* (pp. 562–594). San Diego, CA: Academic Press. http://dx.doi.org/10.1016/B978-0-12-386915-9.00020-6

Paulhus, D. L., & Williams, K. M. (2002). The Dark Triad of personality: Narcissism, Machiavellianism, and psychopathy. *Journal of Research in Personality, 36,* 556–563. http://dx.doi.org/10.1016/S0092-6566(02)00505-6

Rauthmann, J. F. (2012). The Dark Triad and interpersonal perception: Similarities and differences in the social consequences of narcissism, Machiavellianism, and psychopathy. *Social Psychological and Personality Science, 3,* 487–496. http://dx.doi.org/10.1177/1948550611427608

Rauthmann, J. F., & Kolar, G. P. (2012). How "dark" are the Dark Triad traits? Examining the perceived darkness of narcissism, Machiavellianism, and psychopathy. *Personality and Individual Differences, 53*, 884–889. http://dx.doi.org/10.1016/j.paid.2012.06.020

Sparks, J. R. (1994). Machiavellianism and personal success in marketing: The moderating role of latitude for improvisation. *Journal of the Academy of Marketing Science, 22*, 393–400. http://dx.doi.org/10.1177/0092070394224008

Spitzer, M., Fischbacher, U., Herrnberger, B., Grön, G., & Fehr, E. (2007). The neural signature of social norm compliance. *Neuron, 56*, 185–196. http://dx.doi.org/10.1016/j.neuron.2007.09.011

Stylianou, A. C., Winter, S., Niu, Y., Giacalone, R. A., & Campbell, M. (2013). Understanding the behavioral intention to report unethical information technology practices: The role of Machiavellianism, gender, and computer expertise. *Journal of Business Ethics, 117*, 333–343. http://dx.doi.org/10.1007/s10551-012-1521-1

Turner, C. F., & Martinez, D. C. (1977). Socioeconomic achievement and the Machiavellian personality. *Sociometry, 40*, 325–336. http://dx.doi.org/10.2307/3033481

Verbeke, W. J. M. I., Rietdijk, W. J., van den Berg, W. E., Dietvorst, R. C., Worm, L., & Bagozzi, R. P. (2011). The making of the Machiavellian brain: A structural MRI analysis. *Journal of Neuroscience, Psychology, and Economics, 4*, 205–216. http://dx.doi.org/10.1037/a0025802

Vernon, P. A., Villani, V. C., Vickers, L. C., & Harris, J. A. (2008). A behavioral genetic investigation of the Dark Triad and the Big 5. *Personality and Individual Differences, 44*, 445–452. http://dx.doi.org/10.1016/j.paid.2007.09.007

Vladu, A. B. (2013). Machiavellianism and short-term earnings management practices. *Annales Universitatis Apulensis Series Oeconomica, 15*, 467–472.

Wai, M., & Tiliopoulos, N. (2012). The affective and cognitive empathetic nature of the Dark Triad of personality. *Personality and Individual Differences, 52*, 794–799. http://dx.doi.org/10.1016/j.paid.2012.01.008

Wei, H. S., & Chen, J. K. (2012). The moderating effect of Machiavellianism on the relationships between bullying, peer acceptance, and school adjustment in adolescents. *School Psychology International, 33*, 345–363. http://dx.doi.org/10.1177/0143034311420640

Williams, K. M., Nathanson, C., & Paulhus, D. L. (2010). Identifying and profiling scholastic cheaters: Their personality, cognitive ability, and motivation. *Journal of Experimental Psychology: Applied, 16*, 293–307. http://dx.doi.org/10.1037/a0020773

Zagenczyk, T. J., Cruz, K. S., Woodard, A. M., Walker, J. C., Few, W. T., Kiazad, K., & Raja, M. (2013). The moderating effect of Machiavellianism on the psychological contract breach—Organizational identification/disidentification relationships. *Journal of Business and Psychology, 28*, 287–299. http://dx.doi.org/10.1007/s10869-012-9278-1

Zagenczyk, T. J., Restubog, S. L. D., Kiewitz, C., Kiazad, K., & Tang, R. L. (2014). Psychological contracts as a mediator between Machiavellianism and employee citizenship and deviant behaviors. *Journal of Management, 40,* 1098–1122. http://dx.doi.org/10.1177/0149206311415420

Zeigler-Hill, V., Southard, A. C., & Besser, A. (2014). Resource control strategies and personality traits. *Personality and Individual Differences, 66,* 118–123. http://dx.doi.org/10.1016/j.paid.2014.03.037

Zettler, I., & Solga, M. (2013). Not enough of a "dark" trait? Linking Machiavellianism to job performance. *European Journal of Personality, 27,* 545–554. http://dx.doi.org/10.1002/per.1912

5

EVERYDAY SADISM

DELROY L. PAULHUS AND DONALD G. DUTTON

Sadism is the enjoyment of other people's suffering. The phenomenon has traditionally been discussed in its most extreme forms, that is, in criminal and sexual contexts. Increasingly, sadism is being treated as a more common behavior with evolutionary roots (Baumeister & Campbell, 1999; Dutton, 2007; Nell, 2006; Taylor, 2009). Extreme sadism, such as torture of civilians by military and police forces, has been reported so consistently across time and cultures that its origin must lie deeper in the human condition than arbitrary instances of social learning (Dutton, Bond, & Boyanowsky, 2005). In contrast, social prohibitions against exhibitions of sadistic acts have developed incrementally in Western culture beginning around the 14th century (Pinker, 2011). We no longer consider it acceptable to publicly torture cats for amusement, as was the case in medieval France. However, Pinker (2011) conceded that a milder version—"soft sadism"—remains evident in contemporary human societies and may even be normally distributed. In this chapter,

http://dx.doi.org/10.1037/14854-006

The Dark Side of Personality: Science and Practice in Social, Personality, and Clinical Psychology, V. Zeigler-Hill and D. K. Marcus (Editors)

we use the term *everyday sadism* to refer to a similar concept: largely acceptable forms of subclinical sadism that are prevalent in modern culture.

DEFINITION AND BACKGROUND

When people hear the term *sadism*, they typically think of sexual sadism, and may conjure up the notion of a diabolical deviant. High-profile historical examples have contributed to this notion. Gilles de Rais, perhaps the most infamous serial killer in history, was convicted of the rape, torture, and murder of hundreds of boys in 15th-century France. De Rais specifically derived sexual excitement from the pain and suffering of his victims. After confessing, he was hanged in 1440. The transcript of his confession was so lurid it was ordered to be burned. Three centuries later in France, Donatien Francois de Sade, aka the Marquis de Sade, wrote extensively about the sexual pleasures of sadism, leading to the practice adopting his name. His libertine novels, *Justine* and *120 Days of Sodom*, were banned by the Catholic Church, and de Sade was imprisoned and sentenced to death. His extolling of sadomasochism, pedophilia, and sodomy has been defended in modern works by such scholars as T. W. Adorno (1998) and Camille Paglia (1990) as extolling nihilism and moral cynicism.

Such modern-day serial killers as Leonard Lake and Charles Ng specifically used torture of victims as a form of sexual excitement. The fact that their crimes were sensationalistic and received a great deal of media attention may have contributed to the public equation of sadism with criminal sexual sadism. Videos of their crimes were posted online and, like many websites about sadistic killers, continue to draw frequent viewers (see http://www.murderpedia.org).

The assumed interweaving of sadism with sex and criminality has regularly confounded attempts at technical definitions, even among associations of health professionals (Bradley, Shedler, & Westen, 2006). The 1987 edition of the *Diagnostic and Statistical Manual of Mental Disorders* (DSM–III–R; American Psychiatric Association, 1987) included Sadistic Personality Disorder as a category with eight criteria (the diagnosis required that individuals meet at least four of these criteria). Interestingly, none of the criteria included sexual sadism, and the focus was on domination and power over others. However, that global version of sadism was dropped in *DSM–IV* (American Psychiatric Association, 1994), with only sexual sadism remaining as a paraphilia. Later, Millon and Davis (1996) proposed that Millon's nonsexual subtypes (explosive, spineless, enforcing, and tyrannical sadism) be considered for the *DSM–5* (American Psychiatric Association, 2013), but the proposal was rejected. Similarly, the *International Statistical Classification of Diseases and Related Health Problems* (10th rev.; ICD–10; World Health Organization,

1992) has no coding category for global sadism. However, like the *DSM*, it recognizes sexual sadism.

The noncriminal/nonsexual conception of sadism had previously been offered by such influential writers as Fromm (1973), who insisted that sadism is a natural aspect of the human condition. Consistent with that view, Dutton (2007) laid out detailed evidence across time and cultures for the acceptance of sadistic behavior toward outgroup members. Torture of vanquished peoples has been used by preconquest Native Americans, the Japanese army at Nanking during World War II, the El Salvadoran army at El Mozote, the U.S. Army in Vietnam, and Polish civilians against Jewish neighbors during the Nazi occupation (Dutton et al., 2005). The use of torture in these historical examples rarely served a military advantage. Similar gratuitous cruelty has emerged spontaneously across such broad variations in time and geography that the notion of common cultural directives is implausible. Instead, fundamental brain mechanisms have been postulated. Dutton (2007), for example, suggested a neural mechanism that generates pleasure from sadistic violence. Taylor (2009) saw sadism arising as a physiological response to war-induced callousness. To the degree that such indifference to the suffering of others facilitated military objectives, evolutionary selection could then gradually transform that indifference into enjoyment of cruelty. Selection for sadism would be especially efficient when the victims were perceived collectively as dangerous outgroups. In the most detailed treatment, Nell (2006) detailed a three-stage model for this evolutionary process. In the final hominid stage, sadistic behavior promoted fitness via the maintenance of personal and social power.

In sum, evidence from military history and evolutionary psychology suggests that sadism is an innate aspect of the human condition. Indeed, the behavior was widely considered to be acceptable until the Age of Enlightenment (Pinker, 2011). Although suppressed in contemporary civilian society, it appears that milder forms of sadism may continue to flourish.

Contemporary examples of nonsexual sadism are so common that we have applied the term *everyday sadism*. Although a categorical distinction from clinically defined sadism may not be possible, most of the following examples would not meet standard *DSM* or *ICD* criteria. Blatant examples abound in popular entertainment, where sadistic displays are considered to be acceptable entertainment. Violent films have been so appealing that governing bodies such as the Motion Picture Association of America have had to gradually relax earlier restrictions (Vaughn, 2006), whereas sexual content has remained relatively more restricted during the same period (Sandler, 2007). Technological advances in other modes of entertainment have made it even more difficult for authorities to control violent content. For example, the appeal of violent video games is unparalleled (Anderson, Gentile, & Buckley, 2007). Among young males, the most popular are "first-person shooter" games

(Entertainment Software Association, 2015). Newer editions of popular games such as *Grand Theft Auto* continually up the ante of brutality to compete for customers. Internet hubs such as bestgore.com feed viewers with endless volumes of gruesome images. Not limited to passive viewing, some of these sites encourage viewers to torture their virtual victims (see torturegames.net).

Finally, consider the popularity of violent sports. Although some mainstream sports try to contain violence, professional hockey referees allow fighting to continue if the participants appear to be matched in size. In appreciation, the crowds show nearly as much excitement and applause for the fights as they do for a goal scored by their home team. Sports in which fighting is the centerpiece have also become more vicious. Although initially banned in many jurisdictions, mixed martial arts (i.e., cage fighting) has recently risen to become one of North America's most popular sports (Gullo, 2013). Here, the rules are minimal and bloodletting is abundant. Although Roman circuses are long gone, the appeal of sadism as a spectator sport has not subsided.

REVIEW OF THE EMPIRICAL LITERATURE

Such apparent examples of sadistic appeal inspired our empirical endeavors several years ago. This program of research was a natural extension of our earlier work on the *Dark Triad* (Paulhus & Williams, 2002). Those three personality variables—narcissism, Machiavellianism, and psychopathy—each had extensive literatures. The narcissist is a grandiose attention seeker; the Machiavellian, a strategic manipulator; the psychopath, an impulsive thrill seeker. Despite the clear differences among these constructs, they were found to overlap both theoretically and empirically. Intercorrelations of their standard measures range from .20 to .60, depending on the sample (for a review, see Furnham, Richards, & Paulhus, 2013). Note that research on Dark Triad variables has been restricted to subclinical levels—that is, levels observed in individuals at large in the broader community, not those under clinical or criminal supervision. Hence, Dark Triad variables should not be confused with true personality disorders.

Research on a fourth dark personality feature—everyday sadism—did not become viable until the recent development of questionnaire measures (Chabrol, Van Leeuwen, Rodgers, & Séjourné, 2009; O'Meara, Davies, & Hammond, 2011; Paulhus, Jones, Klonsky, & Dutton, 2011).[1] Our laboratory conducted extensive work on the questionnaire labeled the Varieties of Sadistic Tendencies (VAST; available in Paulhus & Jones, 2015). It comprises

---

[1]The Sadistic Personality Disorder scale of the Millon Clinical Inventory—III (Millon & Davis, 1996) is older, but the item content reflects global aggression rather than sadism.

separate subscales for direct and vicarious forms of sadism. Items on the direct subscale include "I like to physically hurt people" and "I like to mock losers to their face," whereas items on the vicarious subscale include "I like to watch YouTube videos of people fighting" and "In car racing, it's the accidents I enjoy most." Although structural analyses revealed separate factors for direct and vicarious sadism, they were highly correlated. Hence, the same people who like to hurt others also like to watch others being hurt. Men tend to score higher than women on both subscales (Paulhus & Jones, 2015).

A later version of the questionnaire, titled the Comprehensive Assessment of Sadistic Tendencies (CAST; Buckels & Paulhus, 2013), comprises three subscales tapping vicarious, physical, and verbal forms of sadism. Although men had higher scores on the first two subscales, female respondents scored as high as male respondents on verbal sadism. Total scores for both the CAST and the VAST have shown moderate positive correlations with the members of the Dark Triad. Together, the four variables have been labeled the *Dark Tetrad* (Buckels, Jones, & Paulhus, 2013; Chabrol et al., 2009; Paulhus, 2014). In distinction from the other members, the everyday sadist seeks opportunities to engage in or view cruel behavior. It is important to note the contrast with the psychopath who simply does not care whether others get hurt during his or her selfish pursuits (for a full review of the Dark Tetrad, see Paulhus, 2014).

Survey Research

Research with the VAST and CAST has already revealed a number of provocative findings. In survey research, we found that these questionnaires predicted reports of animal abuse, fire setting, vandalism, and dominance via threats, including partner abuse (Paulhus, Jones, Klonsky, & Dutton, 2011). One notable finding was a positive correlation between everyday sadism and enjoyment of hurting a partner during sex. This finding should be considered tentative for a number of reasons. One is that the correlation was small and based on a single item measuring sexual sadism. Another is that the finding conflicts with statements from the sadomasochism community arguing that their form of sadism is more a matter of sexual role-playing than actual enjoyment of hurting others (Richters, de Visser, Rissel, Grulich, & Smith, 2008).

Although our surveys found little indication of personal adjustment problems for individuals with sadistic personality features (see more under Adaptive and Maladaptive Features), their interpersonal relationships may not be ideal. For example, we found a link between VAST scores and self-reported partner abuse in a large community sample (Paulhus et al., 2011). Using Dutton's (1995) Partner Abusiveness Scale (PAS), the correlations were significant for both male and female respondents. Note, however, that PAS scores in our community sample may have required speculation about potential for partner abuse; in fact, no link has been found with confirmed spouse abusers (Dutton, 1995). Nonetheless, individuals reporting that they "dominate others using fear" (a VAST item) may not make ideal relationship partners.

Our most recent research on everyday sadism studied the phenomenon of Internet "trolls" (Buckels, Trapnell, & Paulhus, 2014). These are individuals who frequent comment sections on Internet sites to make critical or disturbing comments. In several survey studies, we found associations between CAST scores and reported frequency of such activities. Moreover, enjoyment appeared to mediate the link between sadism and trolling frequency (Buckels et al., 2014).

Laboratory Research

Needless to say, any notion of encouraging sadistic behaviors in the laboratory must confront ethical issues. To avoid such concerns, we developed two behavioral paradigms that mitigate ethical concerns yet are both observable and sadistic in nature (Buckels et al., 2013). To study the enjoyment gained from harming others, we substituted bugs for people. More specifically, we used a bug-crunching machine that allowed people the opportunity to kill bugs in a rather gruesome fashion (in fact, an illusion—no bugs were actually harmed). Participants had to choose among a variety of unsavory tasks (e.g., cleaning toilets, cold-pressor test). Those who chose bug-crunching scored higher on a questionnaire measure of everyday sadism.

The second study sought to verify the motivational nature of everyday sadism by making people work for the opportunity to harm another (human) participant (Buckels et al., 2013). Here we used a variant of the white noise aggression paradigm often used by Anderson and Bushman (2002). Whereas most such studies allow participants to aggress against a victim who had provoked them, the variant developed by Reidy, Zeichner, and Seibert (2011) examined aggression against totally innocent victims. We modified that methodology by requiring subjects to work on a boring task just so they could blast their innocent victim with white noise. As expected, individuals willing to do so scored highest on the CAST, our questionnaire measure of everyday sadism.

ADAPTIVE AND MALADAPTIVE FEATURES

Questions about the adaptiveness of everyday sadism can be posed at both the psychological and evolutionary levels of analysis. Are everyday sadists psychologically disturbed? On the basis of our research, we have to conclude otherwise (Paulhus et al., 2011). Overall adjustment measures such as self-esteem and neuroticism were unrelated to our questionnaire measures of sadism. Nor did measures of self-harm (cutting, burning) show any association with self-report sadism. In short, research with our everyday sadism measures conflicts with evidence from clinical and forensic cases in which sadistic individuals often show signs of psychopathology (Fedoroff, 2008; Knight, 1999; Mokros, Osterheider, Hucker, & Nitschke, 2011).

From an evolutionary perspective, the ubiquity of sadism in human cultures suggests that it has conferred a reproductive advantage. As noted earlier, several recent books have offered these arguments. Their evolutionary account can be summarized as follows: Given that power can be maintained via sadistic behavior and power confers more sexual opportunities, then sadism may have been selected as one reproductive strategy (Dutton, 2007; Nell, 2006; Taylor, 2009). As noted earlier, everyday sadism may not be adaptive for personal relationships. Committed associations (e.g., family, coworkers) give people more power and opportunity to display any dark tendencies. However, sadistic behavior is unlikely to emerge unless the sadistic tendency is accompanied by some other personality deficit (e.g., anger proneness, impulsivity). In any case, partner abuse is not interchangeable with psychopathology (Dutton, 1995; Krupp, Sewall, Lalumière, Sheriff, & Harris, 2013). It is quite possible to have sadistic impulses (sans callousness) while remaining psychologically normal (Hagger-Johnson & Egan, 2010). Unless considered a sufficient criterion for inferring psychopathology, sadism should not be considered inherently abnormal.

DIRECTIONS FOR FUTURE RESEARCH

Future research should attend to a number of open issues. One is the shape of the frequency distributions of everyday sadism measures. To date, our research has shown mixed results, but there is a hint of bimodal distribution (Paulhus et al., 2011). The heritability of this dimension has yet to be pursued (cf. Vernon, Villani, Vickers, & Harris, 2008). Another issue concerns the position of sadism in the higher order structure of the Dark Tetrad. The components of the Dark Triad fall together under the Honesty-Humility dimension of the HEXACO model (Ashton & Lee, 2001). It is not yet clear whether sadism can also be subsumed within that model. Similarly, no evidence is available regarding the location of sadism on the interpersonal circumplex. Its overlap with the Dark Triad suggests that it should fall in Quadrant II (cold agency) of the interpersonal circumplex (Jones & Paulhus, 2011; Lee & Ashton, 2005). In contrast to work on the Dark Triad (Jonason, Li, Webster, & Schmitt, 2009; Jones & Weiser, 2014), mating choices have yet to be explored. Finally, understanding the role of sadism in terrorist groups and street gangs may prove to be the most important application for the broader society (Paulhus & Buckels, 2011).

CLINICAL IMPLICATIONS

Extreme levels of sadistic behavior have both clinical and criminal implications. Interestingly, the current focus remains on sexual sadism, even in the *DSM–5* and the *ICD–10*. Work by Mokros, Nitschke, and colleagues in Germany has investigated that phenomenon in some depth (Mokros et al., 2011), and they have developed a forensic measurement device (Nitschke, Osterheider, & Mokros, 2009). It tabulates concrete aspects of crime scenes, for example, evidence of corpse mutilation. Media focus on sexual and criminal cases may explain why less dramatic cases of sadism have been largely overlooked in the psychological literature.

As detailed earlier, our work on the Dark Tetrad has focused on the subclinical (i.e., everyday) variants of these personality variables. Although having much in common with the clinical variants, the subclinical cases are able to survive, if not flourish, in everyday society. As Hall and Benning (2006) pointed out, several explanations for the success of subclinical cases are viable. One is that the subclinical versions are sufficiently mild that their behavior remains within socially acceptable boundaries. Another is that subclinical cases possess some moderating asset that makes them appealing to society. For example, they may be wealthy, attractive, athletic, or intelligent. The third is a dual process notion: Adaptive features may appear independently of pathological features. For example, the self-confidence of narcissists may not always be accompanied by a maladaptive sense of entitlement. Similarly, the impulsivity of psychopaths may not always be accompanied by antisocial behavior (Hall & Benning, 2006).

In the case of the subclinical sadist, all three of these explanations remain viable. Milder levels of sadistic tendencies may be limited to vicarious aspects: watching violent sports or brutalizing virtual others in video games. The moderator explanation may depend on the desirable asset: Talented athletes with sadistic tendencies may choose cage fighting or the role of a hockey goon because those roles reward sadistic behavior. Finally, the dual process notion may apply to surgeons or police officers who are rewarded for remaining aloof when confronted with gory injuries. Although their empathy deficit helps during surgery, it may detract from their bedside manner (Gleichgerrcht & Decety, 2012).

SUMMARY AND CONCLUSIONS

In the present chapter, we have focused on instances of everyday behaviors that reflect some degree of sadistic tendencies. When conceived as a dimension of normal personality, the tendency may explain common behaviors such as humiliating or bullying others as well as pleasurable reactions to violence in sports, film, and video games. Although contextual triggers such as revenge seem to intensify sadistic behavior (DeLongis, Nathanson, & Paulhus, 2011), our trait conception emphasizes that people differ dramatically in such tendencies. In most people, sadistic fantasies are overridden by the tendency to be revolted by depictions of sadistic behavior and empathize with victims (Buckels & Paulhus, 2013).

Research from our lab and elsewhere has supported the construct validity of this individual difference variable. In the validation process, the construct has been elaborated into three facets: physical, verbal, and vicarious sadism. Several questionnaire measures are now available for use by researchers. Among these, the most elaborate measure, the CAST, provides separate subscales for these three conceptual facets (Buckels & Paulhus, 2013). When aggregated across facets, total scores on the CAST are correlated with—but distinct from—the Dark Triad of narcissism, Machiavellianism, and psychopathy. That finding is both a critical advance and a warning: Observed correlates of everyday sadism may actually be due to its empirical overlap with narcissism, Machiavellianism, or psychopathy. Therefore, we recommend that sadism be evaluated concurrently with the Dark Triad. That approach will clarify any unique contribution of sadism and was used in the studies reviewed in this chapter.

Preliminary research has begun to flesh out the construct validity of everyday sadism. In survey research, we found that questionnaire measures predicted reports of animal abuse, fire setting, vandalism, and dominance via threats. We also found a small association with enjoyment of sexual sadism but no association with self-harm. In laboratory work, questionnaire measures were linked to enjoyment of bug-crunching and willingness to work for an opportunity to harm innocent victims. On the Internet, we found that trolls (nasty commenters) scored high on sadism measures and reported pure pleasure as their primary motivation. In sum, sadistic tendencies may be more common than previously thought.

REFERENCES

Adorno, T. W. (1998). *Critical models: Interventions and catchwords*. New York, NY: Columbia University Press.

American Psychiatric Association. (1987). *Diagnostic and statistical manual of mental disorders* (3rd ed., rev.). Washington, DC: Author.

American Psychiatric Association. (1994). *Diagnostic and statistical manual of mental disorders* (4th ed.). Washington, DC: Author.

American Psychiatric Association. (2013). *Diagnostic and statistical manual of mental disorders* (5th ed.). Arlington, VA: Author.

Anderson, C. A., & Bushman, B. J. (2002). Psychology. The effects of media violence on society. *Science, 295,* 2377–2379. http://dx.doi.org/10.1126/science.1070765

Anderson, C. A., Gentile, D. A., & Buckley, K. E. (2007). *Violent video game effects on children and adolescents: Theory, research, and public policy.* New York, NY: Oxford Press. http://dx.doi.org/10.1093/acprof:oso/9780195309836.001.0001

Ashton, M. C., & Lee, K. (2001). A theoretical basis for the major dimensions of personality. *European Journal of Personality, 15,* 327–353. http://dx.doi.org/10.1002/per.417

Baumeister, R. F., & Campbell, W. K. (1999). The intrinsic appeal of evil: Sadism, sensational thrills, and threatened egotism. *Personality and Social Psychology Review, 3,* 210–221. http://dx.doi.org/10.1207/s15327957pspr0303_4

Bradley, R., Shedler, J., & Westen, D. (2006). Is the appendix a useful appendage? An empirical examination of depressive, passive-aggressive (negativistic), sadistic, and self-defeating personality disorders. *Journal of Personality Disorders, 20,* 524–540. http://dx.doi.org/10.1521/pedi.2006.20.5.524

Buckels, E. E., Jones, D. N., & Paulhus, D. L. (2013). Behavioral confirmation of everyday sadism. *Psychological Science, 24,* 2201–2209. http://dx.doi.org/10.1177/0956797613490749

Buckels, E. E., & Paulhus, D. L. (2013). *Comprehensive Assessment of Sadistic Tendencies (CAST).* Unpublished instrument, University of British Columbia, Vancouver, British Columbia, Canada.

Buckels, E. E., Trapnell, P. D., & Paulhus, D. L. (2014). Trolls just want to have fun. *Personality and Individual Differences, 67,* 97–102. http://dx.doi.org/10.1016/j.paid.2014.01.016

Chabrol, H., Van Leeuwen, N., Rodgers, R., & Séjourné, N. (2009). Contributions of psychopathic, narcissistic, Machiavellian, and sadistic personality traits to juvenile delinquency. *Personality and Individual Differences, 47,* 734–739. http://dx.doi.org/10.1016/j.paid.2009.06.020

DeLongis, A., Nathanson, C., & Paulhus, D. L. (2011). *Revenge: Who, when, and why.* Unpublished manuscript, University of British Columbia, Vancouver, British Columbia, Canada.

Dutton, D. G. (1995). A scale for measuring propensity for abusiveness. *Journal of Family Violence, 10,* 203–221. http://dx.doi.org/10.1007/BF02110600

Dutton, D. G. (2007). *The psychology of genocide, massacres, and extreme violence.* Westport, CT: Praeger International.

Dutton, D. G., Bond, M. H., & Boyanowsky, E. (2005). Extreme mass homicide: From military massacre to genocide. *Aggression and Violent Behavior, 10,* 45–57.

Entertainment Software Association. (2015). *2015 essential facts about the computer and video game industry: Sales, demographic and usage data.* Retrieved from http://www.theesa.com/wp-content/uploads/2015/04/ESA-Essential-Facts-2015.pdf

Fedoroff, J. P. (2008). Sadism, sadomasochism, sex, and violence. *Canadian Journal of Psychiatry, 53,* 637–646.

Fromm, E. (1973). *The anatomy of human destructiveness.* New York, NY: Fawcett Crest.

Furnham, A., Richards, S. C., & Paulhus, D. L. (2013). The Dark Triad of personality: A 10-year review. *Social and Personality Psychology Compass, 7*, 199–216. http://dx.doi.org/10.1111/spc3.12018

Gleichgerrcht, E., & Decety, J. (2012). The costs of empathy among health professionals. In J. Decety (Ed.), *Empathy: From bench to bedside* (pp. 245–262). Boston: Massachusetts Institute of Technology Press.

Gullo, N. (2013). *Into the cage: The rise of UFC nation*. Toronto, Ontario, Canada: Random House.

Hagger-Johnson, G., & Egan, V. (2010). Sadistic personality disorder and sensational interests: What is the size and specificity of the association? *Journal of Forensic Psychiatry & Psychology, 21*, 113–120. http://dx.doi.org/10.1080/14789940903174220

Hall, J. R., & Benning, S. D. (2006). The "successful" psychopath: Adaptive and subclinical manifestations of psychopathy in the general population. In C. J. Patrick (Ed.), *Handbook of psychopathy* (pp. 459–478). New York, NY: Guilford Press.

Jonason, P. K., Li, N. P., Webster, G. D., & Schmitt, D. P. (2009). The Dark Triad: Facilitating a short-term mating strategy in men. *European Journal of Personality, 23*, 5–18. http://dx.doi.org/10.1002/per.698

Jones, D. N., & Paulhus, D. L. (2011). Differentiating the Dark Triad within the interpersonal circumplex. In L. M. Horowitz & S. Strack (Eds.), *Handbook of interpersonal psychology* (pp. 249–268). New York, NY: Wiley.

Jones, D. N., & Weiser, D. (2014). Differential infidelity patterns among the Dark Triad. *Personality and Individual Differences, 57*, 20–24. http://dx.doi.org/10.1016/j.paid.2013.09.007

Knight, R. A. (1999). Validation of a typology for rapists. *Journal of Interpersonal Violence, 14*, 303–329. http://dx.doi.org/10.1177/088626099014003006

Krupp, D. B., Sewall, L. A., Lalumière, M. L., Sheriff, C., & Harris, G. T. (2013). Psychopathy, adaptation, and disorder. *Frontiers in Psychology, 4*, 139. http://dx.doi.org/10.3389/fpsyg.2013.00139

Lee, K., & Ashton, M. C. (2005). Psychopathy, Machiavellianism, and narcissism in the five-factor model and the HEXACO model of personality structure. *Personality and Individual Differences, 38*, 1571–1582. http://dx.doi.org/10.1016/j.paid.2004.09.016

Millon, T., & Davis, R. D. (1996). *Disorders of personality: DSM–IV and beyond*. New York, NY: Wiley Interscience.

Mokros, A., Osterheider, M., Hucker, S. J., & Nitschke, J. (2011). Psychopathy and sexual sadism. *Law and Human Behavior, 35*, 188–199. http://dx.doi.org/10.1007/s10979-010-9221-9

Nell, V. (2006). Cruelty's rewards: The gratifications of perpetrators and spectators. *Behavioral and Brain Sciences, 29*, 211–224. http://dx.doi.org/10.1017/S0140525X06009058

Nitschke, J., Osterheider, M., & Mokros, A. (2009). A cumulative scale of severe sexual sadism. *Sexual Abuse: Journal of Research and Treatment, 21*, 262–278.

O'Meara, A., Davies, J., & Hammond, S. (2011). The psychometric properties and utility of the Short Sadistic Impulse Scale (SSIS). *Psychological Assessment, 23*, 523–531. http://dx.doi.org/10.1037/a0022400

Paglia, C. (1990). *Sexual personae: Art and decadence from Nefertiti to Emily Dickinson*. New York, NY: Vintage Books.

Paulhus, D. L. (2014). Toward a taxonomy of dark personalities. *Current Directions in Psychological Science, 23*, 421–426. http://dx.doi.org/10.1177/0963721414547737

Paulhus, D. L., & Buckels, E. E. (2011, February). *The Dark Tetrad of personality: Relevance to terrorist groups*. Invited address to the Defense Research and Development Canada (DRDC) agency, Toronto, Ontario, Canada.

Paulhus, D. L., & Jones, D. N. (2015). Measures of dark personalities. In G. J. Boyle, E. H. Saklofske, & G. Matthews (Eds.), *Measures of personality and social psychological constructs* (pp. 562–594). San Diego, CA: Academic Press. http://dx.doi.org/10.1016/B978-0-12-386915-9.00020-6

Paulhus, D. L., Jones, D. N., Klonsky, E. D., & Dutton, D. G. (2011). *Sadistic personality and its correlates in community samples*. Unpublished manuscript, University of British Columbia, Vancouver, British Columbia, Canada.

Paulhus, D. L., & Williams, K. M. (2002). The Dark Triad of personality: Narcissism, Machiavellianism, and psychopathy. *Journal of Research in Personality, 36*, 556–563. http://dx.doi.org/10.1016/S0092-6566(02)00505-6

Pinker, S. (2011). *The better angels of our nature: Why violence has declined*. New York, NY: Viking.

Reidy, D. E., Zeichner, A., & Seibert, L. A. (2011). Unprovoked aggression: Effects of psychopathic traits and sadism. *Journal of Personality, 79*, 75–100. http://dx.doi.org/10.1111/j.1467-6494.2010.00691.x

Richters, J., de Visser, R. O., Rissel, C. E., Grulich, A. E., & Smith, A. M. (2008). Demographic and psychosocial features of participants in bondage and discipline, "sadomasochism" or dominance and submission (BDSM): Data from a national survey. *Journal of Sexual Medicine, 5*, 1660–1668. http://dx.doi.org/10.1111/j.1743-6109.2008.00795.x

Sandler, K. (2007). *The naked truth: Why Hollywood doesn't make X-rated movies*. Piscataway, NJ: Rutgers University Press.

Taylor, K. (2009). *Cruelty: Human evil and the human brain*. Oxford, England: Oxford University Press.

Vaughn, S. (2006). *Freedom and entertainment: Rating the new movies in an age of new media*. New York, NY: Cambridge University Press.

Vernon, P. A., Villani, V. C., Vickers, L. C., & Harris, J. A. (2008). A behavioral genetic investigation of the Dark Triad and the Big 5. *Personality and Individual Differences, 44*, 445–452. http://dx.doi.org/10.1016/j.paid.2007.09.007

World Health Organization. (1992). *International statistical classification of diseases and related health problems* (10th rev.). Geneva, Switzerland: Author.

6

SPITE

DAVID K. MARCUS AND ALYSSA L. NORRIS

DEFINITION AND BACKGROUND

What do bacteria and medieval nuns have in common? Some species of bacteria produce toxins (bacteriocins) that are lethal to conspecifics who do not have a gene that makes them immune to the bacteriocin. The act of releasing the bacteriocin is fatal to the actor, but because it kills more distantly related conspecifics while sparing bacteria who share many genes with the actor, this single-cell version of a "suicide bombing" may be biologically adaptive (West & Gardner, 2010). To protect her virginity during an attack on the St. Cyr monastery in France in the 8th century, Eusebia, the abbess of the monastery, cut off her nose and encouraged the other nuns to do the same. Their aim was "to irritate by this bloody spectacle the rage of the barbarians and to extinguish their passions" (de Rey, 1885, as cited in Schulenburg, 1998, p. 145). Although the nuns were massacred, they were

http://dx.doi.org/10.1037/14854-007
The Dark Side of Personality: Science and Practice in Social, Personality, and Clinical Psychology, V. Zeigler-Hill and D. K. Marcus (Editors)

not raped, and thus their gambit to protect their virginity may have succeeded. Similar events involving homicidal invaders and self-mutilating nuns occurred throughout the Middle Ages in Britain, Spain, and Jerusalem (Schulenburg, 1998). If *spite* is understood as behaviors that involve harm to oneself in order to harm another, then both the bacteria and the nuns acted spitefully. In fact, the harm in each case was significant (death, mutilation), with the nuns literally cutting off their noses for spite. Although the specific circumstances and actions have changed, it would not be difficult to generate a timeline of noteworthy acts of spite throughout recorded history. Currently, for example, some analysts (e.g., Krugman, 2013) have suggested that state governments that are refusing federal funds to expand Medicaid coverage are doing so primarily out of spite.

Despite the ubiquity of spite and its potential consequences, spitefulness, as an individual difference variable, has received far less attention in the psychology research literature than other dark personality traits such as narcissism, Machiavellianism, psychopathy, or sadism. The first personality scale designed to assess trait spitefulness was only developed recently (Marcus, Zeigler-Hill, Mercer, & Norris, 2014). There is also no standard definition of spitefulness. *Spite* can be broadly defined to include any vindictive or mean-spirited actions, as appears to be the case in the *Diagnostic and Statistical Manual of Mental Disorders* (5th ed.; *DSM–5*) criteria for oppositional defiant disorder (ODD), which includes "Has been spiteful or vindictive at least twice within the past 6 months" (American Psychiatric Association, 2013, p. 462). Alternatively, a narrower definition includes the requirement that spiteful acts involve some degree of self-harm (e.g., "cutting off one's nose to spite one's face"). This narrower definition has been adopted by a variety of disciplines. In economics, a spiteful act is one in which the actor is willing to incur personal costs in order to impose a cost on another, even when these costs do not result in future rewards to the actor (Cullis, Jones, & Soliman, 2012; Fehr & Fischbacher, 2005). Similarly, in evolutionary biology, "spite involves paying a cost to inflict a cost on another" (Smead & Forber, 2013, p. 698). The current chapter focuses on this narrow definition, both because it distinguishes spite from other related acts of aggression and because it emphasizes the apparently irrational and paradoxical nature of spitefulness.

Part of what makes spite an intriguing topic is that it seems to contradict basic assumptions underlying both classical economics and evolutionary theory. At the heart of classical economic theory is the assumption that people are rational actors who seek to maximize rewards. Behavioral economists have focused on spite precisely because spiteful actors sacrifice benefits to harm another, suggesting that human motives are more complex than simply maximizing acquisitions. Similarly, from a biological perspective, spiteful actions result in negative consequences for both the actor and the recipient (Hamilton, 1970) and thus reduce an individual's fitness by depleting resources or risking harm, without resulting in any apparent gains. Although genuine spite (as opposed to selfish or retaliatory acts that may increase the actor's fitness) appears to be rare among nonhuman species, examples of spiteful behavior have been documented among social insects and bacteria (West & Gardner, 2010). Hamilton (1970) hypothesized that spiteful behavior may occur when the actor is negatively related to the recipient (i.e., the actor shares fewer genes in common with the recipient than with the average member of the population). Wilson (1975) added that spiteful behavior may occur when the harm to the recipient benefits a third party who is related to the actor. Most recently, Smead and Forber (2013) suggested that spite may evolve when individuals interact with others of a different type, regardless of whether the difference is genetically based or instead involves different traits, strategies, or behaviors. This broader concept of *anticorrelation* or negative assortment encompasses negative relatedness but eliminates the need for accurate kin determination as a prerequisite for spite.

REVIEW OF THE RELEVANT LITERATURE

Much of the research that is most relevant to human spitefulness has used variants of the ultimatum game (UG) paradigm. In the basic UG, one player (the proposer) is given the opportunity to divide a set amount of money. The second player (the responder) then gets to decide whether to accept the offer or reject it. If the responder accepts the offer, then both players split the money in the way suggested by the proposer. However, if the responder rejects the offer, then neither player receives anything. This paradigm provides the responder with the opportunity to behave spitefully by rejecting unequal offers. Furthermore, the rejection of a less unequal offer (a 60/40 split) may be considered to be more spiteful than the rejection of a more unequal offer (a 90/10 split). In an iterative version of the UG, the players play multiple rounds, which could provide a rational incentive for spiteful behavior (e.g., if Don rejects Ted's offer of $1/$9 split, perhaps in the next round, Ted will make a more equitable offer). In contrast, in a "one-shot" UG, the responder plays against a different proposer for each turn (or, in studies in which the proposer is actually a computer, the responder is led to believe that the proposer is a different player for each turn). In this design, the rational and selfish strategy is to accept all offers no matter how small and unequal because some money is better than no money. However, it is common for responders to reject uneven offers in these one-shot UG designs (Camerer, 2003). Even children will engage in these spiteful rejections in an UG (Sutter, 2007).

Although not all UG and related game studies were framed as investigations of spiteful behavior, research examining responder behavior in these games may provide clues to individual differences in spitefulness. First, across a wide range of studies, there is clear variability in the rates at which responders reject offers from proposers (e.g., Camerer, 2003; Fehr & Schmidt, 1999), suggesting individual differences in spitefulness. For example, in a modified UG in which some responders still received a small payment even if they rejected the proposer's offer to split $20, roughly one third of the responders rejected a $2 offer and instead opted to receive $1 when they were led to believe that the proposer knew about this fallback option (Pillutla & Murnighan, 1996). In effect, these participants spitefully paid $1 to prevent the proposer from receiving $18. Kimbrough and Reiss (2012) used a bidding game task to measure the distribution of spitefulness. In this auction game, players could bid up the cost of an item without risking any costs to themselves. Roughly 25% of the participants behaved spitefully across multiple trials. Although the rules of this bidding game do not match our definition of spite because the participants could act vindictively without risking harm to themselves, this estimate of the rate of spitefulness is close to the 20% rate that Levine (1998) derived from the mathematical model he developed to explain the results from various resource allocation games. Across a range of UG studies, highly unequal offers (80/20 or less) were rejected at a 50% rate (Camerer, 2003).

If somewhere between one fifth and one third of people behave spitefully in UG and related games, this base rate raises the question of whether there are personality traits or other individual differences that can predict this spiteful behavior. Asked to imagine a hypothetical one-shot UG, individuals high in Machiavellianism expressed a greater willingness to accept unequal offers (to play selfishly instead of spitefully) than those low in Machiavellianism (Meyer, 1992). However, there is little reason to assume that these reports of hypothetical behavior are indicative of people's behavior when there are actual consequences. Brandstätter and Königstein (2001) reported an interaction between emotional stability and extraversion when predicting responses in an UG such that participants who were either emotionally unstable and extraverted or emotionally stable and introverted were the most likely to reject unequal offers. Almakias and Weiss (2012) examined whether attachment style was related to how college students played a UG. An avoidant attachment style (i.e., low anxiety combined with high avoidance) was associated with a greater tendency to reject unequal offers. In contrast, clinically depressed college students in the role of responders were more likely to accept unfair offers (Harlé, Allen, & Sanfey, 2010). Similarly, high levels of trait negative affect and low levels of trait positive affect were associated with a tendency to accept unequal offers in an UG (Dunn, Makarova,

Evans, & Clark, 2010). Overall, these studies suggest that low levels of trait negative affect (and perhaps a lack of interpersonal connection) are most consistently associated with a spiteful response style in UG. However, none of these studies attempted to measure trait spitefulness directly.

Marcus and colleagues (2014) recently developed a 17-item self-report Spitefulness Scale. The scale is composed of items describing situations in which there is the opportunity to harm another but that also entail self-harm (e.g., "I would be willing to pay more for some goods and services if other people I did not like had to pay even more" and "It might be worth risking my reputation in order to spread gossip about someone I did not like"). As part of the initial validation of the scale, Marcus et al. examined the associations between this Spitefulness Scale and related constructs. Individuals who scored higher on the Spitefulness Scale also reported higher levels of aggression and overall psychological distress, and lower levels of agreeableness, conscientiousness, and self-esteem. Although the associations with aggression and agreeableness were to be expected, the positive correlation with psychological distress runs counter to the findings that depressed and anxious individuals are less spiteful in UG studies (e.g., Harlé et al., 2010). Controlling for the shared variance between self-reported guilt and shame, spitefulness was positively associated with shame-proneness and negatively associated with guilt-proneness. Self-reported spitefulness was also associated with the dark personality traits of psychopathy, narcissism, and Machiavellianism, especially the facets of these traits that involve callousness, manipulation, and exploitation. The association between callous-unemotional psychopathic personality traits and spitefulness is consistent with Almakias and Weiss's (2012) finding that an avoidant attachment style predicted spiteful responses in an UG. On the other hand, the positive association between spitefulness and Machiavellianism seems to contradict Meyer's (1992) finding that Machiavellianism was associated with a selfish and not spiteful strategy in a hypothetical UG. Future research examining the association between Machiavellianism and actual play in an UG may help resolve this inconsistency. Given that the associations between self-reported spitefulness and external correlates were not consistently the same as the associations between spiteful UG play and external correlates, it will be especially important to examine whether self-reported spitefulness predicts spiteful UG play.

ADAPTIVE AND MALADAPTIVE FEATURES

Although spitefulness is generally portrayed as a negative personality trait and has the potential to cause considerable suffering to both the spiteful individual and the recipient of the spiteful behavior, it may serve an important adaptive function. Smead and Forber (2013) deemed spite "the shady relative of altruism" (p. 698) and demonstrated how similar mechanisms can account for the evolution of both spite and altruism. In fact, within a population whose size remains constant, "any social trait that is spiteful simultaneously qualifies as altruistic" (Lehmann, Bargum, & Reuter, 2006, p. 1507) because any act that directly harms recipients of the act indirectly helps nonrecipients of the act (e.g., bacteria not killed by the release of the bacteriocin now have access to more resources), and any altruistic acts that directly help recipients indirectly harm nonrecipients. However, if the population size is not fixed, spite is more problematic because it can result in population decline, in contrast to altruistic behavior, which can lead to population growth (Smead & Forber, 2013).

The threat of spiteful retaliation may lead people to treat others more fairly. In other words, spite may limit exploitation and encourage fairness and reciprocity. In a computer simulation study using an UG paradigm, Forber and Smead (2014) found that when players were likely to encounter opponents who used strategies different from their own (i.e., negative assortment), then including some spiteful players in the simulation (i.e., players who rejected unequal offers at a cost to themselves) resulted in fewer inequitable offers. In this simulation, fairness evolved through spite. Thus, despite the potential for harm, spiteful actors may serve as enforcers of important social norms. For example, a spiteful act by a "coercive creditor" (Leff, 1970) who spends more in legal fees or payments to collection agencies than the value of the debt may also have altruistic repercussions by helping to enforce the norm that people honor their obligations.

Of course, despite its potential evolutionary and social value, there is also quite a bit of maladaptive behavior associated with spitefulness. Anecdotal examples of the toll of spitefulness abound, perhaps most prototypically during divorce proceedings. When spouses turn spiteful, divorces run the risk of devolving into a negative sum game in which each party reduces the value of shared assets (e.g., by engaging in protracted and expensive legal proceedings) to prevent the other party from benefiting (Scott, 1992). Divorcing parents may pursue custody to spite their ex-spouses and not because of the children's best interests (Scott 1992). Spitefulness may also motivate "coercive collection" by creditors who spend more in legal fees or payments to collection agencies than the money they expect to recoup (Leff, 1970). In these instances, "the fulfillment of an urge to spite seems no different from the fulfillment of any other human desire" (Leff, 1970, p. 19).

Anecdotal examples of spiteful suicides staged to traumatize the person they blamed for their problems have also been documented. These include cases in which a fired employee shot herself by the house of the person she thought was responsible for her firing and of a man who shot himself in his ex-girlfriend's snowy front yard to highlight the red blood on the white snow

(Joiner, 2010). The most extreme examples of spite may be suicide bombings in which the bombers kill themselves with the goal of simultaneously killing their enemies (Gambetta, 2005). Despite the wealth of anecdotal examples of maladaptive spiteful behavior, there have been no systematic studies of the frequency and costs of spite in everyday life.

DIRECTIONS FOR FUTURE RESEARCH

Although numerous UG studies have implications for spite, and evolutionary biologists have studied and theorized about spite, there is virtually no research on spitefulness as an individual difference variable. As a result, future research is needed to address a wide variety of unanswered questions about trait spitefulness. Marcus et al. (2014) found that spitefulness was negatively associated with agreeableness and conscientiousness, but additional research at the facet level is needed to determine how spitefulness fits into the five-factor model of personality. There are also questions of how distinct spitefulness is from hostility and aggression. Does assessing trait spitefulness contribute additional variance to the prediction of spiteful behavior beyond what may be accounted for by traditional measures of aggressiveness? Is spitefulness a facet of aggressiveness, or is it a blend of aggressiveness and other traits? Does the hostile versus instrumental aggression distinction also apply to spiteful actions?

Little is known about the frequency and context of spiteful behavior in everyday life. Is spiteful behavior a daily occurrence? What types of situations are most likely to elicit spite? How often do people behave in a truly destructive spiteful manner, causing serious harm to either themselves or others? Daily diary studies and ecological momentary assessment studies can provide preliminary answers to these questions. Collecting such data can also be used to assess whether individuals who self-report higher levels of spitefulness actually engage in more frequent or harmful spiteful behavior. These data will also be an important step in validating Marcus et al.'s (2014) Spitefulness Scale and the broader concept of trait spitefulness. Such daily diary data could also be used to examine whether frequent or severely spiteful behavior is associated with psychopathology or whether otherwise well-adjusted individuals are capable of engaging in destructive spite. Considering the evolutionarily adaptive function of spite and its possible role in enforcing social norms, it is noteworthy that trait spitefulness appears to be associated with a range of maladaptive personality traits (Marcus et al., 2014), and this apparent paradox also merits further study.

There are also unanswered questions regarding sex differences in spitefulness that merit further study. Marcus et al. (2014) found that men reported higher levels of spitefulness than women, but it is unclear whether this finding reflects a genuine sex difference in spitefulness or is an artifact of a content validity issue with the Spitefulness Scale. On the one hand, spitefulness was associated with other personality traits that show similar sex differences (e.g., aggression, psychopathy, narcissism). However, the version of the Spitefulness Scale that Marcus and colleagues constructed did not include items addressing relational spitefulness (e.g., "After a bad breakup, I would try to date my ex's best friend even if I wasn't attracted to that person"). Perhaps the inclusion of such items would have attenuated this sex difference. UG studies have yielded inconsistent results regarding sex differences, with some finding that men play more spitefully than women (Eckel & Grossman, 2001), but Solnick (2001) found a trend toward women rejecting more offers than men (i.e., playing more spitefully).

Ethnic or cultural differences in spitefulness may also be worthy of study. Marcus et al. (2014) found that ethnic minority participants reported higher levels of spitefulness. Similarly, Eckel and Grossman (2001) found that African American participants were more likely to reject unequal offers in an UG (although as proposers, they made more generous offers than White participants). In a cross-cultural study, Henrich (2000) found that as proposers in a UG, the Machiguenga people of the Peruvian Amazon made more unequal offers than did players from industrialized countries but that as responders they were also more willing to accept more unequal offers. These results suggest that at least within the context of a UG, there may be cultural differences in spitefulness, although research has yet to identify the possible causes for these group differences.

CLINICAL IMPLICATIONS

Spiteful behavior is one of the diagnostic criteria for ODD in the *DSM–5* (American Psychiatric Association, 2013) and for conduct disorder in the *International Statistical Classification of Diseases and Related Health Problems* (10th rev.; *ICD–10*; World Health Organization, 1992). However, the *DSM* does not define whether such behaviors must involve an element of self-harm, specify what behaviors qualify as spiteful, or provide illustrative examples of spiteful behavior. Furthermore, whereas the other seven *DSM* diagnostic criteria for ODD must occur often (e.g., "*Often* loses temper," "*Often* deliberately annoys others"; American Psychiatric Association, 2013, p. 462, emphasis added), the criterion for spiteful or vindictive behavior is at least twice in the past 6 months (in contrast the *ICD–10* criterion is also "Often spiteful or vindictive"). The imprecision and different temporal format for this spitefulness criterion in the *DSM* may have contributed to the inconsistent findings when researchers have factor analyzed the *DSM* ODD criteria. Some studies have found that spiteful or vindictive behavior loads on a "headstrong" factor along with symptoms such as "annoys others" and "defies adults" (e.g., Rowe, Costello, Angold, Copeland, & Maughan, 2010). In contrast, Burke, Hipwell, and Loeber (2010) found that spitefulness loaded on a negative affect factor along with "touchy" and "angry," but not with the criteria that comprised Rowe et al.'s (2010) headstrong factor. Furthermore, in a factor analysis that included the symptoms of a variety of childhood disorders, spitefulness loaded on a conduct disorder factor and not with many of the other ODD symptoms (Lahey et al., 2004). Perhaps specifying that spiteful behavior must involve some harm to the self may help clarify how this symptom is related to the other symptoms of ODD or whether spitefulness would be better situated with a different externalizing disorder such as conduct disorder.

Elevated hostility and aggression are associated with narcissistic (e.g., Baumeister, Bushman, & Campbell, 2000), borderline (e.g., Tragesser, Lippman, Trull, & Barrett, 2008), and antisocial personality disorders (e.g., Lobbestael, Cima, & Arntz, 2013). However, the extent to which spitefulness, in particular, is associated with these personality disorders is less clear. Some published clinical observations and a scant amount of research has considered the role of spitefulness in both narcissistic and borderline personality disorders. Psychoanalytic theorists (e.g., Shabad, 2000; Stern, 2004) have noted that narcissism, shame, and envy are common among their more spiteful clients. Gottlieb (2004), for example, discussed the challenge of working with narcissistic clients who idealize but then envy their analysts. As a consequence of this dynamic, these clients may spitefully injure themselves (e.g., fail to improve in therapy, terminate prematurely) to injure their analysts. Consistent with these clinical observations, Marcus et al. (2014) found medium-to-large correlations between self-reported spitefulness and narcissistic vulnerability, narcissistic entitlement, and shame-proneness.

Both self-harm ("suicidal behavior, gestures, or threats, or self-mutilating behavior"; American Psychiatric Association, 2013, p. 663) and problems with anger are listed as symptoms of borderline personality disorder in the DSM–5 (and "recurrent threats or acts of self-harm" is one of the criteria for the emotionally unstable personality disorder, borderline type, in the ICD–10), raising the question of whether some of the self-harm found in borderline personality disorder is spiteful. Critchfield, Levy, Clarkin, and Kernberg (2008) examined the association between attachment style and aggression in a sample of 92 female patients diagnosed with borderline personality disorder. Whereas anger and irritability were associated with relationship anxiety, self-harm was associated with relationship avoidance. According to the authors, self-harm in borderline personality disorder may serve a variety of functions, including self-punishment or as a means to elicit forgiveness or support from significant others. However, they noted that it may also "represent an indirect indictment or punishment of others who may care about the individual" (Critchfield et al., 2008, p. 77), suggesting that at times part of the motivation for self-harm in borderline personality disorder may be spite.

Furthermore, using an investment game paradigm, King-Casas and colleagues (2008) found that whereas non–borderline personality disorder individuals responded to low payments with anterior insula activation and attempts to repair the investment relationship, individuals with borderline personality disorder showed no such activation. The authors interpreted these results as evidence that individuals with borderline personality disorder expect to be undercut, so interpersonal slights reinforce their lack of trust and encourage a lack of cooperation. Thus, individuals with borderline personality disorder might be more likely to behave spitefully because they perceive exploitation as normative. In fact, individuals with symptoms of borderline personality disorder are more likely to report "losing a job on purpose" (Sansone & Wiederman, 2013, p. 210), which the authors speculated could be due to poor workplace relationships. Clearly, additional research examining spitefulness in the cluster B personality disorders is needed.

SUMMARY AND CONCLUSIONS

Spiteful behavior has been a subject of study for behavioral economists and evolutionary biologists, but it has received far less attention from psychologists. Thus, whereas a considerable amount has been learned about the role of spite in economic decision making, far less is known about the role of spite in other aspects of daily life. Spitefulness is likely to be of relevance for understanding individual differences, intimate relationships (and their dissolution), social behavior, and some forms of psychopathology. Exactly why spitefulness has not received the same degree of attention as other dark personality traits such as psychopathy, narcissism, and Machiavellianism, is something of a mystery. Perhaps psychologists have assumed that spitefulness is simply synonymous with aggressiveness, an assumption that remains an open question. By emphasizing the centrality of self-harm to the concept of spite and developing a self-report measure of spitefulness, we hope that psychologists pay greater attention to this understudied construct.

REFERENCES

Almakias, S., & Weiss, A. (2012). Ultimatum game behavior in light of attachment theory. *Journal of Economic Psychology, 33,* 515–526. http://dx.doi.org/10.1016/j.joep.2011.12.012

American Psychiatric Association. (2013). *Diagnostic and statistical manual of mental disorders* (5th ed.). Arlington, VA: Author.

Baumeister, R. F., Bushman, B. J., & Campbell, K. W. (2000). Self-esteem, narcissism, and aggression: Does violence result from low self-esteem or from threatened egotism? *Current Directions in Psychological Science, 9,* 26–29. http://dx.doi.org/10.1111/1467-8721.00053

Brandstätter, H., & Königstein, M. (2001). Personality influences on ultimatum bargaining decisions. *European Journal of Personality, 15,* S53–S70. http://dx.doi.org/10.1002/per.424

Burke, J. D., Hipwell, A. E., & Loeber, R. (2010). Dimensions of oppositional defiant disorder as predictors of depression and conduct disorder in preadolescent girls. *Journal of the American Academy of Child & Adolescent Psychiatry, 49,* 484–492.

Camerer, C. F. (2003). *Behavioral game theory: Experiments in strategic interaction.* New York, NY: Princeton University Press.

Critchfield, K. L., Levy, K. N., Clarkin, J. F., & Kernberg, O. F. (2008). The relational context of aggression in borderline personality disorder: Using adult attachment style to predict forms of hostility. *Journal of Clinical Psychology, 64,* 67–82. http://dx.doi.org/10.1002/jclp.20434

Cullis, J., Jones, P., & Soliman, A. (2012). "Spite effects" in tax evasion experiments. *The Journal of Socio-Economics, 41,* 418–423. http://dx.doi.org/10.1016/j.socec.2011.05.011

Dunn, B. D., Makarova, D., Evans, D., & Clark, L. (2010). "I'm worth more than that": Trait positivity predicts increased rejection of unfair financial offers. *PLoS ONE, 5*(12), e15095. http://dx.doi.org/10.1371/journal.pone.0015095

Eckel, C. C., & Grossman, P. J. (2001). Chivalry and solidarity in ultimatum games. *Economic Inquiry, 39,* 171–188. http://dx.doi.org/10.1111/j.1465-7295.2001.tb00059.x

Fehr, E., & Fischbacher, U. (2005). The economics of strong reciprocity. In H. Gintis, S. Bowles, R. Boyd, & E. Fehr (Eds.), *Moral sentiments and material interests: The foundations of cooperation in economic life* (Vol. 6, pp. 151–191). Cambridge: Massachusetts Institute of Technology Press.

Fehr, E., & Schmidt, K. M. (1999). A theory of fairness, competition, and cooperation. *The Quarterly Journal of Economics, 114,* 817–868. http://dx.doi.org/10.1162/003355399556151

Forber, P., & Smead, R. (2014). The evolution of fairness through spite. *Proceedings of the Royal Society B: Biological Sciences, 281,* 20132439.

Gambetta, D. (2005). Can we make sense of suicide missions? In D. Gambetta (Ed.), *Making sense of suicide missions* (pp. 259–299). Oxford, England: Oxford University Press. http://dx.doi.org/10.1093/acprof:oso/9780199276998.003.0008

Gottlieb, R. M. (2004). Refusing the cure: Sophocles's *Philoctetes* and the clinical problems of self-injurious spite, shame, and forgiveness. *The International*

Journal of Psychoanalysis, 85, 669–689. http://dx.doi.org/10.1516/A750-YQQL-NB4C-LLGC

Hamilton, W. D. (1970). Selfish and spiteful behavior in an evolutionary model. *Nature, 228*, 1218–1220. http://dx.doi.org/10.1038/2281218a0

Harlé, K. M., Allen, J. J., & Sanfey, A. G. (2010). The impact of depression on social economic decision making. *Journal of Abnormal Psychology, 119*, 440–446. http://dx.doi.org/10.1037/a0018612

Henrich, J. (2000). Does culture matter in economic behavior? Ultimatum game bargaining among the Machiguenga of the Peruvian Amazon. *The American Economic Review, 90*, 973–979. http://dx.doi.org/10.1257/aer.90.4.973

Joiner, T. (2010). *Myths about suicide.* Cambridge, MA: Harvard University Press.

Kimbrough, E. O., & Reiss, J. P. (2012). Measuring the distribution of spitefulness. *PLoS ONE, 7*(8), e41812. http://dx.doi.org/10.1371/journal.pone.0041812

King-Casas, B., Sharp, C., Lomax-Bream, L., Lohrenz, T., Fonagy, P., & Montague, P. R. (2008). The rupture and repair of cooperation in borderline personality disorder. *Science, 321*, 806–810. http://dx.doi.org/10.1126/science.1156902

Krugman, P. (2013, June 7). The spite club. *The New York Times.* Retrieved from http://www.nytimes.com/2013/06/07/opinion/krugman-the-spite-club.html

Lahey, B. B., Applegate, B., Waldman, I. D., Loft, J. D., Hankin, B. L., & Rick, J. (2004). The structure of child and adolescent psychopathology: Generating new hypotheses. *Journal of Abnormal Psychology, 113*, 358–385.

Leff, A. A. (1970). Injury, ignorance, and spite: The dynamics of coercive collection. *The Yale Law Journal, 80*, 1–46. http://dx.doi.org/10.2307/795095

Lehmann, L., Bargum, K., & Reuter, M. (2006). An evolutionary analysis of the relationship between spite and altruism. *Journal of Evolutionary Biology, 19*, 1507–1516. http://dx.doi.org/10.1111/j.1420-9101.2006.01128.x

Levine, D. K. (1998). Modeling altruism and spitefulness in experiments. *Review of Economic Dynamics, 1*, 593–622. http://dx.doi.org/10.1006/redy.1998.0023

Lobbestael, J., Cima, M., & Arntz, A. (2013). The relationship between adult reactive and proactive aggression, hostile interpretation bias, and antisocial personality disorder. *Journal of Personality Disorders, 27*, 53–66. http://dx.doi.org/10.1521/pedi.2013.27.1.53

Marcus, D. K., Zeigler-Hill, V., Mercer, S. H., & Norris, A. L. (2014). The psychology of spite and the measurement of spitefulness. *Psychological Assessment, 26*, 563–574. http://dx.doi.org/10.1037/a0036039

Meyer, H. D. (1992). Norms and self-interest in ultimatum bargaining: The prince's prudence. *Journal of Economic Psychology, 13*, 215–232. http://dx.doi.org/10.1016/0167-4870(92)90031-2

Pillutla, M. M., & Murnighan, J. K. (1996). Unfairness, anger, and spite: Emotional rejections of ultimatum offers. *Organizational Behavior and Human Decision Processes, 68*, 208–224. http://dx.doi.org/10.1006/obhd.1996.0100

Rowe, R., Costello, E. J., Angold, A., Copeland, W. E., & Maughan, B. (2010). Developmental pathways in oppositional defiant disorder and conduct disorder. *Journal of Abnormal Psychology, 119*, 726–738. http://dx.doi.org/10.1037/a0020798

Sansone, R. A., & Wiederman, M. W. (2013). Losing a job on purpose: Relationships with borderline personality symptomatology. *Early Intervention in Psychiatry, 7*, 210–212. http://dx.doi.org/10.1111/eip.12014

Schulenburg, J. T. (1998). *Forgetful of their sex: Female sanctity and society ca. 500–1100*. Chicago, IL: University of Chicago Press.

Scott, E. S. (1992). Pluralism, parental preference, and child custody. *California Law Review, 80*, 615–672. http://dx.doi.org/10.2307/3480710

Shabad, P. (2000). Giving the devil his due: Spite and the struggle for individual dignity. *Psychoanalytic Psychology, 17*, 690–705. http://dx.doi.org/10.1037/0736-9735.17.4.690

Smead, R., & Forber, P. (2013). The evolutionary dynamics of spite in finite populations. *Evolution: International Journal of Organic Evolution, 67*, 698–707. http://dx.doi.org/10.1111/j.1558-5646.2012.01831.x

Solnick, S. J. (2001). Gender differences in the ultimatum game. *Economic Inquiry, 39*, 189–200. http://dx.doi.org/10.1111/j.1465-7295.2001.tb00060.x

Stern, J. (2004). Of "Sympathy for the Devil" and a question of conscious versus unconscious spite: Comment on Shabad (2000). *Psychoanalytic Psychology, 21*, 655–661. http://dx.doi.org/10.1037/0736-9735.21.4.655

Sutter, M. (2007). Outcomes versus intentions: On the nature of fair behavior and its development with age. *Journal of Economic Psychology, 28*, 69–78. http://dx.doi.org/10.1016/j.joep.2006.09.001

Tragesser, S. L., Lippman, L. G., Trull, T. J., & Barrett, K. C. (2008). Borderline personality disorder features and cognitive, emotional, and predicted behavioral reactions to teasing. *Journal of Research in Personality, 42*, 1512–1523. http://dx.doi.org/10.1016/j.jrp.2008.07.003

West, S. A., & Gardner, A. (2010). Altruism, spite, and greenbeards. *Science, 327*, 1341–1344. http://dx.doi.org/10.1126/science.1178332

Wilson, E. O. (1975). *Sociobiology: A new synthesis*. Cambridge, MA: Harvard University Press.

World Health Organization. (1992). *International statistical classification of diseases and related health problems* (10th rev.). Geneva, Switzerland: Author.

II

DISINHIBITION

7

A REVIEW OF SENSATION SEEKING AND ITS EMPIRICAL CORRELATES: DARK, BRIGHT, AND NEUTRAL HUES

JESSICA L. MAPLES-KELLER, DANIELLE S. BERKE,
LAUREN R. FEW, AND JOSHUA D. MILLER

DEFINITION AND BACKGROUND

Sensation seeking, as defined by Zuckerman (1979), represents "the need for varied, novel, and complex sensations and experiences and the willingness to take physical and social risks for the sake of such experiences" (p. 10). Individuals who score high on measures of this trait are thought to seek these kinds of experiences to maintain or attain optimal levels of arousal. The initial theory surrounding investigations of sensation seeking was based in optimal level of stimulation theory, which posits that a continuum of intensity of sensation exists in which there is an optimal point at which the stimulus is regarded as most pleasurable, as well as optimal level of arousal theory (Breuer & Freud, 1895/1955), in which individuals are posited to vary with regard to the level of arousal that is optimal.

http://dx.doi.org/10.1037/14854-008

The Dark Side of Personality: Science and Practice in Social, Personality, and Clinical Psychology, V. Zeigler-Hill and D. K. Marcus (Editors)

Sensation seeking is a fundamental component of several comprehensive models of general personality, including Eysenck's three-factor model (Eysenck & Eysenck, 1985), Costa and McCrae's description of the five-factor model (FFM; Costa & McCrae, 1992), and Cloninger's seven-factor model (Cloninger, Svrakic, & Przybeck, 1993). This trait can also be found in pathological trait models, including Livesley's four-factor model (Livesley, Jackson, & Schroeder, 1989) and the *Diagnostic and Statistical Manual of Mental Disorders'* (5th ed.; *DSM–5*) new trait model of personality disorders (PDs; American Psychiatric Association, 2013). Although the *International Statistical Classification of Diseases and Related Health Problems* (10th rev.; *ICD–10*; World Health Organization [WHO], 1992) does not explicitly identify trait sensation seeking because it does not include a pathological trait model, both the *ICD–10* and the *DSM–5* include multiple categorical PD diagnoses that have been shown to relate to trait sensation seeking, such as dissocial PD/antisocial PD and histrionic PD (e.g., Samuel & Widiger, 2008).

In many cases, sensation seeking traits are "housed" within the extraversion domain (e.g., FFM), although the manner in which scales measuring this trait load with other traits in factor analyses varies across studies and measures, such that this trait sometimes loads with facets of extraversion and other times with facets of disinhibition (e.g., Markon, Krueger, & Watson, 2005). Biological accounts of extraversion (e.g., Eysenck, 1967) and sensation seeking (Zuckerman, 1979) overlap such that it has been argued that both are related to differing levels of physiological arousal. Zuckerman (1979) theorized that individuals high in sensation seeking may be chronically underaroused and require additional stimulation to reach their optimal level of arousal. As such, underaroused individuals may engage in sensation seeking behaviors as a means of increasing their arousal to their preferred level.

As part of Zuckerman's seminal research on the conceptualization and assessment of sensation seeking (using the Sensation Seeking Scale [SSS]; Zuckerman, Kolin, Price, & Zoob, 1964), he identified four subfactors of sensation seeking. As defined by Zuckerman (2008), thrill and adventure seeking involves "the intent or desire to engage in physical activities or sports involving unusual sensations," whereas experience seeking involves "the intent or desire to have new sensations and experiences through the mind and senses as in music, travel, and an unconventional lifestyle." Disinhibition is conceptualized as "seeking excitement through other people in parties, sex, and alcohol," and boredom susceptibility involves "an aversion to sameness and routine in activities and people, and a restlessness when little variety is present" (Zuckerman, 2008, p. 380). Correlations among these subfactors range from .22 to .57 for males and .21 to .62 for females (Zuckerman, Eysenck, & Eysenck, 1978).

There are a variety of ways to assess sensation seeking-related traits in addition to Zuckerman's SSS, including the use of the Novelty Seeking scale from the Tridimensional Personality Questionnaire (Cloninger, Przybeck, & Svrakic, 1991), the Excitement Seeking subscale of the revised NEO Personality Inventory (Costa & McCrae, 1992), and the Sensation Seeking scale from the UPPS model (Whiteside & Lynam, 2001; U = Urgency; P = lack of Perseverance; P = lack of Premeditation; S = Sensation Seeking). Whiteside and Lynam (2001) argued that the dimensions of the UPPS model represent specific pathways through which traits from a number of different personality domains (Sensation Seeking = extraversion; Urgency = neuroticism; lack of Premeditation and Perseverance = low conscientiousness) can lead to impulsive behavior (for a discussion of urgency, see Chapter 8, this volume). Although small differences likely exist between the various sensation seeking scales, for the sake of this chapter, they are grouped together to provide a review of the literature on sensation seeking.

REVIEW OF THE RELEVANT LITERATURE

Demographic Differences

Men generally score higher on sensation-seeking scales than women, although these differences tend to be small and may vary depending on participant age and measure used (Costa & McCrae, 1992; Zuckerman et al., 1978). Racial differences in sensation seeking have been suggested across several studies. A study using latent growth curve modeling on seven waves of data from a sample of 447 African American and European American individuals suggested higher initial levels of sensation seeking in European Americans, as well as greater growth in sensation seeking over time compared with African Americans (S. L. Pedersen, Molina, Belendiuk, & Donovan, 2012). With respect to age and development, a study using a large sample of twins demonstrated a linear decrease in sensation seeking over time for both sexes, suggesting that sensation seeking decreases over the lifespan (Zuckerman et al., 1978). More recently, data from a diverse sample of 935 individuals found a curvilinear pattern over the lifespan, with sensation seeking increasing between ages 10 and 15 and declining thereafter (Steinberg et al., 2008). These changes over time may not characterize all people; there is some evidence that some individuals' scores remain stably high or low whereas others change over time (e.g., Lynne-Landsman, Graber, Nichols, & Botvin, 2011).

Heritability

Sensation seeking, like most traits (e.g., Bouchard, 2004), is moderately heritable. The SSS subscales manifested heritability estimates that ranged from .48 to .63 in a Dutch sample of twins (Koopmans, Boomsma, Heath, & van Doornen, 1995). In a follow-up study that extended this sample to include nontwin siblings, heritability estimates for the SSS subscales ranged from .29 to .65 for females and .34 and .60 for males (Stoel, De Geus, & Boomsma, 2006). Most recently, a study of 2,562 sibling pairs found evidence of substantial genetic influences on both initial levels and change in sensation seeking over early adolescence, with more than 80% of the change due to genetic factors (Harden, Quinn, & Tucker-Drob, 2012).

Animal Models

Meaningful variations in levels of sensation seeking have been found in nonhuman animal species, supporting its evolutionary and biological basis (Roberti, 2004). Indeed, recent work in affective neuroscience has indicated that sensation seeking is one of six primary emotional traits that are present across species (Davis & Panksepp, 2011). Research using animal models has been useful in elucidating the neurobiological underpinnings of sensation seeking. For example, rats demonstrate varying levels of preference for novelty and activity in new environments, and these differences are related to dopamine activity (Blanchard, Mendelsohn, & Stamp, 2009). Animal models of sensation seeking have indicated an increased dopamine response in the nucleus accumbens similar to that found to reinforce drug intake (e.g., Olsen & Winder, 2009), suggesting that sensation seeking is likely related to reward processing.

Neuroscience

Consistent with these animal models, research with humans provides support for the hypothesis that the dopaminergic system underlies individual variability in sensation seeking because it is associated with genetic differences at certain dopamine receptors (D2 and D4; Derringer et al., 2010). Accumulating evidence suggests that this relationship may be nonlinear, such that healthy males with low or high levels of sensation seeking demonstrate lower dopamine availability than those with average levels (Gjedde, Kumakura, Cumming, Linnet, & Møller, 2010). It is likely that sensation seeking may be polygenetic in nature or related to multiple genes. Consistent with this notion, four dopamine receptor genes account for 5.25% of the variance in Novelty Seeking (Comings, Saucier, & MacMurray, 2002). The relation between sensation seeking and reward circuitry has also been supported using functional magnetic resonance imaging methodology. For instance, changes in the nucleus accumbens, a key component in reward circuitry in the brain, during anticipation of rewards correlated positively with sensation-seeking scores in children of alcoholics (Bjork, Knutson, & Hommer, 2008), providing further support for the relationship between trait sensation seeking and biological processes related to reward pathways and sensitivity.

The Risk-Taking Continuum

Both prosocial and antisocial behaviors are associated with sensation seeking, suggesting that this trait can be manifested in adaptive, neutral, and maladaptive ways. Gomà-i-Freixanet (2001) proposed a *risk-taking continuum* that includes antisociality at one pole, prosociality at the other, and more "neutral" behaviors (e.g., risky sports, aesthetic preference) near the center of the spectrum. Gomà-i-Freixanet (1995) provided support for this notion by comparing risk takers from different categories including prisoners, risky sportsmen, prosocial risk takers (e.g., firefighters, prison warden), and a control group; the only variable that differentiated the control group from all of the other groups in discriminant analyses was the Thrill and Adventure Seeking subscale of the SSS. This finding suggests that sensation-seeking individuals may find a wide array of activities and professions—prosocial, neutral, and antisocial—to satisfy their need for excitement, novelty, and danger. Therefore, a thorough elucidation of the consequences of sensation seeking requires study of its adaptive, neutral, and maladaptive correlates.

ADAPTIVE FEATURES

Civic Engagement

Sensation seeking is related to prosocial behavior such as volunteerism, leadership, and civic participation. Sensation seekers are more likely to be politically progressive and prefer societal change to the status quo (Zuckerman, 1994). Relatedly, sensation seeking-related traits are also positively related to political participation (Kam, 2012) and a preference for leadership positions (Wymer, Self, & Findley, 2008).

Military Service

In a 2008 survey of 28,546 active duty military personnel in the U.S. Armed Services, 78% were classified as high sensation seekers on the basis of their self-report scores, suggesting that this construct is strongly related to voluntary enlistment (Bray et al., 2009). These same data speak to the maladaptive aspects of this trait; sensation seeking among these military personnel was linked to alcohol, drug, and tobacco use and to on-the-job accidents.

Exploration

Consistent with animal models of sensation seeking suggesting its relation to increased preference for novel environments and exploratory behavior (e.g., Blanchard et al., 2009), research in humans suggests a link between trait sensation seeking and a preference for activities related to exploration. For instance, in a study comparing climbers from the 1985 Mount Everest expedition to elite mountain climbers, collegiate sport students, and military recruits, the Mount Everest climbers demonstrated higher levels of sensation seeking (Breivik, 1996). Additionally, in a study of 2,320 individuals from 39 populations and their migration patterns, populations that engaged in long-distance migration had a higher proportion of long alleles for the D4 dopamine receptor, which has been demonstrated to relate to levels of trait sensation seeking (Chen, Burton, Greenberger, & Dmitrieva, 1999). This finding suggests that it may be adaptive, at the societal level, for cultures to contain individuals with varying levels of sensation seeking as individuals with high scores on this trait may, at times, be responsible for monumental shifts in important paradigms (e.g., where to live, how to live).

Creativity

Sensation seeking is related to various tests of cognitive innovation, variety, and originality, suggesting that sensation seekers tend to tolerate ambiguity and are original and innovative in their approach to problem solving (Zuckerman, 1994). Sensation seeking is also associated with a common creativity factor comprising aspects of fluency, flexibility, originality, and elaboration (Okamoto & Takaki, 1992).

NEUTRAL FEATURES

Aesthetic Preference

Gomà-i-Freixanet's (2001) concept of a spectrum of sensation-seeking outcomes suggests the value of investigating this trait not only at its poles but across a continuum. The literature linking sensation seeking to individual differences in aesthetic preference reveals neutral correlates of this trait, positioned at the center of the continuum. With regard to music, sensation seeking is related to a preference for certain genres, such as hard rock (Dollinger,

1993), which may be due to a preference for emotionally evocative and arousing music. For example, Rawlings and Leow (2008) demonstrated that high scorers on the Impulsive Sensation Seeking Scale reported being sadder and less happy than low scorers when listening to relaxing/peaceful music. These findings are consistent with the optimal levels of arousal theory that suggests individuals high in sensation seeking may pursue complex, discordant, or intense stimuli as a means of optimizing their level of arousal. Similar findings have been found with regard to preferences for art and humor. Carretero-Dios and Ruch (2010) demonstrated that sensation seeking-related traits were related to less appreciation of incongruity–resolution humor (i.e., jokes that have punch lines that resolve the incongruity introduced in the setup of a joke) and greater appreciation of nonsense humor, or humor that did not provide resolution. The affinity of those high in sensation seeking for incongruous stimuli is also reflected in studies demonstrating their preference for art that is abstract or surrealistic (Furnham & Avison, 1997).

Extreme Sports

Engagement in "extreme" sports, characterized by such qualities as defiance of gravity, speed, and unusual experiences in unfamiliar environments, comprises both adaptive and maladaptive consequences because these sports may simultaneously serve to increase an individual's physical fitness while also subjecting him or her to heightened risk of physical harm. As such, extreme sports have been posited to lie conceptually at the center of the sensation-seeking spectrum and have received much attention via empirical investigation (Gomà-i-Freixanet, 2001). Several reviews have reported a correlation between sensation seeking and the riskiness of sport activities (e.g., Gomà-i-Freixanet, 2004). Skydiving, hang gliding, white-water rafting, rock-climbing, surfing, and downhill skiing are sports linked to high levels of sensation seeking, whereas moderate levels of the trait appear to be better predictors of engagement in competitive sports (e.g., automobile racing, hockey). Athletic activities that require endurance and commitment (e.g., long-distance running) or are played for an extended period of time at a slower pace (e.g., golf) are negatively associated with sensation seeking.

MALADAPTIVE FEATURES

Aggression and Antisocial Behavior

Sensation seeking is related to a host of maladaptive externalizing behavioral outcomes, although the effects are relatively small and sometimes inconsistent. For instance, two recent meta-analyses examined the relations between sensation seeking and aggression, with one finding a small positive effect ($d = .19$; Wilson & Scarpa, 2011) and the other finding no effect ($r = -.02$; Jones, Miller, & Lynam, 2011). Jones and colleagues (2011) did, however, find a small positive relation between sensation seeking as assessed by measures of FFM Excitement Seeking and antisocial behavior ($r = .14$). To the extent that there is some link between sensation seeking and behavior that is aggressive or antisocial, it may be explained by level of arousal theories. Low resting heart rate, which is a prospective predictor of sensation-seeking scores (Raine, Venables, & Mednick, 1997), is the single best replicated psychophysiological correlate of aggression (Ortiz & Raine, 2004).

Riskier Sex

Given Zuckerman's conceptualization of sensation seeking as a trait defined by desire for varied, novel, and complex sensations and experiences, riskier sexual behavior has been a regular outcome of interest in research on sensation seeking. In a meta-analytic review of the personality correlates of sexual risk taking, small positive effects were found for sensation seeking-related traits ($rs = .15$ to $.19$; Hoyle, Fejfar, & Miller, 2000) and these relations appear to hold across a wide array of samples (e.g., high school students, community participants, gay and straight participants; Zuckerman, 2007). Engagement in these higher risk behaviors may be due, in part, to differences in how risk is appraised because high sensation seekers rate dangerous activities as less risky in hindsight than do low sensation seekers (Zuckerman, 1994).

Risky Driving Behavior

Driving is a readily accessible opportunity for arousal and excitement for individuals predisposed to seek such sensations. In a review of 40 studies (Jonah, 1997), sensation seeking manifested a moderate relation (with correlations in the .30–.40 range) with risky driving behavior (e.g., driving at speeds far beyond the legal limit, driving while intoxicated or high). Risky driving has also been explored using multidimensional trait models of impulsivity; data suggest that all four subfactors of the UPPS, including sensation seeking, predict increased levels of risky driving acts (Bachoo, Bhagwanjee, & Govender, 2013).

Gambling

Although not all forms of gambling are harmful, gambling can become problematic when it exceeds economic means or interferes with occupational or social functioning. Engagement in high-stakes gambling appears to differ from other forms of sensation-seeking behavior. For pathological gamblers (i.e., gamblers who engage in "chasing behavior" in which they continue to place bets, often with increased wagers, after a sequence of losing bets), level of risk appears to be the primary reinforcing factor, whereas for many behaviors discussed thus far (e.g., sex, driving, substance use) level of risk is secondary to the rewarding sensations conferred by stimulating activities (Zuckerman, 1994). The anticipatory arousal involved in gambling appears to be most meaningful for those who engage in the behavior in repetitive or problematic ways. For example, the level of arousal exhibited by gamblers is correlated with the size of bets placed such that higher stakes bets were associated with heart rate increases (Anderson & Brown, 1984). Other studies have focused specifically on the link between trait impulsivity and gambling, as it is plausible that impulsivity may better explain why pathological gamblers continue to place risky bets despite potential negative consequences. Barrault and Varescon (2013) found that although sensation seeking is elevated for online poker players, it did not differentiate nonpathological players from pathological ones. A recent study investigated the relation between pathological gambling, as assessed via a semistructured clinical interview of DSM symptoms, and an array of 19 impulsivity-related measures (MacKillop et al., 2014). Factor analytic techniques identified four latent factors from these impulsivity indices, and the factor related to sensation seeking, titled reward sensitivity, manifested a small positive correlation with pathological gambling ($r = .17$), although the individual UPPS Sensation Seeking subscale was itself uncorrelated with pathological gambling ($r = -.03$). In a study that investigated a semistructured clinical interview of pathological gambling symptoms from the ICD–10 (WHO, 1992), pathological gamblers did not demonstrate higher average levels of sensation seeking compared with matched controls (Michalczuk, Bowden-Jones, Verdejo-Garcia, & Clark, 2011). Future research should simultaneously assess both DSM and ICD–10 pathological gambling symptoms to directly compare their relations with trait sensation seeking.

Substance Abuse

A meta-analysis of studies that used the SSS to assess the association between sensation seeking and alcohol across a range of different types of samples (e.g., patients, college students, adolescents, community members) and alcohol use outcomes (e.g., frequency of drinking, problem drinking, binge drinking, DSM-based alcohol use disorders) reported a small to moderate effect size ($r = .26$; Hittner & Swickert, 2006). In a more recent meta-analytic review of both cross-sectional and prospective studies, Stautz and

Cooper (2013) examined the relations between impulsivity-related traits and alcohol use and found nearly identical effect sizes. For cross-sectional studies, these authors reported small to medium effect sizes between sensation seeking and both alcohol consumption ($r = .28$) and problematic use ($r = .24$). These two meta-analyses provide consistent evidence of an association between sensation seeking and alcohol involvement, although there appear to be important moderators such that sensation seeking is more strongly associated with initiation/onset than pathological alcohol use (Stautz & Cooper, 2013) and is more strongly associated with alcohol use among Caucasians than African Americans (Hittner & Swickert, 2006; Stautz & Cooper, 2013). Hittner and Swickert (2006) hypothesized that sociocultural factors may explain why Caucasian individuals with high levels of sensation seeking are more inclined to engage in heavier alcohol use. It also does not appear that the relation between sensation seeking and alcohol use is limited to one diagnostic system: A previous study that assessed both ICD- and DSM-based substance use disorders identified elevated levels of this trait in hospital patients diagnosed with a lifetime history of alcohol abuse or dependence (Liraud & Verdoux, 2000). Sensation seeking is a consistent predictor of drug use as well, demonstrating medium to strong effect sizes across many studies (Roberti, 2004). In a sample of adolescents, sensation seeking predicted alcohol, tobacco, and marijuana use (Baker & Yardley, 2002). Sensation-seeking scores have been shown to predict drug use over a 20-month period, with the Disinhibition subscale of the SSS emerging as the strongest predictor (W. Pedersen, 1991). Peers' sensation seeking scores have also been shown to predict adolescents' marijuana and alcohol use (Donohew et al., 1999), suggesting that the level of sensation seeking within social networks may affect drug use, in addition to individual-level personality variables.

Relations With PDs

Sensation seeking is a central component of a number of PDs related to externalizing behaviors. Experts view sensation seeking (using FFM Excitement Seeking as the marker) to be a defining characteristic of prototypical cases of psychopathy (Miller, Lynam, Widiger, & Leukefeld, 2001), as well as DSM–5 Cluster B PDs that are also part of the ICD–10, including antisocial, borderline, histrionic, and narcissistic PDs (Lynam & Widiger, 2001; Samuel & Widiger, 2008). Meta-analytic reviews of the FFM-PD literature support most of these hypothesized relations with significant correlations between FFM Excitement Seeking and psychopathy ($r = .31$; Decuyper, DePauw, DeFruyt, DeBolle, & DeClercq, 2009), antisocial PD ($r = .25$), and histrionic PD ($r = .27$; Samuel & Widiger, 2008). The evidence for the role of sensation seeking in narcissistic ($r = .16$) and borderline PD ($r = .06$) is more mixed (Samuel & Widiger,

2008). Although this research demonstrates that sensation seeking is related to a number of PDs, it is important to note that this same research indicates that other personality traits are as or more central to understanding these disorders. For instance, within the meta-analytic review of PDs and FFM facets (Samuel & Widiger, 2008), independent weighted mean effect size correlations for antisocial PD ranged from −.17 to −.37 for Agreeableness facets and −.18 to −.38 for Conscientiousness facets, suggesting that these personality domains are likely the driving force behind this disorder and related externalizing outcomes. It is possible that the relations between sensation seeking and externalizing behaviors (e.g., antisocial behavior; crime) may be moderated by other traits that are stronger predictors of these outcomes—namely, traits from the domains of Agreeableness/Antagonism and Conscientiousness/Disinhibition (Jones et al., 2011; Miller & Lynam, 2001). That is, sensation seeking may be a stronger concurrent correlate or prospective risk factor for these outcomes when paired with traits such as callousness, self-absorption, or impulsivity.

DIRECTIONS FOR FUTURE RESEARCH

Although some studies have suggested differences across racial groups in the relations between sensation seeking and maladaptive outcomes (e.g., S. L. Pedersen et al., 2012), future research should strive to elucidate the nomological network of sensation seeking among different racial or ethnic groups. The ability to study this trait in other cultures depends on the existence of culturally sensitive and validated assessment measures. However, a recent study investigating the validity of a brief measure of the SSS scale (BSSS–4; Stephenson, Hoyle, Palmgreen, & Slater, 2003) demonstrated that it manifested more limited reliability and validity among African Americans compared with both White and Hispanic groups (Vallone, Allen, Clayton, & Xiao, 2007). Although the validity and reliability across racial groups of the SSS and other commonly used measures of this trait has not been directly investigated, this finding suggests that existing scales may be culturally biased and the construction of alternative scales may be required.

Future research could focus on gender differences in sensation seeking as well to parse genetic differences versus cultural factors. In a recent meta-analysis of differences in sensation seeking over time, the mean effect size for sex differences was moderate and stable over 35 years for total score sensation seeking, but the sex difference in the Thrill and Adventuring Seeking subscale has decreased significantly due to a decline in male scores (Cross, Cyrenne, & Brown, 2013). These data provide preliminary support for the notion that cultural factors may affect these traits and that gender socialization processes may affect the likelihood that men or women may engage in specific types of activities. Additionally, the preponderance of research investigating sensation seeking as a risk factor for maladaptive behaviors has used samples of young adults. Future research would benefit from assessing the effects of sensation seeking in older samples to assess the relevance of this trait across the lifespan. Although research suggests that sensation seeking decreases over the lifespan (Steinberg et al., 2008), it is also likely that the trait is expressed differently across various age ranges. Additionally, although research supports a biological underpinning of this trait, future research should focus on demonstrating causality between observed biological differences in individuals high on sensation seeking and risky behaviors. Although single genes and neurotransmitters have been shown to relate to sensation seeking, the inconsistency in findings is likely due to the polygenetic nature of traits, which can be investigated in future studies that use well-powered samples.

The literature reviewed in this chapter demonstrates that sensation seeking is related to multiple maladaptive outcomes, including substance use, risky driving, risky sex, and aggression/antisocial behavior, although these effects tend to be small and can vary across studies (and meta-analytic reviews), in part, depending on how sensation seeking is assessed. Although this idea has received little empirical attention to date, we believe it is possible that sensation seeking's relations with maladaptive outcomes (e.g., problematic risk taking, externalizing behaviors) may be moderated by the level of other relevant personality traits such that sensation seeking is more strongly related to these outcomes when paired with high levels of traits related to interpersonal antagonism or disinhibition. For instance, one study directly investigated whether impulsivity and sensation seeking operate independently or synergistically in relation to risky sexual behaviors and found a significant interaction between these traits in predicting multiple risky sex outcomes (Charnigo et al., 2013). Our understanding of sensation seeking's role in these various outcomes would benefit from future research that examines more systematically whether sensation-seeking relations with maladaptive outcomes are moderated by other known trait correlates of these outcomes.

CLINICAL IMPLICATIONS

Implications for Prevention and Intervention Efforts

Sensation seeking manifests small but relatively reliable positive relations with risky, potentially dangerous, and impairing behaviors, even in prospective studies, which suggests that it is a risk factor that should be included in prevention and intervention strategies attempting to reduce risky behavior. Lynne-Landsman and colleagues (2011) identified different groups of adolescents with varying levels of sensation seeking across time, including a stably low group, a moderately increasing group, and a stably high group. As such, they suggested a "two-pronged approach" (p. 55), such that efforts targeting the high and stable sensation-seeking group may focus specifically on altering how this trait is expressed. Conversely, for the moderately increasing group, they suggest that it will be important to identify and target the factors associated with this increase to attenuate its effect. It may also be effective to direct individuals high on trait sensation seeking toward more prosocial and adaptive outlets for their sensation seeking rather than attempting to change the underlying trait. For instance, this intervention could involve directing individuals toward activities that increase arousal level such as enrollment in the military or engagement in physical/sporting activities that may serve this same function with lower levels of risk of harm for the participant or those around the participant. In a sample of Israeli war veterans, sensation seeking was related to better performance during war and less posttraumatic stress symptoms after war (Neria, Solomon, Ginzburg, & Dekel, 2000), suggesting that individuals high on sensation seeking can function well in relatively neutral or prosocial environments that allow expression of this trait (cf. Bray et al., 2009). It may also be that individuals who are high on sensation seeking need to be targeted for prevention and intervention via different types of messages that play to these personality tendencies. For instance, Donohew and colleagues (2000) found that sensation-seeking individuals prefer antidrug-related messages that were novel, creative, intense, and unconventional. As such, two different antidrug public service announcements were developed, and individuals high on trait sensation seeking reported a greater intent to call a drug hotline offered in the public service announcement if they viewed the more stimulating version.

Implications for Prognostic Indicators

Traits such as sensation seeking can also be used within the context of treatment to anticipate difficulties that may arise. In a study investigating treatment response among a sample of African American individuals addicted to cocaine, sensation seeking was significantly negatively related to days in treatment and positively related to dropout rate and failed drug screenings (Patkar et al., 2004). Sensation seeking is also related to poor medication compliance (Ekselius, Bengtsson, & von Knorring, 2000). Clinicians may find it helpful to screen for sensation seeking when formulating a treatment plan. For instance, clinicians may use novelty and variation in treatment delivery (e.g., changing the modality or location of treatment) and work to identify prosocial alternatives to maladaptive behaviors.

SUMMARY AND CONCLUSIONS

Overall, sensation seeking has a complicated nomological network that includes largely adaptive and prosocial behaviors (e.g., civic engagement, voluntary enlistment in the military), neutral behaviors (e.g., tastes in music, art, or leisure activities), as well as more maladaptive and antisocial behaviors (e.g., substance use, risky sex, antisocial behavior). The effects for these behaviors, however, tend to be small to moderate and should not be overstated. We believe that it is possible that what directs individuals who are high on sensation seeking to these behaviors of varying levels of adaptivity is likely the presence or absence of other critical personality traits including tendencies toward disinhibition and interpersonal orientation (i.e., agreeable vs. antagonistic). For instance, many individuals who are high on sensation seeking are not impulsive; in fact, many sensation seekers demonstrate a great deal of preplanning and deliberation before engaging in dangerous activities (e.g., skydivers who check their equipment carefully before jumping). Similarly, many individuals who are high in sensation seeking are interpersonally agreeable and express these preferences via prosocial outlets (e.g., firefighter). The spectrum of outcomes related to sensation seeking, which includes both prosocial and antisocial outcomes (Gomà-i-Freixanet, 2004), demonstrates this trait is likely to be "dark" only when matched with more consistently maladaptive traits, such as callousness, affective dysregulation, manipulativeness, egocentrism, narcissism, and deficient impulse control.

REFERENCES

American Psychiatric Association. (2013). *Diagnostic and statistical manual of mental disorders* (5th ed.). Arlington, VA: Author.

Anderson, G., & Brown, R. I. F. (1984). Real and laboratory gambling, sensation-seeking and arousal. *British Journal of Psychology, 75,* 401–410. http://dx.doi.org/10.1111/j.2044-8295.1984.tb01910.x

Bachoo, S., Bhagwanjee, A., & Govender, K. (2013). The influence of anger, impulsivity, sensation seeking, and driver attitudes on risky driving behavior among postgraduate university students in Durban, South Africa. *Accident Analysis & Prevention, 55,* 67–76. http://dx.doi.org/10.1016/j.aap.2013.02.021

Baker, J. R., & Yardley, J. K. (2002). Moderating effect of gender on the relationship between sensation seeking-impulsivity and substance use in adolescents. *Journal of Child & Adolescent Substance Abuse, 12,* 27–43. http://dx.doi.org/10.1300/J029v12n01_02

Barrault, S., & Varescon, I. (2013). Impulsive sensation seeking and gambling practice among a sample of online poker players: Comparison between nonpathological, problem, and pathological gamblers. *Personality and Individual Differences, 55*, 502–507. http://dx.doi.org/10.1016/j.paid.2013.04.022

Bjork, J. M., Knutson, B., & Hommer, D. W. (2008). Incentive-elicited striatal activation in adolescent children of alcoholics. *Addiction, 103*, 1308–1319. http://dx.doi.org/10.1111/j.1360-0443.2008.02250.x

Blanchard, M. M., Mendelsohn, D., & Stamp, J. A. (2009). The HR/LR model: Further evidence as an animal model of sensation seeking. *Neuroscience and Biobehavioral Reviews, 33*, 1145–1154. http://dx.doi.org/10.1016/j.neubiorev.2009.05.009

Bouchard, T. J. (2004). Genetic influence on human psychological traits: A survey. *Current Directions in Psychological Science, 13*, 148–151. http://dx.doi.org/10.1111/j.0963-7214.2004.00295.x

Bray, R. M., Pemberton, M. R., Hourani, L. L., Witt, M., Olmsted, K. L. R., Brown, J. M., . . . RTI International. (2009). *2008 Department of Defense survey of health related behaviors among active duty military personnel: A component of the Defense Lifestyle Assessment Program (DLAP)* (Contract No. GS-10F-0097L). Retrieved from http://www.dtic.mil/cgi-bin/GetTRDoc?AD=ADA527178

Breivik, G. (1996). Personality, sensation seeking, and risk-taking among Everest climbers. *International Journal of Sport Psychology, 27*, 308–320.

Breuer, J., & Freud, S. (1955). *Studies on hysteria* (J. Strachey, Trans.). New York, NY: Basic Books. (Original work published 1895)

Carretero-Dios, H., & Ruch, W. (2010). Humor appreciation and sensation seeking: Invariance of findings across culture and assessment instrument. *Humor: International Journal of Humor Research, 23*, 427–445. http://dx.doi.org/10.1515/humr.2010.020

Charnigo, R., Noar, S. M., Garnett, C., Crosby, R., Palmgreen, P., & Zimmerman, R. S. (2013). Sensation seeking and impulsivity: Combined associations with risky sexual behavior in a large sample of young adults. *Journal of Sex Research, 50*, 480–488. http://dx.doi.org/10.1080/00224499.2011.652264

Chen, C., Burton, M., Greenberger, E., & Dmitrieva, J. (1999). Population migration and the variation of dopamine D4 receptor (DRD4) allele frequencies around the globe. *Evolution and Human Behavior, 20*, 309–324. http://dx.doi.org/10.1016/S1090-5138(99)00015-X

Cloninger, C. R., Przybeck, T. R., & Svrakic, D. M. (1991). The Tridimensional Personality Questionnaire: U.S. normative data. *Psychological Reports, 69*, 1047–1057. http://dx.doi.org/10.2466/pr0.1991.69.3.1047

Cloninger, C. R., Svrakic, D. M., & Przybeck, T. R. (1993). A psychobiological model of temperament and character. *Archives of General Psychiatry, 50*, 975–990. http://dx.doi.org/10.1001/archpsyc.1993.01820240059008

Comings, D. E., Saucier, G., & MacMurray, J. P. (2002). Role of DRD2 and other dopamine genes in personality traits. In J. Benjamin, R. P. Ebstein, & R. H. Belmaker (Eds.), *Molecular genetics and the human personality* (pp. 165–192). Washington, DC: American Psychiatric Publishing.

Costa, P. T., & McCrae, R. R. (1992). *Revised NEO Personality Inventory (NEO PI–R) and the NEO Five-Factor Inventory (NEO–FFI) professional manual.* Odessa, FL: PAR.

Cross, C. P., Cyrenne, D. L. M., & Brown, G. R. (2013). Sex differences in sensation-seeking: A meta-analysis. *Scientific Reports, 3,* 2486. http://dx.doi.org/10.1038/srep02486

Davis, K. L., & Panksepp, J. (2011). The brain's emotional foundations of human personality and the Affective Neuroscience Personality Scales. *Neuroscience and Biobehavioral Reviews, 35,* 1946–1958. http://dx.doi.org/10.1016/j.neubiorev.2011.04.004

Decuyper, M., DePauw, S., DeFruyt, F., DeBolle, M., & DeClercq, B. (2009). A meta-analysis of psychopathy, antisocial PD, and FFM associations. *European Journal of Personality, 23,* 531–565. http://dx.doi.org/10.1002/per.729

Derringer, J., Krueger, R. F., Dick, D. M., Saccone, S., Grucza, R. A., Agrawal, A., . . . the Gene Environment Association Studies (GENEVA) Consortium. (2010). Predicting sensation seeking from dopamine genes. A candidate-system approach. *Psychological Science, 21,* 1282–1290.

Dollinger, S. J. (1993). Personality and music preference: Extraversion and excitement seeking or openness to experience. *Psychology of Music, 21,* 73–77. http://dx.doi.org/10.1177/030573569302100105

Donohew, R. L., Hoyle, R. H., Clayton, R. R., Skinner, W. F., Colon, S. E., & Rice, R. E. (1999). Sensation seeking and drug use by adolescents and their friends: Models for marijuana and alcohol. *Journal of Studies on Alcohol, 60,* 622–631. http://dx.doi.org/10.15288/jsa.1999.60.622

Donohew, R. L., Zimmerman, R., Cupp, P. S., Novak, S., Colon, S., & Abell, R. (2000). Sensation seeking, impulsive decision-making, and risky sex: Implications for risk-taking and design of interventions. *Personality and Individual Differences, 28,* 1079–1091. http://dx.doi.org/10.1016/S0191-8869(99)00158-0

Ekselius, L., Bengtsson, F., & von Knorring, L. (2000). Noncompliance with pharmacotherapy of depression is associated with a sensation seeking personality. *International Clinical Psychopharmacology, 15,* 273–278. http://dx.doi.org/10.1097/00004850-200015050-00004

Eysenck, H. J. (1967). *The biological basis of personality.* Springfield, IL: Charles C. Thomas.

Eysenck, S. B., & Eysenck, H. J. (1985). *Personality and individual differences: A natural science approach.* New York, NY: Plenum. http://dx.doi.org/10.1007/978-1-4613-2413-3

Furnham, A., & Avison, M. (1997). Personality and preference for surreal paintings. *Personality and Individual Differences, 23,* 923–935. http://dx.doi.org/10.1016/S0191-8869(97)00131-1

Gjedde, A., Kumakura, Y., Cumming, P., Linnet, J., & Møller, A. (2010). Inverted-U-shaped correlation between dopamine receptor availability in striatum and sensation seeking. *Proceedings of the National Academy of Sciences of the United States of America, 107,* 3870–3875. http://dx.doi.org/10.1073/pnas.0912319107

Gomà-i-Freixanet, M. (1995). Prosocial and antisocial aspects of personality. *Personality and Individual Differences, 19,* 125–134. http://dx.doi.org/10.1016/0191-8869(95)00037-7

Gomà-i-Freixanet, M. (2001). *Prosocial and antisocial risk-taking.* Paper presented at the Tenth Biennial Meeting of the International Society for the Study of Individual Differences, Department of Psychology, University of Edinburgh, Scotland.

Gomà-i-Freixanet, M. M. (2004). Sensation seeking and participation in physical risk sports. In R. M. Stelmack (Ed.), *On the psychobiology of personality: Essays in honor of Marvin Zuckerman* (pp. 185–201). New York, NY: Elsevier Science. http://dx.doi.org/10.1016/B978-008044209-9/50012-9

Harden, K. P., Quinn, P. D., & Tucker-Drob, E. M. (2012). Genetically influenced change in sensation seeking drives the rise of delinquent behavior during adolescence. *Developmental Science, 15,* 150–163. http://dx.doi.org/10.1111/j.1467-7687.2011.01115.x

Hittner, J. B., & Swickert, R. (2006). Sensation seeking and alcohol use: A meta-analytic review. *Addictive Behaviors, 31,* 1383–1401. http://dx.doi.org/10.1016/j.addbeh.2005.11.004

Hoyle, R. H., Fejfar, M. C., & Miller, J. D. (2000). Personality and sexual risk taking: A quantitative review. *Journal of Personality, 68,* 1203–1231. http://dx.doi.org/10.1111/1467-6494.00132

Jonah, B. A. (1997). Sensation seeking and risky driving: A review and synthesis of the literature. *Accident Analysis & Prevention, 29,* 651–665. http://dx.doi.org/10.1016/S0001-4575(97)00017-1

Jones, S. E., Miller, J. D., & Lynam, D. R. (2011). Personality, antisocial behavior, and aggression: A meta-analytic review. *Journal of Criminal Justice, 39,* 329–337. http://dx.doi.org/10.1016/j.jcrimjus.2011.03.004

Kam, C. D. (2012). Risk attitudes and political participation. *American Journal of Political Science, 54,* 817–836.

Koopmans, J. R., Boomsma, D. I., Heath, A. C., & van Doornen, L. J. (1995). A multivariate genetic analysis of sensation seeking. *Behavior Genetics, 25,* 349–356. http://dx.doi.org/10.1007/BF02197284

Liraud, F., & Verdoux, H. (2000). Which temperamental characteristics are associated with substance use in subjects with psychotic and mood disorders? *Psychiatry Research, 93,* 63–72.

Livesley, W. J., Jackson, D. N., & Schroeder, M. L. (1989). A study of the factorial structure of personality pathology. *Journal of Personality Disorders, 3,* 292–306. http://dx.doi.org/10.1521/pedi.1989.3.4.292

Lynam, D. R., & Widiger, T. A. (2001). Using the five-factor model to represent the *DSM–IV* personality disorders: An expert consensus approach.

Journal of Abnormal Psychology, 110, 401–412. http://dx.doi.org/10.1037/0021-843X.110.3.401

Lynne-Landsman, S. D., Graber, J. A., Nichols, T. R., & Botvin, G. J. (2011). Is sensation seeking a stable trait or does it change over time? *Journal of Youth and Adolescence, 40,* 48–58. http://dx.doi.org/10.1007/s10964-010-9529-2

MacKillop, J., Miller, J. D., Fortune, E., Maples, J., Lance, C. E., Campbell, W. K., & Goodie, A. S. (2014). Multidimensional examination of impulsivity in relation to disordered gambling. *Experimental and Clinical Psychopharmacology, 22,* 176–185. http://dx.doi.org/10.1037/a0035874

Markon, K. E., Krueger, R. F., & Watson, D. (2005). Delineating the structure of normal and abnormal personality: An integrative hierarchical approach. *Journal of Personality and Social Psychology, 88,* 139–157.

Michalczuk, R., Bowden-Jones, H., Verdejo-Garcia, A., & Clark, L. (2011). Impulsivity and cognitive distortions in pathological gamblers attending the UK National Problem Gambling Clinic: A preliminary report. *Psychological Medicine, 41,* 2625–2635. http://dx.doi.org/10.1017/S003329171100095X

Miller, J. D., & Lynam, D. R. (2001). Structural models of personality and their relation to antisocial behavior: A meta-analysis. *Criminology, 39,* 765–798. http://dx.doi.org/10.1111/j.1745-9125.2001.tb00940.x

Miller, J. D., Lynam, D. R., Widiger, T. A., & Leukefeld, C. (2001). Personality disorders as extreme variants of common personality dimensions: Can the five-factor model adequately represent psychopathy? *Journal of Personality, 69,* 253–276. http://dx.doi.org/10.1111/1467-6494.00144

Neria, Y., Solomon, X., Ginzburg, K., & Dekel, R. (2000). Sensation seeking, wartime performance, and long-term adjustment among Israeli war veterans. *Personality and Individual Differences, 29,* 921–932. http://dx.doi.org/10.1016/S0191-8869(99)00243-3

Okamoto, K., & Takaki, E. (1992). Structure of creativity measurements and their correlations with sensation seeking and need for uniqueness. *Japanese Journal of Experimental Social Psychology, 31,* 203–210. http://dx.doi.org/10.2130/jjesp.31.203

Olsen, C. M., & Winder, D. G. (2009). Operant sensation seeking engages similar neural substrates to operant drug seeking in C57 mice. *Neuropsychopharmacology, 34,* 1685–1694. http://dx.doi.org/10.1038/npp.2008.226

Ortiz, J., & Raine, A. (2004). Heart rate level and antisocial behavior in children and adolescents: A meta-analysis. *Journal of the American Academy of Child & Adolescent Psychiatry, 43,* 154–162. http://dx.doi.org/10.1097/00004583-200402000-00010

Patkar, A. A., Murray, H. W., Mannelli, P., Gottheil, E., Weinstein, S. P., & Vergare, M. J. (2004). Pretreatment measures of impulsivity, aggression, and sensation seeking are associated with treatment outcome for African American cocaine-dependent patients. *Journal of Addictive Diseases, 23,* 109–122. http://dx.doi.org/10.1300/J069v23n02_08

Pedersen, S. L., Molina, B. S., Belendiuk, K. A., & Donovan, J. E. (2012). Racial differences in the development of impulsivity and sensation seeking from childhood into adolescence and their relation to alcohol use. *Alcoholism: Clinical and Experimental Research, 36,* 1794–1802. http://dx.doi.org/10.1111/j.1530-0277.2012.01797.x

Pedersen, W. (1991). Mental health, sensation seeking, and drug use patterns: A longitudinal study. *British Journal of Addiction, 86,* 195–204. http://dx.doi.org/10.1111/j.1360-0443.1991.tb01769.x

Raine, A., Venables, P. H., & Mednick, S. A. (1997). Low resting heart rate at age 3 years predisposes to aggression at age 11 years: Evidence from the Mauritius Child Health Project. *Journal of American Child & Adolescent Psychiatry, 36,* 1457–1464. http://dx.doi.org/10.1097/00004583-199710000-00029

Rawlings, D., & Leow, S. (2008). Investigating the role of psychoticism and sensation seeking in predicting emotional reactions to music. *Psychology of Music, 36,* 269–287. http://dx.doi.org/10.1177/0305735607086042

Roberti, J. (2004). A review of the behavioral and biological correlates of sensation seeking. *Journal of Research in Personality, 38,* 256–279. http://dx.doi.org/10.1016/S0092-6566(03)00067-9

Samuel, D. B., & Widiger, T. A. (2008). A meta-analytic review of the relationships between the five-factor model and *DSM–IV–TR* personality disorders: A facet level analysis. *Clinical Psychology Review, 28,* 1326–1342. http://dx.doi.org/10.1016/j.cpr.2008.07.002

Stautz, K., & Cooper, A. (2013). Impulsivity-related personality traits and adolescent alcohol use: A meta-analytic review. *Clinical Psychology Review, 33,* 574–592. http://dx.doi.org/10.1016/j.cpr.2013.03.003

Steinberg, L., Albert, D., Cauffman, E., Banich, M., Graham, S., & Woolard, J. (2008). Age differences in sensation seeking and impulsivity as indexed by behavior and self-report: Evidence for a dual systems model. *Developmental Psychology, 44,* 1764–1778. http://dx.doi.org/10.1037/a0012955

Stephenson, M. T., Hoyle, R. H., Palmgreen, P., & Slater, M. D. (2003). Brief measures of sensation seeking for screening and large-scale surveys. *Drug and Alcohol Dependence, 72,* 279–286. http://dx.doi.org/10.1016/j.drugalcdep.2003.08.003

Stoel, R. D., De Geus, E. J., & Boomsma, D. I. (2006). Genetic analysis of sensation seeking with an extended twin design. *Behavior Genetics, 36,* 229–237. http://dx.doi.org/10.1007/s10519-005-9028-5

Vallone, D., Allen, J. A., Clayton, R. R., & Xiao, H. (2007). How reliable and valid is the Brief Sensation Seeking Scale (BSSS–4) for youth of various racial/ethnic groups? *Addiction, 102*(Suppl. 2), 71–78. http://dx.doi.org/10.1111/j.1360-0443.2007.01957.x

Whiteside, S. P., & Lynam, D. R. (2001). The five factor model and impulsivity: Using a structural model of personality to understand impulsivity. *Personality and Individual Differences, 30,* 669–689. http://dx.doi.org/10.1016/S0191-8869(00)00064-7

Wilson, L. C., & Scarpa, A. (2011). The link between sensation seeking and aggression: A meta-analytic review. *Aggressive Behavior, 37*, 81–90. http://dx.doi.org/10.1002/ab.20369

World Health Organization. (1992). *International statistical classification of diseases and related health problems* (10th rev.). Geneva, Switzerland: Author.

Wymer, W., Self, D., & Findley, C. (2008). Sensation seekers and civic participation: Exploring the influence of sensation seeking and gender on intention to lead and volunteer. *International Journal of Nonprofit and Voluntary Sector Marketing, 13*, 287–300. http://dx.doi.org/10.1002/nvsm.330

Zuckerman, M. (1979). *Sensation seeking: Beyond the optimal level of arousal*. Hillsdale, NJ: Erlbaum.

Zuckerman, M. (1994). *Behavioral expressions and biosocial bases of sensation seeking*. New York, NY: Cambridge University Press.

Zuckerman, M. (2007). *Sensation seeking and risky behavior*. Washington, DC: American Psychological Association. http://dx.doi.org/10.1037/11555-005

Zuckerman, M. (2008). Personality and sensation seeking. In G. J. Boyle, G. Matthews, & D. H. Saklofske (Eds.), *The Sage handbook of personality theory and assessment* (pp. 379–398). Los Angeles, CA: Sage. http://dx.doi.org/10.4135/9781849200462.n18

Zuckerman, M., Eysenck, S., & Eysenck, H. J. (1978). Sensation seeking in England and America: Cross-cultural, age, and sex comparisons. *Journal of Consulting and Clinical Psychology, 46*, 139–149. http://dx.doi.org/10.1037/0022-006X.46.1.139

Zuckerman, M., Kolin, E. A., Price, L., & Zoob, I. (1964). Development of a sensation-seeking scale. *Journal of Consulting Psychology, 28*, 477–482. http://dx.doi.org/10.1037/h0040995

8

URGENCY: A COMMON TRANSDIAGNOSTIC ENDOPHENOTYPE FOR MALADAPTIVE RISK TAKING

MELISSA A. CYDERS, AYCA COSKUNPINAR,
AND J. DAVIS VANDERVEEN

DEFINITION AND BACKGROUND

Urgency is a personality trait reflecting the tendency to engage in maladaptive behavior in response to extreme negative (*negative urgency*) or positive (*positive urgency*) affect (Cyders & Smith, 2007; Cyders et al., 2007; Whiteside & Lynam, 2001). Research with urgency grew from the perspective that impulsivity, thought to be one of the most important risk factors for a wide range of risk-taking behaviors (e.g., Evenden, 1999a), is actually composed of multiple separate, although related, tendencies toward rash action, including seeking out new and exciting experiences and sensations (see Chapter 7, this volume), being easily distracted (see Chapter 9, this volume), and having a lack of forethought (e.g., Evenden, 1999b; Reed & Derryberry, 1995). There have been several attempts to conceptualize impulsivity as a personality trait by integrating information from the medical, psychological, behavioral, and social models (Barratt, 1993). One such attempt led to

http://dx.doi.org/10.1037/14854-009

The Dark Side of Personality: Science and Practice in Social, Personality, and Clinical Psychology, V. Zeigler-Hill and D. K. Marcus (Editors)

the development of the UPPS model of impulsivity (Whiteside & Lynam, 2001; U = Urgency; P = lack of Perseverance; P = lack of Premeditation; S = Sensation Seeking), which has gained momentum in clinical and research settings, with almost 700 citations between 2001 and the beginning of 2014.

The UPPS model of impulsivity was developed via a factor analysis of existing personality-based questionnaires of impulsivity and suggested that, across existing measures, four main impulsivity-related traits exist: (a) *sensation seeking*, defined as the tendency to seek out new and exciting experiences and sensations; (b) *lack of perseverance*, defined as the inability to persist in and complete tasks; (c) *lack of planning*, defined as the likelihood not to think carefully before action; and (d) *negative urgency*. Cyders and colleagues (2007) later highlighted the role of a positive mood variant of urgency, *positive urgency*. These five traits have been combined into the UPPS–P Impulsive Behavior Scale (Lynam, Miller, Miller, Bornovalova, & Lejuez, 2011), and work measuring and assessing these traits has overwhelmingly supported the importance of conceptualizing impulsivity as separate dispositions toward rash action (e.g., Smith et al., 2007). In fact, recent work has suggested that the term *impulsivity* is not meaningful (e.g., Cyders & Coskunpinar, 2011; Smith et al., 2007) and that research should instead focus on three main factors: *deficits in conscientiousness* (of which lack of perseverance and lack of planning are subfacets), *emotion-based dispositions to rash action* (of which negative and positive urgency are subfacets), and *sensation seeking* (Cyders & Smith, 2007; see also Chapter 7, this volume). Furthermore, urgency appears to be the most clinically relevant of the impulsivity-related traits because it is most highly related to problematic levels of a wide range of risk-taking behaviors, including problematic alcohol use, risky sexual behavior, illegal drug use, tobacco use, and gambling (e.g., Anestis, Selby, & Joiner, 2007; Coskunpinar, Dir, & Cyders, 2013; Cyders & Smith, 2008b; Cyders et al., 2007; Fischer, Anderson, & Smith, 2004; Fischer, Smith, & Anderson, 2003; Fischer, Smith, Annus, & Hendricks, 2007; J. Miller, Flory, Lynam, & Leukefeld, 2003; Stautz & Cooper, 2014; Zapolski, Cyders, Rainer, & Smith, 2007). However, there are important distinctions between the clinical correlates of positive urgency and negative urgency, for example, with binge eating behaviors (e.g., Fischer & Smith, 2008; Fischer et al., 2007). See Table 8.1 for a comprehensive review of the behavioral correlates of urgency.

REVIEW OF THE RELEVANT LITERATURE

Research examining urgency has been conducted across multiple levels of analysis, including genetic predisposition, developmental trajectories, effects on learning, neurocognitive underpinnings, and physiological reactivity; this vast literature is briefly reviewed here.

TABLE 8.1
Studies Examining External Correlates of Urgency

Study	Sample characteristics	Design	Main study finding
	Studies examining negative urgency		
Adams, Kaiser, Lynam, Charnigo, & Milich (2012)	*N* = 432 college students	SR	(+) with problematic drinking
Alemis & Yap (2013)	*N* = 162 community sample	SR	(+) with compulsive buying
Amlung et al. (2013)	*N* = 273 college students	SR and LT	(+) with frequency of caffeinated alcoholic beverages and greater demand for alcohol
Anestis, Selby, & Joiner (2007)	*N* = 70 college students	SR	(+) with drinking to cope and bulimic symptoms
Bayard, Raffard, & Gely-Nargeot (2011)	*N* = 107 healthy volunteers	SR	(+) with disadvantageous decision on the Game of Dice Task
Billieux, Gay, Rochat, & Van der Linden (2010)	*N* = 95	SR	(+) with compulsive buying, problematic use of cell phones, and problematic use of Internet
Billieux, Rochat, Rebetez, & Van der Linden (2008)	*N* = 150 community volunteers	SR	(+) with compulsive buying
Billieux, Van der Linden, & Ceschi (2007)	*N* = 40 college students	SR	(+) with tobacco cravings
Billieux, Van der Linden, D'Acremont, Ceschi, & Zermatten (2007)	*N* = 108 female college students	SR	(+) with use of mobile phones
Billieux, Van der Linden, & Rochat (2008)	*N* = 339 volunteers	SR	(+) with problematic use of mobile phones
Bresin, Carter, & Gordon (2013)	*N* = 1,612 college students	Longitudinal	(+) with only for those high in NUR
Carlson, Pritchard, & Dominelli (2013)	*N* = 282 college students (50% male)	SR	(+) with aggression
Claes & Muehlen-kamp (2013)	*N* = 613 high school students	SR	(+) with NSSI behaviors
Coskunpinar, Dir, & Cyders (2013)	*N* = 96	Meta-analysis	(+) with drinking problems and alcohol dependence

(*continues*)

TABLE 8.1
Studies Examining External Correlates of Urgency *(Continued)*

Study	Sample characteristics	Design	Main study finding
Cyders & Smith (2010)	$N = 292$ college freshman	Longitudinal	(+) with negative mood-based rash action
Davis & Fischer (2013)	$N = 460$ female college freshman	SR	(+) with global eating pathology and binge eating
Davis-Becker, Peterson, & Fischer (2014)	$N = 884$	SR	(+) with binge eating
Derefinko, DeWall, Metze, Walsh, & Lynam (2011)	$N = 70$ male college students	SR & LT	(+) with intimate partner violence
Dir, Karyadi, & Cyders (2013)	$N = 734$ college students	SR	(+) with self-harming frequency, variety of self-harm methods, number of years of self-harming, problematic alcohol use, and eating problems
Fink, Anestis, Selby, & Joiner (2010)	$N = 217$ college students	SR	(+) with dysregulated behaviors
Fischer, Anderson, & Smith (2004)	$N = 217$ female college students	SR	(+) with problems from alcohol use and binge eating and purging
Fischer, Peterson, & McCarthy (2013)	$N = 355$ female college freshmen	Longitudinal	(+) with later binge eating and purging
Fischer, Settles, Collins, Gunn, & Smith (2012)	$N = 905$ fifth-grade girls	SR	(+) with binge eating, alcohol use, or both
Glenn & Klonsky (2010)	$N = 168$ college students	SR	(+) with nonsuicidal self-injury
Jones, Chryssanthakis, & Groom (2014)	$N = 400$ college students	SR	(+) with tendency to engage in risky behaviors with negative consequences
Kaiser, Milich, Lynam, & Charnigo (2012)	$N = 525$ college freshman	SR	(+) with average weekly alcohol, marijuana, and tobacco use
Karyadi & King (2011)	$N = 442$ college students	SR	(+) with alcohol-related problems
LaBrie, Kenney, Napper, & Miller (2014)	$N = 470$ college students	SR	(+) with greater experience of negative consequences related to alcohol

TABLE 8.1

Study	Sample characteristics	Design	Main study finding
Lucas & Koff (2014)	*N* = 232 female college students	SR	(+) with affective aspect of impulse buying
Lynam, Miller, Miller, Bornovalova, & Lejuez (2011)	*N* = 76 drug abusers	SR	(+) with suicidal behavior and NSSI
Martens, Pedersen, Smith, Stewart, & O'Brien (2011)	*N* = 198 college students	SR	(+) with alcohol-related problems
J. D. Miller, Zeichner, & Wilson (2012)	*N* = 116 college students	SR	(+) with aggression
Mouilso, Calhoun, & Rosenbloom (2013)	*N* = 304 male college students	SR	NUR was higher in perpetrators compared with nonperpetrators
Mullins-Sweatt, Lengel, & Grant (2013)	*N* = 211 college students	SR	Individuals who had a history of non-suicidal self-injury scored higher on NUR
Peterson, Davis-Becker, & Fischer (2014)	*N* = 884 college students	SR	(+) with nonsuicidal self-injury
Peterson & Fischer (2012)	*N* = 489 young adult females	SR	(+) with NSSI and bulimia nervosa
Racine et al. (2013)	*N* = 222 female twin pairs	SR	(+) with dysregulated eating
Robinson, Ladd, & Anderson (2014)	*N* = 1051 high-school students	SR	(+) with greater like-lihood of lifetime and current alcohol use
Settles et al. (2012)	*n* = 1,813 fifth-grade students *n* = 418 college freshman	SR	(+) with drinking problems in preadolescents; aggression, risky sex, illegal drug use, drinking prob-lems, and conduct-disordered behav-ior in college students
Stautz & Cooper (2014)	*N* = 270 adoles-cents	SR	(+) with problematic alcohol and can-nabis use
Timpano et al. (2013)	*N* = 532 American and German young adults	SR	(+) with hoarding
Xiao et al. (2009)	*N* = 181 Chinese adolescents	Longitudinal	(+) with binge drinking

(continues)

TABLE 8.1
Studies Examining External Correlates of Urgency *(Continued)*

Study	Sample characteristics	Design	Main study finding
	Studies examining positive urgency		
Amlung, Few, Howland, Rohsenow, & Metrik (2013)	$N = 273$ college students	SR & LT	(+) with frequency of caffeinated alcoholic beverages and greater demand for alcohol
Claes & Muehlenkamp (2013)	$N = 613$ high school students	SR	(+) with NSSI behaviors
Coskunpinar, Dir, & Cyders (2013)	$N = 96$	Meta-analysis	(+) with drinking problems
Cyders, Flory, Rainer, & Smith (2009)	$N = 293$ college freshman (25% male)	Longitudinal	(+) with quantity of alcohol at any given time and experience of negative outcomes from drinking
Cyders & Smith (2008a)	$N = 418$ college students	Longitudinal	(+) with gambling and risky behavior, and predicted longitudinal increases in gambling behavior
Cyders & Smith (2010)	$N = 292$ college freshman	Longitudinal	(+) with positive mood-based rash action
Cyders et al. (2007)	$N = 326$ college students	SR	(+) with risk-taking behaviors
Cyders et al. (2010)	$N = 94$ college students	SR	(+) with beer consumption
Karyadi & King (2011)	$N = 442$ college students	SR	(+) with alcohol-related problems
LaBrie, Kenney, Napper, & Miller (2014)	$N = 470$ college students	SR	(+) with negative consequences related to alcohol
J. D. Miller, Zeichner, & Wilson (2012)	$N = 116$ college students	SR	(+) with aggression
Robinson, Ladd, & Anderson (2014)	$N = 1,051$ high-school students	SR	(+) with lifetime and current alcohol use and lifetime marijuana use
Stautz & Cooper (2014)	$N = 270$ adolescents	SR	(+) with problematic alcohol and cannabis use
Zapolski, Cyders, & Smith (2009)	$N = 407$ college freshman	Longitudinal	(+) with illegal drug use and risky sexual behavior

Note. SR = self-report; LT = lab task; NUR = negative urgency; NSSI = nonsuicidal self-injury.

Genetic Predisposition

Cyders and Smith (2008b) originally proposed that variability in serotonin and dopamine levels related to gene polymorphisms in the serotonin transporter gene (*5HTTLPR*) and dopamine receptor genes *DRD2*, *DRD3*, and *DRD4* underlie urgency. Although research has yet to examine the genetics of negative urgency, work using the impulsiveness scale from the NEO Personality Inventory—Revised (NEO–PI–R; Costa & McCrae, 2008), which overlaps highly with negative urgency (Whiteside & Lynam, 2001), has suggested that negative urgency is genetically influenced. First, Carver, Johnson, Joormann, Kim, and Nam (2011) found that *5HTTLPR* interacted with the experience of childhood adversity to predict the later development of NEO–PI–R impulsiveness. Second, there is a relationship between NEO–PI–R impulsiveness and the *g* allele of the inhibitory gamma-amino butyric acid (GABA) α2 receptor subunit (*GABRA2*) gene, which encodes the GABAAα2 receptor units and has been consistently related to alcoholism risk (e.g., Edenberg et al., 2004), likely through effects on insula activation in the anticipation of reward (Villafuerte et al., 2012), or through the reduction of GABA in the dorsolateral prefrontal cortex (Boy et al., 2011). More important, the relationship between *GABRA2* and lifetime alcohol problems is mediated by NEO–PI–R impulsiveness, suggesting that genetics play a role in the development of alcohol use problems in part by affecting urgent action (Villafuerte, Strumba, Stoltenberg, Zucker, & Burmeister, 2013).

Developmental Trajectories and Effects on Learning

Urgency has been implicated in the later development of maladaptive behaviors through its direct effect on the behaviors and through its indirect effect on biased learning about the outcomes associated with such behaviors (known as the acquired preparedness model; e.g., Smith & Anderson, 2001). Negative and positive urgency increase prospective risk for increased alcohol consumption in adolescents and young adults, in part through the increased likelihood of learning the positive, reinforcing aspects of alcohol use (e.g., Cyders, Flory, Rainer, & Smith, 2009; Gunn & Smith, 2010; Settles, Cyders, & Smith, 2010). Specifically, negative urgency appears to lead one to learn that drinking helps one cope with negative affect, which subsequently leads to increased drinking behaviors. In contrast, positive urgency leads one to learn that alcohol will enhance a positive mood (Settles et al., 2010). This pattern has also been found for smoking (Spillane, Smith, & Kahler, 2010) and disordered eating in preadolescents (negative urgency only; e.g., Combs, Pearson, & Smith, 2011). Thus, urgency appears to impart risk for development of maladaptive behaviors in part by making one more likely to learn and recall positive outcome expectancies related to such behaviors.

Neurocognitive Underpinnings

It has recently been hypothesized that neurocognition patterns might relate to urgency. Some work has found a relationship between urgency and behavioral tasks related to impulsive behavior (e.g., Billieux, Gay, Rochat, & Van der Linden, 2010), but in general, urgency shows little overlap with these behavioral tasks, likely reflecting underlying construct-based differences (see Cyders & Coskunpinar, 2011). However, positive urgency has been linked to performance on the Balloon Analogue Risk Task (Lejuez et al., 2002), a task designed as a laboratory-based behavioral task of risk taking (Cyders et al., 2010), and negative urgency has been linked to biased attention toward alcohol cues (Coskunpinar, Dir, Karyadi, et al., 2013). These findings suggest that urgency might lead one to be more attentive to reward cues in the environment through biased learning and dopaminergic activity. This hypothesis still needs more empirical support because a recent review found no support for the relationship between urgency and substance-related attentional biases in a limited number of studies (Coskunpinar & Cyders, 2013).

Physiological Reactivity

Cyders and Smith (2008b) suggested that urgency is related to brain systems involved in emotion and action, including the amygdala, as well as the ventromedial and medial portion of the prefrontal cortex. Some work has begun to investigate these possibilities and has suggested a link between negative urgency and the brain's reward and limbic systems. Negative urgency is associated with reduced activation in the anterior and medial orbitofrontal cortex and anterior cingulate in response to positively and negatively valenced stimuli (Joseph, Liu, Jiang, Lynam, & Kelly, 2009), increased activation in the left amygdala and right orbitofrontal cortex in response to negatively valenced images (Cyders et al., 2014a), and increased activation in the amygdala during negative emotion maintenance and reappraisal (Albein-Urios et al., 2013). These findings suggest that negative urgency is likely related to hyperactivity in limbic regions associated with emotional experiences, despite conflicting reports using self-reported mood, which fails to find a relationship between emotional experiences and urgency (e.g., Cyders & Coskunpinar, 2010; Cyders et al., 2010).

Additionally, negative urgency is related to increased ventromedial prefrontal cortex activation to alcoholic drink aromas in social drinkers (Cyders et al., 2014b) and to right insula activation during a decision making task (Xue, Lu, Levin, & Bechara, 2010), suggesting that negative urgency is associated with hyperactivity in the brain's reward motivational circuits. Additionally, two studies (Cyders et al., 2014a, 2014b) find that the relationship between these brain responses and risky behaviors (specifically, problematic alcohol use and general risk taking) is mediated by negative urgency, suggesting that physiological hyperreactivity to emotional stimuli and reward cues is related to later risk taking by increasing the tendency toward rash action in negative emotional states. These studies suggest activity in limbic and reward systems as underlying the trait of negative urgency.

Positive urgency has been, to date, largely unrelated to physiological reactivity to emotion or risk-taking cues (Cyders et al., 2014a, 2014b), although it might be due to failure of positive mood induction techniques (e.g., Cyders & Coskunpinar, 2011). Research needs to examine the relationship between such markers and positive urgency. Additionally, research on other potential markers of physiological response, including positron emission technology, hypothalamic–pituitary–adrenal (HPA) axis activation, heart rate, and galvanic skin response, and how these factors might underlie the risk for urgency and maladaptive risk taking should be conducted. Al'Absi et al. (1997) found that the relationship between mood induction and cortisol release (a common measure of HPA axis activation) was mediated by negative affectivity, thus suggesting that negative urgency, a facet of negative affectivity (Whiteside & Lynam, 2001), might also mediate this relationship. Additionally, negative urgency has been linked to lower rates of [11C]-raclopride binding potentials in problematic gamblers, suggesting differences in dopaminergic function related to negative urgency (Clark et al., 2012). Work examining the relationship between urgency and physiological reactivity to emotion and reward is in its infancy, and it will be exciting as this literature emerges.

ADAPTIVE AND MALADAPTIVE FEATURES

The role of emotion in motivating behavior is generally an adaptive process. The experience of emotion signals to the body and draws attention to emotion-arousing stimuli, preparing the body for action (Frijda, 1986; Lang, 1993; Saami, Mumme, & Campos, 1998). In fact, emotionally arousing stimuli activate the motor cortex, thus preparing the individual to respond to the stimuli that caused the initial emotional response (Bremner et al., 1999; Hajcak et al., 2007; Rauch et al., 1996). One can see how immediate action in response to emotions would be adaptive: It would predict the animal that can escape a feared predator, the pilot who can quickly respond to an emergency in the cockpit, and the financial advisor who is able to make quick, decisive investments after news of an exciting opportunity (see Dickman, 1990). The ability to integrate emotional information into decision making in an adaptive way is referred to as *affect-guided planning* and is related to healthy functioning of the orbitofrontal cortex and the left ventromedial prefrontal cortex (Davidson, 2003), allowing for the maintenance of focus on the salience of behavioral reinforcement options in the working memory (Rolls, Thorpe, & Madison, 1983) and the inhibition of amygdala activity (Davidson, 1998) related to the experience of the emotional response. Indeed, damage to the ventromedial prefrontal cortex results in affective lability and rash action (e.g., Bechara, 2004; Bechara, Damasio, Damasio, & Anderson, 1994; Bechara, Tranel, Damasio, & Damasio, 1996; Cardinal, Parkinson, Hall, & Everitt, 2002).

However, it is also well acknowledged that (a) extreme emotional experiences often result in suboptimal decision making (Bechara, 2004, 2005; Dolan, 2007; Dreisbach, 2006; Shiv, Loewenstein, & Bechara, 2005), especially at higher arousal levels (Forgas, 1992; Forgas & Bower, 1987; Gleicher & Weary, 1991), and (b) often actions in response to emotions do not address the specific stimulus or need that precipitated the emotion in the first place. Many behaviors occur more frequently after negative or positive emotions, including alcohol and drug use (Colder & Chassin, 1997; Cooper, 1994; Cooper, Agocha, & Sheldon, 2000; Del Boca, Darkes, Greenbaum, & Goldman, 2004; Martin & Sher, 1994; Peveler & Fairburn, 1990; Swendsen et al., 2000), gambling (Holub, Hodgins, & Peden, 2005), and bulimic behaviors (Agras & Telch, 1998; Smyth et al., 2007). Such behaviors can serve as short-term distractions from negative emotional states but do so by allowing the individual to avoid considering how to address the cause of the emotion, thus leaving the problem unsolved or disregarding other important goals and priorities in the moment. In addition, these behaviors often make the situation worse, through pharmacological effects of alcohol or drugs, placing oneself in ill-advised or dangerous situations (as is the case with sexual or self-harm behaviors) or financial damage (due to gambling or compulsive shopping). Additionally, the experience of positive emotions makes one more optimistic about positive outcomes of a situation (Nygren, Isen, Taylor, & Dulin, 1996), leading to deficient consideration of the risks involved in these behaviors.

Therefore, although the role of emotions in motivating behaviors is fundamentally adaptive, the choice of ill-advised actions in response to emotions often leads to negative outcomes for individuals. Urgency represents a disposition that increases an individual's likelihood of engaging in maladaptive behaviors in response to emotional states (Cyders & Smith, 2008b). With repetition, these behaviors are reinforced (Heatherton & Baumeister, 1991), and the development of more adaptive responses to emotions is limited.

DIRECTIONS FOR FUTURE RESEARCH

There are many areas for future research with urgency. Previous work has inconsistently supported the role of impulsive personality traits in clinical criteria, which is due in part to the use of traits that comprise multiple tendencies toward rash action that have different relationships with behaviors of risk, which masks important relationships and effects (Smith et al., 2007). Use of a single "impulsivity" score will water down or mask important distinctions among the clinical predictive utility of the separate traits (see Smith et al., 2007). Urgency has a unique and powerful role for a wide range of problematic behaviors, and use of this specific trait in research protocols will improve clinical prediction and utility (Smith et al., 2007). Furthermore, most of the research to date has examined the relationship of urgency with self-reported engagement in risk-taking behaviors. More recent investigations have begun to examine underlying genetic, physiological, and neurocognitive factors associated with this tendency and how these affect risk for maladaptive risk taking. This work is preliminary and should continue, with particular focus on novel genetic and pharmacological targets underlying urgent behaviors. Only by understanding the biological underpinnings of urgency can the identification of targets for treatment and prevention approaches proceed—not for just one disorder but for a wide range of risk-taking and clinical disorders. Such work additionally provides further confidence in urgency's role, unaffected by self-report biases. Finally, work to develop and examine the effectiveness of psychological treatments that aim to modify urgency is necessary to prevent or intervene in a wide range of clinical problems, as we discuss next.

CLINICAL IMPLICATIONS

Urgency is represented across multiple different categories and diagnoses in the *Diagnostic and Statistical Manual of Mental Disorders* (5th ed.; *DSM–5*; American Psychiatric Association, 2013) and the *ICD–10 Classification of Mental and Behavioural Disorders* (World Health Organization, 1992). As noted by Zapolski, Settles, Cyders, and Smith (2010), impulse control is likely

> the most common diagnostic criterion in the manual, appearing in borderline personality disorder, antisocial personality disorder, bulimia nervosa, attention deficit/hyperactivity disorder, mania, dementia, substance use disorders, and paraphilias, along with the whole section devoted to impulse-control disorders (e.g., intermittent explosive disorder, kleptomania, and pyromania). (p. 1)

In addition to its common appearance in diagnostic criteria, many clinical groups have been characterized for their level of urgency and the role urgency plays in their symptoms, including borderline personality disorder, attention-deficit/hyperactivity disorder, and binge eating disorder. Table 8.2 summarizes findings across clinical diagnoses.

TABLE 8.2

Role of Urgency in Clinical Diagnostic Criteria and in Disordered Groups

Disorder class	Disorder	DSM–5 criteria	Supporting studies	Sample	Finding
Neurodevelopmental disorders	Autism spectrum disorder	Criterion A1: Deficits in social-emotional reciprocity Criterion B1: Repetitive motor movements Criterion B3: Hyper-reactivity to sensory input	Bradley & Isaacs (2006)	$n = 31$ with teenagers with autism and $n = 31$ healthy control participants	Inattention, hyperactivity, and impulsiv-ity behaviors higher in subjects with autism vs. healthy control participants
	ADHD	Criterion A2: Hyper-activity and impulsivity Criterion B: Hyperactive-impulsive symptoms were present before age 12 years	Marmorstein (2013)	$N = 144$ middle school students	NUR related to more ADHD symptoms
		Criterion C: Hyperactive-impulsive symptoms are present in two or more settings	A. C. Miller et al. (2013)	$n = 60$ children with ADHD and $n = 21$ children without ADHD	NUR higher in children with ADHD vs. no ADHD
Bipolar and related disorders	Bipolar I, bipolar II, and cyclothymic disorders	Criteria include the presence of manic or hypomanic episodes involving the following: Criterion A: irritable mood Criterion B7: excessive involvement in activi-ties that have a high potential for painful consequences	No current findings related to urgency		

Category	Disorder	Criteria	N	Citation	Findings
Depressive disorders	Premenstrual dysphoric disorders	Criterion B1: marked affective lability; Criterion B2: marked irritability or increased interpersonal conflicts			No current findings related to urgency
Obsessive-compulsive and related disorders	Obsessive-compulsive, body dysmorphic, and hoarding disorders, trichotillomania	Characterized by recurrent repetitive behaviors and repeated attempts to decrease or stop the behaviors	$N = 238$ nonclinical individuals	Cougle, Timpano, & Goetz (2012)	NUR associated with greater obsession symptoms
	Excoriation disorder	Criterion A: recurrent skin picking resulting in skin lesions; Criterion B: repeated attempts to decrease or stop skin picking	$N = 55$ students with pathological skin picking and $N = 55$ healthy control participants	Snorrason, Smári, & Ólafsson (2011)	NUR and PUR higher in students with pathological skin picking vs. control participants
Trauma- and stressor-related disorders	Posttraumatic stress disorder	Criterion D: Negative alterations in cognitions and mood; Criterion E: Marked alterations in arousal and reactivity	$N = 60$ with substance use and PTSD and $N = 146$ with substance use only	Weiss, Tull, Viana, Anestis, & Gratz (2012)	Impulsivity and emotion dysregulation predicted PTSD; Emotion dysregulation moderated the impulsivity–PTSD relationship

(continues)

Disorder class	Disorder	DSM–5 criteria	Supporting studies	Sample	Finding
	Reactive attachment, disinhibited social engagement, acute stress, and adjustment disorders	Criteria include consistent patterns of emotional disturbances and disinhibited behaviors	No current findings related to urgency		
Feeding and eating disorders	Bulimia nervosa	Criterion A2: Sense of lack of control over eating	Anestis, Smith, Fink, & Joiner (2009)	N = 137 outpatients	NUR predicted bulimia nervosa symptoms
		Criterion B: Recurrent inappropriate compensatory behaviors	Claes, Vandereycken, & Vertommen (2005)	N = 146 eating-disordered inpatients	Urgency related to more binge eating, vomiting, and laxative abuse symptoms
	Binge eating disorder	Criterion A2: Sense of lack of control over eating	Fischer & Smith (2008)	N = 246 undergraduate students	Urgency related to binge eating episodes
			Fischer, Smith, Annus, & Hendricks (2007)	n = 32 women with eating disorder symptoms and n = 34 women without eating disorder symptoms	Urgency related to more binge eating symptoms

Disorder category	Disorder	Criterion	Study	Sample	Finding
Disruptive, impulse control, and conduct disorders	Oppositional defiant, intermittent explosive, conduct, pyromania, and kleptomania disorders	Classification of disorders characterized by problems in emotional and/or behavioral regulation	Grant & Kim (2003)	$n = 22$ gambling and impulse control and $n = 74$ gambling only	Greater intensity of urges and thoughts related to comorbid impulse control
Substance-related and addictive disorders	Alcohol use disorder	Criterion A2: unsuccessful efforts to cut down or control use of alcohol	Cyders et al. (2007)	$n = 45$ women with alcohol abuse/dependence and $n = 35$ health controls	PUR higher in alcoholics vs. control group
		Criterion A4: Strong desire or urge to use alcohol	Shin, Hong, & Jeon (2012)	$N = 190$ adolescents	Urgency related to alcohol use frequency, problems, binge drinking, and disorders
	Tobacco use disorder	Criterion A2: unsuccessful efforts to cut down or control use of the substance	Spillane, Smith, & Kahler (2010)	$N = 359$ undergraduate students	PUR related to nicotine dependence
		Criterion A4: strong desire or urge to use the substance	Settles et al. (2012)	$N = 1,810$ pre-adolescents	NUR related to smoking status
	Cannabis use disorder	Criterion A2: unsuccessful efforts to cut down or control use of cannabis Criterion A4: strong desire or urge to use cannabis	Stautz & Cooper (2014)	$N = 270$ sixth-form students	NUR and PUR predict cannabis use

(continues)

TABLE 8.2

Role of Urgency in Clinical Diagnostic Criteria and in Disordered Groups　(Continued)

Disorder class	Disorder	DSM–5 criteria	Supporting studies	Sample	Finding
	Stimulant use disorder	Criterion A2: unsuccessful efforts to cut down or control use of opioids Criterion A4: strong desire or urge to use opioids	Verdejo-García et al. (2013)	N = 72 cocaine users and 52 healthy controls	PUR predicted cocaine use
	Other substance use disorders	Criterion A2: unsuccessful efforts to cut down or control use of the substance Criterion A4: strong desire or urge to use the substance	Verdejo-Garcia, Bechara, Recknor & Pérez-García (2007)	N = 36 inpatients with alcohol, cocaine, heroin, marijuana, or methamphetamine substance dependence and n = 36 healthy control participants	Urgency related to severity of dependence symptoms Urgency higher in inpatient vs. control group
Neurocognitive disorders	Delirium, major and mild neurocognitive, and major or mild frontotemporal neurocognitive disorders	Criteria include decline in executive functioning, perceptual-motor functioning, behavioral disinhibition, and perseverative or compulsive behavior	No current findings related to urgency		
Personality disorders	General personality disorder	Criterion A2: lability of emotional responses Criterion A4: impulse control	No current findings related to urgency		

Cluster A	Schizoid and schizotypal personality disorder	Criteria include inappropriate or flat affect and odd or eccentric behavior	No current findings related to urgency		
Cluster B	Antisocial personality disorder	Criterion A3: impulsivity or failure to plan ahead Criterion A5: reckless disregard for safety of self or others Criterion A6: consistent irresponsibility	Whiteside, Lynam, Miller, & Reynolds (2005)	$n = 33$ outpatients with substance use and $n = 27$ nonpsychiatric clinic controls	Urgency higher in substance use and antisocial personality disorder vs. substance use only and control groups
	Borderline personality disorder	Criterion 4: impulsivity in at least two areas that are potentially self-damaging Criterion 6: affective instability	Anestis, Anestis, & Joiner (2009) Tragesser & Robinson (2009) Peters, Upton, & Baer (2013)	$N = 156$ undergraduates $N = 141$ undergraduate students $N = 227$ undergraduate students	NUR related to more antisocial behaviors NUR related to self-harm behaviors NUR predicts affective instability, identity problems, negative relationships, and self-harm

(continues)

TABLE 8.2
Role of Urgency in Clinical Diagnostic Criteria and in Disordered Groups *(Continued)*

Disorder class	Disorder	DSM–5 criteria	Supporting studies	Sample	Finding
	Histrionic personality disorder	Criteria includes a pervasive pattern of excessive emotionality and attention seeking Criterion 2: Interaction with others is often characterized by inappropriate sexually seductive or provocative behavior Criterion 3: Displays rapidly shifting and shallow expression of emotions	Albein-Urios et al. (2013)	N = 76 cocaine users and N = 34 non-drug-using controls	NUR predicts comorbid Cluster B personality vs cocaine only and control participants

	Narcissistic personality disorder	Criteria includes a pervasive pattern of grandiosity (in fantasy or behavior), need for admiration, and lack of empathy	No current findings related to urgency
Cluster C	Dependent personality disorder	Criterion 7: urgently seeks another relationship as a source of care and support when a close relationship ends	No current findings related to urgency
Paraphilic disorders	Voyeuristic, frotteuristic, sexual masochism, sexual sadism, pedophilic, fetishistic, and transvestic disorders	Characterized by intense and persistent sexual interest other than sexual interest in genital stimulation or preparatory fondling with phenotypically normal, physically mature, consenting human partners	No current findings related to urgency

Note. This table focuses solely on *DSM–5* diagnostic criteria because most of the research in this area has used this diagnostic system. However, many of these disorders and criteria also appear in similar forms in the *International Statistical Classification of Diseases and Related Health Problems*, and it is expected that urgency would similarly relate to clinical diagnoses using this classification system. ADHD = attention-deficit/hyperactivity disorder; *DSM–5* = *Diagnostic and Statistical Manual of Mental Disorders* (5th ed.); NUR = negative urgency; NSSI = nonsuicidal self-injury; PTSD = posttraumatic stress disorder.

Several psychotherapeutic treatments have focused on the modification of emotion-based impulsivity tendencies in the prevention and treatment of various clinical disorders. As reviewed by Zapolski and colleagues (2010), skills such as emotion regulation and distress tolerance training (e.g., Linehan, 1993) directly address impulsive behaviors that might occur in response to an emotional experience. Other treatments, such as mindfulness training (especially training to accept and experience emotions without action), selective serotonin reuptake inhibitors, evaluation of behavioral choices and short- and long-term goals, and the identification of cues or triggers and alternatives to such behaviors are skills that could be helpful to alleviate maladaptive emotion-based rash action (Zapolski et al., 2010). However, research has yet to address whether urgency levels are changed with such interventions and if such reductions in emotion-based rash action correspond with a reduction in clinical diagnoses.

Much work in the field of psychology and psychiatry has focused on identifying risk factors and empirically supported treatments for specific clinical disorders. Although this is an important effort, it often leads to "reinventing of the wheel" when treatments developed for one disorder are not generalized to other disorders that share common underlying factors. In fact, many are suggesting that the focus of treatment on arbitrarily defined and ever-changing clinical diagnostic criteria might be misguided and that instead we should focus treatment on "a clinical target, a well-defined risk state, illness, or symptom complex for which the treatment is meant" (Hyman & Fenton, 2003, p. 350). Our view is that urgency is a prime clinical target, and development of psychotherapy or pharmacological therapies to alleviate emotion-based rash action could be useful across many clinical diagnoses. Indeed, the fact that dialectical behavior therapy (Linehan, 1993) has been effectively applied to other disorders, such as binge eating (Telch, Agras, & Linehan, 2001) and alcohol use (Dimeff & Linehan, 2008) is not surprising, given the focus on avoiding maladaptive and impulsive emotion-based action.

SUMMARY AND CONCLUSIONS

The literature we have reviewed clearly implicates urgency as (a) the most clinically relevant of the impulsivity-related traits and (b) a common, transdiagnostic endophenotype for a wide range of maladaptive behaviors and clinical disorders. This review suggests that urgency is a prime marker of mental health risk, representing increased physiological reactivity to emotional cues and an increased likelihood of responding to emotions with maladaptive and risky behaviors. Urgency is a common risk factor across multiple risk domains, including alcohol and drug abuse, problematic gambling, and sexual risk taking, suggesting that urgency could be a prime point of intervention and identification that is nonspecific to risk type. Urgency is represented in several clinical diagnostic criteria and is related to multiple clinical disordered groups, allowing it to be an easily assessed endophenotypic marker for clinical risk. It is easily assessed via the UPPS–P Impulsive Behavior Scale (Lynam, Smith, Whiteside, & Cyders, 2006), and emerging evidence supports the underlying genetic, neurocognitive, and physiological underpinnings of this trait. Future research should continue to understand how and why urgency imparts such risk and should focus on developing specific interventions to mitigate this risk that could be applied across multiple clinical and nonclinical populations.

REFERENCES

Adams, Z. W., Kaiser, A. J., Lynam, D. R., Charnigo, R. J., & Milich, R. (2012). Drinking motives as mediators of the impulsivity-substance use relation: Pathways for negative urgency, lack of premeditation, and sensation seeking. *Addictive Behaviors, 37*, 848–855. http://dx.doi.org/10.1016/j.addbeh.2012.03.016

Agras, W. S., & Telch, C. F. (1998). The effects of caloric deprivation and negative affect on binge eating in obese binge-eating disordered women. *Behavior Therapy, 29*, 491–503. http://dx.doi.org/10.1016/S0005-7894(98)80045-2

Al'Absi, M., Bongard, S., Buchanan, T., Pincomb, G. A., Licinio, J., & Lovallo, W. R. (1997). Cardiovascular and neuroendocrine adjustment to public speaking and mental arithmetic stressors. *Psychophysiology, 34*, 266–275. http://dx.doi.org/10.1111/j.1469-8986.1997.tb02397.x

Albein-Urios, N., Verdejo-Román, J., Soriano-Mas, C., Asensio, S., Martínez-González, J. M., & Verdejo-García, A. (2013). Cocaine users with comorbid Cluster B personality disorders show dysfunctional brain activation and connectivity in the emotional regulation networks during negative emotion maintenance and reappraisal. *European Neuropsychopharmacology, 23*, 1698–1707. http://dx.doi.org/10.1016/j.euroneuro.2013.04.012

Alemis, M. C., & Yap, K. (2013). The role of negative urgency impulsivity and financial management practices in compulsive buying. *Australian Journal of Psychology, 65*, 224–231. http://dx.doi.org/10.1111/ajpy.12025

American Psychiatric Association. (2013). *Diagnostic and statistical manual of mental disorders* (5th ed.). Arlington, VA: Author.

Amlung, M., Few, L. R., Howland, J., Rohsenow, D. J., Metrik, J., & MacKillop, J. (2013). Impulsivity and alcohol demand in relation to combined alcohol and caffeine use. *Experimental and Clinical Psychopharmacology, 21*, 467–474. http://dx.doi.org/10.1037/a0034214

Anestis, M. D., Anestis, J. C., & Joiner, T. E. (2009). Affective considerations in antisocial behavior: An examination of negative urgency in primary and secondary psychopathy. *Personality and Individual Differences, 47,* 668–670. http://dx.doi.org/ 10.1016/j.paid.2009.05.013

Anestis, M. D., Selby, E. A., & Joiner, T. E. (2007). The role of urgency in maladaptive behaviors. *Behaviour Research and Therapy, 45,* 3018–3029. http://dx.doi.org/ 10.1016/j.brat.2007.08.012

Anestis, M. D., Smith, A. R., Fink, E. L., & Joiner, T. E. (2009). Dysregulated eating and distress: Examining the specific role of negative urgency in a clinical sample. *Cognitive Therapy and Research, 33,* 390–397. http://dx.doi.org/10.1007/ s10608-008-9201-2

Barratt, E. S. (1993). Impulsivity: Integrating cognitive, behavioral, biological, and environmental data. In W. G. McCown, J. L. Johnson, & M. B. Shure (Eds.), *The impulsive client: Theory, research, and treatment* (pp. 39–56). Washington, DC: American Psychological Association. http://dx.doi.org/10.1037/10500-003

Bayard, S., Raffard, S., & Gely-Nargeot, M. C. (2011). Do facets of self-reported impulsivity predict decision-making under ambiguity and risk? Evidence from a community sample. *Psychiatry Research, 190,* 322–326. http://dx.doi.org/ 10.1016/j.psychres.2011.06.013

Bechara, A. (2004). The role of emotion in decision-making: Evidence from neurological patients with orbitofrontal damage. *Brain and Cognition, 55,* 30–40. http://dx.doi.org/10.1016/j.bandc.2003.04.001

Bechara, A. (2005). Decision making, impulse control and loss of willpower to resist drugs: A neurocognitive perspective. *Nature Neuroscience, 8,* 1458–1463. http:// dx.doi.org/10.1038/nn1584

Bechara, A., Damasio, A. R., Damasio, H., & Anderson, S. W. (1994). Insensitivity to future consequences following damage to human prefrontal cortex. *Cognition, 50,* 7–15. http://dx.doi.org/10.1016/0010-0277(94)90018-3

Bechara, A., Tranel, D., Damasio, H., & Damasio, A. R. (1996). Failure to respond autonomically to anticipated future outcomes following damage to prefrontal cortex. *Cerebral Cortex, 6,* 215–225. http://dx.doi.org/10.1093/cercor/6.2.215

Billieux, J., Gay, P., Rochat, L., & Van der Linden, M. (2010). The role of urgency and its underlying psychological mechanisms in problematic behaviors. *Behaviour Research and Therapy, 48,* 1085–1096. http://dx.doi.org/10.1016/ j.brat.2010.07.008

Billieux, J., Rochat, L., Rebetez, M. M. L., & Van der Linden, M. (2008). Are all facets of impulsivity related to self-reported compulsive buying behavior? *Personality and Individual Differences, 44,* 1432–1442. http://dx.doi.org/10.1016/ j.paid.2007.12.011

Billieux, J., Van der Linden, M., & Ceschi, G. (2007). Which dimensions of impulsivity are related to cigarette craving? *Addictive Behaviors, 32,* 1189–1199. http:// dx.doi.org/10.1016/j.addbeh.2006.08.007

Billieux, J., Van der Linden, M., D'Acremont, M., Ceschi, G., & Zermatten, A. (2007). Does impulsivity relate to perceived dependence on and actual use of the mobile phone? *Applied Cognitive Psychology, 21,* 527–537. http://dx.doi.org/10.1002/acp.1289

Billieux, J., Van der Linden, M., & Rochat, L. (2008). The role of impulsivity in actual and problematic use of the mobile phone. *Applied Cognitive Psychology, 22,* 1195–1210. http://dx.doi.org/10.1002/acp.1429

Boy, F., Evans, C. J., Edden, R. A., Lawrence, A. D., Singh, K. D., Husain, M., & Sumner, P. (2011). Dorsolateral prefrontal γ-aminobutyric acid in men predicts individual differences in rash impulsivity. *Biological Psychiatry, 70,* 866–872. http://dx.doi.org/10.1016/j.biopsych.2011.05.030

Bradley, E. A., & Isaacs, B. J. (2006). Inattention, hyperactivity, and impulsivity in teenagers with intellectual disabilities, with and without autism. *Canadian Journal of Psychiatry, 51,* 598–606.

Bremner, J. D., Staib, L. H., Kaloupek, D., Southwick, S. M., Soufer, R., & Charney, D. S. (1999). Neural correlates of exposure to traumatic pictures and sound in Vietnam combat veterans with and without posttraumatic stress disorder: A positron emission tomography study. *Biological Psychiatry, 45,* 806–816. http://dx.doi.org/10.1016/S0006-3223(98)00297-2

Bresin, K., Carter, D. L., & Gordon, K. H. (2013). The relationship between trait impulsivity, negative affective states, and urge for nonsuicidal self-injury: A daily diary study. *Psychiatry Research, 205,* 227–231.

Cardinal, R. N., Parkinson, J. A., Hall, J., & Everitt, B. J. (2002). Emotion and motivation: The role of the amygdala, ventral striatum, and prefrontal cortex. *Neuroscience and Biobehavioral Reviews, 26,* 321–352. http://dx.doi.org/10.1016/S0149-7634(02)00007-6

Carlson, S. R., Pritchard, A. A., & Dominelli, R. M. (2013). Externalizing behaviors, the UPPS–P Impulsive Behavior scale and reward and punishment sensitivity. *Personality and Individual Differences, 54,* 202–207. http://dx.doi.org/10.1016/j.paid.2012.08.039

Carver, C. S., Johnson, S. L., Joormann, J., Kim, Y., & Nam, J. Y. (2011). Serotonin transporter polymorphism interacts with childhood adversity to predict aspects of impulsivity. *Psychological Science, 22,* 589–595. http://dx.doi.org/10.1177/0956797611404085

Claes, L., & Muehlenkamp, J. (2013). The relationship between the UPPS–P impulsivity dimensions and nonsuicidal self-injury characteristics in male and female high-school students. *Psychiatry Journal, 2013.* Retrieved from http://www.hindawi.com/journals/psychiatry/2013/654847

Claes, L., Vandereycken, W., & Vertommen, H. (2005). Impulsivity-related traits in eating disorder patients. *Personality and Individual Differences, 39,* 739–749. http://dx.doi.org/10.1016/j.paid.2005.02.022

Clark, L., Stokes, P. R., Wu, K., Michalczuk, R., Benecke, A., Watson, B. J., . . . Lingford-Hughes, A. R. (2012). Striatal dopamine D2/D3 receptor binding in pathological gambling is correlated with mood-related impulsivity. *NeuroImage, 63,* 40–46. http://dx.doi.org/10.1016/j.neuroimage.2012.06.067

Colder, C. R., & Chassin, L. (1997). Affectivity and impulsivity: Temperament risk for adolescent alcohol involvement. *Psychology of Addictive Behaviors, 11,* 83–97. http://dx.doi.org/10.1037/0893-164X.11.2.83

Combs, J. L., Pearson, C. M., & Smith, G. T. (2011). A risk model for preadolescent disordered eating. *International Journal of Eating Disorders, 44,* 596–604. http://dx.doi.org/10.1002/eat.20851

Cooper, M. L. (1994). Motivations for alcohol use among adolescents: Development and validation of a four-factor model. *Psychological Assessment, 6,* 117–128. http://dx.doi.org/10.1037/1040-3590.6.2.117

Cooper, M. L., Agocha, V. B., & Sheldon, M. S. (2000). A motivational perspective on risky behaviors: The role of personality and affect regulatory processes. *Journal of Personality, 68,* 1059–1088. http://dx.doi.org/10.1111/1467-6494.00126

Coskunpinar, A., & Cyders, M. A. (2013). Impulsivity and substance-related attentional bias: A meta-analytic review. *Drug and Alcohol Dependence, 133,* 1–14. http://dx.doi.org/10.1016/j.drugalcdep.2013.05.008

Coskunpinar, A., Dir, A. L., & Cyders, M. A. (2013). Multidimensionality in impulsivity and alcohol use: A meta-analysis using the UPPS model of impulsivity. *Alcoholism: Clinical and Experimental Research, 37,* 1441–1450. http://dx.doi.org/10.1111/acer.12131

Coskunpinar, A., Dir, A. L., Karyadi, K. A., Koo, C. S., & Cyders, M. A. (2013). Mechanisms underlying the relationship between negative affectivity and problematic alcohol use. *Journal of Experimental Psychopathology, 4,* 263–278. http://dx.doi.org/10.5127/jep.029612

Costa, P. T., Jr., & McCrae, R. R. (2008). The Revised NEO Personality Inventory (NEO–PI–R). In G. J. Boyle, G. Matthews, & D. H. Saklofske (Eds.), *The Sage handbook of personality theory and assessment: Vol. 2. Personality Measurement and Testing* (pp. 179–198). London, England: Sage.

Cougle, J. R., Timpano, K. R., & Goetz, A. R. (2012). Exploring the unique and interactive roles of distress tolerance and negative urgency in obsessions. *Personality and Individual Differences, 52,* 515–520. http://dx.doi.org/10.1016/j.paid.2011.11.017

Cyders, M. A., & Coskunpinar, A. (2010). Is urgency emotionality? Separating urgent behaviors from effects of emotional experiences. *Personality and Individual Differences, 48,* 839–844. http://dx.doi.org/10.1016/j.paid.2010.02.009

Cyders, M. A., & Coskunpinar, A. (2011). Measurement of constructs using self-report and behavioral lab tasks: Is there overlap in nomothetic span and construct representation for impulsivity? *Clinical Psychology Review, 31,* 965–982. http://dx.doi.org/10.1016/j.cpr.2011.06.001

Cyders, M. A., Dzemidzic, M., Eiler, W. J., Coskunpinar, A., Karyadi, K. A., & Kareken, D. A. (2014a). Negative urgency mediates the relationship between amygdala and orbitofrontal cortex activation to negative emotional stimuli and general risk-taking stimuli. *Cerebral Cortex.* Advance online publication. http://dx.doi.org/10.1093/cercor/bhu123

Cyders, M. A., Dzemidzic, M., Eiler, W. J., Coskunpinar, A., Karyadi, K. A., & Kareken, D. A. (2014b). Negative urgency and ventromedial prefrontal cortex responses to alcohol cues: FMRI evidence of emotion-based impulsivity. *Alcoholism: Clinical and Experimental Research, 38,* 409–417. http://dx.doi.org/10.1111/acer.12266

Cyders, M. A., Flory, K., Rainer, S., & Smith, G. T. (2009). The role of personality dispositions to risky behavior in predicting first-year college drinking. *Addiction, 104,* 193–202. http://dx.doi.org/10.1111/j.1360-0443.2008.02434.x

Cyders, M. A., & Smith, G. T. (2007). Mood-based rash action and its components: Positive and negative urgency. *Personality and Individual Differences, 43,* 839–850. http://dx.doi.org/10.1016/j.paid.2007.02.008

Cyders, M. A., & Smith, G. T. (2008a). Clarifying the role of personality dispositions in risk for increased gambling behavior. *Personality and Individual Differences, 45,* 503–508. http://dx.doi.org/10.1016/j.paid.2008.06.002

Cyders, M. A., & Smith, G. T. (2008b). Emotion-based dispositions to rash action: Positive and negative urgency. *Psychological Bulletin, 134,* 807–828. http://dx.doi.org/10.1037/a0013341

Cyders, M. A., & Smith, G. T. (2010). Longitudinal validation of the urgency traits over the first year of college. *Journal of Personality Assessment, 92,* 63–69. http://dx.doi.org/10.1080/00223890903381825

Cyders, M. A., Smith, G. T., Spillane, N. S., Fischer, S., Annus, A. M., & Peterson, C. (2007). Integration of impulsivity and positive mood to predict risky behavior: Development and validation of a measure of positive urgency. *Psychological Assessment, 19,* 107–118. http://dx.doi.org/10.1037/1040-3590.19.1.107

Cyders, M. A., Zapolski, T. C. B., Combs, J. L., Settles, R. F., Fillmore, M. T., & Smith, G. T. (2010). Experimental effect of positive urgency on negative outcomes from risk taking and on increased alcohol consumption. *Psychology of Addictive Behaviors, 24,* 367–375. http://dx.doi.org/10.1037/a0019494

Davidson, R. J. (1998). *Prefrontal cortex and amygdala contributions to emotion and affective style.* Hove, England: Psychology Press.

Davidson, R. J. (2003). Darwin and the neural bases of emotion and affective style. *Annals of the New York Academy of Sciences, 1000,* 316–336. http://dx.doi.org/10.1196/annals.1280.014

Davis, L. R., & Fischer, S. (2013). The influence of trait anger, trait anxiety and negative urgency on disordered eating. *Personality and Individual Differences, 54,* 307–310. http://dx.doi.org/10.1016/j.paid.2012.08.036

Davis-Becker, K., Peterson, C. M., & Fischer, S. (2014). The relationship of trait negative urgency and negative affect to disordered eating in men and women. *Personality and Individual Differences, 56,* 9–14. http://dx.doi.org/10.1016/j.paid.2013.08.010

Del Boca, F. K., Darkes, J., Greenbaum, P. E., & Goldman, M. S. (2004). Up close and personal: Temporal variability in the drinking of individual college students during their first year. *Journal of Consulting and Clinical Psychology, 72*, 155–164. http://dx.doi.org/10.1037/0022-006X.72.2.155

Derefinko, K., DeWall, C. N., Metze, A. V., Walsh, E. C., & Lynam, D. R. (2011). Do different facets of impulsivity predict different types of aggression? *Aggressive Behavior, 37*, 223–233. http://dx.doi.org/10.1002/ab.20387

Dickman, S. J. (1990). Functional and dysfunctional impulsivity: Personality and cognitive correlates. *Journal of Personality and Social Psychology, 58*, 95–102. http://dx.doi.org/10.1037/0022-3514.58.1.95

Dimeff, L. A., & Linehan, M. M. (2008). Dialectical behavior therapy for substance abusers. *Addiction Science & Clinical Practice, 4*, 39–47. http://dx.doi.org/10.1151/ascp084239

Dir, A. L., Karyadi, K., & Cyders, M. A. (2013). The uniqueness of negative urgency as a common risk factor for self-harm behaviors, alcohol consumption, and eating problems. *Addictive Behaviors, 38*, 2158–2162. http://dx.doi.org/10.1016/j.addbeh.2013.01.025

Dolan, R. J. (2007). The human amygdala and orbital prefrontal cortex in behavioral regulation. *Philosophical Transactions of the Royal Society B: Biological Sciences, 362*, 787–799. http://dx.doi.org/10.1098/rstb.2007.2088

Dreisbach, G. (2006). How positive affect modulates cognitive control: The costs and benefits of reduced maintenance capability. *Brain and Cognition, 60*, 11–19. http://dx.doi.org/10.1016/j.bandc.2005.08.003

Edenberg, H. J., Dick, D. M., Xuei, X., Tian, H., Almasy, L., Bauer, L. O., . . . Begleiter, H. (2004). Variations in GABRA2, encoding the α 2 subunit of the GABA(A) receptor, are associated with alcohol dependence and with brain oscillations. *American Journal of Human Genetics, 74*, 705–714. http://dx.doi.org/10.1086/383283

Evenden, J. L. (1999a). Impulsivity: A discussion of clinical and experimental findings. *Journal of Psychopharmacology, 13*, 180–192. http://dx.doi.org/10.1177/026988119901300211

Evenden, J. L. (1999b). Varieties of impulsivity. *Psychopharmacology, 146*, 348–361. http://dx.doi.org/10.1007/PL00005481

Fink, E. L., Anestis, M. D., Selby, E. A., & Joiner, T. E. (2010). Negative urgency fully mediates the relationship between alexithymia and dysregulated behaviors. *Personality and Mental Health, 4*, 284–293. http://dx.doi.org/10.1002/pmh.138

Fischer, S., Anderson, K. G., & Smith, G. T. (2004). Coping with distress by eating or drinking: Role of trait urgency and expectancies. *Psychology of Addictive Behaviors, 18*, 269–274. http://dx.doi.org/10.1037/0893-164X.18.3.269

Fischer, S., Peterson, C. M., & McCarthy, D. (2013). A prospective test of the influence of negative urgency and expectancies on binge eating and purging. *Psychology of Addictive Behaviors, 27*, 294–300. http://dx.doi.org/10.1037/a0029323

Fischer, S., Settles, R., Collins, B., Gunn, R., & Smith, G. T. (2012). The role of negative urgency and expectancies in problem drinking and disordered eating:

Testing a model of comorbidity in pathological and at-risk samples. *Psychology of Addictive Behaviors, 26*, 112–123. http://dx.doi.org/10.1037/a0023460

Fischer, S., & Smith, G. T. (2008). Binge eating, problem drinking, and pathological gambling: Linking behavior to shared traits and social learning. *Personality and Individual Differences, 44*, 789–800. http://dx.doi.org/10.1016/j.paid.2007.10.008

Fischer, S., Smith, G. T., & Anderson, K. G. (2003). Clarifying the role of impulsivity in bulimia nervosa. *International Journal of Eating Disorders, 33*, 406–411. http://dx.doi.org/10.1002/eat.10165

Fischer, S., Smith, G. T., Annus, A. M., & Hendricks, M. (2007). The relationship of neuroticism and urgency to negative consequences of alcohol use in women with bulimic symptoms. *Personality and Individual Differences, 43*, 1199–1209. http://dx.doi.org/10.1016/j.paid.2007.03.011

Forgas, J. P. (1992). Affect in social judgments and decisions: A multiprocess model. In M. Zanna (Ed.), *Advances in experimental social psychology* (pp. 227–275). San Diego, CA: Academic Press. http://dx.doi.org/10.1016/S0065-2601(08)60285-3

Forgas, J. P., & Bower, G. H. (1987). Mood effects on person-perception judgments. *Journal of Personality and Social Psychology, 53*, 53–60. http://dx.doi.org/10.1037/0022-3514.53.1.53

Frijda, N. H. (1986). *The emotions.* New York, NY: Cambridge University Press.

Gleicher, F., & Weary, G. (1991). Effect of depression on quantity and quality of social inferences. *Journal of Personality and Social Psychology, 61*, 105–114. http://dx.doi.org/10.1037/0022-3514.61.1.105

Glenn, C. R., & Klonsky, E. D. (2010). A multimethod analysis of impulsivity in nonsuicidal self-injury. *Personality Disorders: Theory, Research, and Treatment, 1*, 67–75. http://dx.doi.org/10.1037/a0017427

Grant, J. E., & Kim, S. W. (2003). Comorbidity of impulse control disorders in pathological gamblers. *Acta Psychiatrica Scandinavica, 108*, 203–207. http://dx.doi.org/10.1034/j.1600-0447.2003.00162.x

Gunn, R. L., & Smith, G. T. (2010). Risk factors for elementary school drinking: Pubertal status, personality, and alcohol expectancies concurrently predict fifth grade alcohol consumption. *Psychology of Addictive Behaviors, 24*, 617–627. http://dx.doi.org/10.1037/a0020334

Hajcak, G., Molnar, C., George, M. S., Bolger, K., Koola, J., & Nahas, Z. (2007). Emotion facilitates action: A transcranial magnetic stimulation study of motor cortex excitability during picture viewing. *Psychophysiology, 44*, 91–97. http://dx.doi.org/10.1111/j.1469-8986.2006.00487.x

Heatherton, T. F., & Baumeister, R. F. (1991). Binge eating as escape from self-awareness. *Psychological Bulletin, 110*, 86–108. http://dx.doi.org/10.1037/0033-2909.110.1.86

Holub, A., Hodgins, D. C., & Peden, N. E. (2005). Development of the temptations for gambling questionnaire: A measure of temptation in recently quit gamblers. *Addiction Research & Theory, 13*, 179–191. http://dx.doi.org/10.1080/16066350412331314902

Hyman, S. E., & Fenton, W. S. (2003). Medicine. What are the right targets for psychopharmacology? *Science, 299*, 350–351. http://dx.doi.org/10.1126/science.1077141

Jones, K. A., Chryssanthakis, A., & Groom, M. J. (2014). Impulsivity and drinking motives predict problem behaviors relating to alcohol use in university students. *Addictive Behaviors, 39*, 289–296. http://dx.doi.org/10.1016/j.addbeh.2013.10.024

Joseph, J. E., Liu, X., Jiang, Y., Lynam, D., & Kelly, T. H. (2009). Neural correlates of emotional reactivity in sensation seeking. *Psychological Science, 20*, 215–223. http://dx.doi.org/10.1111/j.1467-9280.2009.02283.x

Kaiser, A. J., Milich, R., Lynam, D. R., & Charnigo, R. J. (2012). Negative urgency, distress tolerance, and substance abuse among college students. *Addictive Behaviors, 37*, 1075–1083. http://dx.doi.org/10.1016/j.addbeh.2012.04.017

Karyadi, K. A., & King, K. M. (2011). Urgency and negative emotions: Evidence for moderation on negative alcohol consequences. *Personality and Individual Differences, 51*, 635–640. http://dx.doi.org/10.1016/j.paid.2011.05.030

LaBrie, J. W., Kenney, S. R., Napper, L. E., & Miller, K. (2014). Impulsivity and alcohol-related risk among college students: Examining urgency, sensation seeking, and the moderating influence of beliefs about alcohol's role in the college experience. *Addictive Behaviors, 39*, 159–164. http://dx.doi.org/10.1016/j.addbeh.2013.09.018

Lang, P. J. (1993). The motivational organization of emotion: Affect reflex connections. In S. van Goozen, N. E. van der Poll, & J. A. Sergeant (Eds.), *The emotions: Essays on emotion theory* (pp. 61–96). Hillsdale, NJ: Erlbaum.

Lejuez, C. W., Read, J. P., Kahler, C. W., Richards, J. B., Ramsey, S. E., Stuart, G. L., . . . Brown, R. A. (2002). Evaluation of a behavioral measure of risk taking: The Balloon Analogue Risk Task (BART). *Journal of Experimental Psychology: Applied, 8*, 75–84. http://dx.doi.org/10.1037/1076-898X.8.2.75

Linehan, M. M. (1993). *Cognitive–behavioral treatment of borderline personality disorder.* New York, NY: Guilford Press.

Lucas, M., & Koff, E. (2014). The role of impulsivity and of self-perceived attractiveness in impulse buying in women. *Personality and Individual Differences, 56*, 111–115. http://dx.doi.org/10.1016/j.paid.2013.08.032

Lynam, D. R., Miller, J. D., Miller, D. J., Bornovalova, M. A., & Lejuez, C. W. (2011). Testing the relations between impulsivity-related traits, suicidality, and nonsuicidal self-injury: A test of the incremental validity of the UPPS model. *Personality Disorders: Theory, Research, and Treatment, 2*, 151–160. http://dx.doi.org/10.1037/a0019978

Lynam, D. R., Smith, G. T., Whiteside, S. P., & Cyders, M. A. (2006). *The UPPS–P: Assessing five personality pathways to impulsive behavior.* West Lafayette, IN: Purdue University.

Marmorstein, N. R. (2013). Associations between dispositions to rash action and internalizing and externalizing symptoms in children. *Journal of Clinical*

Child and Adolescent Psychology, 42, 131–138. http://dx.doi.org/10.1080/15374416.2012.734021

Martens, M. P., Pedersen, E. R., Smith, A. E., Stewart, S. H., & O'Brien, K. (2011). Predictors of alcohol-related outcomes in college athletes: The roles of trait urgency and drinking motives. *Addictive Behaviors, 36*, 456–464. http://dx.doi.org/10.1016/j.addbeh.2010.12.025

Martin, E. D., & Sher, K. J. (1994). Family history of alcoholism, alcohol use disorders, and the five-factor model of personality. *Journal of Studies on Alcohol, 55*, 81–90. http://dx.doi.org/10.15288/jsa.1994.55.81

Miller, A. C., Keenan, J. M., Betjemann, R. S., Willcutt, E. G., Pennington, B. F., & Olson, R. K. (2013). Reading comprehension in children with ADHD: Cognitive underpinnings of the centrality deficit. *Journal of Abnormal Child Psychology, 41*, 473–483.

Miller, J. D., Flory, K., Lynam, D., & Leukefeld, C. (2003). A test of the four-factor model of impulsivity-related traits. *Personality and Individual Differences, 34*, 1403–1418. http://dx.doi.org/10.1016/S0191-8869(02)00122-8

Miller, J. D., Zeichner, A., & Wilson, L. F. (2012). Personality correlates of aggression: Evidence from measures of the five-factor model, UPPS model of impulsivity, and BIS/BAS. *Journal of Interpersonal Violence, 27*, 2903–2919. http://dx.doi.org/10.1177/0886260512438279

Mouilso, E. R., Calhoun, K. S., & Rosenbloom, T. G. (2013). Impulsivity and sexual assault in college men. *Violence and Victims, 28*, 429–442. http://dx.doi.org/10.1891/0886-6708.VV-D-12-00025

Mullins-Sweatt, S. N., Lengel, G. J., & Grant, D. M. (2013). Nonsuicidal self-injury: The contribution of general personality functioning. *Personality and Mental Health, 7*, 56–68. http://dx.doi.org/10.1002/pmh.1211

Nygren, T. E., Isen, A. M., Taylor, P. J., & Dulin, J. (1996). The influence of positive affect on the decision rule in risk situations: Focus on outcome (and especially avoidance of loss) rather than probability. *Organizational Behavior and Human Decision Processes, 66*, 59–72. http://dx.doi.org/10.1006/obhd.1996.0038

Peters, J. R., Upton, B. T., & Baer, R. A. (2013). Brief report: Relationships between facets of impulsivity and borderline personality features. *Journal of Personality Disorders, 27*, 547–552. http://dx.doi.org/10.1521/pedi_2012_26_044

Peterson, C. M., Davis-Becker, K., & Fischer, S. (2014). Interactive role of depression, distress tolerance, and negative urgency on nonsuicidal self-injury. *Personality and Mental Health, 8*, 151–160. http://dx.doi.org/10.1002/pmh.1256

Peterson, C. M., & Fischer, S. (2012). A prospective study of the influence of the UPPS model of impulsivity on the co-occurrence of bulimic symptoms and nonsuicidal self-injury. *Eating Behaviors, 13*, 335–341. http://dx.doi.org/10.1016/j.eatbeh.2012.05.007

Peveler, R., & Fairburn, C. (1990). Eating disorders in women who abuse alcohol. *British Journal of Addiction, 85,* 1633–1638. http://dx.doi.org/10.1111/j.1360-0443.1990.tb01653.x

Racine, S. E., Keel, P. K., Burt, S. A., Sisk, C. L., Neale, M., Boker, S., & Klump, K. L. (2013). Exploring the relationship between negative urgency and dysregulated eating: Etiologic associations and the role of negative affect. *Journal of Abnormal Psychology, 122,* 433–444. http://dx.doi.org/10.1037/a0031250

Rauch, S. L., van der Kolk, B. A., Fisler, R. E., Alpert, N. M., Orr, S. P., Savage, C. R., . . . Pitman, R. K. (1996). A symptom provocation study of posttraumatic stress disorder using positron emission tomography and script-driven imagery. *Archives of General Psychiatry, 53,* 380–387. http://dx.doi.org/10.1001/archpsyc.1996.01830050014003

Reed, M. A., & Derryberry, D. (1995). Temperament and response processing: Facilitatory and inhibitory consequences of positive and negative motivational states. *Journal of Research in Personality, 29,* 59–84. http://dx.doi.org/10.1006/jrpe.1995.1004

Robinson, J. M., Ladd, B. O., & Anderson, K. G. (2014). When you see it, let it be: Urgency, mindfulness and adolescent substance use. *Addictive Behaviors, 39,* 1038–1041. http://dx.doi.org/10.1016/j.addbeh.2014.02.011

Rolls, E. T., Thorpe, S. J., & Maddison, S. P. (1983). Responses of striatal neurons in the behaving monkey: 1. Head of the caudate nucleus. *Behavioural Brain Research, 7,* 179–210. http://dx.doi.org/10.1016/0166-4328(83)90191-2

Saami, C., Mumme, D. L., & Campos, J. J. (1998). *Emotional development: Action, communication, and understanding.* Hoboken, NJ: Wiley.

Settles, R. E., Fischer, S., Cyders, M. A., Combs, J. L., Gunn, R. L., & Smith, G. T. (2012). Negative urgency: A personality predictor of externalizing behavior characterized by neuroticism, low conscientiousness, and disagreeableness. *Journal of Abnormal Psychology, 121,* 160–172. http://dx.doi.org/10.1037/a0024948

Settles, R. F., Cyders, M., & Smith, G. T. (2010). Longitudinal validation of the acquired preparedness model of drinking risk. *Psychology of Addictive Behaviors, 24,* 198–208. http://dx.doi.org/10.1037/a0017631

Shin, S. H., Hong, H. G., & Jeon, S. M. (2012). Personality and alcohol use: The role of impulsivity. *Addictive Behaviors, 37,* 102–107. http://dx.doi.org/10.1016/j.addbeh.2011.09.006

Shiv, B., Loewenstein, G., & Bechara, A. (2005). The dark side of emotion in decision-making: When individuals with decreased emotional reactions make more advantageous decisions. *Cognitive Brain Research, 23,* 85–92. http://dx.doi.org/10.1016/j.cogbrainres.2005.01.006

Smith, G. T., & Anderson, K. G. (2001). Personality and learning factors combine to create risk for adolescent problem drinking: A model and suggestions for intervention. In P. M. Monti, S. M. Colby, & T. A. O'Leary (Eds.), *Adolescents, alcohol, and substance abuse: Reaching teens through brief interventions* (pp. 109–144). New York, NY: Guilford Press.

Smith, G. T., Fischer, S., Cyders, M. A., Annus, A. M., Spillane, N. S., & McCarthy, D. M. (2007). On the validity and utility of discriminating among impulsivity-like traits. *Assessment, 14,* 155–170. http://dx.doi.org/10.1177/1073191106295527

Smyth, J. M., Wonderlich, S. A., Heron, K. E., Sliwinski, M. J., Crosby, R. D., Mitchell, J. E., & Engel, S. G. (2007). Daily and momentary mood and stress are associated with binge eating and vomiting in bulimia nervosa patients in the natural environment. *Journal of Consulting and Clinical Psychology, 75,* 629–638. http://dx.doi.org/10.1037/0022-006X.75.4.629

Snorrason, Í., Smári, J., & Ólafsson, R. P. (2011). Motor inhibition, reflection impulsivity, and trait impulsivity in pathological skin picking. *Behavior Therapy, 42,* 521–532.

Spillane, N. S., Smith, G. T., & Kahler, C. W. (2010). Impulsivity-like traits and smoking behavior in college students. *Addictive Behaviors, 35,* 700–705. http://dx.doi.org/10.1016/j.addbeh.2010.03.008

Stautz, K., & Cooper, A. (2014). Urgency traits and problematic substance use in adolescence: Direct effects and moderation of perceived peer use. *Psychology of Addictive Behaviors, 28,* 487–497.

Swendsen, J. D., Tennen, H., Carney, M. A., Affleck, G., Willard, A., & Hromi, A. (2000). Mood and alcohol consumption: An experience sampling test of the self-medication hypothesis. *Journal of Abnormal Psychology, 109,* 198–204. http://dx.doi.org/10.1037/0021-843X.109.2.198

Telch, C. F., Agras, W. S., & Linehan, M. M. (2001). Dialectical behavior therapy for binge eating disorder. *Journal of Consulting and Clinical Psychology, 69,* 1061–1065. http://dx.doi.org/10.1037/0022-006X.69.6.1061

Timpano, K. R., Rasmussen, J., Exner, C., Rief, W., Schmidt, N. B., & Wilhelm, S. (2013). Hoarding and the multifaceted construct of impulsivity: A cross-cultural investigation. *Journal of Psychiatric Research, 47,* 363–370. http://dx.doi.org/10.1016/j.jpsychires.2012.10.017

Tragesser, S. L., & Robinson, R. J. (2009). The role of affective instability and UPPS impulsivity in borderline personality disorder features. *Journal of Personality Disorders, 23,* 370–383. http://dx.doi.org/10.1521/pedi.2009.23.4.370

Verdejo-García, A., Albein-Urios, N., Molina, E., Ching-López, A., Martínez-González, J. M., & Gutiérrez, B. (2013). A MAOA gene*cocaine severity interaction on impulsivity and neuropsychological measures of orbitofrontal dysfunction: Preliminary results. *Drug and Alcohol Dependence, 133,* 287–290. http://dx.doi.org/10.1016/j.drugalcdep.2013.04.031

Verdejo-García, A., Bechara, A., Recknor, E. C., & Pérez-García, M. (2007). Negative emotion-driven impulsivity predicts substance dependence problems. *Drug and Alcohol Dependence, 91,* 213–219. http://dx.doi.org/10.1016/j.drugalcdep.2007.05.025

Villafuerte, S., Heitzeg, M. M., Foley, S., Yau, W. Y., Majczenko, K., Zubieta, J. K., . . . Burmeister, M. (2012). Impulsiveness and insula activation during reward anticipation are associated with genetic variants in *GABRA2* in a family sample enriched for alcoholism. *Molecular Psychiatry, 17*, 511–519. http://dx.doi.org/10.1038/mp.2011.33

Villafuerte, S., Strumba, V., Stoltenberg, S. F., Zucker, R. A., & Burmeister, M. (2013). Impulsiveness mediates the association between *GABRA2* SNPs and lifetime alcohol problems. *Genes, Brain & Behavior, 12*, 525–531. http://dx.doi.org/10.1111/gbb.12039

Weiss, N. H., Tull, M. T., Viana, A. G., Anestis, M. D., & Gratz, K. L. (2012). Impulsive behaviors as an emotion regulation strategy: Examining associations between PTSD, emotion dysregulation, and impulsive behaviors among substance dependent inpatients. *Journal of Anxiety Disorders, 26*, 453–458. http://dx.doi.org/10.1016/j.janxdis.2012.01.007

Whiteside, S. P., & Lynam, D. R. (2001). The five-factor model and impulsivity: Using a structural model of personality to understand impulsivity. *Personality and Individual Differences, 30*, 669–689. http://dx.doi.org/10.1016/S0191-8869(00)00064-7

Whiteside, S. P., Lynam, D. R., Miller, J. D., & Reynolds, S. K. (2005). Validation of the UPPS impulsive behavior scale: A four-factor model of impulsivity. *European Journal of Personality, 19*, 559–574. http://dx.doi.org/10.1002/per.556

World Health Organization. (1992). *The ICD–10 classification of mental and behavioural disorders: Clinical descriptions and diagnostic guidelines.* Geneva, Switzerland: Author.

Xiao, L., Bechara, A., Grenard, L. J., Stacy, W. A., Palmer, P., Wei, Y., . . . Johnson, C. A. (2009). Affective decision-making predictive of Chinese adolescent drinking behaviors. *Journal of the International Neuropsychological Society, 15*, 547–557. http://dx.doi.org/10.1017/S1355617709090808

Xue, G., Lu, Z., Levin, I. P., & Bechara, A. (2010). The impact of prior risk experiences on subsequent risky decision-making: The role of the insula. *NeuroImage, 50*, 709–716. http://dx.doi.org/10.1016/j.neuroimage.2009.12.097

Zapolski, T. C. B., Cyders, M. A., Rainer, S., & Smith, G. T. (2007, August). *Examination of the relationship between positive urgency, drug use, and risky sex.* Paper presented at the annual meeting of the American Psychological Association, San Francisco, CA.

Zapolski, T. C. B., Cyders, M. A., & Smith, G. T. (2009). Positive urgency predicts illegal drug use and risky sexual behavior. *Psychology of Addictive Behaviors, 23*, 348–354. http://dx.doi.org/10.1037/a0014684

Zapolski, T. C. B., Settles, R. E., Cyders, M. A., & Smith, G. T. (2010). Borderline personality disorder, bulimia nervosa, antisocial personality disorder, ADHD, substance use: Common threads, common treatment needs, and the nature of impulsivity. *Independent Practitioner, 30*, 20–23.

9

DISTRACTIBILITY: INTERRUPTED BY AN INABILITY TO IGNORE

TAMMY D. BARRY, KARIN FISHER, KRISTY M. DISABATINO, AND THEODORE S. TOMENY

DEFINITION AND BACKGROUND

According to the National Highway Traffic Safety Administration (n.d.), there were 3,328 deaths and an estimated 421,000 individuals injured in distracted driving crashes in the United States in 2012 alone. Unfortunately, distractibility thwarts staying on task. Anyone's attention to a task can be diverted by other events (e.g., we may stop reading a book when our roommate or spouse comes into the room to talk with us), and, indeed, set-shifting (or moving one's focus of attention from one task to the other; Kalkut, Han, Lansing, Holdnack, & Delis, 2009) is adaptive. However, a proneness to *distractibility* refers particularly to individuals' attention being shifted to small and irrelevant stimuli and implies that there are other more important stimuli (such as the road on which one is driving) to which they should be attending at the moment (Forster & Lavie, 2008). Given its definition, distractibility is often referred to as

http://dx.doi.org/10.1037/14854-010

The Dark Side of Personality: Science and Practice in Social, Personality, and Clinical Psychology, V. Zeigler-Hill and D. K. Marcus (Editors)

inattentiveness, particularly in studies examining clinical populations. The current chapter focuses on research regarding both distractibility and inattentiveness, including research on attention-deficit/hyperactivity disorder (ADHD), which includes distractibility and inattentiveness as core symptoms within the inattention domain (American Psychiatric Association, 2013). The disorder known as ADHD is also referred to as hyperkinetic disorder with disturbance of activity and attention, per the *ICD–10 Classification of Mental and Behavioural Disorders* (World Health Organization, 1992).

Whereas distractibility is not typically deadly, public service announcements (PSAs) on texting and driving underscore how important staying on task can be. For example, in a clever PSA sponsored by Volkswagen, moviegoers in a Hong Kong theatre watch from first-person point-of-view as a man starts a car, turns up the upbeat song playing on the radio, and takes off at a quick pace on a narrow road lined with trees. For us, the action cuts to an individual in the movie control room using a location-based broadcaster and a laptop to text the audience members at a certain point in the advertisement; meanwhile, the moviegoers are still intently watching the rather mundane event, all eyes fixed on the screen. The text is sent and dozens of audience members simultaneously retrieve their phones and read the text just received. As they do, the sound of the catchy tune turns to squealing brakes and then a crash and breaking glass, as the car lunges from the road and smashes into a tree. Everyone looks up from their phones to the wreckage on the screen as it fades to a message about the use of mobile phones being the leading cause of motor vehicle casualties—and "a reminder to keep your eyes on the road" (Stone, 2014). Unlike the many other PSAs on the subject that use mortality salience to discourage texting and driving by showing someone else in a horrific crash after texting (Kareklas & Muehling, 2014), this one put members of the movie audience (virtually) in the driver's seat so they could experience firsthand what happened when they, themselves, got distracted evenly briefly. Staged or not (a point debated on the Internet; Mackie, 2014), the advertisement makes an important point to the real audience (not necessarily the moviegoers but us, the ones watching the PSA): Being distracted—at least at the wrong time—can kill you.

Distractibility can be both external (based on stimuli coming from the environment outside of the individual, such as sights, sounds, and smells) and internal (based on stimuli coming from within the individual, such as thoughts, emotions, and internal states such as hunger). Typically, *external distractibility* refers to a difficulty with blocking out irrelevant auditory or visual stimuli (Forster & Lavie, 2014; Silver, 2004). Individuals distracted by external stimuli seem to hear and see everything. Distracted children may not be able to focus at school due to other children sharpening their pencils or going to the front of the room to turn in a test paper. Distracted adults may not be able to focus at work due to coworkers talking or typing on their computers. In short, externally distracted individuals seem to notice everything around them and, consequently, become immobilized to deal with a target task at hand. Internal distractibility typically refers to a difficulty with blocking out unimportant thoughts and mind wandering (Forster & Lavie, 2014; Silver, 2004), although it can also include being distracted by emotions or internal states. Often, individuals who are internally distracted report having two or more competing thoughts—or having their minds quickly rush from one thought to another. It becomes difficult to maintain attention on one thought or task, which markedly interferes with productivity in terms of both accuracy and efficiency. Of course, most individuals prone to distractibility experience both external and internal distractibility. Thus, an individual may be working on an important task with a firm midday deadline at work, for example, but be highly distracted by the noise caused by coworkers in the hallway, the humming of the air-conditioning overhead, the racing thoughts about the errands that need to be completed during the lunch break, and the constant pangs of hunger felt as the clock grows closer to noon.

By its definition, being "distracted" means failing to selectively pay full attention to a target stimulus when presented with multiple stimuli (Berti, Grunwald, & Schröger, 2013). This lack of selective attention can have significant negative consequences, given that attention is a basic prerequisite for higher order executive functioning and learning (Cuevas & Bell, 2014). For example, in his theory of social or observational learning, Bandura (1965) indicated that attention was the initial and foremost stage that must be present for learning to take place. Without undistracted attention, learning cannot occur. Given the interruptions it produces in learning, shaping, and acquisition of new information and skills from environmental experiences, distractibility can cause numerous academic, occupational, interpersonal, and intrapersonal difficulties for individuals experiencing it. Distractibility is among the top three problems experienced by children and adolescents (examined separately) as reported by teachers in general education classrooms across the United States, with almost 30% of children being either almost always or often generally distracted (Harrison, Vannest, Davis, & Reynolds, 2012). Such prevalence rates of rather significant distractibility highlight the importance of considering this construct and its potential negative consequences further.

REVIEW OF THE RELEVANT LITERATURE

Biologically Based Correlates of Distractibility

All individuals will be distracted at times; however, some individuals have a specific propensity toward distractibility. Thus, it is important to understand the factors that are associated with, and potentially cause, individual differences in the manifestation of this trait. As with many individual difference traits, there appears to be a genetic component to distractibility. Etiological studies on distractibility and other symptoms of ADHD show that it runs in families; furthermore, when a family member has ADHD, there are genetic characteristics that occur at a higher frequency among those families, pointing to a distinct genetic association (e.g., American Psychiatric Association, 2013; Thissen, Rommelse, Altink, Oosterlaan, & Buitelaar, 2014). Moreover, the genetic component for distractibility/inattentiveness appears to be distinct from hyperactivity/impulsivity (i.e., the sister domain of ADHD), suggesting a distinct genetic pathway underlying distractibility (Kuntsi et al., 2014).

Genetic risk may lead to neurological irregularities that affect distractibility. At the neurotransmitter level, lower levels of dopamine predict higher levels of distractibility, which is why stimulant medications that block dopamine transporters, and thus slow the removal of dopamine from the synapse, are effective in reducing distractibility and other symptoms of ADHD (Volkow, Wang, Fowler, & Ding, 2005). Abnormal functioning in the neurological pathways that regulate selective attention may also cause distractibility. Although both human and nonhuman research indicates that the parietal lobe is implicated in selective attention and distractibility (Bisley & Goldberg, 2006), frontal lobe functioning appears to be primary in these processes (Suzuki & Gottlieb, 2013), and distractibility is clearly linked to frontal lobe dysfunction (Berlin, Bohlin, Nyberg, & Janols, 2004).

Between the genetic predisposition and the phenotypical expressed behavior of distractibility lies the neurocognitive endophenotype (Kendler & Neale, 2010). For example, an endophenotype for distractibility would include poor performance on neuropsychological measures assessing the ability to selectively attend and filter distractors (described in more detail later in the chapter). Research indicates that genetic risk is more directly associated with neurocognitive functions—and, for distractibility, perhaps particularly risk passed from the biological mother—than with behaviorally defined distractibility (and other symptoms of ADHD) directly (Thissen et al., 2014). The importance of the relation between neuropsychological functioning and symptoms of distractibility/inattentiveness is well documented, with a recent longitudinal study showing that neuropsychological functioning at earlier time points among preschoolers at high risk for ADHD symptoms predicted the severity of distractibility and other symptoms of ADHD at latter time points (assessed up to 4 years later; Rajendran et al., 2013).

Environmental Correlates of Distractibility

Despite the strong evidence for an inheritable amount of distractibility, a proneness to distractibility is also influenced by an individual's environment, even prenatally. For example, a child is more likely to have a propensity toward distractibility/inattentiveness if a mother smoked or used alcohol or illicit drugs during her pregnancy (e.g., Sagiv, Epstein, Bellinger, & Korrick, 2013), often leading to preterm delivery or low birth weight that has a direct neurobiological impact on brain development (Loe, Lee, & Feldman, 2013). Certainly after birth, other lifestyle, family, and environmental risk factors continue to play a role in the development of distractibility. One such risk factor is exposure to lead, which was shown via a recent meta-analysis to have a similar magnitude in relation to increased inattentiveness (which includes distractibility) as it does with decreased IQ (Goodlad, Marcus, & Fulton, 2013). A home that is unorganized or poor in quality also increases the risk of developing distractibility/inattentiveness (Sagiv et al., 2013). A susceptibility toward distractibility has also been related to a variety of parental factors, such as low parental education (Sagiv et al., 2013), high parental psychopathology (e.g., depression, anxiety; Barry, Dunlap, Cotten, Lochman, & Wells, 2005), and certain parental interaction styles, including low warmth, high hostility, or high parental strain (Linares et al., 2010; Yates, Obradovic, & Egeland, 2010). Often the findings relating parental psychopathology and parenting practices with child distractibility are bidirectional in nature (e.g., Yates et al., 2010).

Many foods and dietary ingredients (e.g., sugar, food dyes, artificial additives) have been targeted as possibly contributing to behavioral symptoms such as distractibility, although research has not supported a clear link, and more studies are required to draw conclusions on the efficacy of eliminating any specific types of foods (Stevenson et al., 2014). However, recent research, including a two-part meta-analysis, has provided evidence for a negative association between omega-3 fatty acids and symptoms of ADHD such as distractibility/inattentiveness, with dietary supplements improving omega-3 levels and subsequently reducing symptoms (Hawkey & Nigg, 2014). This research is promising, but, notably, the improvements were seen more widely in hyperactivity and less so (only per parent report) for distractibility/inattentiveness.

Even otherwise beneficial behaviors can lead to at least transient decrements in effortful control and increased rates of certain types of distractibility. For example, a recent study found that an acute bout of physical exertion in which the participants achieved up to 85% of their maximum heart rate (compared with those reaching only up to 35%) was associated with higher distractibility for extraneous emotional stimuli for a transient period (Brunyé, Howe, Walker, & Mahoney, 2013). Although only associated with a brief change in distractibility, this finding demonstrates how our own voluntary behaviors can affect our ability to implicitly focus our attention selectively to a target task and ignore irrelevant stimuli. Another voluntary behavior many individuals choose is multitasking, which has become a common way of life in our busy, multimedia, high-technology, portable world and one that appears to predict an increase in distractibility. Indeed, multitasking has been linked to higher levels of *trait* distractibility (i.e., not just distractibility linked to the use of devices; Levine, Waite, & Bowman, 2012). Among Western industrialized cultures, more individuals are doing more multitasking at younger ages (Blaser, 2014), a trend that no doubt will continue to influence distractibility among these cultures.

Individual Differences Correlates of Distractibility

Relating to both individual differences and a biological predisposition, distractibility was considered one of nine core temperamental traits in early conceptualizations of temperament (Thomas & Chess, 1977), and a subscale assessing distractibility—or attentional focus—is typically included on most measures of infant/preschool temperament today (e.g., Huelsman, Gagnon, Kidder-Ashley, & Griggs, 2014; Rothbart, Ahadi, Hershey, & Fisher, 2001).

Distractibility is associated with a number of other individual differences. It is an individual difference variable itself, and, certainly, other individual difference variables may predict higher or lower levels of distractibility. For example, boys have higher rates of ADHD, broadly, than girls; that said, however, gender differences may be most pronounced for hyperactivity/impulsivity and less apparent for distractibility/inattentiveness (Hasson & Fine, 2012). Age has a curvilinear relation with distractibility under typical, nonpathological circumstances—with a clear developmental trajectory of improved executive control from infancy through adolescence that is maintained until later adulthood, when distractibility generally increases again, according to both behavioral and neurological data (Berti et al., 2013; Pozuelos, Paz-Alonso, Castillo, Fuentes, & Rueda, 2014). Specific personality features (e.g., neuroticism) also routinely predict a propensity toward distractibility (Paulhus, Aks, & Coren, 1990).

Measuring Distractibility

Distractibility—or inattentiveness—can be examined using a variety of methods and measures. Behavioral rating forms concerning symptoms of distractibility for the self or others are often evaluated on a Likert scale. Most broadband child and adolescent clinical rating forms (such as the Behavioral Assessment System for Children, Second Edition, and the Child Behavior Checklist from the Achenbach System of Empirically Based Assessment) contain an attention problems scale with items specifically tapping distractibility (Frick, Barry, & Kamphaus, 2010). Forms are typically available for completion by parents, teachers, or children and adolescents, and extensive normative data are available. ADHD-specific rating scales (e.g., Barkley's Adult ADHD Rating

Scale—IV; Barkley, 2011) are commonly used to assess for distractibility among adults, with versions to differentiate both self and other informant reports as well as to distinguish childhood and current functioning. Neuropsychological tests also can be used to measure levels of selective attention and distractibility. For example, the NEPSY–II (which stands for "A Developmental NEuroPSYchological Assessment") for children (Korkman, Kirk, & Kemp, 2007) and the Repeatable Battery for the Assessment of Neuropsychological Status (Update version) for adolescents and adults (Randolph, 2012) both include subtests specifically assessing for distractibility/inattentiveness within the context of broader neuropsychological assessment. Many of these subtests are adaptations of classic neuropsychological measures of distractibility, such as paper-and-pencil canceling tasks with distractors (e.g., for which the participant is asked to cancel a target letter in an array of many letters, the others of which are distractors), connecting trails of numbers then numbers and letters in an array of distractors, or verbal and nonverbal fluency tests (e.g., Reitan & Wolfson, 1993). Some available neuropsychological tests of attention have subtests designed specifically with ecological validity by having examinees complete tasks that they may have to do in their everyday life (e.g., visually searching for symbols on a map or listening for their winning lottery number; Robertson, Ward, Ridgeway, & Nimmo-Smith, 1994).

Computerized tasks are regularly used to assess distractibility both for clinical and research purposes. For example, the Conners Continuous Performance Test is often used to measure distractibility as well as sustained attention and impulsivity and, most recently with the release of Version 3, vigilance (Conners, 2014b). Examinees must press the spacebar on the keyboard when they see the letter X but do nothing when they see any other letter (most stimuli are nontarget distractors). The task lasts approximately 14 minutes and presents many trials across various blocks with randomly presented interstimulus intervals at varied lengths increasing the difficulty level to sustain attention without acting on the distractors. A recently released add-on is the Conners Continuous Auditory Test, measuring the same constructs through the auditory rather than the visual channel and requiring individuals to respond to certain tones, some warned and some unwarned (Conners, 2014a). Both of these tests have considerable research with normative samples so that a multitude of scores are offered about examinees. Distractibility is also regularly measured through computer paradigms developed idiosyncratically for certain research studies, all with the common goal of focusing attention to a target while filtering extraneous stimuli (e.g., Friedman-Hill et al., 2010). Variations on this theme are used to assess specific aspects of distractibility, with accuracy and reaction time (measured to the millisecond) often the outcome measures in such paradigms. Forster and Lavie (2008) demonstrated that stimuli completely unrelated to a task can be as distracting and interfere with task performance as much as a response-competing distractor. This finding is important because the task they developed has more external, ecological validity to everyday distractors that are most often completely irrelevant to our target task and only "compete" with the target because we become distracted by these irrelevant stimuli.

ADAPTIVE AND MALADAPTIVE FEATURES

The (Potential) Adaptive Side of Distractibility

As we have just reviewed, there appears to be a preponderance of evidence in support of a genetic predisposition for the development of distractibility. Not surprisingly, there are evolutionary theories that consider distractibility to be an inherited and potentially useful condition under certain circumstances, thus explaining its continued survival in the human gene pool. For example, Hartmann (2003) proposed the idea that distractibility—among other characteristics of ADHD—can be considered highly adaptive and useful and that it was critical for survival in our evolutionary, hunter-gatherer past. Shelley-Tremblay and Rosén (1996) also suggested that distractibility could be part of a set of adaptive genetic characteristics—including ADHD and aggressive behaviors more globally—that has been selected by the environment for survival. Distractible hunters, for example, would be more sensitive to noticing a sudden noise or flash of light potentially indicative of their prey and thus would more rapidly locate the prey. Therefore, hunters would be more successful when they were distracted by small potentially irrelevant stimuli that become relevant in the hunting context.

Hartmann (2003) also suggested that such abilities will be necessary in the future as new challenges emerge within our society. An empirical study of the advantages of distractibility showed that a novel sound preceding visual stimuli significantly reduced errors of omission in responding to the visual stimuli but only for individuals who were more distractible in the first place (van Mourik, Oosterlaan, Heslenfeld, Konig, & Sergeant, 2007). That is, the distracting, albeit informative, auditory information appeared to enhance their performance on the visual task relative to individuals with lower levels of distractibility. The distracted participants noticed the informative "distractors," but the nondistracted participants largely missed them and did not discern a pattern accordingly. Similarly, another study found that under instructions to ignore distractors (that were actually clues to solve a task), older adults who failed to ignore the distractors performed better than younger adults who ignored them (Kim, Hasher, & Zacks, 2007). Findings such as this may tie to research on inattentional blindness where a normative perceptual phenomenon exists such that individuals tend to fail to recognize an unexpected stimulus (e.g., a man in a gorilla suit walking through a group playing basketball), perhaps due to overfocusing on expected stimuli (e.g., counting how many times individuals dressed in white pass the ball; Simons & Chabris, 1999).

Distractibility may also help individuals be more creative. A plethora of popular press books espouse, based largely on anecdotes, how distracted children with attention problems and overactivity are only misunderstood, mislabeled creative children. Yet most such claims have been made in the absence of any empirical data. Recently, however, researchers have addressed this issue empirically and found support for the claim that distractibility may improve creativity. For example, one study found that engaging in an undemanding task that allows the mind to wander during an incubation period was related to better creativity than other conditions (including having a break) and that the mind wandering (i.e., internal distractibility) accounted for more variance in creative problem solving on the task than thinking about the task at hand during the incubation period (Baird et al., 2012). However, other research has shown that although distraction during an incubation period may improve accessibility to problem-solving content, it does not improve accuracy when specific answers are required (Zhong, Dijksterhuis, & Galinsky, 2008). Still, a period of unconscious distractibility may help individuals select their most creative idea (Ritter, van Baaren, & Dijksterhuis, 2012). Despite some of these findings supporting a role of distractibility in creativity, a study examining data from 16 studies using Bayesian t tests, which allow an assessment of the evidence for the null hypothesis, found no effect of distraction on creative decision making or problem solving (Newell & Rakow, 2011). Thus, despite the promise and popularity of the Baird et al. study and others, the jury is still out on the link between distractibility and creativity.

The Maladaptive Side of Distractibility

On the surface, distractibility may seem more innocuous than some of the other dark personality traits discussed in this book, such as narcissism and callousness, because it may bring to mind an unfocused kindergartner missing the story during circle time. Nevertheless, as noted at the start of this chapter, distractibility can meet with potentially calamitous consequences. Likewise, distractibility has many associated features that can be seriously maladaptive. For example, distractibility may contribute to a general sense of unhappiness. Killingsworth and Gilbert (2010) found that in most tasks, "people are thinking about what is not happening almost as often as they are thinking about what is" and that "doing so typically makes them unhappy" (p. 932). Along with distractibility being related to a general sense of malcontent, it is also connected with low rates of persistence and high levels of procrastination

(LaLonde, Powers, & Solanto, 2013). Perhaps it is no surprise, then, that distractibility/inattentiveness predicts a host of negative academic (e.g., more frequently retained a grade, lower academic achievement, greater high school dropout rates) and, later, occupational (e.g., job instability, poorer pay) outcomes (Barriga et al., 2002; Fredriksen et al., 2014). Similarly, distractibility and other symptoms of ADHD are linked to peer relationship problems and social isolation or rejection in childhood that appear to carry over into longstanding relationship problems during adulthood (Hoza, 2007). In fact, the general instability experienced by children with such problems places them on "a perhaps irreversible negative trajectory" (Hoza, 2007, p. 660).

Children and adolescents with a propensity toward distractibility are more likely to have not only an ADHD diagnosis but also other disruptive behavior disorders, such as oppositional defiant disorder or conduct disorder (Harty, Miller, Newcorn, & Halperin, 2009). Along those lines, potentially risky driving behaviors among teens and adults, including variable speed and lane-switching behavior, both of which are exacerbated by actions such as texting while driving, are associated with symptoms of ADHD like distractibility (Narad et al., 2013). Finally, distractibility itself is a symptom of an array of clinical diagnoses that are discussed further in the Clinical Implications section.

One may think, given the negative associations with distractibility/ inattentiveness, that individuals high in these traits would suffer from concomitant low self-esteem due to problems and failures. To the contrary, many individuals with high levels of distractibility/inattentiveness have what is often referred to as a positive illusory bias (PIB), or an inflated view of one's standing in some domain of functioning relative to the perceptions of others (e.g., Hoza et al., 2004) or relative to some objective criterion (e.g., test scores; Heath & Glen, 2005). When PIB is present, not only do impaired individuals fail to see their own impairments, they also view themselves as actually more competent than others by an absolute standard (Owens, Goldfine, Evangelista, Hoza, & Kaiser, 2007). Although several theories suggest possible causes for PIB, Dunning and colleagues imply that distractibility itself could contribute to the cause and have coined the phrase the *ignorance of incompetence* phenomenon to explain PIB (Dunning, Johnson, Ehrlinger, & Kruger, 2003, p. 83). Specifically, it is thought that individuals who are incompetent across specific domains simply lack awareness of deficits resulting from the deficits themselves (for a further discussion of PIB, see Chapter 12, this volume). Distractibility could be one such deficit in that highly inattentive individuals fail to attend to a feedback loop about their negative performance that is itself caused by distractibility. Without attending to the feedback about failures because they are distracted by other thoughts or events, there is no motivation for improvement or modification of the behaviors that were originally deficient (Owens et al., 2007). Thus, the problems themselves, as well as the illusion that all is better than it is, cycle on.

CLINICAL IMPLICATIONS

The symptoms of ADHD, which include distractibility/inattentiveness, have been shown to have a dimensional latent structure (Marcus & Barry, 2011) and thus occur on a continuum. Thus, distractibility is something that everyone experiences at some level under certain circumstances. Even for individuals who experience relatively low levels of distractibility compared with the general population, those specific experiences may still lead to impairment (remember the texting and driving example?). In addition, there are those individuals who are on the higher end of the continuum and experience clinically significant levels of distractibility that are frequent and severe. Nevertheless, even when frequent and severe, distractibility is a nonspecific symptom that is present in a variety of clinical disorders, which complicates differential diagnosis (First, 2014). Certainly, as discussed, distractibility and inattentiveness with an onset in early childhood are hallmarks of ADHD. Some specific ADHD symptoms that directly concern distractibility include failing to pay close attention, trouble holding attention, not listening when spoken to, not following through with instructions because sidetracked, not wanting to put forth sustained mental effort, being distracted, and being forgetful (American Psychiatric Association, 2013; World Health Organization, 1992). Distractibility is also a common presenting problem among patients with substance use, including both intoxication and withdrawal states (American Psychiatric Association, 2013; World Health Organization, 1992). In addition to the general tendency for individuals to feel less happy when distracted as described earlier (Killingsworth & Gilbert, 2010), distractibility assessed via laboratory experiments has been linked with major depressive disorder (Lemelin, Baruch, Vincent, Everett, & Vincent, 1997) and is associated with other internalizing disorders, including generalized anxiety disorder, acute stress disorder, and posttraumatic stress disorder (First, 2014). A differential diagnosis for symptoms of distractibility would also include bipolar disorder (i.e., distractibility is often associated with elevated mood; First, 2014) and schizophrenia or schizoaffective disorder (American Psychiatric Association, 2013). Finally, delirium, dementia, and a host of other neurocognitive disorders may be associated with the generalized symptom of distractibility. Given distractibility's association with such varied clinical disorders, it would be paramount to obtain data on the age of onset and the severity and persistence of distractibility, whether distractibility was triggered or exacerbated by external stimuli or stressors, the associated symptoms and features with which distractibility co-occurs, and the extent of clinically significant impairment or distress caused by distractibility to make a differential diagnosis. Of course, a clear assessment regarding use of prescription medications or illicit drugs as well as any general medication conditions is also important when determining the relevance of distractibility clinically (First, 2014).

DIRECTIONS FOR FUTURE RESEARCH

Because distractibility is a common general symptom or associated feature across so many clinical disorders, research on distractibility fits well with the strategic plan of the National Institute of Mental Health (NIMH) to focus on research domain criteria (RDoc; i.e., classifying psychopathology based on observable behavior and neurological/biological measures rather than diagnostic categories; NIMH, n.d.). Furthermore, attention (i.e., the opposite pole would be distractibility) is one of the constructs included on the NIMH's draft RDoc matrix (NIMH, n.d.). Thus, it would be well advised to use the construct of distractibility/inattentiveness to guide classification of patients for research studies when studying populations susceptible to distractibility. More research that is consistent with NIMH's RDoc, whether the research is funded by NIMH or not, would potentially inform clinical work—including differential diagnosis—with patients with distractibility.

The preponderance of research on distractibility has focused on external environmental distractors and additional research concerning internal distractors, such as mind wandering, is warranted, particularly given the ubiquitous nature of mind wandering (Forster & Lavie, 2014). Research has shown that a tendency toward sleepiness, being lost in thought, and daydreaming (often referred to as having a sluggish cognitive tempo) is a correlated but distinct factor from the inattention domain of ADHD that also relates independently to specific types of functional and neuropsychological impairment (Willcutt et al., 2014). Thus, more research should be conducted to better understand sluggish cognitive tempo, including how it may contribute to internal distractibility. Likewise, more studies on the differences in impact of task-relevant versus task-irrelevant distractors on selective attention are needed (Forster & Lavie, 2014).

More research is merited regarding the potential for cognitive overload and distractibility with the intentional division and diffusion of attention, given our current culture's reliance on so many electronic devices (Levine et al., 2012). Such device use may be causing chronic changes to the way we pay attention by developing "a cognitive style of short and shifting attention" that may be increasing distractibility (Levine, Waite, & Bowman, 2007, p. 565). Furthermore, it is imperative that future research clarifies the risk for dire, and even deadly, consequences of distraction, including finding ways to prevent such consequences (Levine et al., 2012).

SUMMARY AND CONCLUSIONS

In summary, distractibility is an interruption in selective attention caused by an inability to ignore extraneous stimuli—both external and internal. The correlates and potential causes of distractibility are numerous and include biologically based, environmental, and individual difference factors. Although distractibility/inattentiveness is a hallmark of ADHD, it is also a nonspecific symptom that occurs in a variety of clinical disorders. Despite some research suggesting there may be some positive outcomes (e.g., creativity) associated with distractibility, a propensity toward distractibility is linked clearly with many maladaptive outcomes—some distressing and irritating, some impeding and debilitating, and some potentially devastating. The latter point, combined with the fact that distractibility is ubiquitous and is something that we all encounter at some level in our everyday lives, makes future research and clinical attention on distractibility something we cannot ignore.

REFERENCES

American Psychiatric Association. (2013). *Diagnostic and statistical manual of mental disorders* (5th ed.). Arlington, VA: Author.

Baird, B., Smallwood, J., Mrazek, M. D., Kam, J. W., Franklin, M. S., & Schooler, J. W. (2012). Inspired by distraction: Mind wandering facilitates creative incubation. *Psychological Science, 23,* 1117–1122. http://dx.doi.org/10.1177/0956797612446024

Bandura, A. (1965). Influence of models' reinforcement contingencies on the acquisition of imitative responses. *Journal of Personality and Social Psychology, 1,* 589–595. http://dx.doi.org/10.1037/h0022070

Barkley, R. A. (2011). *Barkley adult ADHD rating scale—IV (BAARS–IV).* New York, NY: Guilford Press.

Barriga, A. Q., Doran, J. W., Newell, S. R., Morrison, E. M., Barbetti, V., & Robbins, B. D. (2002). Relationships between problem behaviors and academic achievement in adolescents: The unique role of attention problems. *Journal of Emotional and Behavioral Disorders, 10,* 233–240. http://dx.doi.org/10.1177/10634266020100040501

Barry, T. D., Dunlap, S. T., Cotten, S. J., Lochman, J. E., & Wells, K. C. (2005). The influence of maternal stress and distress on disruptive behavior problems in boys. *Journal of the American Academy of Child & Adolescent Psychiatry, 44,* 265–273. http://dx.doi.org/10.1097/00004583-200503000-00011

Berlin, L., Bohlin, G., Nyberg, L., & Janols, L. O. (2004). How well do measures of inhibition and other executive functions discriminate between children with ADHD and controls? *Child Neuropsychology, 10,* 1–13. http://dx.doi.org/10.1076/chin.10.1.1.26243

Berti, S., Grunwald, M., & Schröger, E. (2013). Age dependent changes of distractibility and reorienting of attention revisited: An event-related potential study. *Brain Research, 1491,* 156–166. http://dx.doi.org/10.1016/j.brainres.2012.11.009

Bisley, J. W., & Goldberg, M. E. (2006). Neural correlates of attention and distractibility in the lateral intraparietal area. *Journal of Neurophysiology, 95,* 1696–1717. http://dx.doi.org/10.1152/jn.00848.2005

Blaser, K. (2014). No mindfulness without self-boundaries. In K. Murata-Soraci (Ed.), *Psychology of mindfulness* (pp. 23–34). Hauppauge, NY: Nova Science.

Brunyé, T. T., Howe, J. L., Walker, L. A., & Mahoney, C. R. (2013). Acute bouts of endurance exercise increase distractibility to emotional stimuli. *International Journal of Sport Psychology, 44,* 471–492.

Conners, C. K. (2014a). *Conners CATA: Conners Continuous Auditory Test of Attention.* Toronto, Ontario, Canada: Multi-Health Systems.

Conners, C. K. (2014b). *Conners CPT3: Conners Continuous Performance Test* (3rd ed.). Toronto, Ontario, Canada: Multi-Health Systems.

Cuevas, K., & Bell, M. A. (2014). Infant attention and early childhood executive function. *Child Development, 85,* 397–404. http://dx.doi.org/10.1111/cdev.12126

Dunning, D., Johnson, K., Ehrlinger, J., & Kruger, J. (2003). Why people fail to recognize their own incompetence. *Current Directions in Psychological Science, 12,* 83–87. http://dx.doi.org/10.1111/1467-8721.01235

First, M. B. (2014). DSM–5 *handbook of differential diagnosis.* Arlington, VA: American Psychiatric Publishing.

Forster, S., & Lavie, N. (2008). Failures to ignore entirely irrelevant distractors: The role of load. *Journal of Experimental Psychology: Applied, 14,* 73–83. http://dx.doi.org/10.1037/1076-898X.14.1.73

Forster, S., & Lavie, N. (2014). Distracted by your mind? Individual differences in distractibility predict mind wandering. *Journal of Experimental Psychology: Learning, Memory, and Cognition, 40,* 251–260. http://dx.doi.org/10.1037/a0034108

Fredriksen, M., Dahl, A. A., Martinsen, E. W., Klungsoyr, O., Faraone, S. V., & Peleikis, D. E. (2014). Childhood and persistent ADHD symptoms associated with educational failure and long-term occupational disability in adult ADHD. *ADHD Attention Deficit Hyperactivity Disorders, 6,* 87–99. http://dx.doi.org/10.1007/s12402-014-0126-1

Frick, P. J., Barry, C. T., & Kamphaus, R. W. (2010). *Clinical assessment of child and adolescent personality and behavior* (3rd ed.). New York, NY: Springer Science+Business Media. http://dx.doi.org/10.1007/978-1-4419-0641-0

Friedman-Hill, S. R., Wagman, M. R., Gex, S. E., Pine, D. S., Leibenluft, E., & Unger-leider, L. G. (2010). What does distractibility in ADHD reveal about mechanisms for top-down attentional control? *Cognition, 115*, 93–103. http://dx.doi.org/10.1016/j.cognition.2009.11.013

Goodlad, J. K., Marcus, D. K., & Fulton, J. J. (2013). Lead and attention-deficit/hyperactivity disorder (ADHD) symptoms: A meta-analysis. *Clinical Psychology Review, 33*, 417–425. http://dx.doi.org/10.1016/j.cpr.2013.01.009

Harrison, J. R., Vannest, K., Davis, J., & Reynolds, C. (2012). Common problem behaviors of children and adolescents in general education classrooms in the United States. *Journal of Emotional and Behavioral Disorders, 20*, 55–64. http://dx.doi.org/10.1177/1063426611421157

Hartmann, T. (2003). *The Edison gene: ADHD and the gift of the hunter child.* Rochester, VT: Park Street Press.

Harty, S. C., Miller, C. J., Newcorn, J. H., & Halperin, J. M. (2009). Adolescents with childhood ADHD and comorbid disruptive behavior disorders: Aggression, anger, and hostility. *Child Psychiatry and Human Development, 40*, 85–97. http://dx.doi.org/10.1007/s10578-008-0110-0

Hasson, R., & Fine, J. G. (2012). Gender differences among children with ADHD on continuous performance tests: A meta-analytic review. *Journal of Attention Disorders, 16*, 190–198. http://dx.doi.org/10.1177/1087054711427398

Hawkey, E., & Nigg, J. T. (2014). Omega-3 fatty acid and ADHD: Blood level analysis and meta-analytic extension of supplementation trials. *Clinical Psychology Review, 34*, 496–505. http://dx.doi.org/10.1016/j.cpr.2014.05.005

Heath, N. L., & Glen, T. (2005). Positive illusory bias and the self-protective hypothesis in children with learning disabilities. *Journal of Clinical Child and Adolescent Psychology, 34*, 272–281. http://dx.doi.org/10.1207/s15374424jccp3402_6

Hoza, B. (2007). Peer functioning in children with ADHD. *Journal of Pediatric Psychology, 32*, 655–663. http://dx.doi.org/10.1093/jpepsy/jsm024

Hoza, B., Gerdes, A. C., Hinshaw, S. P., Arnold, L. E., Pelham, W. E., Jr., Molina, B. S. G., . . . Wigal, T. (2004). Self-perceptions of competence in children with ADHD and comparison children. *Journal of Consulting and Clinical Psychology, 72*, 382–391. http://dx.doi.org/10.1037/0022-006X.72.3.382

Huelsman, T. J., Gagnon, S., Kidder-Ashley, P., & Griggs, M. (2014). Preschool temperament assessment: A quantitative assessment of the validity of Behavioral Style Questionnaire data. *Early Education and Development, 25*, 71–92. http://dx.doi.org/10.1080/10409289.2013.770636

Kalkut, E. L., Han, S. D., Lansing, A. E., Holdnack, J. A., & Delis, D. C. (2009). Development of set-shifting ability from late childhood through early adulthood. *Archives of Clinical Neuropsychology, 24*, 565–574. http://dx.doi.org/10.1093/arclin/acp048

Kareklas, I., & Muehling, D. D. (2014). Addressing the texting and driving epidemic: Mortality salience priming effects on attitudes and behavioral intentions. *Journal of Consumer Affairs, 48,* 223–250. http://dx.doi.org/10.1111/joca.12039

Kendler, K. S., & Neale, M. C. (2010). Endophenotype: A conceptual analysis. *Molecular Psychiatry, 15,* 789–797. http://dx.doi.org/10.1038/mp.2010.8

Killingsworth, M. A., & Gilbert, D. T. (2010). A wandering mind is an unhappy mind. *Science, 330,* 932. http://dx.doi.org/10.1126/science.1192439

Kim, S., Hasher, L., & Zacks, R. T. (2007). Aging and a benefit of distractibility. *Psychonomic Bulletin & Review, 14,* 301–305. http://dx.doi.org/10.3758/BF03194068

Korkman, M., Kirk, U., & Kemp, S. (2007). *NEPSY–II: A developmental neuropsychological assessment* (2nd ed.). San Antonio, TX: Harcourt Assessment.

Kuntsi, J., Pinto, R., Price, T. S., van der Meere, J. J., Frazier-Wood, A. C., & Asherson, P. (2014). The separation of ADHD inattention and hyperactivity-impulsivity symptoms: Pathways from genetic effects to cognitive impairments and symptoms. *Journal of Abnormal Child Psychology, 42,* 127–136. http://dx.doi.org/10.1007/s10802-013-9771-7

LaLonde, M. M., Powers, L., & Solanto, M. V. (2013). A 26-year-old male with distractibility, disorganization, and chronic unemployment. *Psychiatric Annals, 43,* 15–19. http://dx.doi.org/10.3928/00485713-20130109-04

Lemelin, S., Baruch, P., Vincent, A., Everett, J., & Vincent, P. (1997). Distractibility and processing resource deficit in major depression. Evidence for two deficient attentional processing models. *Journal of Nervous and Mental Disease, 185,* 542–548. http://dx.doi.org/10.1097/00005053-199709000-00002

Levine, L. E., Waite, B. M., & Bowman, L. L. (2007). Electronic media use, reading, and academic distractibility in college youth. *CyberPsychology & Behavior, 10,* 560–566. http://dx.doi.org/10.1089/cpb.2007.9990

Levine, L. E., Waite, B. M., & Bowman, L. L. (2012). Mobile media use, multitasking and distractibility. *International Journal of Cyber Behavior, Psychology and Learning, 2,* 15–29. http://dx.doi.org/10.4018/ijcbpl.2012070102

Linares, L. O., Li, M., Shrout, P. E., Ramirez-Gaite, M., Hope, S., Albert, A., & Castellanos, F. X. (2010). The course of inattention and hyperactivity/impulsivity symptoms after foster placement. *Pediatrics, 125,* e489–e498. http://dx.doi.org/10.1542/peds.2009-1285

Loe, I. M., Lee, E. S., & Feldman, H. M. (2013). Attention and internalizing behaviors in relation to white matter in children born preterm. *Journal of Developmental and Behavioral Pediatrics, 34,* 156–164. http://dx.doi.org/10.1097/DBP.0b013e3182842122

Mackie, D. (2014, June 13). You'll never text and drive again after watching this PSA. *People.* Retrieved from http://www.people.com/article/volkswagen-texting-while-driving-psa-hong-kong

Marcus, D. K., & Barry, T. D. (2011). Does attention-deficit/hyperactivity disorder have a dimensional latent structure? A taxometric analysis. *Journal of Abnormal Psychology, 120*, 427–442. http://dx.doi.org/10.1037/a0021405

Narad, M., Garner, A. A., Brassell, A. A., Saxby, D., Antonini, T. N., O'Brien, K. M., . . . Epstein, J. N. (2013). Impact of distraction on the driving performance of adolescents with and without attention-deficit/hyperactivity disorder. *JAMA Pediatrics, 167*, 933–938. http://dx.doi.org/10.1001/jamapediatrics. 2013.322

National Highway Traffic Safety Administration. (n.d.). *What is distracted driving?* Retrieved from http://www.distraction.gov/content/get-the-facts/facts-and-statistics.html

National Institute of Mental Health. (n.d.). *NIMH research domain criteria.* Retrieved from http://www.nimh.nih.gov/research-priorities/rdoc/nimh-research-domain-criteria-rdoc.shtml

Newell, B. R., & Rakow, T. (2011). Revising beliefs about the merit of unconscious thought: Evidence in favor of the null hypothesis. *Social Cognition, 29*, 711–726. http://dx.doi.org/10.1521/soco.2011.29.6.711

Owens, J. S., Goldfine, M. E., Evangelista, N. M., Hoza, B., & Kaiser, N. M. (2007). A critical review of self-perceptions and the positive illusory bias in children with ADHD. *Clinical Child and Family Psychology Review, 10*, 335–351. http://dx.doi.org/10.1007/s10567-007-0027-3

Paulhus, D. L., Aks, D. J., & Coren, S. (1990). Independence of performance and self-report measures of distractibility. *The Journal of Social Psychology, 130*, 781–787. http://dx.doi.org/10.1080/00224545.1990.9924630

Pozuelos, J. P., Paz-Alonso, P. M., Castillo, A., Fuentes, L. J., & Rueda, M. R. (2014). Development of attention networks and their interactions in childhood. *Developmental Psychology, 50*, 2405–2415. http://dx.doi.org/10.1037/a0037469

Rajendran, K., Rindskopf, D., O'Neill, S., Marks, D. J., Nomura, Y., & Halperin, J. M. (2013). Neuropsychological functioning and severity of ADHD in early childhood: A four-year cross-lagged study. *Journal of Abnormal Psychology, 122*, 1179–1188. http://dx.doi.org/10.1037/a0034237

Randolph, C. (2012). *Repeatable battery for the assessment of neuropsychological status update (RBANS Update).* San Antonio, TX: Psychological Corporation.

Reitan, R. M., & Wolfson, D. (1993). *The Halstead-Reitan neuropsychological test battery: Theory and clinical interpretation* (2nd ed.). South Tucson, AZ: Neuropsychology Press.

Ritter, S. M., van Baaren, R. B., & Dijksterhuis, A. (2012). Creativity: The role of unconscious processes in idea generation and idea selection. *Thinking Skills and Creativity, 7*, 21–27. http://dx.doi.org/10.1016/j.tsc.2011.12.002

Robertson, I. H., Ward, T., Ridgeway, V., & Nimmo-Smith, I. (1994). *Test of everyday attention.* London, England: Psychological Corporation.

Rothbart, M. K., Ahadi, S. A., Hershey, K. L., & Fisher, P. (2001). Investigations of temperament at three to seven years: The Children's Behavior Questionnaire. *Child Development, 72,* 1394–1408. http://dx.doi.org/10.1111/1467-8624.00355

Sagiv, S. K., Epstein, J. N., Bellinger, D. C., & Korrick, S. A. (2013). Pre- and postnatal risk factors for ADHD in a nonclinical pediatric population. *Journal of Attention Disorders, 17,* 47–57. http://dx.doi.org/10.1177/1087054711427563

Shelley-Tremblay, J. F., & Rosén, L. A. (1996). Attention-deficit/hyperactivity disorder: An evolutionary perspective. *The Journal of Genetic Psychology: Research and Theory on Human Development, 157,* 443–453. http://dx.doi.org/10.1080/00221325.1996.9914877

Silver, L. (2004). *Attention-deficit/hyperactivity disorder: A clinical guide to diagnosis and treatment for health and mental health professionals* (3rd ed.). Washington, DC: American Psychiatric Press.

Simons, D. J., & Chabris, C. F. (1999). Gorillas in our midst: Sustained inattentional blindness for dynamic events. *Perception, 28,* 1059–1074. http://dx.doi.org/10.1068/p2952

Stevenson, J., Buitelaar, J., Cortese, S., Ferrin, M., Konofal, E., Lecendreux, M., . . . Sonuga-Barke, E. (2014). Research review: The role of diet in the treatment of attention-deficit/hyperactivity disorder—An appraisal of the evidence on efficacy and recommendations on the design of future studies. *Journal of Child Psychology and Psychiatry, 55,* 416–427. http://dx.doi.org/10.1111/jcpp.12215

Stone, A. (2014, June 11). If you've ever texted while driving, you should see this. *Huffington Post.* Retrieved from http://www.huffingtonpost.com/2014/06/10/volkswagen-distracted-driving_n_5482847.html

Suzuki, M., & Gottlieb, J. (2013). Distinct neural mechanisms of distractor suppression in the frontal and parietal lobe. *Nature Neuroscience, 16,* 98–104. http://dx.doi.org/10.1038/nn.3282

Thissen, A. J., Rommelse, N. N., Altink, M. E., Oosterlaan, J., & Buitelaar, J. K. (2014). Parent-of-origin effects in ADHD: Distinct influences of paternal and maternal ADHD on neuropsychological functioning in offspring. *Journal of Attention Disorders, 18,* 521–531. http://dx.doi.org/10.1177/1087054712443159

Thomas, A., & Chess, S. (1977). *Temperament and development.* Oxford, England: Brunner/Mazel.

van Mourik, R., Oosterlaan, J., Heslenfeld, D. J., Konig, C. E., & Sergeant, J. A. (2007). When distraction is not distracting: A behavioral and ERP study on distraction in ADHD. *Clinical Neurophysiology, 118,* 1855–1865. http://dx.doi.org/10.1016/j.clinph.2007.05.007

Volkow, N. D., Wang, G. J., Fowler, J. S., & Ding, Y. S. (2005). Imaging the effects of methylphenidate on brain dopamine: New model on its therapeutic actions for attention-deficit/hyperactivity disorder. *Biological Psychiatry, 57,* 1410–1415. http://dx.doi.org/10.1016/j.biopsych.2004.11.006

Willcutt, E. G., Chhabildas, N., Kinnear, M., DeFries, J. C., Olson, R. K., Leopold, D. R., . . . Pennington, B. F. (2014). The internal and external validity of sluggish cognitive tempo and its relation with *DSM–IV* ADHD. *Journal of Abnormal Child Psychology, 42*, 21–35. http://dx.doi.org/10.1007/s10802-013-9800-6

World Health Organization. (1992). *The* ICD–10 *classification of mental and behavioural disorders: Clinical descriptions and diagnostic guidelines*. Geneva, Switzerland: Author.

Yates, T. M., Obradovic, J., & Egeland, B. (2010). Transactional relations across contextual strain, parenting quality, and early childhood regulation and adaptation in a high-risk sample. *Development and Psychopathology, 22*, 539–555. http://dx.doi.org/10.1017/S095457941000026X

Zhong, C. B., Dijksterhuis, A., & Galinsky, A. D. (2008). The merits of unconscious thought in creativity. *Psychological Science, 19*, 912–918. http://dx.doi.org/10.1111/j.1467-9280.2008.02176.x

III

RIGIDITY

10

DEEP, DARK, AND DYSFUNCTIONAL: THE DESTRUCTIVENESS OF INTERPERSONAL PERFECTIONISM

GORDON L. FLETT, PAUL L. HEWITT, AND SIMON S. SHERRY

Perfectionists are generally portrayed as people who desire social approval and recognition; they are seen typically in positive terms as goal-directed people who engage in forms of striving that reflect the shared goals of individualistic, achievement-oriented societies. Unfortunately, this highly sanitized view fails to take into account some problematic aspects of perfectionism. Our goal in the current chapter is to advance the theme of "perfectionism as destructive" by examining it within the context of interpersonal perfectionism. Our willingness to characterize interpersonal perfectionism as "deep, dark, and dysfunctional" reflects our conviction that although interpersonal perfectionism is deeply ingrained in perfectionists, it can be a dark orientation, especially when it is combined with other dark elements. We do this with the full realization that the notion that perfectionism has a dark side is a theme that may come as a surprise to many readers. First, extreme perfectionism involves a sense of compulsiveness and a sense of being driven to the extent that the person cannot stop striving

http://dx.doi.org/10.1037/14854-011
The Dark Side of Personality: Science and Practice in Social, Personality, and Clinical Psychology, V. Zeigler-Hill and D. K. Marcus (Editors)

and thinking about the need to be perfect. Perfectionists do not simply wish for perfection. Rather, they feel that they "must" be perfect, and this same sense of insistence and urgency applies when they require other people to be perfect.

Second, extreme perfectionists tend to be rigid and inflexible in their thoughts, feelings, and actions. Thus, they attempt to be perfect even when doing so is neither relevant nor required. This inability to be flexible and tailor one's thoughts, feelings, and actions to the situation is a primary indicator of personality dysfunction. This rigidity and inability to be flexible can become generalized and other-directed in ways that alienate other people.

Finally, an emphasis on perfectionism as desirable does not allow for the less socially desirable interpersonal aspects of perfectionism, including the tendency for many disagreeable perfectionists to demand perfection from other people. Research has confirmed that underlying such demands is a strong desire for control (for a review, see Flett, Hewitt, Blankstein, & Mosher, 1995). We emphasize this need for control because the potential for perfectionism to have a discernible dark side becomes much more apparent when perfectionism is paired with an overcontrolling nature. When these attributes are found among overcontrolling perfectionists who have considerable power and influence, such as Steve Jobs or Gordon Ramsay, it is a troubling combination that can greatly influence the lives of other people. Biographical and autobiographical accounts of Jobs and Ramsay contain numerous descriptions of their tendency to be self-involved yet still demand absolute perfection from others; this tendency is often combined with a narcissistic tendency to react harshly when others fall short of these expectations.

Two things become evident when we consider case accounts of extremely perfectionistic people. First, the interpersonal side of perfectionists is quite salient and poses profound problems for many perfectionists and the people around them. Indeed, interpersonal perfectionism often serves as a stress generator that creates conflict and problems in relationships and organizations (e.g., Flett & Hewitt, 2006; Mackinnon et al., 2012). Problems ensue when the interpersonal perfectionist is critical of others and when people who perceive that they are the target of socially prescribed perfectionism feel threatened and controlled by imposed expectations.

Second, there is heterogeneity among perfectionists such that two perfectionists can differ substantially in the nature of their perfectionism as well as the factors that coexist with their perfectionism and that contribute to their perfectionism. This heterogeneity is important to acknowledge because it sets up one of our basic premises in this chapter, which is that there is an identifiable subset of perfectionists who are angry, highly disagreeable, hostile, and potentially antisocial. These individuals are often narcissistically self-focused on their own goals and are driven to attain them no matter the cost. This narcissism involves heightened grandiosity that is underscored by narcissistic vulnerability (e.g., Flett, Sherry, Hewitt, & Nepon, 2014; Nealis, Sherry, Sherry, Stewart, & Macneil, 2015; see also Chapter 1, this volume). They often have little empathy or consideration for other people. When other people do garner attention, they can be objects of scorn who are seen as competitors and human obstacles to the success of the perfectionist. This orientation can apply to the hypercompetitive, elite perfectionistic athlete who will do whatever it takes to win, including using performance-enhancing substances (Flett & Hewitt, 2014), but it can also apply to the driven student who must get accepted into the best schools even if it means having to be Machiavellian and doing whatever it takes to be successful (for a review of Machiavellianism, see Chapter 4, this volume).

The examples of the "success at any cost" athlete and the driven, determined student are mild in comparison to some of the most heinous and extreme illustrations of the dark side of perfectionism. An extreme illustration of "dark perfectionism" was provided in the 2014 movie *Whiplash*, which portrayed the tyrannical perfectionism and abusiveness of a music teacher named Fletcher who was played by actor J. K. Simmons. This movie was inspired by high school experiences of the movie's director, Damien Chazelle. Unfortunately, there are several "real-life" accounts of perfectionists who have engaged in antisocial and sometimes murderous acts. For instance, mathematics professor Walter Petryshyn was charged with murdering his wife Arcadia in 1996 after bludgeoning her to death. According to media accounts, the perfectionistic Petryshyn was agitated in anticipation of being ridiculed by colleagues for making what turned out to be a minor mistake in his textbook. Petryshyn was eventually found not guilty by reason of insanity. Apparently, he developed a psychotic depression after sensing that Arcadia was going to have him committed (Wynnyckyj, 1997).

The dark side of perfectionism is also on display among the ranks of terrorists. One notorious example is Theodore Kaczynski, the Unabomber. Kaczynski expressed his upset with intrusive technological developments by sending mail bombs that resulted in the deaths of three people and injuries to 29 others. Adlerian analyses of Kaczynski focus on his behaviors as a classic example of what happens in extreme cases when a person expresses the superiority complex as a deep form of overcompensation (Leeper, Carwile, & Huber, 2002). Kaczynski belittled others in a way that ironically suggests he expected others to be perfect, but he regarded them as far from perfect. Kaczynski, a former mathematics professor, is a methodical and exacting perfectionist as symbolized by the precision he used to craft the bombs he sent to unsuspecting recipients. His isolation also stands as an example of perfectionistic social disconnection.

There are other examples of antisocial, sadistic perfectionists. We learned in 2010 of Colonel Russell Williams, who sadistically raped and killed two women in Canada after he had committed sexual assaults against other women and had broken into the homes of dozens of girls and women (Appleby, 2011). Williams is someone with a long history of being a meticulous, methodical planner and an impeccable dresser. There are suggestions his perfectionism was part of an obsessive-compulsive personality disorder (see Appleby, 2011). Perhaps his perfectionism served Williams well in his former role as commander of a large Canadian Forces base, but when it was combined with his malevolent and sadistic urges, it contributed to one of the clearest displays of dark, dysfunctional perfectionism. The double life of Williams should be kept in mind later in this chapter when we discuss how presenting oneself as perfect can be a facade that covers up socially unacceptable aspects of the self.

Other case accounts further illustrate the anger and hostility found in certain perfectionists. Albert Ellis (2002) described John, a man who was set to get "a double divorce" because both his wife and his business partners had become exasperated by his perfectionistic demands and tendency to become enraged when others fell short of his expectations. Flett and Hewitt (2001) described a narcissistic, perfectionistic spouse abuser who threw his former wife through a glass door. This narcissistic perfectionist often reminded his former wife that he was perfect and, according to him, the only mistake he had ever made was marrying her.

All of these examples described men. Frei, Völlm, Graf, and Dittmann (2006) showed in their analysis of a perfectionistic female serial killer that perfectionism can also fuel the violence committed by women. At the root of this serial killer's violence was her other-oriented tendency to abhor weakness in other women. She was surprised when one of her victims did not die because she prided herself on being a thorough, competent perfectionist.

These case accounts are consistent with a growing empirical literature linking personal and interpersonal perfectionism with personality dysfunction, including the features of the dark triad described by Paulhus and Williams (2002). We summarize this literature to illustrate the deep, dark, and dysfunctional aspects of interpersonal perfectionism. First, we provide an overview of our conceptual model of personal and interpersonal perfectionism. We then discuss how classic observations by Adler (1938/1998) and Horney (1950) help account for the dark side of certain perfectionists.

DEFINITION AND BACKGROUND

Multidimensional Perfectionism: An Expanded Conceptualization

The concept of multidimensional perfectionism was introduced in 1990 by separate research teams (Frost, Marten, Lahart, & Rosenblate, 1990; Hewitt & Flett, 1990). Our current analysis focuses on the framework advanced by

Hewitt and Flett (1991). Initially, they described three trait dimensions—self-oriented, other-oriented, and socially prescribed. Self-oriented perfectionism includes a strong motivation to be perfect, setting unrealistic self-standards, compulsive striving, and dichotomous thinking where only total success or total failure exist as outcomes. Although self-oriented perfectionism is characterized by some authors as "adaptive," as noted earlier, extreme self-oriented perfectionism involves a form of all-or-none thinking and sense of being driven that can prove exhausting for perfectionists and people in their lives. Extreme self-oriented perfectionism is often at the root of extreme work addiction.

Other-oriented perfectionism involves exacting standards for other people and is often accompanied by the tendency to be extrapunitive and hostile toward others. Initial scale development research showed that other-oriented perfectionism is linked with domineering and authoritarian tendencies along with narcissistic features including a sense of entitlement and a tendency to blame others (Hewitt & Flett, 1991). Although five-factor model analyses typically link other-oriented perfectionism with heightened disagreeableness (Hill, McIntire, & Bacharach, 1997), our conceptualization of people who have extreme levels of other-oriented perfectionism focus on an extrapunitive form of hostility that goes well beyond describing someone as disagreeable.

Socially prescribed perfectionism is defined as the generalized perception that others demand perfection from the self. Individuals with high levels of this orientation are hypersensitive to criticism and have a strong need for approval (Hewitt & Flett, 1991). Socially prescribed perfectionism tends to be accompanied by deficits in trait self-control (Tangney, Baumeister, & Boone, 2004) and cognitive emotional regulation (Rudolph, Flett, & Hewitt, 2007). This sense of being chronically exposed to unfair, extreme pressure promotes resentment and anger as well as helplessness and hopelessness due to the feeling that it is impossible to please people who are exceptionally demanding.

Hewitt et al. (2003) introduced the construct of perfectionistic self-presentation as a supplement to the focus on trait perfectionism. Perfectionistic self-presentation is a maladaptive interpersonal style with three facets: perfectionistic self-promotion, nondisplay of imperfection, and nondisclosure of imperfection. Perfectionistic self-promotion involves actively displaying and proclaiming one's "perfection." This perfectionistic self-promotion is motivated by self-image goals and can take many forms including having perfect appearance and manners but also projecting a picture of being flawlessly capable, moral, socially skilled, and highly successful. The purpose of trying to seem perfect is to maximize recognition, admiration, and respect. Unfortunately, perfectionistic self-promoters seem unaware of how their behaviors alienate other people. This self-presentational style is seen as pathologically driven and interpersonally aversive in ways that can create interpersonal stress.

The other facets of perfectionistic self-presentation reflect the need to minimize and not display or disclose any imperfections that reveal that the individual is "less than perfect." Mistakes and shortcomings are covered up, and situations that might reveal imperfections are avoided. People with this interpersonal style respond quite strongly in terms of negative emotional and physiological reactions when they are required to describe the biggest mistakes they ever made (Hewitt, Habke, Lee-Baggley, Sherry, & Flett, 2008).

When it comes to perfectionistic self-presentation, the public image of people highly invested in this style may represent a facade that entirely covers up their true nature. Extreme forms of perfectionistic self-presentation displayed by someone with reasonable social skills can resemble a chameleon-like form of behavior that conceals the true self. Most accounts of the perfectionistic self-presenter portray defensive people who are hiding undesirable aspect of themselves due to a sense of shame and inadequacy. We maintain that there is also a subset of perfectionistic self-presenters who are fueled by hostility, hypercompetitiveness, and darker urges, and—at least on the surface—an inflated sense of self. As we see next, classic theorists allowed for the dark side of perfectionists.

The Dark Side of Perfectionism: The Views of Adler and Horney

Adler (1938/1998) argued that feelings of inferiority are a basic element of human existence that everyone experiences and that we all strive to overcome feelings of inferiority by striving for perfection and superiority. He posited that some people develop a superiority complex that can involve a complete lack of social interest as the individual "aims for the glitter of personal conquest" (p. 38). The superiority complex involves a conscious sense of possessing superhuman abilities and a tendency to make extreme demands of self and others while striving for godlike perfection. Adler (1938/1998) posited that these individuals are "perpetually comparing themselves with the unattainable ideal of perfection, are always possessed and spurred on by a sense of inferiority" (pp. 35–36).

Horney's (1950) observations seem most relevant when considering the darker aspects of perfectionism. She saw perfectionism as rooted not only in anxiety and fear but also based deeply in hostility and resentment. According to Horney, neurosis reflects early life experiences that give rise to basic anxiety and hostility. Basic anxiety is a fear of helplessness and worries about abandonment. It occurs if important needs are not met. Many children also develop basic hostility as a response to parental indifference and neglect or more overt forms of mistreatment, but this hostility is often concealed due to the anticipated negative consequences of expressing it.

Horney posited further that neurosis underscores 10 neurotic needs that reflect our conflicting desires to simultaneously move toward people, away from people, and against people. The neurotic need for perfection and unassailability is one of these needs. Horney (1945/1972) suggested that one way to resolve neurotic conflicts is to create an idealized image of the perfect self that can perhaps be attained at some point. This idealized image can be taken to the extreme, as shown by an abiding sense of infallibility that characterizes figures such as Adolf Hitler (Langer, 1972; Waite, 1972). Horney (1950) emphasized the compulsive striving for glory that can result in an utter disregard for the self and others. Clearly, Horney emphasized the folly of striving for perfection, which she characterized as dooming an individual to failure and reflecting an intolerable life situation that restricts personal development.

Regarding other-oriented perfectionism, Horney (1945/1972) suggested that addressing neurotic conflicts via perfectionism often takes the form of "swinging those standards as a whip over others" (p. 113). She noted further that

> a person may impose his standards upon others and make relentless demands to *their* perfection. The more he feels himself to be the measure of all things, the more he *insists*—not upon general perfection but upon his particular norms being measured up to. The failure of others to do so arouses his contempt or anger. (Horney, 1950, p. 78)

Robinson (2000) echoed these sentiments in his description of the workaholic perfectionist who is hypercritical of the self and other people. He noted that "both the self and others are judged unmercifully. . . . Because of these superhuman standards, failure and anger at others for not meeting high standards are superhuman companions" (p. 49).

REVIEW OF RELEVANT LITERATURE

Perfectionism in Anger and Hostility

Consistent with Horney's analysis, links between perfectionism and self-reported anger and hostility have indeed been documented (e.g., Hewitt & Flett, 1991; Wiebe & McCabe, 2002). These self-report studies have been supplemented by experimental work showing that perfectionists experience hostility after making mistakes in an ego-involving task situation (Besser, Flett, & Hewitt, 2004).

Hostile perfectionism is best illustrated by interpersonal circumplex analyses of perfectionism. The interpersonal circumplex is a circle of interpersonal styles that involves two major dimensions (Wiggins & Broughton,

1985). The first dimension involves themes of love, warmth, and nurturance at one end versus being interpersonally cold and quarrelsome at the other end. The other main axis or dimension reflects being dominant and ambitious at one end or pole versus lazy and submissive at the other end. The interpersonal circumplex is further divided into eight major octants that represent blends of the nurturance and dominance dimensions.

How does the interpersonal circumplex relate to perfectionism? Hill, Zrull, and Turlington (1997) administered the Multidimensional Perfectionism Scale (Hewitt & Flett, 1991) and two interpersonal circumplex measures to university students. Men who were high in self-oriented and other-oriented perfectionism tended to have hostile and dominant interpersonal traits. Self-oriented perfectionism in women was less problematic such that it was linked with an overly nurturant interpersonal style. However, other-oriented perfectionism in women was linked with the same hostile and dominant interpersonal tendencies found among men. Overall, the evidence suggested self-oriented and other-oriented perfectionists have rigid and extreme interpersonal styles. Finally, socially prescribed perfectionism in men was "associated with arrogant, socially distant, and maladaptive interpersonal characteristics for men, similar to other-oriented perfectionism" (Hill, Zrull, et al., 1997, p. 100) as well as a diverse array of interpersonal problems for women.

Slaney, Pincus, Uliaszek, and Wang (2006) reported that those people who fell short of their need to be perfect were characterized by greater interpersonal problems and interpersonal distress. Supplementary analyses distinguished two perfectionistic types: friendly, submissive perfectionists and hostile perfectionists. Hostile perfectionists had a marked tendency to see their partners as falling short of their demanding expectations. Wiebe and McCabe (2002) reported data showing in the relationship context that hostility is linked with other-directed relationship perfectionism, and related research shows that other-directed relationship perfectionism is linked with trait disagreeableness and relationship dissatisfaction (Matte & Lafontaine, 2012).

Perfectionism and Personality Disorder and Dysfunction

Although our focus is primarily on multidimensional perfectionism, recent work with unidimensional measures of rigid self-oriented perfectionism shows that this kind of perfectionism can also be quite dysfunctional in ways that have interpersonal consequences. For instance, a study with clinical outpatients linked perfectionism with intense anger and a related tendency to bear grudges and retaliate for perceived wrongs (Ansell et al., 2010). Similarly, Wright et al. (2012) found that rigid perfectionism was linked with the narcissistic grandiosity and narcissistic vulnerability described by Pincus et al. (2009). There was also a link with dysfunctional interpersonal style of being cold and domineering as assessed by the interpersonal circumplex. Finally, a study with 434 adolescents found that rigid perfectionism was correlated with narcissism, disagreeableness, irritable and aggressive traits, dominance, compulsivity, and externalizing symptoms (De Clercq et al., 2014).

Ayearst, Flett, and Hewitt (2012) documented how perfectionism has a more pervasive role in personality dysfunction when the interpersonal perfectionism dimensions are considered. Our work on multidimensional perfectionism and personality disorder began when Hewitt and Flett (1991) explored the correlates of the Millon Clinical Multiaxial Inventory (MCMI) subscales. We found few significant associations involving self-oriented perfectionism. However, other-oriented perfectionism was linked with the MCMI personality disorder subscales tapping histrionic, narcissistic, and antisocial personalities (rs ranging from .26 to .31). Socially prescribed perfectionism was associated robustly with borderline, passive-aggressive, avoidant, schizotypal, and schizoid personality patterns. A subsequent study of Minnesota Multiphasic Personality Inventory personality disorder correlates in 90 psychiatric patients found that other-oriented perfectionism was associated significantly with 8 of 11 subscales, including antisocial, histrionic, narcissistic, and passive-aggressive personality disorder subscales (Hewitt, Flett, & Turnbull, 1992). Socially prescribed perfectionism was associated significantly with antisocial personality disorder, and paranoid personality disorder from Cluster A, and other Cluster C subscales (i.e., avoidant, compulsive, dependent, and passive aggressive).

This research has primarily examined personality disorder symptoms instead of people with personality disorder diagnoses. However, people with borderline personality disorder diagnoses tend to have elevated levels of socially prescribed perfectionism (Hewitt, Flett, & Turnbull, 1994). Similarly, McCown and Carlson's (2004) analysis of cocaine abusers undergoing treatment linked narcissistic personality disorder with other-oriented and socially prescribed perfectionism. Most notably, antisocial personality disorder was associated with levels of other-oriented perfectionism that substantially exceeded clinical norms (Hewitt & Flett, 2004), which suggests that some other-oriented perfectionists are highly punitive toward others and that they do so without conscience or empathy for those individuals. This pattern fits with accounts of perfectionistic spouse abusers with clear features of narcissism who demand perfection from others and who will use extrapunitive behavior to "correct" partners whom they deem to be flawed (see Flett & Hewitt, 2001; Lohr, Hamberger, & Bonge, 1988; Rothschild, Dimson, Storaasli, & Clapp, 1997).

Research by Sherry, Hewitt, Flett, Lee-Baggley, and Hall (2007) on perfectionism and personality disorder symptoms is particularly noteworthy because of its broad assessment of the perfectionism construct. Sherry et al. (2007) conducted two studies in which undergraduates completed the Multidimensional Perfectionism Scale (MPS; Hewitt & Flett, 1991, 2004) and the Perfectionistic Self-Presentation Scale (PSPS; Hewitt et al., 2003). One sample of 532 students also completed the Personality Disorder Questionnaire—4+ (PDQ–4; Hyler, 1994), whereas another 350 students completed the Dimensional Assessment of Personality Pathology (DAPP; Livesley, Jackson, & Schroeder, 1992). In the first sample, all six perfectionism measures (the three MPS and the three PSPS subscales) were associated significantly with the Cluster A, Cluster B, and Cluster C summary measures. The second sample showed extensive links between perfectionism and the DAPP pathology measures. For instance, a higher order measure of dissociality was associated significantly with other-oriented perfectionism, socially prescribed perfectionism, and all PSPS facets. Similarly, dysregulation was linked robustly with socially prescribed perfectionism and all PSPS facets (rs ranging from .37 to .55).

Stoeber (2014b) examined the association between trait perfectionism dimensions and the various scales from the Personality Inventory for *DSM–5* (PID–5; Krueger, Derringer, Markon, Watson, & Skodol, 2012) in over 300 students. This inventory taps five broad personality domains (negative affect, detachment, antagonism, disinhibition, and psychoticism). Socially prescribed perfectionism was associated with all five personality disorder domains. Other-oriented perfectionism was associated predominantly with the higher order measure of antagonism and subscales tapping hostility, callousness, deceitfulness, manipulativeness, and narcissistic grandiosity. These results once again indicate that interpersonal perfectionism has pervasive links with personal and interpersonal dysfunction.

Perfectionism and the Dark Triad

Research is beginning to accumulate concerning perfectionism and the components of the Dark Triad (i.e., Machiavellianism, narcissism, and psychopathy). Some of the case accounts outlined earlier point to the need to consider whether there exist certain individuals who are characterized jointly by angry forms of other-directed perfectionism along with features of the Dark Triad; in such instances, perfectionism would provide a tendency to plan and an antisocial form of striving that includes an active willingness to put dark plans into action.

One of our first studies relevant to the Dark Triad focused on the associations among Machiavellianism, trait perfectionism, and perfectionistic self-presentation in 483 undergraduates (Sherry, Hewitt, Besser, Flett, & Klein, 2006). Machiavellianism in men was associated with socially prescribed perfectionism and all facets of perfectionistic self-presentation. The same associations were found among women along with an association with other-oriented perfectionism. The links with perfectionistic self-presentation and Machiavellianism were stronger among women. Furthermore, socially prescribed perfectionism mediated the association between Machiavellianism and perfectionistic self-presentation. Overall, Sherry et al. (2006) concluded that "Machiavellian perfectionists (a) perceive others as demanding, controlling, punitive, and hostile toward them, (b) promote an image of perfection, capability, and strength to others, and (c) conceal any hint of imperfection, vulnerability, and weakness from others" (p. 838).

Nathanson, Paulhus, and Williams (2006) reported correlations between perfectionism and all components of the Dark Triad (i.e., Machiavellianism, narcissism, and psychopathy) while studying scholastic cheating in 291 undergraduates. Self-oriented perfectionism was associated significantly with narcissism and Machiavellianism. Other-oriented perfectionism was significantly correlated only with narcissism. Socially prescribed perfectionism was unrelated to narcissism but associated significantly with both Machiavellianism and subclinical psychopathy.

Stoeber (2014a) also examined perfectionism and the Dark Triad in undergraduates. All three Dark Triad traits were associated significantly with other-oriented perfectionism. Other-oriented perfectionism was also linked negatively with the honesty-humility HEXACO trait dimension. Finally, small but significant positive links were also found between socially prescribed perfectionism and both narcissism and Machiavellianism. A follow-up investigation by Stoeber (2015) found among students that two measures of other-oriented perfectionism were associated with elevated levels of callousness toward others.

Recent attempts to extend the Dark Triad have incorporated the additional dimension of sadism (Buckels, Jones, & Paulhus, 2013; see also Chapter 5, this volume). It is clear from this work and subsequent work that this added element is meaningful. We suggest that this work would also be advanced substantially by considering the possibility that interpersonal perfectionism (especially other-oriented perfectionism) merits consideration as well. The case accounts that we outlined earlier and suggestions that perfectionism can be found among people with extreme forms of psychopathy (e.g., Gacono & Meloy, 2012) point to the likelihood of person-centered analyses being able to detect a group of individuals who are characterized jointly by the Dark Triad and hostile forms of perfectionism. Perfectionism combined with these other attributes could result in highly destructive outcomes, at the individual level or at a broader societal level, due to the determination, planfulness, compulsion to strive, and the willingness to act that tends to be found among highly perfectionistic individuals. These tendencies would be even more problematic if hidden behind a facade of perfectionistic self-presentation. Clearly, a manager in a workplace with these attributes could wreak havoc in a manner that is consistent with past accounts of the dark side of perfectionism in the workplace (see Flett & Hewitt, 2006).

Finally, regarding the possible role of perfectionistic self-presentation as a form of "dark perfectionism," Hewitt et al. (2011) established links between perfectionistic self-presentation and the subscales that comprise the Youth Psychopathic Inventory (YPI; Andershed, Kerr, Stattin, & Levander, 2002) in more than 200 adolescents. The YPI assesses dishonest charm, grandiosity, lying, manipulativeness, callousness, lack of emotionality, remorselessness, impulsiveness, thrill seeking, and irresponsibility. Collectively, the picture that emerged from this study was that the adolescent perfectionistic self-promoter is someone with disarming charm and a tendency to be manipulative, callous, and remorseless. These results counter the idea that people who are trying to seem perfect are merely trying to get approval and be accepted by others. There is a subset of perfectionistic self-presenters who are highly self-invested and are seemingly willing to do things that will advance their self-interests and public image with some of them having the superficial charm that is a hallmark of psychopathy.

DIRECTIONS FOR FUTURE RESEARCH

We contend that the findings described in this chapter illustrate the need for programmatic research on interpersonal perfectionism as a form of personality dysfunction and that there is a particular need for research conducted with clinical samples. Research that goes beyond self-report and includes informant reports and takes both a variable-centered and a person-centered perspective would be particularly valuable and revealing, given that people characterized by hostile forms of interpersonal perfectionism likely lack the insight needed to describe their interpersonal tendencies.

If research and theory on perfectionism and personality dysfunction are to advance, it must be shown that interpersonal perfectionism is a unique predictor of personality disturbances in ways that are not redundant with broader personality frameworks. In recent years, several studies in various contexts have shown that perfectionism can predict outcomes beyond what can be explained by the five-factor model of personality. In this regard, it is worth noting an important element of the Sherry et al. (2007) study: Trait perfectionism and perfectionistic self-presentation predicted unique variance in personality dysfunction beyond the variance attributable to neuroticism and conscientiousness. Additional research with a comparative focus is needed to illustrate further the uniqueness of dysfunctional perfectionism.

CLINICAL IMPLICATIONS

The findings described here have clear implications for the clinical assessment and treatment of people with dysfunctional interpersonal perfectionism. People high in socially prescribed perfectionism are typically self-conscious and hypersensitive to criticism. Because socially prescribed perfectionism is generalized, they come to believe that the therapist also expects them to be perfect. It is important that these clients experience the empathy and nonjudgmental support of their therapists so that they feel safe enough to explore personal identity issues and interpersonal relationships, both past and present. An appropriate and supportive therapeutic alliance is essential, particularly when these clients are vulnerable and preoccupied with feelings of shame. This type of atmosphere must be present for perfectionists to drop their facades if they are hiding behind a constructed image that reflects their needs to seem perfect.

The situation is considerably more challenging when the client is a hostile, other-oriented perfectionist. These individuals often do not want to be in treatment; some are present only under conditions in which something (e.g., a court) or someone (e.g., an irate boss or spouse) has compelled them to attend or they have reached a point of being totally perplexed and disquieted by their interpersonal difficulties and lack of insight. Initially, autonomous motivation is low. Extensive work is needed to instill a more positive motivational orientation. In many instances, expressed hostility toward the therapist is high, and the therapeutic alliance is difficult to establish and maintain. These clients can be openly oppositional in ways that are not conducive to successful treatment outcomes. The significant challenges involved here were highlighted by McCown and Carlson (2004), who found evidence indicating that narcissistic, other-oriented perfectionists had a marked tendency to terminate their treatment. Several factors likely operate here, including the aversive self-awareness and self-scrutiny that can come as a result of treatment, but there are more basic problems such as not respecting and trusting other people.

Perfectionists in general—and hostile perfectionists in particular—often try to intellectualize their problems in ways that enable them to avoid fully experiencing their negative emotions. Indeed, one way of viewing the anger of the hostile perfectionist is that it diverts attention away from the vulnerabilities of the self as the focus shifts to other people's misdeeds and inadequacies. An important goal in treatment is to develop the other-oriented perfectionist's capacity to examine, experience, and express the negative emotions that underscore their extrapunitiveness. Resistance is quite common here because perfectionists with grandiose goals and a history of self-promotion may reveal their need to seem perfect by fostering the appearance of perfect emotional control.

Some authors have reported success in treating perfectionists with diagnosed personality disorders with a metacognitive interpersonal approach. Dimaggio et al. (2014) documented the treatment progress of a narcissistic perfectionist. Initially, the client was emotionally detached, but he eventually became more open to his emotions and vulnerabilities and more willing to evaluate how he had contributed to his interpersonal difficulties. What is evident from this account of 2 years of therapy is that the darker aspects of perfectionism require extensive treatment that is broad in scope in that it considers cognitive, emotional, and interpersonal themes.

SUMMARY AND CONCLUSIONS

There is a dark side to perfectionism that is seldom considered by the lay public or researchers focused on perfectionists' positive achievement strivings. We began our analysis with a description of numerous case examples of angry, extrapunitive perfectionists. The image that emerged from these accounts of "dark perfectionism" is quite dissonant with seeing perfectionism as socially desirable. Perfectionistic self-presentation and interpersonal perfectionism are accompanied by a range of negative interpersonal tendencies and personality dysfunction. Clearly, not all perfectionists have a dark side. Many perfectionists resemble neurotic perfectionists who are described as friendly and submissive (Slaney et al., 2006), seek approval and recognition and will likely engage in self-silencing to promote relationship harmony. These people are quite different from the hostile, disagreeable perfectionists who are highly invested in self-promotion and aggressively pursue their goals.

Collectively, there is now enough evidence to suggest that people should think twice before describing themselves as perfectionists, and it is important to distinguish between perfectionists who are friendly and agreeable versus those who are disagreeable and potentially hostile. When considering someone who has self-identified as a perfectionist, people who are in a position to select from several applicants for an opening should determine which personality features go along with this perfectionism. It may not, however, be a simple task to detect dark side features if the applicant is charming and skilled in perfectionistic self-presentation.

REFERENCES

Adler, A. (1998). *Social interest: Adler's key to the meaning of life*. Oxford, England: Oneworld. (Original work published 1938)

Andershed, H., Kerr, M., Stattin, H., & Levander, S. (2002). Psychopathic traits in nonreferred youths: A new assessment tool. In E. Blaauw & L. Sheridan (Eds.),

Psychopaths: Current international perspectives (pp. 131–158). The Hague, The Netherlands: Elsevier.

Ansell, E. B., Pinto, A., Crosby, R. D., Becker, D. F., Añez, L. M., Paris, M., & Grilo, C. M. (2010). The prevalence and structure of obsessive-compulsive personality disorder in Hispanic psychiatric outpatients. *Journal of Behavior Therapy and Experimental Psychology, 41*, 275–281. http://dx.doi.org/10.1016/j.jbtep.2010.02.005

Appleby, T. (2011). *A new kind of monster: The secret life and chilling crimes of Colonel Russell Williams.* Toronto, Ontario, Canada: Random House Canada.

Ayearst, L. E., Flett, G. L., & Hewitt, P. L. (2012). Where is multidimensional perfectionism in *DSM–5?* A question posed to the *DSM–5* personality and personality disorders work group. *Personality Disorders: Theory, Research, and Treatment, 3*, 458–469. http://dx.doi.org/10.1037/a0026354

Besser, A., Flett, G. L., & Hewitt, P. L. (2004). Perfectionism, cognition, and affect in response to performance failure versus success. *Journal of Rational-Emotive & Cognitive-Behavior Therapy, 22*, 301–328.

Buckels, E. E., Jones, D. N., & Paulhus, D. L. (2013). Behavioral confirmation of everyday sadism. *Psychological Science, 24*, 2201–2209. http://dx.doi.org/10.1177/0956797613490749

De Clercq, B., De Fruyt, F., De Bolle, M., Van Hiel, A., Markon, K. E., & Krueger, R. F. (2014). The hierarchical structure and construct validity of the PID–5 trait measure in adolescence. *Journal of Personality, 82*, 158–169. http://dx.doi.org/10.1111/jopy.12042

Dimaggio, G., Valeri, S., Salvatore, G., Popolo, R., Montano, A., & Ottavi, P. (2014). Adopting metacognitive interpersonal therapy to treat narcissistic personality disorder with somatization. *Journal of Contemporary Psychotherapy, 44*, 85–95. http://dx.doi.org/10.1007/s10879-013-9254-8

Ellis, A. E. (2002). The role of irrational beliefs in perfectionism. In G. L. Flett & P. L. Hewitt (Eds.), *Perfectionism: Theory, research, and treatment* (pp. 217–229). Washington, DC: American Psychological Association. http://dx.doi.org/10.1037/10458-009

Flett, G. L., & Hewitt, P. L. (2001). Personality factors and substance abuse in relationship violence and child abuse: A review and theoretical analysis. In C. Wekerle & A. M. Wall (Eds.), *The violence and addiction equation: Theoretical and clinical issues in substance abuse and relationship violence* (pp. 66–102). Philadelphia, PA: Brunner/Mazel.

Flett, G. L., & Hewitt, P. L. (2006). Perfectionism as a detrimental factor in leadership: A multidimensional analysis. In R. J. Burke & C. L. Cooper (Eds.), *Inspiring leaders* (pp. 247–272). London, England: Routledge.

Flett, G. L., & Hewitt, P. L. (2014). "The perils of perfectionism in sports" revisited: Toward a broader understanding of the pressure to be perfect and its impact on athletes and dancers. *International Journal of Sport Psychology, 45*, 395–407.

Flett, G. L., Hewitt, P. L., Blankstein, K. R., & Mosher, S. W. (1995). Perfectionism, life events, and depressive symptoms: A test of a diathesis-stress model. *Current Psychology, 14,* 112–137. http://dx.doi.org/10.1007/BF02686885

Flett, G. L., Sherry, S. B., Hewitt, P. L., & Nepon, T. (2014). Understanding the narcissistic perfectionists among us: Grandiosity, vulnerability, and the quest for the perfect self. In A. Besser (Ed.), *Handbook of the psychology of narcissism: Diverse perspectives* (pp. 43–66). New York, NY: Nova Science.

Frei, A., Völlm, B., Graf, M., & Dittmann, V. (2006). Female serial killing: Review and case report. *Criminal Behaviour and Mental Health, 16,* 167–176. http://dx.doi.org/10.1002/cbm.615

Frost, R. O., Marten, P., Lahart, C., & Rosenblate, R. (1990). Perfectionism and evaluative threat. *Cognitive Therapy and Research, 14,* 559–572. http://dx.doi.org/10.1007/BF01173364

Gacono, C. B., & Meloy, R. B. (2012). *The Rorschach assessment of aggressive and psychopathic personalities.* New York, NY: Routledge.

Hewitt, P. L., Blasberg, J. S., Flett, G. L., Besser, A., Sherry, S. B., Caelian, C., . . . Birch, S. (2011). Perfectionistic self-presentation in children and adolescents: Development and validation of the Perfectionistic Self-Presentation Scale—Junior Form. *Psychological Assessment, 23,* 125–142. http://dx.doi.org/10.1037/a0021147

Hewitt, P. L., & Flett, G. L. (1990). Perfectionism and depression: A multidimensional analysis. *Journal of Social Behavior & Personality, 5,* 423–438.

Hewitt, P. L., & Flett, G. L. (1991). Perfectionism in the self and social contexts: Conceptualization, assessment, and association with psychopathology. *Journal of Personality and Social Psychology, 60,* 456–470. http://dx.doi.org/10.1037/0022-3514.60.3.456

Hewitt, P. L., & Flett, G. L. (2004). *The Multidimensional Perfectionism Scale: Technical manual.* Toronto, Ontario, Canada: Multi-Health Systems.

Hewitt, P. L., Flett, G. L., Sherry, S. B., Habke, M., Parkin, M., Lam, R. W., . . . Stein, M. B. (2003). The interpersonal expression of perfection: Perfectionistic self-presentation and psychological distress. *Journal of Personality and Social Psychology, 84,* 1303–1325. http://dx.doi.org/10.1037/0022-3514.84.6.1303

Hewitt, P. L., Flett, G. L., & Turnbull, W. (1992). Perfectionism and Multiphasic Personality Inventory (MMPI) indices of personality disorder. *Journal of Psychopathology and Behavioral Assessment, 14,* 323–335. http://dx.doi.org/10.1007/BF00960777

Hewitt, P. L., Flett, G. L., & Turnbull, W. (1994). Borderline personality disorder: An investigation with the Multidimensional Perfectionism Scale. *European Journal of Psychological Assessment, 10,* 28–33.

Hewitt, P. L., Habke, A. M., Lee-Baggley, D. L., Sherry, S. B., & Flett, G. L. (2008). The impact of perfectionistic self-presentation on the cognitive, affective, and physiological experience of a clinical interview. *Psychiatry: Interpersonal and Biological Processes, 71,* 93–122. http://dx.doi.org/10.1521/psyc.2008.71.2.93

Hill, R. W., McIntire, K., & Bacharach, V. R. (1997). Perfectionism and the Big Five factors. *Journal of Social Behavior & Personality, 12*, 257–270.

Hill, R. W., Zrull, M. C., & Turlington, S. (1997). Perfectionism and interpersonal problems. *Journal of Personality Assessment, 69*, 81–103. http://dx.doi.org/10.1207/s15327752jpa6901_5

Horney, K. (1950). *Neurosis and human growth*. New York, NY: Norton.

Horney, K. (1972). *Our inner conflicts: A constructive theory of neurosis*. New York, NY: Norton. (Original work published 1945)

Hyler, S. (1994). *The Personality Diagnostic Questionnaire—4*. New York: New York State Psychiatric Institute.

Krueger, R. F., Derringer, J., Markon, K. E., Watson, D., & Skodol, A. E. (2012). Initial construction of a maladaptive personality trait model and inventory for *DSM–5*. *Psychological Medicine, 42*, 1879–1890. http://dx.doi.org/10.1017/S0033291711002674

Langer, W. C. (1972). *The mind of Adolf Hitler*. London, England: Pan Books.

Leeper, A., Carwile, S., & Huber, J. R. (2002). An Adlerian analysis of the Unabomber. *The Journal of Individual Psychology, 58*, 169–176.

Livesley, W. J., Jackson, D. N., & Schroeder, M. L. (1992). Factorial structure of traits delineating personality disorders in clinical and general population samples. *Journal of Abnormal Psychology, 101*, 432–440. http://dx.doi.org/10.1037/0021-843X.101.3.432

Lohr, J. M., Hamberger, L. K., & Bonge, D. (1988). The nature of irrational beliefs in different personality clusters of spouse abusers. *Journal of Rational-Emotive & Cognitive-Behavior Therapy, 6*, 273–285. http://dx.doi.org/10.1007/BF01061293

Mackinnon, S. P., Sherry, S. B., Antony, M. M., Stewart, S. H., Sherry, D. L., & Hartling, N. (2012). Caught in a bad romance: Perfectionism, conflict, and depression in romantic relationships. *Journal of Family Psychology, 26*, 215–225. http://dx.doi.org/10.1037/a0027402

Matte, M., & Lafontaine, M.-F. (2012). Assessment of romantic perfectionism: Psychometric properties of the Romantic Relationship Perfectionism Scale. *Measurement and Evaluation in Counseling and Development, 45*, 113–132. http://dx.doi.org/10.1177/0748175611429303

McCown, W., & Carlson, G. (2004). Narcissism, perfectionism, and self-termination from treatment in outpatient cocaine abusers. *Journal of Rational-Emotive & Cognitive-Behavior Therapy, 22*, 325–336. http://dx.doi.org/10.1023/B:JORE.0000047314.90953.c9

Nathanson, C., Paulhus, D. L., & Williams, K. M. (2006). Predictors of a behavioral measure of scholastic cheating: Personality and competence but not demographics. *Contemporary Educational Psychology, 31*, 97–122. http://dx.doi.org/10.1016/j.cedpsych.2005.03.001

Nealis, L. J., Sherry, S. B., Sherry, D. L., Stewart, S. H., & Macneil, M. A. (2015). Toward a better understanding of narcissistic perfectionism: Evidence of factorial validity, incremental validity, and mediating mechanisms. *Journal of Research in Personality*, *57*, 11–25. http://dx.doi.org/10.1016/j.jrp.2015.02.006

Paulhus, D. L., & Williams, K. M. (2002). The dark triad of personality: Narcissism, Machiavellianism, and psychopathy. *Journal of Research in Personality*, *36*, 556–563. http://dx.doi.org/10.1016/S0092-6566(02)00505-6

Pincus, A. L., Ansell, E. B., Pimentel, C. A., Cain, N. M., Wright, A. G., & Levy, K. N. (2009). Initial construction and validation of the Pathological Narcissism Inventory. *Psychological Assessment*, *21*, 365–379. http://dx.doi.org/10.1037/a0016530

Robinson, B. E. (2000). *Chained to the desk: A guidebook for workaholics, their partners and children, and the clinicians who treat them*. New York: New York University Press.

Rothschild, B., Dimson, C., Storaasli, R., & Clapp, L. (1997). Personality profiles of veterans entering treatment in domestic violence. *Journal of Family Violence*, *12*, 259–274. http://dx.doi.org/10.1023/A:1022896704136

Rudolph, S. G., Flett, G. L., & Hewitt, P. L. (2007). Perfectionism and deficits in cognitive emotion regulation. *Journal of Rational-Emotive & Cognitive-Behavior Therapy*, *25*, 343–357. http://dx.doi.org/10.1007/s10942-007-0056-3

Sherry, S. B., Hewitt, P. L., Besser, A., Flett, G. L., & Klein, C. (2006). Machiavellianism, trait perfectionism, and perfectionistic self-presentation. *Personality and Individual Differences*, *40*, 829–839. http://dx.doi.org/10.1016/j.paid.2005.09.010

Sherry, S. B., Hewitt, P. L., Flett, G. L., Lee-Baggley, D. L., & Hall, P. A. (2007). Trait perfectionism and perfectionistic self-presentation in personality pathology. *Personality and Individual Differences*, *42*, 477–490. http://dx.doi.org/10.1016/j.paid.2006.07.026

Slaney, R. B., Pincus, A. L., Uliaszek, A. A., & Wang, K. T. (2006). Conceptions of perfectionism and interpersonal problems: Evaluating groups using the structural summary method for circumplex data. *Assessment*, *13*, 138–153. http://dx.doi.org/10.1177/1073191105284878

Stoeber, J. (2014a). How other-oriented perfectionism differs from self-oriented and socially prescribed perfectionism. *Journal of Psychopathology and Behavioral Assessment*, *36*, 329–338. http://dx.doi.org/10.1007/s10862-013-9397-7

Stoeber, J. (2014b). Multidimensional perfectionism and the DSM–5 personality traits. *Personality and Individual Differences*, *64*, 115–120. http://dx.doi.org/10.1016/j.paid.2014.02.031

Stoeber, J. (2015, May 15). How other-oriented perfectionism differs from self-oriented and socially prescribed perfectionism: Further findings. *Journal of Psychopathology and Behavioral Assessment*. Advance online publication. http://dx.doi.org/10.1007/s10862-015-9485-y

Tangney, J. P., Baumeister, R. F., & Boone, A. L. (2004). High self-control predicts good adjustment, less pathology, better grades, and interpersonal success. *Journal of Personality*, *72*, 271–324. http://dx.doi.org/10.1111/j.0022-3506.2004.00263.x

Waite, R. G. L. (1972). Afterword. In W. C. Langer (Ed.), *The mind of Adolf Hitler* (pp. 219–242). London, England: Pan Books.

Wiebe, R. E., & McCabe, S. B. (2002). Relationship perfectionism, dysphoria, and hostile interpersonal behaviors. *Journal of Social and Clinical Psychology, 21,* 67–91. http://dx.doi.org/10.1521/jscp.21.1.67.22406

Wiggins, J. S., & Broughton, R. (1985). The interpersonal circle: A structural model for the integration of personality research. In R. Hogan & W. H. Jones (Eds.), *Perspectives in personality* (Vol. 1, pp. 1–47). Greenwich, CT: JAI Press.

Wright, A. G. C., Pincus, A. L., Hopwood, C. J., Thomas, K. M., Markon, K. E., & Krueger, R. F. (2012). An interpersonal analysis of pathological personality traits in *DSM–5. Assessment, 19,* 263–275. http://dx.doi.org/10.1177/1073191112446657

Wynnyckyj, A. K. (1997, August 31). Prof. Petryshyn legally insane, not guilty of wife's murder. *The Ukrainian Weekly, 65*(35).

11

AUTHORITARIANISM: POSITIVES AND NEGATIVES

STEVEN LUDEKE

In both the psychological literature and in broader intellectual and political discussions, authoritarianism has a pronounced negative valence. The tendency to obey established authorities is, to be sure, linked with a wide range of unpalatable outcomes, particularly in the social and political spheres. Less attention has been paid to its links with some outcomes that are positive both for the individual and for society at large, including lower rates of substance abuse and criminal behavior. This chapter provides a broader picture of authoritarianism's nomological net than is typically presented by highlighting not only its important and well-recognized costs but also its occasional upsides.

http://dx.doi.org/10.1037/14854-012

The Dark Side of Personality: Science and Practice in Social, Personality, and Clinical Psychology, V. Zeigler-Hill and D. K. Marcus (Editors)

DEFINITION AND BACKGROUND

Authoritarianism first attracted widespread attention in the psychological literature with the publication of *The Authoritarian Personality* (TAP; Adorno, Frenkel-Brunswik, Levinson, & Sanford, 1950) shortly after World War II. Current research continues to draw heavily on several themes found in TAP, even though the psychodynamic approach taken in TAP has limited the appeal it has for modern researchers, and the primary measure to come out of TAP (the F-Scale) has been found to have serious limitations. Of the nine core features of authoritarianism identified in TAP, six have been either discarded or have been shifted to the periphery. For example, TAP identified a *rigid* frame of mind as a primary characteristic of authoritarianism, whereas today it is seen instead as a precursor to authoritarianism (Jugert, Cohrs, & Duckitt, 2009). Authoritarianism is generally defined by three central components derived from TAP. These are *authoritarian submission* (i.e., the tendency to submit to established authorities), *authoritarian aggression* (i.e., a willingness to aggress against those condemned by those authorities), and *conventionalism* (i.e., a preference for traditional values).

Altemeyer (1981, 1988, 1996) is responsible both for many of the modifications to the authoritarian construct since TAP and for reviving interest in authoritarianism among psychologists in the wake of severe criticism of TAP. Altemeyer's measure, the Right-Wing Authoritarianism (RWA) scale, is so named to specify its focus as the tendency to display obedience to established ("right-wing") rather than revolutionary ("left wing") authorities (Altemeyer, 1996). Altemeyer's RWA measure offered several improvements over the much-maligned F-Scale created by Adorno and colleagues (1950), including a balance between positively and negatively worded items, improved reliability, and apparent unidimensionality (discussed later). Most important, although the most appropriate measurement of authoritarianism remains a topic of debate, the core disposition appears to be measured effectively using a range of instruments (Duckitt, Bizumic, Krauss, & Heled, 2010; Feldman, 2003; Ludeke, Johnson, & Bouchard, 2013; Van Hiel, Cornelis, Roets, & De Clercq, 2007). For our purposes, the distinctions between the various instruments are not important.

A recent objection to Altemeyer's perspective concerns his conceptualization of authoritarianism as a personality trait, a view he preserved from TAP. Although a full treatment of this topic is beyond the scope of this chapter, it is worth noting some important support for his position. Altemeyer (1996) assessed the stability of his measure over 12- and 18-year intervals in samples first assessed at the beginning of college; the test–retest coefficients of .62 and .59, respectively, compares favorably to that observed for personality traits such as the Big Five (Roberts & DelVecchio, 2000). As is typical of personality traits (Roberts & DelVecchio, 2000), the rank-order stability of authoritarianism appears to be even higher in older samples: a large twin sample assessed in middle age and then again nearly two decades later exhibited a high correlation ($r = .74$) between the two assessments, with genetic influences accounting for a majority of the stability in the trait (Ludeke & Krueger, 2013). The role of genetics in authoritarianism was not predicted by Altemeyer (1988, 1996), who favored a social learning account. However, a significant role for genetics in authoritarianism has been documented in several studies (Ludeke & Krueger, 2013; McCourt, Bouchard, Lykken, Tellegen, & Keyes, 1999; Shikishima & Ando, 2004), and a genetic perspective is perhaps better able than social learning theory to account for differences in the expression of authoritarianism recently observed among preschoolers (Reifen Tagar, Federico, Lyons, Ludeke, & Koenig, 2014). Importantly, many personality theorists argue that a genetic basis is an important criterion for distinguishing personality traits from psychological features that are more culturally contingent and susceptible to environmental influence (e.g., DeYoung, 2015; McAdams & Pals, 2006; McCrae & Costa, 2008). Furthermore, although Altemeyer's RWA measure requires some modification for use in different cultural contexts (for example, items from the measure concerning religion functioned differently in Soviet culture; McFarland, Ageyev, & Abalakina-Paap, 1992), differences in authoritarianism remain salient across cultures, which is consistent with the trait conception of authoritarianism (DeYoung, 2015).

There have been several important critiques of the trait conception of authoritarianism (e.g., Duckitt & Sibley, 2010), highlighting that authoritarianism is not completely resistant to manipulation, undergoes significant changes over the life course, and is assessed using items that do not exclusively measure behavior. These criticisms merit a fuller response than can be provided here; I note only that these critiques would seem to exclude even the Big Five from being considered personality traits, given the substantial mean-level changes observed over the life course (Roberts, Walton, & Viechtbauer, 2006), the use of nonbehavioral items in assessing the Big Five (Pytlik Zillig, Hemenover, & Dienstbier, 2002), and the susceptibility of Big Five traits to experimental manipulation (White, Kenrick, Li, Mortensen, Neuberg, & Cohen, 2012). For the purposes of the present chapter, I thus retain the original trait conception of authoritarianism because I believe its stability, presence across cultures, and predictive power merit such a treatment.

REVIEW OF THE RELEVANT LITERATURE

Authoritarianism is one of the most researched constructs within psychology, with more than 2,000 publications on the topic appearing before 1990 (Meloen, 1993). Accordingly, any review of the literature must be selective.

In this section, I use two recent theoretical attempts to account for right-wing beliefs to guide an overview of major findings related to the origins of authoritarianism.

Both of the accounts used to guide this review were directed not at explaining authoritarianism in particular but instead treated authoritarianism as one among many indicators of general left–right differences on political and social issues.[1] The first of these (Jost, Glaser, Kruglanski, & Sulloway, 2003) synthesized the previous literature on the various correlates of left–right differences, arguing that this literature was best understood as illustrating two primary differences between the left and the right. Specifically, right-wing beliefs were argued to be adopted to help an individual manage feelings of uncertainty and feelings of threat.

Orientation Toward Uncertainty

Jost and colleagues (2003) highlighted the relevance of feelings of uncertainty by using a wide array of measures assessing an individual's comfort with and willingness to tolerate uncertainty and ambiguity. A more comprehensive meta-analysis of the relationship between these domains and right-wing beliefs reported similar if more modest associations (Van Hiel, Onraet, & De Pauw, 2010; see also Van Hiel & Crowson, in press). Authoritarians were consistently less tolerant of ambiguity—for example, having more difficulty recognizing both positive and negative characteristics in the same object, or sticking for a longer period of time to an original perception of a changing object (e.g., an image of a dog gradually morphing into an image of a cat). Authoritarianism is also positively correlated with a preference for quick and decisive answers as opposed to extended deliberation with possibly inconclusive results (Van Hiel & Crowson, in press).[2] These results are consistent with the negative associations between authoritarianism and the Big Five trait of Openness to Experience, which a recent meta-analysis

---

[1]More extensive discussions of the justification for this strategy are provided elsewhere (Bouchard, 2009; Ludeke, Johnson, et al., 2013).

[2]It is important to note that these associations were stronger in studies in which the measure of "cognitive style" was assessed with self-report surveys rather than with behavioral measures. The authors identify several possible explanations for this finding, including common method variance and content overlap between the dependent and independent variables (Van Hiel & Crowson, in press; Van Hiel et al., 2010). A recent study (Ludeke, Reifen Tagar, & DeYoung, 2014) identified an additional likely explanation, highlighting how value differences between those scoring high and low on authoritarianism measures lead to different patterns of misrepresentation in self-report measures. Because authoritarians tend to place less value on Openness to Experience than do nonauthoritarians (Ludeke et al., 2014), we should expect that authoritarians are less likely to overclaim Openness-related characteristics such as a willingness to tolerate uncertainty and ambiguity (Ludeke, Weisberg, & DeYoung, 2013).

identified as the most pronounced predictor of authoritarianism within the Big Five (Sibley & Duckitt, 2008). Finally, meta-analysis also indicated that authoritarianism is predicted by cognitive ability and educational attainment (Van Hiel et al., 2010), with more authoritarian individuals performing less well on intelligence tests and completing fewer years of formal education. Considered together, the resulting picture is one in which authoritarian individuals are relatively uninterested in and incapable of cognitive exploration: They prefer simple and definite answers and to obtain them quickly and permanently. These differences are vividly demonstrated by the preference of those on the right for simple rather than complex art (Wilson, Ausman, & Mathews, 1973), familiar as opposed to unfamiliar foods (Hibbing, Smith, & Alford, 2014), and novels that come to closure (Hibbing et al., 2014).

Recent research has mapped the causal pathways among these characteristics. For example, a portion of the effect of intelligence on right-wing attitudes appears to be mediated by years of education completed (Schoon, Cheng, Gale, Batty, & Deary, 2010): British children scoring high on a cognitive ability measure at age 11 tended to complete more years of advanced education, and these extra years of education partially accounted for the more left-wing beliefs reported by those high-ability children at age 33.

Orientation Toward Threat

In arguing that right-wing beliefs derived from an elevated response to feelings of threat, Jost and colleagues (2003) highlighted both dispositional and situational evidence. For example, those who see the world as a more dangerous place and those who report higher fear of death tend to score higher on measures of right-wing beliefs. Situational changes may also be important: Individuals asked to imagine their beliefs in an apocalyptic future imagine their future selves to be more authoritarian than do those asked to imagine their beliefs in a world more like the present (Duckitt & Fisher, 2003; Jugert & Duckitt, 2009). Deteriorating economic and social conditions have also been argued to correlate with broader societal shifts toward more authoritarian views and behaviors (Doty, Peterson, & Winter, 1991; Sales, 1973).

These ideas have recently been incorporated into an account arguing that left–right differences such as authoritarianism derive from differences with respect to the salience and importance of negative events for an individual (Hibbing et al., 2014). Although all individuals may be prone to prioritize attention to the negative rather than the positive (e.g., people generally experience more pain from a loss than pleasure from a comparable gain), Hibbing and colleagues suggested that this is particularly the case for those with right-wing beliefs. In addition to the evidence discussed earlier, Hibbing et al. (2014) claimed that right-wing individuals

> display elevated physiological response to negative stimuli, devote more attention to negative stimuli, possess distinct self-reported psychological patterns when asked to imagine negative stimuli (i.e., give evidence of high disgust and high threat sensitivity), and perhaps harbor recognizable structural features consistent with elevated responsiveness to negative situations (distinctive substructures of the amygdala and perhaps even genetic differences such as a "short" allele of the dopamine receptor gene DRD4). (p. 303)

This account has limitations to be worked out by future research; for example, it is not consistent with all observed structural differences in the brains of those on the left and right, and it may be better suited to explain characteristics such as authoritarianism than antiegalitarianism, even though both orientations are associated with general differences between the left and right (Ludeke & DeYoung, 2014). Nevertheless, the account offered by Hibbing et al. (2014) remains an impressive act of synthesis, drawing on a range of important findings. In addition to those highlighted by Jost and colleagues (2003), Hibbing and colleagues (2014) highlight experimental findings in which those with right-wing beliefs exhibited elevated responses to threatening stimuli (e.g., more pronounced blinks in response to unexpected loud noises; Oxley et al., 2008). When tracking the eye movements of participants, Dodd et al. (2012) also found that right-wing individuals pay more attention to aversive images (such as a spider on a man's face) than do those on the left. Right-wing beliefs are associated with the tendency to pay attention to negative stimuli to such an extent that performance on basic cognitive tasks can be impaired; for example, when asked to identify the color of the letters used to display words, conservatives were particularly slow to perform the task for negative words (e.g., vomit, suffering; Carraro, Castelli, & Macchiella, 2011). Finally, those on the right are particularly prone to restrict their exploration when that exploration can bring losses as well as gains (Shook & Fazio, 2009).

ADAPTIVE AND MALADAPTIVE FEATURES

Because much of the initial impetus for research on authoritarianism was an effort to understand and identify differences in the tendency to support Fascist regimes and anti-Semitism, most research on the consequences of authoritarianism has focused on its (negative) effects on other people. This review does not reflect this focus of the literature, instead devoting roughly equal attention to the effects of authoritarianism on oneself as on others, and on both positive and negative consequences of authoritarianism. This emphasis is primarily a product of space constraints, although it also reflects the broader goals of this book: The political implications of authoritarian beliefs are less important for clinicians than are the mental health implications. Finally, it also reflects the author's belief that (perhaps reflecting the scarcity of right-wing social psychologists; Haidt, 2011) the positive aspects of authoritarianism have been comparatively neglected by psychological researchers, with some notable exceptions (e.g., Kessler & Cohrs, 2008).

Authoritarianism in Political and Social Contexts

Despite the challenges in obtaining significant samples of those with explicit affiliations with Fascist parties, the studies conducted to date support the view that such individuals score high on measures of authoritarianism. McFarland (in press) reviewed studies from a range of cultures, including evidence of elevated levels of authoritarianism among fascist party members in Britain (Eysenck & Coulter, 1972), among Soviet ultranationalists (McFarland, Ageyev, & Abalakina, 1993), former Nazi officers in Germany (Steiner & Fahrenberg, 1970, as cited in McFarland, in press), and militant nationalists in both Israel and Palestine (Rubinstein, 1996).

Authoritarians are not only more likely to support the establishment of dangerous political regimes but also to participate in the more heinous acts perpetrated by such regimes. Although Milgram's (1973) famous program of research on obedience suggested that the willingness to obey immoral orders from authorities was far more widespread than most would have suspected, not all individuals were equally willing to "follow orders." In Milgram's experiments, participants were asked to deliver electric "shocks" to another "participant" (actually an actor, who received no shocks in the experiment) in response to the participant's failure to complete a simple memory task. When instructed to do so, many participants were willing to administer extraordinary levels of "electric shock" despite the actor's screams of agony or feigned unconsciousness, with authoritarians more likely to obey the orders to do so (Elms & Milgram, 1966). Other classic research on the misbehavior of authorities may also reveal the import of differences in authoritarianism. For example, the famous Stanford prison experiment (Haney, Banks, & Zimbardo, 1973) has been thought to illustrate the degree to which any individual may abuse authority and denigrate those over whom they have power, as individuals randomly assigned to be guards significantly mistreated fellow students who were randomly assigned to be prisoners. However, recent research highlighting the importance of personality has suggested participants in these experiments may have been particularly disposed to behave in this fashion, given that students signing up for a "prison experiment" (advertised similarly to the Stanford experiment) tended to be relatively elevated on authoritarianism, social dominance, and aggression, while tending to score low on empathy and altruism (Carnahan & McFarland, 2007).

It is important to note that authoritarianism does not predict a tendency to indiscriminately abuse others. First, although authoritarianism is generally associated with punitive attitudes (supporting, for example, harsher punishments for most criminal convictions), authoritarianism is negatively correlated with a willingness to punish authority figures who break the law, whether in the case of police brutality or for illegal wiretapping by law enforcement (Altemeyer, 1981). Second, authoritarianism exhibits significant correlations with prejudice against a wide range of groups: Authoritarianism predicts low feelings of warmth toward those who are viewed as either dangerous (those involved in drugs or crime) or as dissident (protestors, feminists), though not (on the whole) toward derogated groups such as the unattractive, obese, or mentally handicapped (Duckitt & Sibley, 2007). An exception to this trend that will prove to be important later in the chapter concerns individuals with mental illness. Although attitudes toward the mentally ill tend to covary with attitudes about other derogated groups (i.e., those who hold negative views of the obese and unattractive also hold negative views of the mentally ill), authoritarianism is positively linked to prejudice against the mentally ill (Duckitt & Sibley, 2007; Fodor, 2006).

Criminality and Substance Abuse

Authoritarianism researchers have tended to use "narrow-bandwidth" instruments (which measure a small number of traits rather than providing a comprehensive picture of an individual's personality) such as Altemeyer's RWA scale or the Adorno F-Scale in their research. However, the authoritarian construct is also effectively assessed by scales within broader bandwidth measures, which seek to provide a more comprehensive assessment of the individual by assessing many different traits. One example is the Multidimensional Personality Questionnaire (MPQ; Tellegen & Waller, 2008). The Traditionalism scale of this instrument (originally named Authoritarianism because many of its items were derived from the F-Scale and similar measures; Tellegen & Waller, 2008) correlates highly with other measures: unpublished analyses by the author on three large community samples yield an average correlation between Altemeyer's (1996) RWA measure and MPQ Traditionalism of .73, which (because of the imperfect reliability of these measures and the nonsimultaneous assessment in these samples) indicates that almost all of the reliable variance is shared between the two measures (see also Ludeke, Johnson, et al., 2013). Because the Traditionalism scale is part of broader personality measure used in a wide variety of research contexts, it makes it possible to explore authoritarianism's relationship with outcomes outside of those areas most commonly focused on by authoritarianism researchers (i.e., politics and prejudice).

Authoritarianism appears to be negatively correlated with rates of substance abuse. Kohn and Mercer (1971) found that scores on a modified and balanced version of the F-scale had markedly negatively correlations with self-reported use of illicit substances. Authoritarianism is also negatively correlated with other forms of antisocial behavior. For example, scores on MPQ Traditionalism were significantly negatively correlated with self-reported rule-breaking behavior over the previous 6 months in a sample of undergraduates as assessed by questions concerning drug and alcohol use, trouble with the law, and general rule breaking (Burt & Donnellan, 2008).

A causal role for authoritarianism in affecting substance abuse was supported by a large, community-based longitudinal study in which MPQ Traditionalism scores at age 17 predicted the absence of nicotine dependence as well as disorders relating to alcohol and illicit substances at age 20 (Elkins, King, McGue, & Iacono, 2006). The relationships that authoritarianism had with illicit substance use disorders were particularly pronounced. Because authoritarianism is positively associated with the tendency to present oneself in a "saint-like" fashion (Altemeyer, 1996; Ludeke et al., 2014; Meston, Heiman, Trapnell, & Paulhus, 1998), one might wonder whether these results reflected reality or misrepresentation on self-report measures. However, a large community-based study of 18-year-olds found that MPQ Traditionalism was negatively associated not only with self-reports of delinquency in the past year but also with informant reports of antisocial behaviors as well as with the number of convictions revealed by court records (Krueger et al., 1994), which supports the results found in self-report studies.

Subjective Well-Being

Early work on authoritarianism suggested that it would be positively correlated with psychological dysfunction and distress, with Adorno and colleagues (1950) arguing that feelings of personal insecurity played a major role in the development of authoritarianism. More recently, others have suggested that right-wing beliefs are in fact positively associated with subjective feelings of well-being. Rather than deriving from feelings of insecurity and conflict, Napier and Jost (2008) argued that right-wing views promoted individuals' happiness by inuring them to dissatisfaction with economic inequality. However, a recent meta-analysis (Onraet, Van Hiel, & Dhont, 2013) noted that such findings were contradicted as often as they were supported by other studies. Results from the meta-analysis indicated that right-wing beliefs bear little to no association with various measures of psychological well-being. More specifically, authoritarianism bore no consistent relation with any of the constructs studied, including positive affect, negative affect, life satisfaction, and self-esteem.

DIRECTIONS FOR FUTURE RESEARCH

Research on authoritarianism can be considered mature in many ways: authoritarianism has been investigated in a wide range of cultural contexts, avoiding overreliance on student populations, and in connection with an impressive diversity of important outcomes. At the same time, the lack of consensus regarding both the conceptualization and measurement of authoritarianism is surprising and indicative of a far less mature construct. Future research is needed to resolve these basic questions.

With regard to authoritarianism's conceptualization, important questions remain about particularly basic issues, such as whether authoritarianism is most accurately perceived as a highly stable personality trait (Altemeyer, 1996; Ludeke & Krueger, 2013) or whether it is more accurately understood as a feature that is more flexible and influenced by the environment (Duckitt & Sibley, 2010). Resolution of this dispute will help guide future research on how to prevent the harms associated with authoritarianism. For example, those who consider authoritarianism to be a relatively malleable feature may favor research into the best way to change an individual's level of authoritarianism, whereas those who take individual differences in authoritarianism to be more stable will also see promise in research concerning how to reduce the harm that authoritarians can cause to others.

With regard to the measurement of authoritarianism, future research should aim to address two issues. First, it should evaluate the ways in which authoritarianism has been measured. Previous summaries of the authoritarianism literature have overlooked the substantial body of research produced using the Traditionalism scale of the MPQ (Tellegen & Waller, 2008). This omission is unfortunate because most research using single-construct measures of authoritarianism have tended to focus on its most obvious associated constructs such as political views and prejudice, whereas research using the MPQ has (as one would expected of a broad-bandwidth personality instrument) been applied to a particularly wide range of domains, including the literature reviewed here concerning mental health and antisocial behavior. Thus, far more is known about the relationship between authoritarianism and other domains of functioning than is commonly recognized at present.

A second question concerns the most effective assessment of the construct for future research. There is much to be said for Altemeyer's (1996) argument that an individual's level of authoritarianism is effectively revealed in his or her responses to attitudinal questions covering a wide range of topics, and this view is consistent with more recent theoretical (Bouchard, 2009) and empirical (Ludeke, Johnson, et al., 2013) work. At the same time, recent research has demonstrated weaknesses in Altemeyer's measure: For example, the unidimensionality of his measure is somewhat illusory, derived as it was from a reliance on double- and even triple-barreled items (i.e., items that simultaneously assess multiple components of authoritarianism; Funke, 2005).[3] Other researchers, interested in identifying the association between an authoritarian predisposition and opinions on certain political topics (e.g., on the rights of sexual minorities), are troubled by the inclusion of such items within the RWA measure itself. Future research on authoritarianism may be better served by measures of authoritarianism that omit reference to most particular issues (Feldman & Stenner, 1997), measures that allow separate assessment of authoritarian aggression, authoritarian submission, and conventionalism (Duckitt et al., 2010), or Saucier's (2000, 2013) attitude measure that parallels the "Big Five" of personality in its lexical basis, comprehensiveness, and power to capture the true underlying structure of the domain. Resolving these basic challenges of conceptualization and assessment will allow research on authoritarianism to proceed more quickly and on a surer footing with researchers being more aware of what has been discovered and what remains to be learned.

CLINICAL IMPLICATIONS

Although the most frequently studied outcomes associated with authoritarianism have been social and political in nature, several studies have explored how authoritarianism relates to mental health and treatment. In this area, authoritarianism may be seen as a protective factor. The tendency of authoritarians to obey established authorities and follow societal conventions may account for the findings reviewed in this chapter concerning their relatively low rates of substance use disorders and antisocial behavior. Authoritarianism may also operate as a buffer against stress: Van Hiel and De Clercq (2009) found that stressful life events, typically seen as a risk factor for psychological health, were associated with an increase in health problems (including insomnia, anxiety, social dysfunction, and depression) only among those scoring low on an authoritarianism measure. High scorers on an authoritarianism measure were modestly less likely to suffer from depression and showed no increase in health problems as a function of stressful life events. The authors suggested authoritarians may derive protection from the impact of stressful life events due to a tendency to justify the state of the world, although they challenged these ideas in a later meta-analysis (Onraet et al., 2013). These results were recently contradicted by a study showing authoritarianism predicted a

---

[3]For example, one item reads: "Our country will be great if we honor the ways of our forefathers, do what the authorities tell us to do, and get rid of the 'rotten apples' who are ruining everything." This item simultaneously assesses conventionalism, authoritarian submission, and authoritarian aggression, respectively.

modestly elevated risk for developing depression over a 3-month and 1-year period, which additionally found no evidence that authoritarianism buffered individuals from the impact of negative life events (Duriez, Klimstra, Luyckx, Beyers, & Soenens, 2012). Although the relation between authoritarianism and depression remains somewhat uncertain and is likely to be modest, its connection with other disorders is less equivocal and more pronounced: Results from a representative birth cohort (Krueger, Caspi, Moffitt, Silva, & McGee, 1996) indicated that authoritarianism (as assessed by MPQ Traditionalism) was associated with only a modestly decreased risk for depression but had more pronounced connections with low rates of substance abuse and antisocial behavior disorders. However, future research is needed to reconcile these findings with a recent meta-analysis that indicated authoritarianism is a poor predictor of personality disorders, including antisocial personality disorder (Samuel & Widiger, 2008). The measure of authoritarianism used in this meta-analysis was the Openness to Values facet from the revised NEO Personality Inventory (Costa & McCrae, 2008), which Sibley and Duckitt (in press) reported to be substantially, but not perfectly, associated with Altemeyer's measure of authoritarianism. Further research is needed to identify whether this discrepancy is due to differences in the operationalization of authoritarianism or the measure of antisociality.

Authoritarianism has been studied not only in relation to psychopathology but also as a predictor of attitudes toward psychotherapy. On the basis of the prejudice that individuals with high levels of authoritarianism express toward those with mental illness (Duckitt & Sibley, 2007; Fodor, 2006), one might expect authoritarianism to be negatively correlated with positive attitudes toward personally using mental health services. Several studies support this expectation. A study using the F-Scale (Fischer & Turner, 1970) found that authoritarianism was positively correlated with concern about stigmatization if one's use of psychotherapy became known, as well as with the belief that individuals should be able to overcome mental health challenges without the aid of a mental health practitioner. Further, the F-Scale was negatively correlated with a willingness to talk about personally sensitive issues with others. Perhaps because of authoritarianism's deference to authority, the F-Scale was unassociated with ratings of confidence in mental health practitioners. However, a more recent study (McGowan & Midlarsky, 2012) reported substantially higher intercorrelations between these various components of attitudes toward mental health use than was observed by Fischer and Turner (1970). It is thus perhaps unsurprising that they found authoritarianism to predict not only attitudes toward stigma, discussing sensitive issues, and overcoming mental health challenges alone but also ratings of confidence in mental health practitioners. These confidence ratings were lower among authoritarians, which indicates that negative attitudes toward mental illness were stronger than the deference to the authority of mental health professionals (McGowan & Midlarsky, 2012). On the basis of these results, it is not surprising that authoritarians have been observed to be more reluctant to personally use mental health services (Furr, Usui, & Hines-Martin, 2003). Authoritarians may also be less likely to benefit from mental health treatment. For example, Quilty et al. (2008) found that improvement during treatment for depression was positively correlated with the Big Five trait of Openness to Experience, and authoritarians tend to have low scores on this trait (Sibley & Duckitt, 2008).

SUMMARY AND CONCLUSIONS

Authoritarianism was originally conceived as a highly stable personality trait with pathological implications for a wide range of personal and social outcomes. More recent research has tended to dispute the stability of authoritarianism, critically examine the possible positive and negative consequences of authoritarianism, and focus primarily on its political consequences (an excellent review of this latter literature is provided by McFarland, in press). The present chapter has aimed to preserve the broad focus and "trait" conception of authoritarianism while incorporating the more balanced evaluation of authoritarianism that is present in some corners of the contemporary literature, although space constraints limited the breadth and depth with which these topics could be addressed.

Because even the most even-handed evaluation of authoritarianism is likely to conclude that its negatives (especially for the lives of others) significantly outweigh its positives, research on how to shift an individual's authoritarianism level or constrain its negative impact on others is of particular importance. Education (Petzel & Crowson, in press) and exposure to diversity (Hodson, in press) present promising approaches to this end. However, the pernicious aspects of authoritarianism present themselves most clearly when considering political behaviors and expressions of prejudice. In the context of mental health or obedience to prosocial norms and laws, authoritarianism has some noteworthy positive characteristics. In particular, the emphasis of highly authoritarian individuals on obeying established authorities may serve to reduce their rates of substance abuse and criminal activities. However, it is important to note that even though highly authoritarian individuals may exhibit no difference from others in their need for treatment for other common mental disorders (somewhat contrary to earlier thinking, which saw authoritarianism as inherently pathological), they are less likely to seek out such treatment and may be less likely to benefit when receiving it. Highly authoritarian individuals may thus be an underserved population with respect to mental health, and future research should consider strategies for convincing such individuals of the benefits of psychological treatment.

REFERENCES

Adorno, T., Frenkel-Brunswik, E., Levinson, D. J., & Sanford, N. (1950). *The authoritarian personality*. Oxford, England: Harpers.

Altemeyer, R. (1981). *Right-wing authoritarianism*. Winnipeg, Manitoba, Canada: University of Manitoba Press.

Altemeyer, R. (1988). *Enemies of freedom: Understanding right-wing authoritarianism*. San Francisco, CA: Jossey-Bass.

Altemeyer, R. (1996). *The authoritarian specter*. Cambridge, MA: Harvard University Press.

Bouchard, T. J. (2009). Authoritarianism, religiousness, and conservatism: Is "Obedience to Authority" the explanation for their clustering, universality, and evolution? In E. Voland & W. Schiefenhövel (Eds.), *The biological evolution of religious mind and behavior* (pp. 165–180). Berlin, Germany: Springer-Verlag. http://dx.doi.org/10.1007/978-3-642-00128-4_11

Burt, S. A., & Donnellan, M. B. (2008). Personality correlates of aggressive and non-aggressive antisocial behavior. *Personality and Individual Differences, 44*, 53–63. http://dx.doi.org/10.1016/j.paid.2007.07.022

Carnahan, T., & McFarland, S. (2007). Revisiting the Stanford prison experiment: Could participant self-selection have led to the cruelty? *Personality and Social Psychology Bulletin, 33*, 603–614. http://dx.doi.org/10.1177/0146167206292689

Carraro, L., Castelli, L., & Macchiella, C. (2011). The automatic conservative: Ideology-based attentional asymmetries in the processing of valenced information. *PLoS ONE, 6*(11), e26456. http://dx.doi.org/10.1371/journal.pone.0026456

Costa, P. T., Jr., & McCrae, R. R. (2008). The Revised NEO Personality Inventory (NEO–PI–R). In G. J. Boyle, G. Matthews, & D. H. Saklofske (Eds.), *The Sage handbook of personality theory and assessment: Vol. 2. Personality Measurement and Testing* (pp. 179–198). Los Angeles, CA: Sage.

DeYoung, C. G. (2015). Cybernetic Big Five theory. *Journal of Research in Personality, 56*, 33–58.

Dodd, M., Balzer, A., Jacobs, C. M., Gruszczynski, M. W., Smith, K. B., & Hibbing, J. R. (2012). The political left rolls with the good and the political right confronts the bad: Connecting physiology and cognition to preferences. *Philosophical Transactions of the Royal Society B: Biological Sciences, 367*, 640–649.

Doty, R. M., Peterson, B. E., & Winter, D. G. (1991). Threat and authoritarianism in the United States, 1978–1987. *Journal of Personality and Social Psychology, 61*, 629–640. http://dx.doi.org/10.1037/0022-3514.61.4.629

Duckitt, J., Bizumic, B., Krauss, S., & Heled, E. (2010). A tripartite approach to right-wing authoritarianism: The authoritarianism-conservatism-traditionalism model. *Political Psychology, 31,* 685–715. http://dx.doi.org/10.1111/j.1467-9221.2010.00781.x

Duckitt, J., & Fisher, K. (2003). The impact of social threat on worldview and ideological attitudes. *Political Psychology, 24,* 199–222. http://dx.doi.org/10.1111/0162-895X.00322

Duckitt, J., & Sibley, C. G. (2007). Right-wing authoritarianism, social dominance orientation and the dimensions of generalized prejudice. *European Journal of Personality, 21,* 113–130. http://dx.doi.org/10.1002/per.614

Duckitt, J., & Sibley, C. G. (2010). Personality, ideology, prejudice, and politics: A dual-process motivational model. *Journal of Personality, 78,* 1861–1894. http://dx.doi.org/10.1111/j.1467-6494.2010.00672.x

Duriez, B., Klimstra, T., Luyckx, K., Beyers, W., & Soenens, B. (2012). Right-wing authoritarianism: Protective factor against or risk factor for depression? *European Journal of Personality, 26,* 536–549. http://dx.doi.org/10.1002/per.853

Elkins, I. J., King, S. M., McGue, M., & Iacono, W. G. (2006). Personality traits and the development of nicotine, alcohol, and illicit drug disorders: Prospective links from adolescence to young adulthood. *Journal of Abnormal Psychology, 115,* 26–39. http://dx.doi.org/10.1037/0021-843X.115.1.26

Elms, A., & Milgram, S. (1966). Personality characteristics associated with obedience and defiance toward authoritative command. *Journal of Experimental Research in Personality, 1,* 282–289.

Eysenck, H. J., & Coulter, T. T. (1972). The personality and attitudes of working-class British Communists and Fascists. *The Journal of Social Psychology, 87,* 59–73. http://dx.doi.org/10.1080/00224545.1972.9918648

Feldman, S. (2003). Enforcing social conformity: A theory of authoritarianism. *Political Psychology, 24,* 41–74. http://dx.doi.org/10.1111/0162-895X.00316

Feldman, S., & Stenner, K. (1997). Perceived threat and authoritarianism. *Political Psychology, 18,* 741–770. http://dx.doi.org/10.1111/0162-895X.00077

Fischer, E. H., & Turner, J. L. (1970). Orientations to seeking professional help: Development and research utility of an attitude scale. *Journal of Consulting and Clinical Psychology, 35,* 79–90. http://dx.doi.org/10.1037/h0029636

Fodor, E. M. (2006). Right-wing authoritarianism and managerial assessment of a schizophrenic candidate. *Journal of Applied Social Psychology, 36,* 953–978. http://dx.doi.org/10.1111/j.0021-9029.2006.00051.x

Funke, F. (2005). The dimensionality of right-wing authoritarianism: Lessons from the dilemma between theory and measurement. *Political Psychology, 26,* 195–218. http://dx.doi.org/10.1111/j.1467-9221.2005.00415.x

Furr, L. A., Usui, W., & Hines-Martin, V. (2003). Authoritarianism and attitudes toward mental health services. *American Journal of Orthopsychiatry, 73,* 411–418. http://dx.doi.org/10.1037/0002-9432.73.4.411

Haidt, J. (2011, January). *The bright future of post-partisan social psychology*. Presented at the Annual Meeting of the Society for Personality and Social Psychology, San Antonio, TX.

Haney, C., Banks, C., & Zimbardo, P. (1973). Interpersonal dynamics in a simulated prison. *International Journal of Criminology & Penology, 1*, 69–97.

Hibbing, J. R., Smith, K. B., & Alford, J. R. (2014). Differences in negativity bias underlie variations in political ideology. *Behavioral and Brain Sciences, 37*, 297–307. http://dx.doi.org/10.1017/S0140525X13001192

Hodson, G. (in press). Authoritarian contact—From "tight circles" to cross-group friendship. In F. Funke, T. Petzel, C. Cohrs, & J. Duckitt (Eds.), *Perspectives on authoritarianism* (Politische Psychologie series). Berlin, Germany: Verlag.

Jost, J. T., Glaser, J., Kruglanski, A. W., & Sulloway, F. J. (2003). Political conservatism as motivated social cognition. *Psychological Bulletin, 129*, 339–375. http://dx.doi.org/10.1037/0033-2909.129.3.339

Jugert, P., Cohrs, J. C., & Duckitt, J. (2009). Inter- and intrapersonal processes underlying authoritarianism: The role of social conformity and personal need for structure. *European Journal of Personality, 23*, 607–621. http://dx.doi.org/10.1002/per.735

Jugert, P., & Duckitt, J. (2009). A motivational model of authoritarianism: Integrating personal and situational determinants. *Political Psychology, 30*, 693–719. http://dx.doi.org/10.1111/j.1467-9221.2009.00722.x

Kessler, T., & Cohrs, J. C. (2008). The evolution of authoritarian processes: Fostering cooperation in large-scale groups. *Group Dynamics: Theory, Research, and Practice, 12*, 73–84. http://dx.doi.org/10.1037/1089-2699.12.1.73

Kohn, P. M., & Mercer, G. W. (1971). Drug use, drug-use attitudes, and the authoritarianism-rebellion dimension. *Journal of Health and Social Behavior, 12*, 125–131. http://dx.doi.org/10.2307/2948519

Krueger, R. F., Caspi, A., Moffitt, T. E., Silva, P. A., & McGee, R. (1996). Personality traits are differentially linked to mental disorders: A multitrait–multidiagnosis study of an adolescent birth cohort. *Journal of Abnormal Psychology, 105*, 299–312. http://dx.doi.org/10.1037/0021-843X.105.3.299

Krueger, R. F., Schmutte, P. S., Caspi, A., Moffitt, T. E., Campbell, K., & Silva, P. A. (1994). Personality traits are linked to crime among men and women: Evidence from a birth cohort. *Journal of Abnormal Psychology, 103*, 328–338. http://dx.doi.org/10.1037/0021-843X.103.2.328

Ludeke, S. G., & DeYoung, C. G. (2014). Differences in negativity bias probably underlie variation in attitudes toward change generally, not political ideology specifically. *Behavioral and Brain Sciences, 37*, 319–320. http://dx.doi.org/10.1017/S0140525X13002641

Ludeke, S. G., Johnson, W., & Bouchard, T. J., Jr. (2013). "Obedience to traditional authority": A heritable factor underlying authoritarianism, conservatism, and religiousness. *Personality and Individual Differences, 55*, 375–380. http://dx.doi.org/10.1016/j.paid.2013.03.018

Ludeke, S. G., & Krueger, R. F. (2013). Authoritarianism as a personality trait: Evidence from a longitudinal behavior genetic study. *Personality and Individual Differences, 55*, 480–484. http://dx.doi.org/10.1016/j.paid.2013.04.015

Ludeke, S. G., Reifen Tagar, M., & DeYoung, C. G. (2014, May 15). Not as different as we want to be: Attitudinally consistent trait desirability leads to exaggerated associations between personality and sociopolitical attitudes. *Political Psychology.* Advance online publication. http://dx.doi.org/10.1111/pops.12221

Ludeke, S. G., Weisberg, Y. J., & DeYoung, C. G. (2013). Idiographically desirable responding: Individual differences in perceived trait desirability predict over-claiming. *European Journal of Personality, 27*, 580–592. http://dx.doi.org/10.1002/per.1914

McAdams, D. P., & Pals, J. L. (2006). A new Big Five: Fundamental principles for an integrative science of personality. *American Psychologist, 61*, 204–217. http://dx.doi.org/10.1037/0003-066X.61.3.204

McCourt, K., Bouchard, T. J., Jr., Lykken, D. T., Tellegen, A., & Keyes, M. (1999). Authoritarianism revisited: Genetic and environmental influences examined in twins reared apart and together. *Personality and Individual Differences, 27*, 985–1014. http://dx.doi.org/10.1016/S0191-8869(99)00048-3

McCrae, R. R., & Costa, P. T., Jr. (2008). The five-factor theory of personality. In O. P. John, R. W. Robins, & L. A. Pervin (Eds.), *Handbook of personality: Theory and research* (3rd ed., pp. 159–181). New York, NY: Guilford Press.

McFarland, S. G. (in press). Consequences of authoritarianism for political attitudes and behaviors. In F. Funke, T. Petzel, C. Cohrs, & J. Duckitt (Eds.), *Perspectives on authoritarianism* (Politische Psychologie series). Berlin, Germany: Verlag.

McFarland, S. G., Ageyev, V., & Abalakina, M. (1993). The authoritarian personality in the United States and former Soviet Union: Comparative studies. In W. F. Stone, G. Lederer, & R. Christie (Eds.), *Strength and weakness: The authoritarian personality today* (pp. 199–225). New York, NY: Springer. http://dx.doi.org/10.1007/978-1-4613-9180-7_10

McFarland, S. G., Ageyev, V. S., & Abalakina-Paap, M. A. (1992). Authoritarianism in the former Soviet Union. *Journal of Personality and Social Psychology, 63*, 1004–1010. http://dx.doi.org/10.1037/0022-3514.63.6.1004

McGowan, J. C., & Midlarsky, E. (2012). Religiosity, authoritarianism, and attitudes toward psychotherapy in later life. *Aging & Mental Health, 16*, 659–665. http://dx.doi.org/10.1080/13607863.2011.653954

Meloen, J. D. (1993). The F-scale as a predictor of fascism: An overview of 40 years of authoritarianism research. In W. F. Stone, G. Lederer, & R. Christie (Eds.), *Strength and weakness: The authoritarian personality today* (pp. 47–69). New York, NY: Springer. http://dx.doi.org/10.1007/978-1-4613-9180-7_3

Meston, C. M., Heiman, J. R., Trapnell, P. D., & Paulhus, D. L. (1998). Socially desirable responding and sexuality. *Journal of Sex Research, 35*, 148–157. http://dx.doi.org/10.1080/00224499809551928

Milgram, S. (1973). The perils of obedience. *Harper's, 1483*, 62–77.

Napier, J. L., & Jost, J. T. (2008). Why are conservatives happier than liberals? *Psychological Science, 19*, 565–572. http://dx.doi.org/10.1111/j.1467-9280.2008.02124.x

Onraet, E., Van Hiel, A., & Dhont, K. (2013). The relationship between right-wing ideological attitudes and psychological well-being. *Personality and Social Psychology Bulletin, 39*, 509–522. http://dx.doi.org/10.1177/0146167213478199

Oxley, D. R., Smith, K. B., Alford, J. R., Hibbing, M. V., Miller, J. L., Scalora, M., . . . Hibbing, J. R. (2008, September 19). Political attitudes vary with physiological traits. *Faculty Publications: Political Science*. Retrieved from http://digitalcommons.unl.edu/cgi/viewcontent.cgi?article=1026&context=poliscifacpub

Petzel, T., & Crowson, H. M. (in press). Schools against authoritarianism: An examination of possible avenues to reduce antidemocratic dispositions in educational institutions. In F. Funke, T. Petzel, C. Cohrs, & J. Duckitt (Eds.), *Perspectives on authoritarianism* (Politische Psychologie series). Berlin, Germany: Verlag.

Pytlik Zillig, L. M., Hemenover, S. H., & Dienstbier, R. A. (2002). What do we assess when we assess a Big 5 trait? A content analysis of the affective, behavioral, and cognitive processes represented in Big 5 personality inventories. *Personality and Social Psychology Bulletin, 28*, 847–858. http://dx.doi.org/10.1177/0146167202289013

Quilty, L. C., De Fruyt, F., Rolland, J.-P., Kennedy, S. H., Rouillon, P. F., & Bagby, R. M. (2008). Dimensional personality traits and treatment outcome in patients with major depressive disorder. *Journal of Affective Disorders, 108*, 241–250. http://dx.doi.org/10.1016/j.jad.2007.10.022

Reifen Tagar, M., Federico, C. M., Lyons, K. E., Ludeke, S., & Koenig, M. A. (2014). Heralding the authoritarian? Orientation toward authority in early childhood. *Psychological Science, 25*, 883–892. http://dx.doi.org/10.1177/0956797613516470

Roberts, B. W., & DelVecchio, W. F. (2000). The rank-order consistency of personality traits from childhood to old age: A quantitative review of longitudinal studies. *Psychological Bulletin, 126*, 3–25. http://dx.doi.org/10.1037/0033-2909.126.1.3

Roberts, B. W., Walton, K. E., & Viechtbauer, W. (2006). Patterns of mean-level change in personality traits across the life course: A meta-analysis of longitudinal studies. *Psychological Bulletin, 132*, 1–25.

Rubinstein, G. (1996). Two peoples in one land: A validation study of Altemeyer's Right-Wing Authoritarianism Scale in the Palestinian and Jewish societies in Israel. *Journal of Cross-Cultural Psychology, 27*, 216–230. http://dx.doi.org/10.1177/0022022196272005

Sales, S. M. (1973). Threat as a factor in authoritarianism: An analysis of archival data. *Journal of Personality and Social Psychology, 28*, 44–57. http://dx.doi.org/10.1037/h0035588

Samuel, D. B., & Widiger, T. A. (2008). A meta-analytic review of the relationships between the five-factor model and *DSM–IV–TR* personality disorders: A facet level analysis. *Clinical Psychology Review, 28*, 1326–1342. http://dx.doi.org/10.1016/j.cpr.2008.07.002

Saucier, G. (2000). Isms and the structure of social attitudes. *Journal of Personality and Social Psychology, 78,* 366–385. http://dx.doi.org/10.1037/0022-3514.78.2.366

Saucier, G. (2013). Isms dimensions: Toward a more comprehensive and integrative model of belief-system components. *Journal of Personality and Social Psychology, 104,* 921–939. http://dx.doi.org/10.1037/a0031968

Schoon, I., Cheng, H., Gale, C. R., Batty, G. D., & Deary, I. J. (2010). Social status, cognitive ability, and educational attainment as predictors of liberal social attitudes and political trust. *Intelligence, 38,* 144–150. http://dx.doi.org/10.1016/j.intell.2009.09.005

Shikishima, C., & Ando, J. (2004). Transmission of social attitudes in a family: A behavioral genetic approach. *Japanese Journal of Family Sociology, 16,* 12–20. http://dx.doi.org/10.4234/jjoffamilysociology.16.12

Shook, N. J., & Fazio, R. H. (2009). Political ideology, exploration of novel stimuli, and attitude formation. *Journal of Experimental Social Psychology, 45,* 995–998. http://dx.doi.org/10.1016/j.jesp.2009.04.003

Sibley, C. G., & Duckitt, J. (in press). Personality geneses of authoritarianism—The form and function of openness to experience. In F. Funke, T. Petzel, C. Cohrs, & J. Duckitt (Eds.), *Perspectives on authoritarianism* (Politische Psychologie series). Berlin, Germany: Verlag.

Sibley, C. G., & Duckitt, J. (2008). Personality and prejudice: A meta-analysis and theoretical review. *Personality and Social Psychology Review, 12,* 248–279. http://dx.doi.org/10.1177/1088868308319226

Steiner, J. M., & Fahrenberg, J. (1970). Die auspragung autoritarer einstellung bei ehemaligen angehorigen der SS und der Wehrmacht [The authoritarian views of former members of the SS and the Wehrmacht]. *Kölner Zeitschrift für Soziologie und Sozialpsychologie* [Cologne Journal of Sociology and Social Psychology], *22,* 551–566.

Tellegen, A., & Waller, N. G. (2008). Exploring personality through test construction: Development of the Multidimensional Personality Questionnaire. In G. J. Boyle, G. Matthews, & D. Saklofske (Eds.), *The Sage handbook of personality theory and assessment* (pp. 261–292). Thousand Oaks, CA: Sage. http://dx.doi.org/10.4135/9781849200479.n13

Van Hiel, A., Cornelis, I., Roets, A., & De Clercq, B. (2007). A comparison of various authoritarianism scales in Belgian Flanders. *European Journal of Personality, 21,* 149–168. http://dx.doi.org/10.1002/per.617

Van Hiel, A., & Crowson, H. M. (in press). The relation between right-wing attitudes and cognitive style. In F. Funke, T. Petzel, C. Cohrs, & J. Duckitt (Eds.), *Perspectives on authoritarianism* (Politische Psychologie series). Berlin, Germany: Verlag.

Van Hiel, A., & De Clercq, B. (2009). Authoritarianism is good for you: Right-wing authoritarianism as a buffering factor for mental distress. *European Journal of Personality, 23,* 33–50. http://dx.doi.org/10.1002/per.702

Van Hiel, A., Onraet, E., & De Pauw, S. (2010). The relationship between social-cultural attitudes and behavioral measures of cognitive style: A meta-analytic integration of studies. *Journal of Personality, 78*, 1765–1799. http://dx.doi.org/10.1111/j.1467-6494.2010.00669.x

White, A. E., Kenrick, D. T., Li, Y. J., Mortensen, C. R., Neuberg, S. L., & Cohen, A. B. (2012). When nasty breeds nice: Threats of violence amplify agreeableness at national, individual, and situational levels. *Journal of Personality and Social Psychology, 103*, 622–634. http://dx.doi.org/10.1037/a0029140

Wilson, G. D., Ausman, J., & Mathews, T. R. (1973). Conservatism and art preferences. *Journal of Personality and Social Psychology, 25*, 286–288. http://dx.doi.org/10.1037/h0033972

12

THE DARK (AND LIGHT) SIDES OF OVERCONFIDENCE

JOYCE EHRLINGER AND ALEX EICHENBAUM

DEFINITION AND BACKGROUND

In the single deadliest accident in Mount Everest's history, an avalanche fell on a group of 50 climbers in 2004, killing 12 and wounding more. Since 1950, more than 800 people have died during attempts to scale the Nepali mountains, including Everest. Thousands more have suffered injury in pursuing the same goal (Salisbury & Hawley, 2011). Presumably few of those who have been injured or died expected their venture to end in tragedy. Had they anticipated these outcomes, they might have found other ways in which to spend their time. Everest stands as a particularly salient example of the sometimes-deadly consequences of overconfidence.

In its broadest form, *overconfidence* can be defined as an overly positive perception of oneself relative to some comparison standard. Confidence can carry many benefits (for a review, see Bandura, 1997). However, overconfidence

http://dx.doi.org/10.1037/14854-013
The Dark Side of Personality: Science and Practice in Social, Personality, and Clinical Psychology, V. Zeigler-Hill and D. K. Marcus (Editors)

refers to the type of confidence that exceeds one's abilities, sometimes to a large degree. Overconfidence refers to the tendency for individuals to view themselves more favorably than others, hold unrealistically high opinions of their own positive traits and abilities, possess overly high estimates of the likelihood that they will experience primarily positive events in the future, and have unrealistically high impressions of the accuracy of their beliefs and opinions. Perhaps the best-known findings in the literature on overconfidence are the tendencies for people to view themselves as consistently better than average with respect to their intellectual abilities (Alicke, Klotz, Breitenbecher, Yurak, & Vredenburg, 1995), job performance (e.g., Harrison & Shaffer, 1994; Oskam, Kingma, & Klasen, 2000), and social skills (College Board, 1976–1977). For example, in one company, 42% of engineers rated their work in the top 5% relative to their peers (Zenger, 1992). Similarly, on average, 90% of drivers rate themselves as above average in their driving ability (Svenson, 1981). Although some people are, presumably, smarter or more productive than the average person, it is statistically impossible for greater than half of the relevant population to be "above average" for any given dimension.

As the literature on the better-than-average effect suggests, people routinely view themselves in more positive terms than can be justified given objective metrics. In this chapter, we discuss when and why people tend to be overconfident, as well as the adaptive and maladaptive features of this robust characteristic of self-assessments.

REVIEW OF THE RELEVANT LITERATURE

Overconfidence has been operationally defined in multiple ways by different researchers. The better-than-average effect is perhaps the best known example of what Moore and Healy (2008) have categorized as *overplacement* in a recent review of the literature on overconfidence. *Overplacement* is defined as an overly positive perception that one is superior to others in a given domain. This can be contrasted with *overestimation*, which is defined as a person's exaggerated perception of his or her own ability or chance of success relative to an objective measure. Finally, Moore and Healy defined *overprecision* as undue confidence in the accuracy of one's beliefs. We use these categories to summarize the literature on overconfidence.

Overplacement has been demonstrated in studies that measure (a) people's perceptions of how they have performed relative to a specific reference group (e.g., one's classmates) and (b) how well participants and others in the relevant reference group have actually performed. People also show significant patterns of overplacement when evaluating their performance on academic exams, their ability to evaluate jokes, and their performance in debate competitions (e.g., Ehrlinger, Johnson, Banner, Dunning, & Kruger, 2008; Kruger & Dunning, 1999).

Whereas overplacement refers to overconfidence in perceptions of how one compares with other people, overestimation refers to the tendency to evaluate one's performances, skills, or personal qualities more positively than can be justified when compared with an objective score or reference point. For example, a student might estimate that he performed well on an exam, answering at least 95% of the questions correctly. If this student answered only 70% of the questions correctly, the student can be said to have overestimated the quality of his test performance. Indeed, past research suggests that students often overestimate the quality of their test performances (Ehrlinger et al., 2008). Overestimation is also common in people's judgments of how they are seen by others. In particular, people tend to overestimate the degree to which others describe their personality in positive ways (Malloy & Janowski, 1992). People also tend to overestimate the degree to which they have control over other people, external variables, and even chance-based events (Langer, 1975). Overestimation is also prevalent when predicting one's own future behavior. We expect that we will behave more charitably (Epley & Dunning, 2000) and that we will be more productive (Buehler, Griffin, & Ross, 1994) than often turns out to be the case.

Finally, the third type of overconfidence identified by Moore and Healy (2008) is *overprecision*—the tendency to have undue confidence in the accuracy of one's judgments or estimates. To quantify overprecision, researchers ask participants to provide a numerical estimate of, for example, the size of a city or the number of weeks it might take to complete a project. Participants are also asked to create a confidence interval around their estimate by naming the lowest likely value for their estimate and the highest likely value. This literature suggests that people tend to be vastly overconfident in the precision of their judgments and beliefs. For example, one study asking traders to estimate 90% confidence intervals of stock prices 6 months in the future found that fewer than 50% estimated an interval that contained the eventual stock price (Deaves, Lüders, & Schröder, 2010). Even when offered feedback, individuals tend to adjust their confidence only marginally, and not nearly as much as they should (Mannes & Moore, 2013).

Causes of Overconfidence

There are at least two broad types of explanations for the frequency with which self-assessments are overly positive. First, it just feels good to think well of the self. People see themselves as better than most others, to some degree, because they are motivated to believe positive things about the self (Taylor & Brown, 1988). Consistent with this explanation, the better-than-average effect is seen most often for characteristics that are viewed as highly desirable (Alicke, 1985) and important (Brown, 2012). In other words, people tend to be most overconfident in exactly the ways that might feel the best.

Despite the tendency for overconfidence, few of us believe that we are Einstein's intellectual equal or that our singing and dancing abilities merit a career on Broadway. As nice as it feels to believe positive things about ourselves, this motivation is tempered by the day-to-day feedback that most of us receive suggesting that we are not perfect. Although we cannot completely ignore the presence of negative feedback in our lives, people do hold negative information about the self to a higher standard than positive information. We more often pay attention to (Ehrlinger, Mitchum, & Dweck, in press), remember (Kunda, 1990), and give greater weight to (Dunning, Meyerowitz, & Holzberg, 1989) flattering over unflattering information. These practices make it easier to maintain overly positive views of the self.

A second category of explanations for the frequency of overconfidence in self-assessments relates to important social cognitive features of how the mind works. For example, confidence judgments are strongly anchored by whatever information is more focal for the individual at the time of judgments. People tend to give too much weight to their own experiences and too little weight to the likely experiences of others when making judgments about how their own performance or likely outcomes might compare to that of other people (Chambers & Windschitl, 2004). This cognitive bias leads to tendencies to view oneself as above average for easy tasks. People anchor on the fact that a task is easy for them and give too little weight to the fact that this same task is likely easy for others (Kruger, 1999).

Individual Differences

One important way of discovering additional contributors to overconfidence is to identify which individuals tend to show the most overconfidence and use this knowledge to understand how these individuals differ from those showing less overconfidence. Kruger and Dunning (1999) discovered that those who lack skill tend to be far more overconfident than their more competent peers. A particularly troubling example of this tendency is that gun owners performing in the bottom quartile on a test of gun use and safety rated their test performance as above average relative to their gun-owning peers (Ehrlinger et al., 2008). The primary reason that those who lack skill remain grossly overconfident is that they lack the knowledge necessary to recognize when they are mistaken and in what ways they need improvement.

Using a similar individual differences approach, Ehrlinger et al. (in press) discovered that people's beliefs about the malleability of intelligence have an important impact on rates of overconfidence. People who view intelligence as fixed account for most of the overconfidence effect for academic performances, whereas those who view intelligence as malleable make far more accurate self-assessments. People with a fixed view of intelligence feel more threatened by feelings of difficulty than those with a malleable view (e.g., Blackwell, Trzesniewski, & Dweck, 2007). For this reason, those with a fixed view allocate their attention away from challenging portions of tasks and toward easier questions. This practice leaves fixed theorists overconfident in the quality of their performances, whereas malleable theorists hold more accurate perceptions of their work (Ehrlinger et al., in press).

Underconfidence

Although underconfidence is far less common than overconfidence, there are several important instances in which it reliably occurs. One of the most troubling examples of underconfidence is the tendency for women and underrepresented minorities to lack confidence in their abilities to succeed in important science, technology, engineering, and math (STEM) domains. From a young age, boys often perceive themselves as more academically competent and capable than girls, even in the absence of any real difference in ability (Phillips & Zimmerman, 1990). Women tend to be less confident than men and, often, less confident than their abilities would merit, especially in STEM fields (Hackett, 1985). This lack of confidence leads to fewer women than men pursuing opportunities and careers in STEM fields (Betz & Hackett, 1981; Ehrlinger & Dunning, 2003).

ADAPTIVE AND MALADAPTIVE FEATURES

There is one important benefit of a certain type of overconfidence that has been demonstrated time and time again. To the degree that people possess high feelings of self-efficacy—a sense that one will be able to take on and complete the actions necessary to attain one's goals—they are more willing to take on challenges and, ultimately, they achieve more than those with lower feelings of self-efficacy (for a review, see Bandura, 1997). The benefits of self-efficacy can be self-fulfilling in that someone who is overconfident will be more willing to apply for high-level jobs, attempt challenging classes, and take risks. Although these people might not achieve everything that they hope or expect, just by virtue of trying, they will achieve considerably more than those who do not try at all. As such, self-efficacy correlates positively with a host of successful athletic (Kane, Marks, Zaccaro, & Blair, 1996), educational (Schunk, 1996), occupational (Latham & Saari, 1979; Porras & Anderson, 1981), and health outcomes (Carey & Carey, 1993).

The literature on self-efficacy suggests that a certain type of confidence, and even overconfidence, might be beneficial. Bandura (1997) referred to these confident, successful people as *resolute strivers*. They are people who are not crushed by minor rejections in part because they believe that, with considered effort, they might succeed. This type is different from other types of overconfident people, including those who believe that they already possess considerable skills and talent or who believe that their past accomplishments have been more impressive than objective metrics would warrant.

The maladaptive features of overconfidence are also plentiful. As noted in the opening example, thousands have been injured or died in overconfident attempts to scale Everest and other Nepali mountains (Salisbury & Hawley, 2011). Overconfidence can also result in less strong performance compared with a more accurate view of the self (Stone, 1994; Vancouver, Thompson, Tischner, & Putka, 2002). For example, one study asked undergraduates to assume the role of a high school principal tasked with improving students' standardized test scores. Those participants who displayed more overconfidence in their solutions provided persuasive statements regarding the likelihood of plan success but were less likely than their less overconfident peers to see the potential deficiencies in their plan (Shipman & Mumford, 2011). Overconfidence can also lead to disappointment that might come when one recognizes that an actual outcome is considerably less positive than the expected outcome (McGraw, Mellers, & Ritov, 2004).

Equally important are the interpersonal consequences of overconfidence. It is true that an overconfident lawyer might experience incrementally more success in winning her cases compared with a less confident lawyer. However, there is little relationship between lawyers' predictions of case outcomes and what actually occurs (Goodman-Delahunty, Granhag, Hartwig, & Loftus, 2010). The clients of these lawyers might prefer a lawyer who is well calibrated about the odds of success over one that is overconfident. Similarly, if asked to choose between a well-calibrated and an overconfident surgeon, we know whom we would prefer to hold the knife.

Overconfidence can also be maladaptive at the group level, often with disastrous consequences. *Groupthink* results when groups dismiss or fail to voice dissenting opinions, instead encouraging concordance or harmony within the individuals composing the group. What often results in these cases is an insulation of the group from "outsiders," as well as from individuals within the group itself, who have points of view or even relevant data that do not conform to the group consensus. Irving Janis (1972) was the first to coin the term and to model and explain the behavior in practical terms. The canonical example he used to illustrate both the process and the effects of groupthink was the Bay of Pigs invasion, when President John F. Kennedy initiated a botched invasion of Cuba in 1961. Janis, and others more recently (e.g., Hermann &

Rammal, 2010), identified a few hallmarks of groupthink in this context; the most important of these are a feeling of invincibility and a certainty in the morality of the group. Kennedy was new in office, and his advisors did not feel comfortable disagreeing with him (or he with them), they underestimated Castro, and marginalized those in the administration who advised caution. Others have reanalyzed many of Janis's examples and suggested that a need for cohesion is not primary in groupthink. Rather, groups may be quicker than individuals acting alone to make decisions that lead to "closure" (Kruglanski, Pierro, Mannetti, & De Grada, 2006), or that threats to the shared social identity of the group better account for the phenomenon, when it occurs (Baron, 2005). The common outcome, however, is a flawed and dangerous decision-making process that can blind individuals to important risks.

In sum, overconfidence can be seen as a double-edged sword, allowing us to set our sights high (for a review, see Bandura, 1997) and to protect our fragile egos (Brown, 2012) while simultaneously robbing us from the opportunity to learn (Ehrlinger et al., in press). Perhaps the ideal state, then, might be one of slight overconfidence—enough to reap the benefits without risking significant costs.

DIRECTIONS FOR FUTURE RESEARCH

Perhaps the most important avenue for future research on overconfidence is to better understand when and how overconfidence can be adaptive rather than maladaptive. As suggested in this chapter, we could imagine that it might be beneficial to be a little overconfident, but not vastly overconfident. Although others have argued this point (Baumeister, 1989), we know of no research that has tested this assertion or clearly outlined the ideal relationship between one's confidence and one's abilities. As our review suggests, there are clear costs and benefits to overconfidence, but researchers have not yet identified how people can best maximize those benefits while minimizing potential costs.

To the degree that research has, and will continue to, identify maladaptive features of overconfidence, an important goal for future research will be to identify means of reducing overconfidence. Previous research has given some insight into strategies that might be effective for encouraging accuracy in self-assessments. However, this work is still in its infancy. For example, there are several mechanisms for reducing people's motivation to self-enhance. To the degree that overconfidence reflects a simple desire to think well of the self, then, one might inspire greater accuracy in self-assessments by making people accountable for their self-assessments (Sedikides, Herbst, Hardin, & Dardis, 2002) or by allowing people to affirm positive aspects of their identity before they give confidence assessments (Blanton, Pelham, DeHart, & Carvallo, 2001). That said, it is clear that overconfidence stems from more than just simple enhancement. Indeed, participants in one study were offered $100 as an incentive to provide accurate estimates of how well they had performed on a set of logic problems. Even this large financial incentive had no impact on the accuracy of students' assessments (Ehrlinger et al., 2008).

CLINICAL IMPLICATIONS

In this section, we offer a brief overview of four areas where research on overconfidence has influenced (and been influenced by) real-world applications and outcomes.

Clinical Psychology

On the basis of the research and prevailing models discussed earlier, it should come as no surprise that individuals' self-perceptions deviate from the perceptions held by others, but research has shown that certain characteristics, especially narcissism, have the potential to eclipse these more general effects (for a review, see Chapter 1, this volume). Individuals scoring high on four measures of narcissism showed significantly greater overconfidence than their less narcissistic peers when predicting their performance in a group-decision task (John & Robins, 1994). Others have also found that overconfidence correlates with nonclinical narcissism; individuals higher in narcissism show no greater accuracy than those low in narcissism when predicting future performance, but they exhibit more confidence in those predictions (Campbell, Goodie, & Foster, 2004). Those high in narcissism tended to base their predictions of future outcomes on inflated expectations instead of past performance on the task in question. A pattern of overconfidence can be seen in other clinical populations. For example, individuals with schizophrenia were more overconfident than controls in their incorrect assessments of another's emotional state (Köther et al., 2012), and patients with borderline personality disorder showed increased overconfidence relative to nonpatients on a theory of mind test (Schilling et al., 2012).

Clinicians themselves are not immune to professional errors of overconfidence. In a classic study, Oskamp (1965) offered clinicians case studies and asked for diagnoses. As participants were given more and more information about each case, their confidence in their diagnoses grew significantly. However, additional information had little impact on the accuracy of the clinicians' diagnoses, such that most of the clinicians studied were unduly overconfident in the accuracy of their impressions. It is important to note, however, that clinical confidence levels are sometimes effective predictors of patient risk (McNiel, Sandberg, & Binder, 1998) and that tendencies toward overconfidence can be combated. Sripada et al. (2011) showed that when psychiatry residents who are engaged in psychotherapy review their ratings of patient functioning with the patients themselves, the therapists' overconfidence in treatment effects can be significantly mitigated.

Health

A body of research demonstrates overconfidence among doctors, nurses, and other health professionals (e.g., Marteau, Johnston, Wynne, & Evans, 1989; Tracey, Arroll, Richmond, & Barham, 1997), but we focus here on the related issue of laypersons' overconfidence as it relates to their personal health decisions. Regarding general health, as well as a host of specific health issues, people underestimate their overall risk relative to the population (Weinstein, 1980, 1987) and show overoptimistic views of their health given facts about their specific risk factors (e.g., Sutton & Bolling, 2003). The obvious implication for these beliefs is that many individuals will continue to engage in risky or unhealthy behaviors because individuals' perceptions of their own vulnerability is a prerequisite for engaging in preventative measures or the cessation of unhealthy ones (e.g., Becker, 1974; Weinstein, 1987). Although some techniques have been found to mitigate this excessive optimism (such as personal counseling and buttressing an individual's self-worth), arguably the most effective counterbalance is personal experience. Individuals who have experienced a negative health incident or life event (e.g., heart attack or auto accident) are more realistic in their personal assessments of the likelihood of experiencing relatively common and relatively uncommon events (Weinstein, 1987), although the effect is comparatively short-lived, and individuals tend to quickly regress to an overly optimistic state. This inflated self-view, however, can also be valuable in certain circumstances. When facing extremely trying life events, such as serious health problems or even war, one's ability to cope with the struggles and the aftermath are related to overconfidence and high optimism (Bonanno, Field, Kovacevic, & Kaltman, 2002; Taylor & Brown, 1988).

Management

Project management leads to profound consequences of overconfidence. New projects suffer from the planning fallacy, in which managers systematically underestimate the time and cost of completion (Buehler et al., 1994). Entering new markets and starting a new business can be similarly problematic. Would-be entrepreneurs tend to overestimate their likelihood of success in lines of business that require relatively greater skill (Camerer

& Lovallo, 1999). Some adaptive features of overconfidence can be seen in these examples as well. Entrepreneurs who showed greater self-confidence tended to work harder on their new businesses and tended to rely more on self-financing than less-confident business owners (Landier & Thesmar, 2003). This confidence allowed them greater flexibility and control over the business but also led to greater risk and loss of capital in more cases than their less-confident peers.

The top of the corporate ladder is not immune to the costly consequences of overconfidence. Consider that high-level managers are in a particularly precarious position with regard to the "risk factors" associated with overconfidence: For example, they have relatively few opportunities for honest feedback from superiors (Morrison & Milliken, 2000), and they tend to receive a disproportionate amount of credit for successes (Meindl, Ehrlich, & Dukerich, 1985). The inflated beliefs about their managerial ability lead many CEOs to make errors of judgment that are dangerous for their organizations and extremely expensive.

Education

Education relies on a student's ability to assess her competence on a topic and then decide whether further study is warranted. Education thus stands to suffer to the degree students are unable to evaluate their learning accurately. Indeed, much research paints a bleak picture on this topic. Students consistently give themselves higher grades than they receive from their instructors (Falchikov & Boud, 1989). More recently, however, laboratory and applied studies have demonstrated the ways in which students can mitigate some of the negative consequences of overconfidence in education. Specifically, work on metacognition in young learners is promising, showing that activities that encourage reflection on what one knows (and does not yet know)—through activities such as self-quizzing and writing targeted summaries in the student's own words—can lead to more accurate self-assessment of knowledge (Roediger & Karpicke, 2006; Thiede, Anderson, & Therriault, 2003). Data on student outcomes have confirmed the importance of strategies such as delayed self-testing and spaced study for fostering more accurate self-assessment and, consequently, success in learning (e.g., Thiede & Dunlosky, 1994).

SUMMARY AND CONCLUSIONS

Collectively, the literature on overconfidence suggests that it is an ever-present feature of human judgment, leaking into our perceptions of our own abilities, our beliefs about our chances for success, our comparisons to other people, and our confidence in our beliefs. Overconfidence stems from both motivated desires to think well of the self and cognitive features of how people organize information. Because overconfidence stems from multiple causes, it is somewhat resistant to efforts to eradicate it from our judgments. Overconfidence is not all bad. In fact, it carries benefits in terms of encouraging effort and persistence. Overconfidence in the form of self-efficacy can lead to real-world success. However, other forms of confidence likely carry more costs than benefits, including increased risk and loss of opportunities to improve. Future research should improve our understanding of when and how much overconfidence can foster success.

REFERENCES

Alicke, M. D. (1985). Global self-evaluation as determined by the desirability and controllability of trait adjectives. *Journal of Personality and Social Psychology, 49*, 1621–1630. http://dx.doi.org/10.1037/0022-3514.49.6.1621

Alicke, M. D., Klotz, M. L., Breitenbecher, D. L., Yurak, T. J., & Vredenburg, D. S. (1995). Personal contact, individuation, and the better-than-average effect. *Journal of Personality and Social Psychology, 68*, 804–825. http://dx.doi.org/10.1037/0022-3514.68.5.804

Bandura, A. (1997). *Self-efficacy: The exercise of control.* New York, NY: W. H. Freeman.

Baron, R. S. (2005). So right it's wrong: Groupthink and the ubiquitous nature of polarized group decision making. *Advances in Experimental Social Psychology, 37*, 219–253. http://dx.doi.org/10.1016/S0065-2601(05)37004-3

Baumeister, R. F. (1989). The optimal margin of illusion. *Journal of Social and Clinical Psychology, 8*, 176–189. http://dx.doi.org/10.1521/jscp.1989.8.2.176

Becker, M. H. (1974). The health belief model and personal health behavior. *Health Education Monographs, 2*, 324–473.

Betz, N. E., & Hackett, G. (1981). The relationship of career-related self-efficacy expectations to perceived career options in college women and men. *Journal of Counseling Psychology, 28*, 399–410. http://dx.doi.org/10.1037/0022-0167.28.5.399

Blackwell, L. S., Trzesniewski, K. H., & Dweck, C. S. (2007). Implicit theories of intelligence predict achievement across an adolescent transition: A longitudinal study and an intervention. *Child Development, 78*, 246–263. http://dx.doi.org/10.1111/j.1467-8624.2007.00995.x

Blanton, H., Pelham, B. W., DeHart, T., & Carvallo, M. (2001). Overconfidence as dissonance reduction. *Journal of Experimental Social Psychology, 37*, 373–385. http://dx.doi.org/10.1006/jesp.2000.1458

Bonanno, G. A., Field, N. P., Kovacevic, A., & Kaltman, S. (2002). Self-enhancement as a buffer against extreme adversity: Civil war in Bosnia and traumatic loss in the United States. *Personality and Social Psychology Bulletin, 28*, 184–196. http://dx.doi.org/10.1177/0146167202282005

Brown, J. D. (2012). Understanding the better than average effect: Motives (still) matter. *Personality and Social Psychology Bulletin, 38,* 209–219. http://dx.doi.org/10.1177/0146167211432763

Buehler, R., Griffin, D., & Ross, M. (1994). Exploring the "planning fallacy": Why people underestimate their task completion times. *Journal of Personality and Social Psychology, 67,* 366–381. http://dx.doi.org/10.1037/0022-3514.67.3.366

Camerer, C., & Lovallo, D. (1999). Overconfidence and excess entry: An experimental approach. *The American Economic Review, 89,* 306–318. http://dx.doi.org/10.1257/aer.89.1.306

Campbell, W. K., Goodie, A. S., & Foster, J. D. (2004). Narcissism, confidence, and risk attitude. *Journal of Behavioral Decision Making, 17,* 297–311. http://dx.doi.org/10.1002/bdm.475

Carey, K. B., & Carey, M. P. (1993). Changes in self-efficacy resulting from unaided attempts to quit smoking. *Psychology of Addictive Behaviors, 7,* 219–224. http://dx.doi.org/10.1037/0893-164X.7.4.219

Chambers, J. R., & Windschitl, P. D. (2004). Biases in social comparative judgments: The role of nonmotivated factors in above-average and comparative-optimism effects. *Psychological Bulletin, 130,* 813–838. http://dx.doi.org/10.1037/0033-2909.130.5.813

College Board. (1976–1977). *Student descriptive questionnaire.* Princeton, NJ: Educational Testing Service.

Deaves, R., Lüders, E., & Schröder, M. (2010). The dynamics of overconfidence: Evidence from stock market forecasters. *Journal of Economic Behavior & Organization, 75,* 402–412. http://dx.doi.org/10.1016/j.jebo.2010.05.001

Dunning, D., Meyerowitz, J. A., & Holzberg, A. D. (1989). Ambiguity and self-evaluation: The role of idiosyncratic trait definitions in self-serving assessments of ability. *Journal of Personality and Social Psychology, 57,* 1082–1090. http://dx.doi.org/10.1037/0022-3514.57.6.1082

Ehrlinger, J., & Dunning, D. (2003). How chronic self-views influence (and potentially mislead) estimates of performance. *Journal of Personality and Social Psychology, 84,* 5–17. http://dx.doi.org/10.1037/0022-3514.84.1.5

Ehrlinger, J., Johnson, K., Banner, M., Dunning, D., & Kruger, J. (2008). Why the unskilled are unaware: Further explorations of (absent) self-insight among the incompetent. *Organizational Behavior and Human Decision Processes, 105,* 98–121. http://dx.doi.org/10.1016/j.obhdp.2007.05.002

Ehrlinger, J., Mitchum, A. L., & Dweck, C. S. (in press). Understanding overconfidence: Implicit theories, preferential attention, and distorted self-assessment. *Journal of Experimental Social Psychology.*

Epley, N., & Dunning, D. (2000). Feeling "holier than thou": Are self-serving assessments produced by errors in self- or social prediction? *Journal of Personality and Social Psychology, 79,* 861–875. http://dx.doi.org/10.1037/0022-3514.79.6.861

Falchikov, N., & Boud, D. (1989). Student self-assessment in higher education: A meta-analysis. *Review of Educational Research, 59*, 395–430. http://dx.doi.org/10.3102/00346543059004395

Goodman-Delahunty, J., Granhag, P. A., Hartwig, M., & Loftus, E. F. (2010). Insightful or wishful: Lawyers' ability to predict case outcomes. *Psychology, Public Policy, and Law, 16*, 133–157. http://dx.doi.org/10.1037/a0019060

Hackett, G. (1985). The role of mathematics self-efficacy in the choice of math-related majors of college women and men: A path analysis. *Journal of Counseling Psychology, 32*, 47–56. http://dx.doi.org/10.1037/0022-0167.32.1.47

Harrison, D. A., & Shaffer, M. A. (1994). Comparative examinations of self-reports and perceived absenteeism norms: Wading through Lake Wobegon. *Journal of Applied Psychology, 79*, 240–251. http://dx.doi.org/10.1037/0021-9010.79.2.240

Hermann, A., & Rammal, H. G. (2010). The grounding of the "flying bank." *Management Decision, 48*, 1048–1062. http://dx.doi.org/10.1108/00251741011068761

Janis, I. (1972). *Victims of groupthink*. Boston, MA: Houghton-Mifflin.

John, O. P., & Robins, R. W. (1994). Accuracy and bias in self-perception: Individual differences in self-enhancement and the role of narcissism. *Journal of Personality and Social Psychology, 66*, 206–219. http://dx.doi.org/10.1037/0022-3514.66.1.206

Kane, T. D., Marks, M. A., Zaccaro, S. J., & Blair, V. (1996). Self-efficacy, personal goals, and wrestlers' self-regulation. *Journal of Sport & Exercise Psychology, 19*, 36–48.

Köther, U., Veckenstedt, R., Vitzthum, F., Roesch-Ely, D., Pfueller, U., Scheu, F., & Moritz, S. (2012). "Don't give me that look"—overconfidence in false mental state perception in schizophrenia. *Psychiatry Research, 196*, 1–8. http://dx.doi.org/10.1016/j.psychres.2012.03.004

Kruger, J. (1999). Lake Wobegon be gone! The "below-average effect" and the egocentric nature of comparative ability judgments. *Journal of Personality and Social Psychology, 77*, 221–232. http://dx.doi.org/10.1037/0022-3514.77.2.221

Kruger, J., & Dunning, D. (1999). Unskilled and unaware of it: How difficulties in recognizing one's own incompetence lead to inflated self-assessments. *Journal of Personality and Social Psychology, 77*, 1121–1134. http://dx.doi.org/10.1037/0022-3514.77.6.1121

Kruglanski, A. W., Pierro, A., Mannetti, L., & De Grada, E. (2006). Groups as epistemic providers: Need for closure and the unfolding of group-centrism. *Psychological Review, 113*, 84–100. http://dx.doi.org/10.1037/0033-295X.113.1.84

Kunda, Z. (1990). The case for motivated reasoning. *Psychological Bulletin, 108*, 480–498. http://dx.doi.org/10.1037/0033-2909.108.3.480

Landier, A., & Thesmar, D. (2003). *Financial contracting with optimistic entrepreneurs: Theory and evidence*. London, England: Centre for Economic Policy Research.

Langer, E. J. (1975). The illusion of control. *Journal of Personality and Social Psychology, 32*, 311–328. http://dx.doi.org/10.1037/0022-3514.32.2.311

Latham, G. P., & Saari, L. M. (1979). Application of social learning theory to training supervisors through behavioral modeling. *Journal of Applied Psychology, 64,* 239–246. http://dx.doi.org/10.1037/0021-9010.64.3.239

Malloy, T. E., & Janowski, C. L. (1992). Perceptions and metaperceptions of leadership: Components, accuracy, and dispositional correlates. *Personality and Social Psychology Bulletin, 18,* 700–708. http://dx.doi.org/10.1177/0146167292186006

Mannes, A. E., & Moore, D. A. (2013). A behavioral demonstration of overconfidence in judgment. *Psychological Science, 24,* 1190–1197. http://dx.doi.org/10.1177/0956797612470700

Marteau, T. M., Johnston, M., Wynne, G., & Evans, T. R. (1989). Cognitive factors in the explanation of the mismatch between confidence and competence in performing basic life support. *Psychology & Health, 3,* 173–182. http://dx.doi.org/10.1080/08870448908400377

McGraw, A. P., Mellers, B. A., & Ritov, I. (2004). The affective costs of overconfidence. *Journal of Behavioral Decision Making, 17,* 281–295. http://dx.doi.org/10.1002/bdm.472

McNiel, D. E., Sandberg, D. A., & Binder, R. L. (1998). The relationship between confidence and accuracy in clinical assessment of psychiatric patients' potential for violence. *Law and Human Behavior, 22,* 655–669. http://dx.doi.org/10.1023/A:1025754706716

Meindl, J. R., Ehrlich, S. B., & Dukerich, J. M. (1985). The romance of leadership. *Administrative Science Quarterly, 30,* 78–102. http://dx.doi.org/10.2307/2392813

Moore, D. A., & Healy, P. J. (2008). The trouble with overconfidence. *Psychological Review, 115,* 502–517. http://dx.doi.org/10.1037/0033-295X.115.2.502

Morrison, E. W., & Milliken, F. J. (2000). Organizational silence: A barrier to change and development in a pluralistic world. *The Academy of Management Review, 25,* 706–725.

Oskam, J., Kingma, J., & Klasen, H. J. (2000). Clinicians' recognition of 10 different types of distal radial fractures. *Perceptual and Motor Skills, 91,* 917–924. http://dx.doi.org/10.2466/pms.2000.91.3.917

Oskamp, S. (1965). Overconfidence in case-study judgments. *Journal of Consulting Psychology, 29,* 261–265. http://dx.doi.org/10.1037/h0022125

Phillips, D. A., & Zimmerman, M. (1990). The developmental course of perceived competence and incompetence among competent children. In R. J. Sternberg & J. Kolligian, Jr., (Eds.), *Competence considered* (pp. 41–66). New Haven, CT: Yale University Press.

Porras, J. I., & Anderson, B. (1981). Improving managerial effectiveness through modeling-based training. *Organizational Dynamics, 9,* 60–77. http://dx.doi.org/10.1016/0090-2616(81)90026-7

Roediger, H. L., & Karpicke, J. D. (2006). Test-enhanced learning: Taking memory tests improves long-term retention. *Psychological Science, 17,* 249–255. http://dx.doi.org/10.1111/j.1467-9280.2006.01693.x

Salisbury, R., & Hawley, E. (2011). *The Himalaya by the numbers: A statistical analysis of mountaineering in the Nepal Himalaya.* Kathmandu, Nepal: Vajra.

Schilling, L., Wingenfeld, K., Löwe, B., Moritz, S., Terfehr, K., Köther, U., & Spitzer, C. (2012). Normal mind-reading capacity but higher response confidence in borderline personality disorder patients. *Psychiatry and Clinical Neurosciences, 66,* 322–327. http://dx.doi.org/10.1111/j.1440-1819.2012.02334.x

Schunk, D. H. (1996). Goal and self-evaluative influences during children's cognitive skill learning. *American Educational Research Journal, 33,* 359–382. http://dx.doi.org/10.3102/00028312033002359

Sedikides, C., Herbst, K. C., Hardin, D. P., & Dardis, G. J. (2002). Accountability as a deterrent to self-enhancement: The search for mechanisms. *Journal of Personality and Social Psychology, 83,* 592–605. http://dx.doi.org/10.1037/0022-3514.83.3.592

Shipman, A. S., & Mumford, M. D. (2011). When confidence is detrimental: Influence of overconfidence on leadership effectiveness. *The Leadership Quarterly, 22,* 649–665. http://dx.doi.org/10.1016/j.leaqua.2011.05.006

Sripada, B. N., Henry, D. B., Jobe, T. H., Winer, J. A., Schoeny, M. E., & Gibbons, R. D. (2011). A randomized controlled trial of a feedback method for improving empathic accuracy in psychotherapy. *Psychology and Psychotherapy: Theory, Research and Practice, 84,* 113–127. http://dx.doi.org/10.1348/147608310X495110

Stone, D. N. (1994). Overconfidence in initial self-efficacy judgments: Effects on decision processes and performance. *Organizational Behavior and Human Decision Processes, 59,* 452–474. http://dx.doi.org/10.1006/obhd.1994.1069

Sutton, S., & Bolling, K. D. (2003). Adolescents' perceptions of the risks and prevalence of smoking. *Zeitschrift für Gesundheitspsychologie, 11,* 107–111. http://dx.doi.org/10.1026//0943-8149.11.3.107

Svenson, O. (1981). Are we all less risky and more skillful than our fellow drivers? *Acta Psychologica, 47,* 143–148. http://dx.doi.org/10.1016/0001-6918(81)90005-6

Taylor, S. E., & Brown, J. D. (1988). Illusion and well-being: A social psychological perspective on mental health. *Psychological Bulletin, 103,* 193–210. http://dx.doi.org/10.1037/0033-2909.103.2.193

Thiede, K. W., Anderson, M., & Therriault, D. (2003). Accuracy of metacognitive monitoring affects learning of texts. *Journal of Educational Psychology, 95,* 66–73. http://dx.doi.org/10.1037/0022-0663.95.1.66

Thiede, K. W., & Dunlosky, J. (1994). Delaying students' metacognitive monitoring improves their accuracy at predicting their recognition performance. *Journal of Educational Psychology, 86,* 290–302. http://dx.doi.org/10.1037/0022-0663.86.2.290

Tracey, J. M., Arroll, B., Richmond, D. E., & Barham, P. M. (1997). The validity of general practitioners' self assessment of knowledge: Cross sectional study. *British Medical Journal, 315,* 1426–1428. http://dx.doi.org/10.1136/bmj.315.7120.1426

Vancouver, J. B., Thompson, C. M., Tischner, E. C., & Putka, D. J. (2002). Two studies examining the negative effect of self-efficacy on performance. *Journal of Applied Psychology, 87,* 506–516. http://dx.doi.org/10.1037/0021-9010.87.3.506

Weinstein, N. D. (1980). Unrealistic optimism about future life events. *Journal of Personality and Social Psychology, 39,* 806–820. http://dx.doi.org/10.1037/0022-3514.39.5.806

Weinstein, N. D. (1987). Unrealistic optimism about susceptibility to health problems: Conclusions from a community-wide sample. *Journal of Behavioral Medicine, 10,* 481–500. http://dx.doi.org/10.1007/BF00846146

Zenger, T. R. (1992). Why do employers only reward extreme performance? Examining the relationships among performance, pay, and turnover. *Administrative Science Quarterly, 37,* 198–219. http://dx.doi.org/10.2307/2393221

IV
NEGATIVE AFFECTIVITY

13

DARK SIDE OF THE MOOD OR SWEET EMOTION? TOWARD A MORE NUANCED UNDERSTANDING OF EMOTIONAL LABILITY

KIM L. GRATZ, KATHERINE L. DIXON-GORDON, AND DIANA WHALEN

Emotional lability is a prominent feature of many psychiatric disorders and has been linked with a variety of negative outcomes. Although historically viewed as a vulnerability factor that increases risk for psychopathology, a review of the literature supports a more nuanced understanding of emotional lability. Specifically, literature suggests that heightened levels of this trait increase the risk for psychopathology only in the context of other risk and vulnerability factors and that both high and low levels of this trait (vs. simply the former) may serve as vulnerability factors. Consequently, we propose a curvilinear model of the adaptive nature of emotional lability and identify relevant factors that may moderate the impact of emotional lability on outcomes. Future directions for this area of research are also discussed.

http://dx.doi.org/10.1037/14854-014

The Dark Side of Personality: Science and Practice in Social, Personality, and Clinical Psychology, V. Zeigler-Hill and D. K. Marcus (Editors)

DEFINITION AND BACKGROUND

The literature on emotional lability is complicated by the absence of a consistent and agreed-on definition of this construct. Further confusing this literature is the use of several different terms to denote this phenomenon, including emotional lability, affective lability, and affective instability (all of which are often used interchangeably to refer to the same construct). Thus, establishing a working definition of emotional lability is crucial to the aggregation and progression of research in this area.

In line with others (e.g., American Psychiatric Association, 2013; R. J. Thompson, Dizén, & Berenbaum, 2009), we define *emotional lability* as intense, frequent, and reactive shifts in emotions. As such, emotional lability encompasses both emotional intensity (i.e., the general tendency to experience emotions strongly; Larsen & Diener, 1987) and emotional reactivity (i.e., the degree of emotional response to internal or external stimuli across subjective, physiological, or expressive domains; Rothbart & Derryberry, 1981). This definition is consistent with extant definitions of affective lability and instability (which also tend to emphasize both intense and reactive shifts in mood; American Psychiatric Association, 2013; Gunderson, Zanarini, & Kisiel, 1996; Koenigsberg, 2010). From our perspective, the experience of both intense emotions and marked reactivity is central to the construct of emotional lability. In the absence of either emotional intensity or reactivity, emotional lability would not be considered present.

Thus, according to this definition, minor fluctuations in affect would not constitute emotional lability. For this reason, and in contrast to others (Coccaro, Ong, Seroczynski, & Bergeman, 2012), we do not view emotional lability as synonymous with the construct of emotional variability (defined as within-person variability in affective states; Coccaro et al., 2012). Although emotional lability encompasses emotional variability, emotional variability in the absence of high magnitude (i.e., intense) responses would not meet our definition of emotional lability (consistent with definitions set forth by others; e.g., R. J. Thompson et al., 2009). Finally, it warrants mention that emotional lability as defined here constitutes one aspect of emotional dysfunction within the larger construct of neuroticism, sharing some variance with this higher order trait (Maples, Miller, Hoffman, & Johnson, 2014) but being a distinct construct (Miller & Pilkonis, 2006).

EMOTIONAL LABILITY AS A HERITABLE PERSONALITY TRAIT

Existing literature provides support for emotional lability as a heritable biologically based personality trait (Skodol et al., 2002). For example, emotional lability has been found to have a heritability estimate of 45% to 48%

(Jang, Livesley, & Vernon, 1996; Livesley, Jang, Jackson, & Vernon, 1993; Skodol et al., 2002), comparable to those of other psychobiological dispositions or endophenotypes theorized to underlie personality disorders (Gunderson et al., 2011; Jang et al., 1996; Siever, Torgersen, Gunderson, Livesley, & Kendler, 2002; Skodol et al., 2002). Moreover, research provides support for both the early expression of this trait in infancy and its relative continuity across time. For example, emotional lability and its components (e.g., peak excitement, rapidity of buildup) can be reliably and validly measured in infants as young as 7 to 10 days old (see Lorber & Egeland, 2011). Furthermore, literature supports the relative stability of emotional lability during infancy (Gunnar, Mangelsdorf, Larson, & Hertsgaard, 1989), childhood (De Clercq, Van Leeuwen, Van Den Noortgate, De Bolle, & De Fruyt, 2009), and adulthood (Carstensen et al., 2011). Indeed, in a prospective study of adult patients, emotional lability was found to demonstrate greater stability than any other feature of borderline personality disorder (BPD) over a 2-year period (McGlashan et al., 2005).

ADAPTIVE AND MALADAPTIVE FEATURES

Maladaptive Correlates

Although the relation of emotional lability to psychopathology and negative outcomes is likely more complex than previously thought, there is a relatively large body of literature linking emotional lability to a number of deleterious outcomes, including psychopathology and maladaptive and self-destructive behaviors. In fact, emotional lability has been found to be an important transdiagnostic vulnerability factor for a range of psychopathology, evidencing significant associations with both internalizing and externalizing disorders in children and adolescents (Stringaris & Goodman, 2009) and numerous psychiatric disorders in adults (including personality, mood, and anxiety disorders; e.g., Angst, Gamma, & Endrass, 2003; Henry et al., 2001, 2008; Koenigsberg, 2010; Sherry et al., 2014; Tragesser & Robinson, 2009).

Despite its relation to numerous forms of psychopathology, however, emotional lability may be most well known as a feature of BPD and bipolar disorder. With regard to the former, emotional lability is among the most frequently endorsed BPD criteria (McGlashan et al., 2005) and, together with impulsivity, is considered one of the core features of the disorder (e.g., Koenigsberg et al., 2001; Tragesser & Robinson, 2009). Notably, emerging evidence suggests that certain forms of emotional lability, particularly shifts from anxious to depressed states and euthymic to angry states, may be especially relevant to BPD. These specific shifts in mood (vs. shifts from euthymia to depression, elation, or anxiety) have been found to be significantly associated with BPD symptoms in undergraduates (Tragesser & Robinson, 2009) and significantly more intense and frequent in BPD than bipolar II disorder (Henry et al., 2001; Reich, Zanarini, & Fitzmaurice, 2012). Likewise, research has provided strong support for a robust relation between emotional lability and bipolar disorder. For example, research provides support for heightened levels of both self-reported emotional intensity and subjective and physiological emotional reactivity among individuals with bipolar disorder, compared with controls (Henry et al., 2008; M'Bailara et al., 2009). Moreover, bipolar II disorder has been linked to emotional lability in the form of shifts from euthymic to elated or depressed states, with individuals with bipolar II disorder reporting higher levels of these forms of emotional lability than a clinical comparison group of patients with BPD (Henry et al., 2001; Reich et al., 2012). In addition to highlighting the particular patterns of emotional lability that may be most relevant to specific disorders, these findings suggest the potential utility of examining emotional lability across specific emotions and contexts.

The relevance of emotional lability to depressive disorders is less clear. Two studies provide some support for a relation between emotional lability and depressive disorders, with one study finding that reported "ups and downs in mood" was the strongest predictor of depressive disorders in a large community sample (Angst et al., 2003) and another finding heightened levels of emotional lability among individuals with (vs. without) a lifetime depressive disorder (R. J. Thompson, Berenbaum, & Bredemeier, 2011). Other studies, however, suggest that emotional lability (as defined here) is not related to depressive disorders. For instance, in two of their three studies, R. J. Thompson and colleagues (2011) found that only emotional variability (and not emotional intensity) was associated with depressive symptoms.

Apart from these established associations with certain forms of psychopathology, emotional lability has been associated with a number of other concerning outcomes in both youth and adults. In a large sample of Spanish students, emotional lability demonstrated positive associations with aggressive behaviors (Carlo et al., 2012). Self-reported emotional lability has also been found to relate positively to both reported health anxiety (Sherry et al., 2014) and problems related to marijuana use (Simons & Carey, 2002) in undergraduates. Furthermore, among adults with psychopathology, emotional lability has been linked to maladaptive behaviors. For instance, in a study of women with bulimia nervosa, emotional lability (assessed via both self-report and ecological momentary assessment) predicted number of binge-eating episodes each day, even when controlling for a number of demographic and affect-related variables (Anestis et al., 2010). Moreover, in a clinical sample of adults, emotional lability predicted later romantic impairment (Miller & Pilkonis, 2006).

Of particular concern, high levels of emotional lability demonstrate strong associations with suicidality. Although a diagnosis of BPD confers risk for suicide attempts (e.g., Soloff, Lis, Kelly, Cornelius, & Ulrich, 1994), in a sample of adolescent inpatients, only the emotional lability criterion of BPD (indicative of pathological levels of emotional lability) predicted suicide-related variables and distinguished suicide attempters from ideators (Glenn, Bagge, & Osman, 2013). Likewise, of all the BPD criteria, only heightened emotional lability was prospectively associated with suicide attempts in a sample of current or past patients with a personality disorder (Yen et al., 2004). Indeed, a meta-analysis of existing studies ($N = 20$) revealed a significant relation between heightened emotional lability and suicide-related outcomes (associated with a medium-sized effect of $Z = 0.35$; Palmier-Claus, Taylor, Varese, & Pratt, 2012). Taken together, these studies underscore the association between clinically relevant levels of emotional lability and heightened suicide risk.

Adaptive Correlates

Although high levels of emotional lability have been found to be related to numerous negative outcomes, research on the relation of high emotional lability to positive outcomes suggests that emotional lability may confer benefits as well. In particular, emotional lability evidences positive and direct associations with creativity (Frantom & Sherman, 1999), consistent with findings that emotional lability is one factor of creativity (Martinsen, 2011). Furthermore, overall self-reported emotional lability was related to greater attention to emotional experiences within undergraduate and community samples (R. J. Thompson et al., 2009).

Research on outcomes related to particularly low levels of emotional lability provides further support for the adaptive nature and potential benefits of at least moderate levels of emotional lability. Specifically, emotional inertia (i.e., the persistence of mood states over time) has been operationalized as the degree of autocorrelation between emotions over time (e.g., Koval, Pe, Meers, & Kuppens, 2013; Kuppens, Allen, & Sheeber, 2010; R. J. Thompson et al., 2012), with high levels of emotional inertia indicative of a relative absence of emotional lability (or the antithesis of this construct). Notably, emotional inertia has been linked to a number of problematic outcomes. For instance, in an ecological momentary assessment study of university students, emotional inertia specific to a range of both positive (e.g., happiness, excitement) and negative (e.g., anger, anxiety, depression) emotions was linked to lower self-reported self-esteem (Kuppens et al., 2010). Furthermore, emotional inertia has been associated with depressive symptoms in a number of studies (e.g., Koval et al., 2013; Kuppens et al., 2010, 2012; cf. R. J. Thompson et al., 2012) and found to predict the onset of depressive episodes over a 2-year period in adolescents (Kuppens et al., 2012). Likewise, emotion context insensitivity (defined as attenuated emotional reactivity to stimuli; Rottenberg, 2005) is considered to be a key mechanism underlying depression (Bylsma, Morris, & Rottenberg, 2008; Rottenberg, 2005) and has been linked to both functional impairment and poor clinical outcomes in individuals with depression (Rottenberg, Kasch, Gross, & Gotlib, 2002). An absence of expressive reactivity to emotional stimuli has also been linked to schizophrenia (Berenbaum & Oltmanns, 1992). Taken together, these data underscore the potentially problematic nature of particularly low levels of emotional lability.

A MORE NUANCED MODEL OF EMOTIONAL LABILITY

Against the backdrop of extant research, we propose a more nuanced model of emotional lability and its relation to both risk and resiliency. Specifically, we propose that emotional lability may be conceptualized as demonstrating a curvilinear relationship to adaptive functioning. At each end of the spectrum, and in the context of other vulnerability factors, either extreme emotional lability or extreme emotional stability may be associated with dysfunction and psychopathology.

Curvilinear Relationship of Emotional Lability to Dysfunction

As noted earlier, extant literature suggests that extremely high levels of emotional lability are indeed associated with a variety of problematic outcomes, including psychopathology, maladaptive behaviors, and even suicide attempts (e.g., Glenn et al., 2013; Henry et al., 2001; Koenigsberg, 2010). The heightened emotional intensity and reactivity associated with emotional lability likely imposes greater demands on emotion regulatory resources. In the absence of skills for managing this emotional lability effectively, it is easy to see how emotional lability could confer vulnerability for diverse forms of psychopathology. This model is consistent with Linehan's (1993) biosocial theory of the pathogenesis of BPD. From this perspective, a biological predisposition toward intense, unstable affect is a risk factor for BPD in the context of key environmental risk factors (see also Crowell, Beauchaine, & Linehan, 2009). Specifically, heightened emotional vulnerability in the form of intense and reactive emotions (i.e., emotional lability) is thought to increase the risk for BPD when combined with an invalidating environment wherein the communication of emotions is met by erratic, inappropriate, or extreme negative responses (Linehan, 1993). Of relevance to our model, however, it is only in the context of an ongoing transaction with an invalidating environment that heightened emotional lability may increase risk for BPD.

In contrast, and consistent with preliminary research (e.g., Koval et al., 2013; Rottenberg et al., 2002), extremely low levels of emotional lability may also increase risk for psychopathology and related dysfunction. Emotions are multicomponential coordinated processes encompassing physiological, subjective, and behavioral response systems that are both necessary and adaptive (Bradley & Lang, 2000; Ekman, 1999). For example, fear can prepare an individual for escape, and sadness can communicate a need for social support. From this perspective, instability and change in one's emotional responses can provide essential information and prepare an individual for the waxing and waning demands of the environment, thereby facilitating adaptive responding (Ekman, 1999; R. A. Thompson, 2011). Thus, a restricted range of emotional experience or lack of sensitivity to environmental cues could lead to substantial impairment across a range of domains. For example, emotional responses provide important information about the incentive value of specific choices and can signal prospective penalties of risky decisions (consistent with the somatic marker hypothesis; Damasio, Everitt, & Bishop, 1996). Therefore, the absence of reactivity to fearful or aversive stimuli could lead to engagement in impulsive, relationship-damaging, or antisocial behaviors (e.g., Benning, Patrick, & Iacono, 2005) that typical fear responses may serve as a cue to inhibit (for a further discussion of the potential adverse consequences of fearlessness, see Chapter 3, this volume). Conversely, sensitivity to emotional cues and the presence of emotional reactions in response may motivate individuals to make rewarding choices and increase adaptive responding.

With either extreme of emotional lability increasing vulnerability for potentially negative outcomes, this curvilinear model implies an optimal level of emotional lability. Although this model has not yet been tested directly, research on emotional expressivity in young children provides preliminary support for the notion of an advantageous level of emotional lability that is associated with less psychopathology and enhanced emotion regulation. Specifically, compared to both high and low levels of emotional expressivity, modulated emotional expressivity in children has been associated with fewer internalizing and externalizing problems and more adaptive emotional development and adjustment (Cole, Zahn-Waxler, Fox, Usher, & Welsh, 1996). Furthermore, in a sample of mother–infant dyads, maternal emotion regulation difficulties were associated with both heightened emotional expressivity and inexpressivity (but not modulated expressivity) in infants (Gratz, Kiel, et al., 2014). Thus, at least with regard to expressive indicators of emotional lability and its components, moderate levels of this trait may be more adaptive than either high or low levels.

Potential Moderators of the Association Between Emotional Lability and Dysfunction

As noted earlier, even at the more extreme ends of the emotional lability spectrum, it is only in the context of other risk and vulnerability factors that either high or low levels of emotional lability would be expected to relate to dysfunction. Although few studies have examined moderators of the relation between emotional lability and dysfunction, theoretical literature in addition to preliminary research in this area point to several factors that may attenuate or potentiate the impact of emotional lability on functioning.

Emotion Regulation

Emotion regulation warrants particular consideration as an important factor in this regard. Although high emotional lability places greater demands on the emotion regulatory system, individuals with the requisite emotion regulation repertoire are likely to be able to cope with these demands. Consistent with the biosocial theory of BPD (Crowell et al., 2009), a predisposition toward emotional intensity, reactivity, or lability is unlikely to lead to problematic outcomes in the absence of difficulties regulating these emotions, with the presence of adaptive emotion regulation skills ameliorating any potential negative consequences of emotional lability. Indeed, the dimension of emotion dysregulation (Gratz & Roemer, 2004), involving difficulties controlling impulsive behaviors in the context of intense emotions (also known as urgency; see Chapter 8, this volume; Whiteside & Lynam, 2001), has been found to moderate the association between emotional lability and aggressive behaviors (Dvorak, Pearson, & Kuvaas, 2013). Specifically, Dvorak et al. (2013) found an interactive effect of negative urgency and emotional lability on aggressive behaviors, such that the association between emotional lability and aggressive behaviors was only significant in the context of high (vs. low) negative urgency.

Environmental Stressors

Emerging evidence also suggests that psychosocial stressors may influence the relation between emotional lability and psychopathology. As noted earlier, theory suggests that emotional lability increases risk for psychopathology only in the context of key environmental stressors (Crowell et al., 2009; Linehan, 1993), and preliminary evidence supports this theory. For example, Gratz (2006) found that a composite of emotional intensity and reactivity was related to frequent deliberate self-harm only when combined with high levels of childhood maltreatment; there was no main effect of emotional intensity and reactivity on self-harm. Likewise, further support for the moderating role of psychosocial stressors on the lability–pathology relation comes from an ecological momentary assessment study of individuals with high levels of behavioral dysregulation (across at least four behavioral domains, i.e., binge eating, purging, self-injury, substance use, or aggressive behaviors; Yu & Selby, 2013). Although the findings from this study revealed a direct relation of emotional lability to binge-eating episodes, this relation was moderated by exposure to interpersonal stressors, such that the relation between emotional lability and binge eating was significant only among those with high levels of interpersonal stress (Yu & Selby, 2013).

Parenting Behaviors

Despite strong evidence for the genetic basis of emotional lability and its intergenerational transmission (see Gunderson et al., 2011; Skodol et al., 2002; White, Gunderson, Zanarini, & Hudson, 2003), gene–environment interaction models highlight the importance of unique environmental contributions to emotional lability, with parenting behaviors serving as one such environmental contributor. Indeed, theoretical and empirical literature suggest that parenting behaviors in general and emotion socialization strategies in particular may influence child emotional lability and its consequences through a transactional process (Crowell et al., 2009; Fruzzetti, Shenk, & Hoffman, 2005; Kiel, Gratz, Moore, Latzman, & Tull, 2011; Linehan, 1993). Specifically, whereas sensitive parenting behaviors facilitate adaptive emotion regulation and may buffer emotionally labile children from the development of psychopathology (Crowell et al., 2009; Eisenberg, Cumberland, & Spinrad, 1998), maladaptive parenting behaviors have been found to exacerbate emotional lability (Smith, Calkins, & Keane, 2006) and increase the risk for psychopathology in emotionally labile youth (De Clercq, Van Leeuwen, De Fruyt, Van Hiel, & Mervielde, 2008).

DIRECTIONS FOR FUTURE RESEARCH

Although researchers have predominantly viewed emotional lability in relation to psychopathology and functional impairment, a closer examination of related literature highlights the adaptive nature and functional consequences of moderate levels of emotional lability and responsiveness to emotional cues. Despite the prominence of emotional lability in existing personality and psychopathology research, the existing literature in this area has been hindered in several ways. First, the various definitions of emotional lability, as well as the numerous terms used to denote this construct, have resulted in a discontinuous body of research. Second, the absence of research examining the full continuum of emotional lability has impeded our ability to detect the functional implications of each end of the emotional lability spectrum. Third, there is little research examining factors that may strengthen or attenuate the association between emotional lability and dysfunction. Further research in this area is urgently needed.

The advancement of research in this area will be facilitated by the use of clear and consistent definitions of this construct, greater attention to precision in terminology when discussing this construct and its overlap with and distinctions from other emotion-related traits (e.g., distinguishing emotional lability from the overlapping constructs of emotional variability and neuroticism; distinguishing emotional lability from either emotional intensity or emotional reactivity alone), and a more comprehensive and nuanced examination of the full spectrum of emotional lability (from very high to very low levels). Studies examining the relations of varying levels of emotional lability to both adaptive and maladaptive outcomes will be particularly important. Research examining the potential moderators of the emotional lability–dysfunction relation outlined above is also needed, and has the potential to improve our understanding of the benefits and costs of varying levels of emotional lability. Finally, prospective longitudinal studies examining the developmental trajectory of emotional lability across the life span and the factors that may influence this trajectory (e.g., parenting, attachment, psychological treatment, environmental stressors) would be particularly helpful.

CLINICAL IMPLICATIONS

This emerging research on emotional lability has important implications for both the prevention and treatment of psychopathology. First, further evidence in support of our proposed curvilinear model would suggest the utility of interventions targeting an optimal range of emotional lability and responsiveness to the environment. Specifically, rather than focusing on the control of emotions and reduction of emotional arousal, useful interventions may focus on increasing emotional awareness and understanding and promoting nonreactive observing of intense emotions and the control of behaviors in the context of such emotions. Acceptance- and mindfulness-based treatments (e.g., acceptance and commitment therapy, dialectical behavior therapy, acceptance-based behavioral therapy for generalized anxiety disorder, and mindfulness-based cognitive therapy; see Hayes, Strosahl, & Wilson, 1999; Linehan, 1993; Roemer, Orsillo, & Salters-Pedneault, 2008; Segal, Williams, & Teasdale, 2002) may be particularly useful in this regard because the process of observing and describing one's emotions mindfully is expected to promote both emotional clarity (as clients are encouraged to observe their emotions as they occur in the moment and to label them objectively) and the decoupling of emotions and behaviors (as clients learn that emotions can be experienced and tolerated without necessarily acting on them). Second, given the potential moderating role of emotion regulation in the relation between high emotional lability and dysfunction, interventions that target emotion regulation may be particularly useful for individuals with high levels of emotional lability. In particular, interventions focused on promoting adaptive ways of approaching, responding to, and regulating emotions (regardless of their intensity/reactivity) may facilitate adaptive emotion regulation in emotionally vulnerable populations (e.g., emotion regulation group therapy; Gratz & Gunderson, 2006; Gratz, Tull, & Levy, 2014).

Third, findings that parenting practices may either attenuate or exacerbate the risks conferred by child emotional lability highlight the potential utility of both prevention and early intervention efforts aimed at promoting adaptive parenting behaviors and emotion socialization strategies in parents of emotionally labile youth. In particular, parent training programs focused on promoting the use of sensitive emotion socialization strategies with children may support the development of adaptive emotion regulation in emotionally vulnerable youth, thereby decreasing the risks associated with even high levels of emotional lability (e.g., Herbert, Harvey, Roberts, Wichowski, & Lugo-Candelas, 2013). Finally, given evidence that certain environmental stressors (particularly childhood maltreatment and other interpersonal stressors) may increase the risk for psychopathology among individuals with high levels of emotional lability, individuals exposed to such stressors may benefit from targeted prevention programs aimed at facilitating adaptive emotion regulation.

SUMMARY AND CONCLUSIONS

Taken together, extant research and theory suggest the need for a more complex model of emotional lability. Despite the tendency to view emotional lability in the context of psychopathology and other negative outcomes, evidence supports the adaptive nature and utility of moderate levels of emotional lability. Whereas pathologically high levels of emotional lability may indeed serve as a vulnerability factor for some forms of psychopathology (particularly in the context of other risk or vulnerability factors), extremely low levels of emotional lability may confer risk for the pathological persistence of mood and/or an inability to respond to emotionally salient cues in the immediate environment. With regard to the latter, future research is needed to characterize the functional impairments associated with pathologically low levels of emotional lability. Furthermore, additional studies are needed to elucidate relevant moderators of the relation of emotional lability to dysfunction.

REFERENCES

American Psychiatric Association. (2013). *Diagnostic and statistical manual of mental disorders* (5th ed.). Arlington, VA: Author.

Anestis, M. D., Selby, E. A., Crosby, R. D., Wonderlich, S. A., Engel, S. G., & Joiner, T. E. (2010). A comparison of retrospective self-report versus ecological momentary assessment measures of affective lability in the examination of its relationship with bulimic symptomatology. *Behaviour Research and Therapy, 48,* 607–613. http://dx.doi.org/10.1016/j.brat.2010.03.012

Angst, J., Gamma, A., & Endrass, J. (2003). Risk factors for the bipolar and depression spectra. *Acta Psychiatrica Scandinavica, 108,* 15–19. http://dx.doi.org/10.1034/j.1600-0447.108.s418.4.x

Benning, S. D., Patrick, C. J., & Iacono, W. G. (2005). Psychopathy, startle blink modulation, and electrodermal reactivity in twin men. *Psychophysiology, 42,* 753–762. http://dx.doi.org/10.1111/j.1469-8986.2005.00353.x

Berenbaum, H., & Oltmanns, T. F. (1992). Emotional experience and expression in schizophrenia and depression. *Journal of Abnormal Psychology, 101,* 37–44. http://dx.doi.org/10.1037/0021-843X.101.1.37

Bradley, M. M., & Lang, P. J. (2000). Measuring emotion: Behavior, feeling, and physiology. In R. D. Lane & L. Nadel (Eds.), *Cognitive neuroscience of emotion* (pp. 242–276). New York, NY: Oxford University Press.

Bylsma, L. M., Morris, B. H., & Rottenberg, J. (2008). A meta-analysis of emotional reactivity in major depressive disorder. *Clinical Psychology Review, 28,* 676–691. http://dx.doi.org/10.1016/j.cpr.2007.10.001

Carlo, G., Mestre, M. V., McGinley, M. M., Samper, P., Tur, A., & Sandman, D. (2012). The interplay of emotional instability, empathy, and coping on prosocial and aggressive behaviors. *Personality and Individual Differences, 53,* 675–680. http://dx.doi.org/10.1016/j.paid.2012.05.022

Carstensen, L. L., Turan, B., Scheibe, S., Ram, N., Ersner-Hershfield, H., Samanez-Larkin, G. R., . . . Nesselroade, J. R. (2011). Emotional experience improves with age: Evidence based on over 10 years of experience sampling. *Psychology and Aging, 26,* 21–33. http://dx.doi.org/10.1037/a0021285

Coccaro, E. F., Ong, A. D., Seroczynski, A. D., & Bergeman, C. S. (2012). Affective intensity and lability: Heritability in adult male twins. *Journal of Affective Disorders, 136,* 1011–1016. http://dx.doi.org/10.1016/j.jad.2011.06.042

Cole, P. M., Zahn-Waxler, C., Fox, N. A., Usher, B. A., & Welsh, J. D. (1996). Individual differences in emotion regulation and behavior problems in preschool children. *Journal of Abnormal Psychology, 105,* 518–529. http://dx.doi.org/10.1037/0021-843X.105.4.518

Crowell, S. E., Beauchaine, T. P., & Linehan, M. M. (2009). A biosocial developmental model of borderline personality: Elaborating and extending Linehan's theory. *Psychological Bulletin, 135,* 495–510. http://dx.doi.org/10.1037/a0015616

Damasio, A. R., Everitt, B. J., & Bishop, D. (1996). The somatic marker hypothesis and the possible functions of the prefrontal cortex. *Philosophical Transactions of the Royal Society B: Biological Sciences, 351,* 1413–1420. http://dx.doi.org/10.1098/rstb.1996.0125

De Clercq, B., Van Leeuwen, K., De Fruyt, F., Van Hiel, A., & Mervielde, I. (2008). Maladaptive personality traits and psychopathology in childhood and adolescence: The moderating effect of parenting. *Journal of Personality, 76,* 357–383. http://dx.doi.org/10.1111/j.1467-6494.2007.00489.x

De Clercq, B., Van Leeuwen, K., Van Den Noortgate, W., De Bolle, M., & De Fruyt, F. (2009). Childhood personality pathology: Dimensional stability and change. *Development and Psychopathology, 21,* 853–869. http://dx.doi.org/10.1017/S0954579409000467

Dvorak, R. D., Pearson, M. R., & Kuvaas, N. J. (2013). The five-factor model of impulsivity-like traits and emotional lability in aggressive behavior. *Aggressive Behavior, 39,* 222–228. http://dx.doi.org/10.1002/ab.21474

Eisenberg, N., Cumberland, A., & Spinrad, T. L. (1998). Parental socialization of emotion. *Psychological Inquiry, 9,* 241–273. http://dx.doi.org/10.1207/s15327965pli0904_1

Ekman, P. (1999). Basic emotions. In T. Dalgleish & M. Power (Eds.), *Handbook of cognition and emotion* (pp. 45–60). Chichester, England: Wiley.

Frantom, C., & Sherman, M. F. (1999). At what price art? Affective instability within a visual art population. *Creativity Research Journal, 12,* 15–23. http://dx.doi.org/10.1207/s15326934crj1201_3

Fruzzetti, A. E., Shenk, C., & Hoffman, P. D. (2005). Family interaction and the development of borderline personality disorder: A transactional model. *Development and Psychopathology, 17,* 1007–1030. http://dx.doi.org/10.1017/S0954579405050479

Glenn, C. R., Bagge, C. L., & Osman, A. (2013). Unique associations between borderline personality disorder features and suicide ideation and attempts in adolescents. *Journal of Personality Disorders, 27,* 604–616. http://dx.doi.org/10.1521/pedi_2013_27_102

Gratz, K. L. (2006). Risk factors for deliberate self-harm among female college students: The role and interaction of childhood maltreatment, emotional inexpressivity, and affect intensity/reactivity. *American Journal of Orthopsychiatry, 76,* 238–250. http://dx.doi.org/10.1037/0002-9432.76.2.238

Gratz, K. L., & Gunderson, J. G. (2006). Preliminary data on an acceptance-based emotion regulation group intervention for deliberate self-harm among women with borderline personality disorder. *Behavior Therapy, 37,* 25–35. http://dx.doi.org/10.1016/j.beth.2005.03.002

Gratz, K. L., Kiel, E. J., Latzman, R. D., Elkin, T. D., Moore, S. A., & Tull, M. T. (2014). Emotion: Empirical contribution. Maternal borderline personality pathology and infant emotion regulation: Examining the influence of maternal emotion-related difficulties and infant attachment. *Journal of Personality Disorders, 28,* 52–69. http://dx.doi.org/10.1521/pedi.2014.28.1.52

Gratz, K. L., & Roemer, L. (2004). Multidimensional assessment of emotion regulation and dysregulation: Development, factor structure, and initial validation of the difficulties in emotion regulation scale. *Journal of Psychopathology and Behavioral Assessment, 26,* 41–54. http://dx.doi.org/10.1023/B:JOBA.0000007455.08539.94

Gratz, K. L., Tull, M. T., & Levy, R. L. (2014). Randomized controlled trial and uncontrolled 9-month follow-up of an adjunctive emotion regulation group therapy for deliberate self-harm among women with borderline personality pathology. *Psychological Medicine, 44,* 2099–2112. http://dx.doi.org/10.1017/S0033291713002134

Gunderson, J. G., Zanarini, M. C., Choi-Kain, L. W., Mitchell, K. S., Jang, K. L., & Hudson, J. I. (2011). Family study of borderline personality disorder and its sectors of psychopathology. *Archives of General Psychiatry, 68,* 753–762. http://dx.doi.org/10.1001/archgenpsychiatry.2011.65

Gunderson, J. G., Zanarini, M. C., & Kisiel, C. (1996). Borderline personality disorder. In T. A. Widiger (Ed.), DSM–IV *sourcebook* (Vol. 2, pp. 717–733). Washington, DC: American Psychiatric Association Press.

Gunnar, M. R., Mangelsdorf, S., Larson, M., & Hertsgaard, L. (1989). Attachment, temperament, and adrenocortical activity in infancy: A study of psychoendocrine regulation. *Developmental Psychology, 25,* 355–363. http://dx.doi.org/10.1037/0012-1649.25.3.355

Hayes, S. C., Strosahl, K. D., & Wilson, K. G. (1999). *Acceptance and commitment therapy: An experiential approach to behavior change.* New York, NY: Guilford Press.

Henry, C., Mitropoulou, V., New, A. S., Koenigsberg, H. W., Silverman, J., & Siever, L. J. (2001). Affective instability and impulsivity in borderline personality and bipolar II disorders: Similarities and differences. *Journal of Psychiatric Research, 35,* 307–312. http://dx.doi.org/10.1016/S0022-3956(01)00038-3

Henry, C., Van den Bulke, D., Bellivier, F., Roy, I., Swendsen, J., M'Baïlara, K., . . . Leboyer, M. (2008). Affective lability and affect intensity as core dimensions of bipolar disorders during euthymic period. *Psychiatry Research, 159,* 1–6. http://dx.doi.org/10.1016/j.psychres.2005.11.016

Herbert, S. D., Harvey, E. A., Roberts, J. L., Wichowski, K., & Lugo-Candelas, C. I. (2013). A randomized controlled trial of a parent training and emotion socialization program for families of hyperactive preschool-aged children. *Behavior Therapy, 44,* 302–316. http://dx.doi.org/10.1016/j.beth.2012.10.004

Jang, K. L., Livesley, W. J., & Vernon, P. A. (1996). Heritability of the Big Five personality dimensions and their facets: A twin study. *Journal of Personality, 64,* 577–591. http://dx.doi.org/10.1111/j.1467-6494.1996.tb00522.x

Kiel, E. J., Gratz, K. L., Moore, S. A., Latzman, R. D., & Tull, M. T. (2011). The impact of borderline personality pathology on mothers' responses to infant distress. *Journal of Family Psychology, 25,* 907–918. http://dx.doi.org/10.1037/a0025474

Koenigsberg, H. W. (2010). Affective instability: Toward an integration of neuroscience and psychological perspectives. *Journal of Personality Disorders, 24,* 60–82. http://dx.doi.org/10.1521/pedi.2010.24.1.60

Koenigsberg, H. W., Harvey, P. D., Mitropoulou, V., New, A. S., Goodman, M., Silverman, J., . . . Siever, L. J. (2001). Are the interpersonal and identity disturbances in the borderline personality disorder criteria linked to the traits of affective instability and impulsivity? *Journal of Personality Disorders, 15,* 358–370. http://dx.doi.org/10.1521/pedi.15.4.358.19181

Koval, P., Pe, M. L., Meers, K., & Kuppens, P. (2013). Affect dynamics in relation to depressive symptoms: Variable, unstable, or inert? *Emotion, 13,* 1132–1141. http://dx.doi.org/10.1037/a0033579

Kuppens, P., Allen, N. B., & Sheeber, L. B. (2010). Emotional inertia and psychological maladjustment. *Psychological Science, 21,* 984–991. http://dx.doi.org/10.1177/0956797610372634

Kuppens, P., Sheeber, L. B., Yap, M. B., Whittle, S., Simmons, J. G., & Allen, N. B. (2012). Emotional inertia prospectively predicts the onset of depressive disorder in adolescence. *Emotion, 12,* 283–289. http://dx.doi.org/10.1037/a0025046

Larsen, R. J., & Diener, E. (1987). Affect intensity as an individual difference characteristic: A review. *Journal of Research in Personality, 21,* 1–39. http://dx.doi.org/10.1016/0092-6566(87)90023-7

Linehan, M. M. (1993). *Cognitive–behavioral treatment of borderline personality disorder.* New York, NY: Guilford Press.

Livesley, W. J., Jang, K. L., Jackson, D. N., & Vernon, P. A. (1993). Genetic and environmental contributions to dimensions of personality disorder. *The American Journal of Psychiatry, 150,* 1826–1831. http://dx.doi.org/10.1176/ajp.150.12.1826

Lorber, M. F., & Egeland, B. (2011). Parenting and infant difficulty: Testing a mutual exacerbation hypothesis to predict early onset conduct problems. *Child Development, 82,* 2006–2020. http://dx.doi.org/10.1111/j.1467-8624.2011.01652.x

Maples, J., Miller, J. D., Hoffman, B. J., & Johnson, S. L. (2014). A test of the empirical network surrounding affective instability and the degree to which it is independent from neuroticism. *Personality Disorders: Theory, Research, and Treatment, 5,* 268–277. http://dx.doi.org/10.1037/per0000019

Martinsen, O. L. (2011). The creative personality: A synthesis and development of the creative person profile. *Creativity Research Journal, 23,* 185–202. http://dx.doi.org/10.1080/10400419.2011.595656

M'Bailara, K., Demotes-Mainard, J., Swendsen, J., Mathieu, F., Leboyer, M., & Henry, C. (2009). Emotional hyper-reactivity in normothymic bipolar patients. *Bipolar Disorders, 11,* 63–69. http://dx.doi.org/10.1111/j.1399-5618.2008.00656.x

McGlashan, T. H., Grilo, C. M., Sanislow, C. A., Ralevski, E., Morey, L. C., Gunderson, J. G., . . . Pagano, M. (2005). Two-year prevalence and stability of individual *DSM–IV* criteria for schizotypal, borderline, avoidant, and obsessive-compulsive personality disorders: Toward a hybrid model of Axis II disorders. *The American Journal of Psychiatry, 162,* 883–889. http://dx.doi.org/10.1176/appi.ajp.162.5.883

Miller, J. D., & Pilkonis, P. A. (2006). Neuroticism and affective instability: The same or different? *The American Journal of Psychiatry, 163,* 839–845. http://dx.doi.org/10.1176/ajp.2006.163.5.839

Palmier-Claus, J. E., Taylor, P. J., Varese, F., & Pratt, D. (2012). Does unstable mood increase risk of suicide? Theory, research, and practice. *Journal of Affective Disorders, 143,* 5–15. http://dx.doi.org/10.1016/j.jad.2012.05.030

Reich, D. B., Zanarini, M. C., & Fitzmaurice, G. (2012). Affective lability in bipolar disorder and borderline personality disorder. *Comprehensive Psychiatry, 53,* 230–237. http://dx.doi.org/10.1016/j.comppsych.2011.04.003

Roemer, L., Orsillo, S. M., & Salters-Pedneault, K. (2008). Efficacy of an acceptance-based behavior therapy for generalized anxiety disorder: Evaluation in a randomized controlled trial. *Journal of Consulting and Clinical Psychology, 76,* 1083–1089. http://dx.doi.org/10.1037/a0012720

Rothbart, M. K., & Derryberry, D. (1981). Development of individual differences in temperament. In M. E. Lamb & A. L. Brown (Eds.), *Advances in developmental psychology* (Vol. 1, pp. 37–86). Hillsdale, NJ: Erlbaum.

Rottenberg, J. (2005). Mood and emotion in major depression. *Current Directions in Psychological Science, 14,* 167–170. http://dx.doi.org/10.1111/j.0963-7214.2005.00354.x

Rottenberg, J., Kasch, K. L., Gross, J. J., & Gotlib, I. H. (2002). Sadness and amusement reactivity differentially predict concurrent and prospective functioning in major depressive disorder. *Emotion, 2,* 135–146. http://dx.doi.org/10.1037/1528-3542.2.2.135

Segal, Z., Williams, M., & Teasdale, J. (2002). *Mindfulness-based cognitive therapy for depression.* New York, NY: Guilford Press.

Sherry, D. L., Sherry, S. B., Vincent, N. A., Stewart, S. H., Hadjistavropoulos, H. D., Doucette, S., & Hartling, N. (2014). Anxious attachment and emotional instability interact to predict health anxiety: An extension of the interpersonal model of health anxiety. *Personality and Individual Differences, 56,* 89–94. http://dx.doi.org/10.1016/j.paid.2013.08.025

Siever, L. J., Torgersen, S., Gunderson, J. G., Livesley, W. J., & Kendler, K. S. (2002). The borderline diagnosis III: Identifying endophenotypes for genetic studies. *Biological Psychiatry, 51,* 964–968. http://dx.doi.org/10.1016/S0006-3223(02)01326-4

Simons, J. S., & Carey, K. B. (2002). Risk and vulnerability for marijuana use problems: The role of affect dysregulation. *Psychology of Addictive Behaviors, 16,* 72–75. http://dx.doi.org/10.1037/0893-164X.16.1.72

Skodol, A. E., Siever, L. J., Livesley, W. J., Gunderson, J. G., Pfohl, B., & Widiger, T. A. (2002). The borderline diagnosis II: Biology, genetics, and clinical course. *Biological Psychiatry, 51,* 951–963. http://dx.doi.org/10.1016/S0006-3223(02)01325-2

Smith, C. L., Calkins, S. D., & Keane, S. P. (2006). The relation of maternal behavior and attachment security to toddlers' emotions and emotion regulation. *Research in Human Development, 3,* 21–31. http://dx.doi.org/10.1207/s15427617rhd0301_3

Soloff, P. H., Lis, J. A., Kelly, T., Cornelius, J., & Ulrich, R. (1994). Risk factors for suicidal behavior in borderline personality disorder. *The American Journal of Psychiatry, 151,* 1316–1323. http://dx.doi.org/10.1176/ajp.151.9.1316

Stringaris, A., & Goodman, R. (2009). Mood lability and psychopathology in youth. *Psychological Medicine, 39,* 1237–1245. http://dx.doi.org/10.1017/S0033291708004662

Thompson, R. A. (2011). Emotion and emotion regulation: Two sides of the developing coin. *Emotion Review, 3,* 53–61. http://dx.doi.org/10.1177/1754073910380969

Thompson, R. J., Berenbaum, H., & Bredemeier, K. (2011). Cross-sectional and longitudinal relations between affective instability and depression. *Journal of Affective Disorders, 130,* 53–59. http://dx.doi.org/10.1016/j.jad.2010.09.021

Thompson, R. J., Dizén, M., & Berenbaum, H. (2009). The unique relations between emotional awareness and facets of affective instability. *Journal of Research in Personality, 43,* 875–879. http://dx.doi.org/10.1016/j.jrp.2009.07.006

Thompson, R. J., Mata, J., Jaeggi, S. M., Buschkuehl, M., Jonides, J., & Gotlib, I. H. (2012). The everyday emotional experience of adults with major depressive disorder: Examining emotional instability, inertia, and reactivity. *Journal of Abnormal Psychology, 121,* 819–829. http://dx.doi.org/10.1037/a0027978

Tragesser, S. L., & Robinson, R. J. (2009). The role of affective instability and UPPS impulsivity in borderline personality disorder features. *Journal of Personality Disorders, 23,* 370–383. http://dx.doi.org/10.1521/pedi.2009.23.4.370

White, C. N., Gunderson, J. G., Zanarini, M. C., & Hudson, J. I. (2003). Family studies of borderline personality disorder: A review. *Harvard Review of Psychiatry, 11,* 8–19.

Whiteside, S. P., & Lynam, D. R. (2001). The five factor model and impulsivity: Using a structural model of personality to understand impulsivity. *Personality and Individual Differences, 30,* 669–689. http://dx.doi.org/10.1016/S0191-8869(00)00064-7

Yen, S., Shea, M. T., Sanislow, C. A., Grilo, C. M., Skodol, A. E., Gunderson, J. G., . . . Morey, L. C. (2004). Borderline personality disorder criteria associated with prospectively observed suicidal behavior. *The American Journal of Psychiatry, 161,* 1296–1298. http://dx.doi.org/10.1176/appi.ajp.161.7.1296

Yu, J., & Selby, E. A. (2013). The interaction between affective lability and interpersonal problems in binge eating. *Journal of Social and Clinical Psychology, 32,* 465–481. http://dx.doi.org/10.1521/jscp.2013.32.5.465

14

ANXIOUSNESS AND NEGATIVE AFFECTIVITY IN THE PERSONALITY AND INTERNALIZING DISORDERS

ANTHONY J. ROSELLINI AND TIMOTHY A. BROWN

Anxiety is usually discussed as an acute emotional experience, typically in relation to one of the several internalizing disorders (e.g., anxiety, mood, trauma, and obsessive-compulsive disorders) described in the *Diagnostic and Statistical Manual of Mental Disorders* (5th ed.; *DSM–5*; American Psychiatric Association, 2013) and the *International Statistical Classification of Diseases and Related Health Problems* (10th rev.; *ICD–10*; World Health Organization, 1992). However, there is also a long history of *anxiousness* being conceptualized as a personality trait (e.g., Cattell & Scheier, 1961).

In this chapter, we begin by reviewing the conceptual basis and definition of anxiousness. We then present findings from research examining the associations of anxiousness and negative affectivity (NA) with the personality disorders (PDs) and internalizing disorders (IDs). We end the chapter by discussing clinical implications, including the role of anxiousness and NA in treatment prognosis and diagnostic classification as well as recently

http://dx.doi.org/10.1037/14854-015
The Dark Side of Personality: Science and Practice in Social, Personality, and Clinical Psychology, V. Zeigler-Hill and D. K. Marcus (Editors)

developed treatments that may reduce psychopathology by directly targeting anxious personality traits.

DEFINITION AND BACKGROUND

Anxiousness has been described in several of the most prominent theories of personality over the past 50 years. In one of the earliest conceptualizations of anxiousness as a personality trait, Cattell and Scheier (1961) defined *trait anxiety* as a stable tendency to (a) view stressors as dangerous and (b) respond to stressful situations with more intense and frequent anxiety. Five-factor models of personality define *anxiety* or *anxiousness*—a lower order facet of neuroticism—in a nearly identical fashion (Digman, 1990; McCrae & Costa, 1987). Anxiousness is also similar to the construct of *harm avoidance* that was discussed by Cloninger (1986) as a temperamental disposition to experience excessive worrying, shyness, and fear. In contrast, in Gray's biopsychological reinforcement sensitivity theory (Gray & McNaughton, 1996), anxiousness is represented by a combination of the *behavioral inhibition system* (i.e., sensitivity to be inhibited when exposed to novel stimuli) and *fight–flight system* (i.e., fight or flight in response to punishment or frustrative nonrewards). Further, Clark and Watson's (1991) tripartite model includes dimensions of NA and *autonomic arousal*, both of which have anxiousness-like qualities. Whereas NA is defined as a trait sensitivity to experience negative emotional states (including, but not limited to anxiety), autonomic arousal represents a propensity to experience physiological arousal such as increased heart rate, trembling, and dizziness (Clark, Watson, & Mineka, 1994).

Although there are nuanced differences (Heubeck, Wilkinson, & Cologon, 1998; Matthews & Gilliland, 1999), a large literature suggests that NA, neuroticism, anxiousness, harm avoidance, and behavioral inhibition are closely related at both the conceptual and empirical levels (Campbell-Sills, Liverant, & Brown, 2004; Carver & White, 1994; Clark et al., 1994; Erdle & Rushton, 2010; Keiser & Ross, 2011). However, it is important to note that some theories of personality do not clearly distinguish anxiousness from other facets of NA and neuroticism (e.g., sadness, irritability). For example, Eysenck's (1981) three-factor theory of personality underscores the importance of neuroticism but does not clearly delineate or distinguish a lower order trait of anxiousness. Overall, the personality-psychopathology literature has focused much more on the higher order traits of NA and neuroticism rather than specific constructs of anxious personality.

The personality theories just described strongly influenced the inclusion of anxiousness in the trait model of personality that is described in Section III of *DSM–5* ("Emerging Measures and Models" in need of further study; Krueger et al., 2011; see also the dimensional personality model expected to be included in the 2017 release of the 11th revision of the *ICD* [*ICD–11*]; Kim, Blashfield, Tyrer, Hwang, & Lee, 2014; Tyrer et al., 2014). Specifically, *DSM–5* identifies anxiousness as one of nine facets of NA. Most similar to Cattell and Scheier's (1961) conception of *trait anxiety* and McCrae and Costa's (1987) five-factor model facet definition of *anxiety*, *DSM–5* defines *anxiousness* as "Feelings of nervousness, tenseness, or panic in reaction to diverse situations; frequent worry about the negative effects of past unpleasant experiences and future negative possibilities; feeling fearful and apprehensive about uncertainty; expecting the worst to happen" (p. 779). Collectively, the aforementioned conceptualizations suggest that individuals with high levels of anxious personality are characterized by a dispositional tendency to experience anxiety-related physiological reactions (e.g., increased heart rate, muscle tension), cognitions (e.g., worry thoughts), and behaviors (e.g., avoidance) when confronted with events or circumstances that are subjectively perceived to be stressful. Numerous self-report instruments have been developed and validated to assess the aforementioned constructs of anxious personality, including but not limited to the Personality Inventory for *DSM–5* (Krueger, Derringer, Markon, Watson, & Skodol, 2012), the popular NEO instruments (Costa & McCrae, 1992), the State-Trait Anxiety Inventory (Spielberger, Gorsuch, Lushene, Vagg, & Jacobs, 1983), and the Behavioral Inhibition/Activation Scales (Carver & White, 1994).

Anxiousness and the Personality and Internalizing Disorders

Most of the anxious personality-psychopathology literature has focused on *DSM*-defined PD and ID outcomes. Although a large portion of the PD research has focused on studying anxiousness as it specifically relates to the "anxious cluster" of PDs (cluster C: dependent, avoidant, and obsessive-compulsive PD), a continually growing literature has more broadly examined the differential associations of anxiousness across the range of PDs. In regard to the IDs, the tripartite model of anxiety and depression has served as a catalyst for research examining the relationships between anxiousness/NA and the severity and course of different disorders (Clark & Watson, 1991). Most of the research reviewed in this chapter has been descriptive and cross-sectional. As discussed by Clark et al. (1994), although some longitudinal studies have been conducted, they have relied heavily on treatment-seeking samples to study anxiousness as a predictor of disorder course and treatment response (i.e., pathoplastic relationship of anxiousness modifying the temporal expression of psychopathology). Thus, research has not been able to draw firm conclusions about directional effects of anxiousness as a causal premorbid risk factor in the development of psychopathology (i.e., predispositional relations) or whether the experience of psychopathology causes temporary or permanent changes in anxious personality traits (complication/scar relations).

Personality Disorders

DSM–III (American Psychiatric Association, 1980) was the first edition to define "clusters" of PDs based on shared phenomenological features. Although there have been some minor changes over the years (e.g., compulsive PD renamed obsessive-compulsive PD), the distinction between these clusters has largely been retained. Research on Cluster C suggests that they are the most common PDs (lifetime prevalence of 6.0%) and, unsurprisingly, have high rates of comorbidity with anxiety and depressive disorders (Lenzenweger, Lane, Loranger, & Kessler, 2007). Cluster C has also been linked to several specific anxious personality traits. Numerous studies have found Cluster C disorders to be associated with higher levels of neuroticism than Cluster A and B disorders (Jylhä, Melartin, & Isometsä, 2009; Moran, Coffey, Mann, Carlin, & Patton, 2006). Such findings are why Tyrer (2005) suggested unifying the frequently comorbid Cluster C, anxiety, and depressive disorders by labeling them all expressions of a *general neurotic syndrome* (i.e., high NA). Other studies have also found the Cluster C PDs to be associated with high levels of harm avoidance (Svrakic et al., 2002) and behavioral inhibition (Ross, Keiser, Strong, & Webb, 2013). For example, in a sample of patients with mood disorders with and without comorbid PDs, Jylhä and colleagues (2013) used logistic regression models to show that the presence of cluster C PDs were uniquely predicted by high levels of harm avoidance. Furthermore, Caseras, Torrubia, and Farré (2001) suggested that behavioral inhibition may be a core vulnerability to the anxious PDs after finding that outpatients with Cluster C PDs had significantly higher levels of behavioral inhibition than those with other PDs.

Studies of *DSM*'s PD clusters are inherently limited by the fact that there is mixed evidence to support the validity of the cluster distinction, particularly Cluster C (Bell & Jackson, 1992; Fossati et al., 2006). Whereas dependent and avoidant PDs typically load onto a shared factor in exploratory and confirmatory factor analytic studies; obsessive-compulsive PD often loads elsewhere (Fossati et al., 2000; Hyler & Lyons, 1988). Moreover, research suggests that patients with borderline PD (a Cluster B disorder) display similar levels of anxious personality traits as those with Cluster C PDs (e.g., Jylhä et al., 2013; Samuel & Widiger, 2008). There is also limited evidence for the genetic overlap among Cluster C PDs. For example, in a sample of 1,386 twins, Reichborn-Kjennerud et al. (2007) found that anxious cluster PDs were moderately heritable (27%–35%) but that shared genetic and environmental factors accounted for only 11% of the variance in obsessive-compulsive PD (opposed to 64% and 54% for dependent and avoidant PDs). Indeed, although the notion of the three PD clusters remains in *DSM–5*, the manual is also transparent about the limited support for its validity.

In recent years, these limitations have led to a slight decline in PD research focused on the cluster distinction. In contrast, there has been an increase in research focused on examining the phenomenology of PDs using five-factor conceptualizations of personality. Despite initial apprehension that the five-factor model traits would not be meaningfully linked to the PDs because it was intended to describe "normal" personality functioning, research in the early 1990s began to identify associations between neuroticism and several PDs (Costa & McCrae, 1990). Numerous studies have since used the NEO inventories to examine differential associations of the PDs with five-factor model traits at both the domain and facet levels. This literature was synthesized in Samuel and Widiger's (2008) meta-analysis of 16 studies ($N = 3,207$). Neuroticism was found to be associated with six of 10 *DSM–IV* PDs (American Psychiatric Association, 1994; weighted effect size correlation range = .22–.54), including avoidant PD (.54) and dependent PD (.44). In addition, subsequent facet-level analyses demonstrated anxiousness to be significantly associated with five PDs: avoidant, dependent, borderline, schizotypal, and paranoid (see Table 14.1). Such findings have led to proposals to classify the PDs using a five-factor approach (e.g., Miller, 2013) and ultimately influenced the integration of five-factor model domains and traits in Section III of *DSM–5* (see Anxiousness and Classification later in the chapter).

TABLE 14.1
Relations Between the Five-Factor Model Facet of Anxiousness
and *DSM* Personality and Internalizing Disorders

Personality disorder	Effect size[a]	Internalizing disorder	Mean (*SD*)[b]
Paranoid[c]	.27	Panic disorder	66.95 (9.25)
Schizoid[c]	.13	Social phobia	67.96 (10.01)
Schizotypal	.27	Posttraumatic stress disorder	58.90 (13.00)
Antisocial	.00	Obsessive-compulsive disorder	66.95 (10.92)
Borderline[d]	.38	Major depression	63.50 (10.50)
Histrionic[c]	.00		
Narcissistic	.02		
Avoidant[d]	.41		
Dependent	.39		
Obsessive	.16		

Note. The NEO Personality Inventory—Revised was used to assess the facet of Anxiety (Costa & McCrae, 1992). All effect size *r*s > .04 were significant at *p* < .05.
[a]Independent weighted mean effect size correlations are from Samuel and Widiger's (2008) meta-analysis of 16 studies. [b]Mean scores are from Rector, Bagby, Huta, and Ayearst (2012) multivariate analysis of variance of 610 internalizing disorder outpatients. [c]Disorders for which no Criterion B traits are defined in Section III. [d]Disorders for which anxiousness is identified as a Criterion B personality disorder trait in Section III of the *Diagnostic and Statistical Manual of Mental Disorders* (5th ed.).

Internalizing Disorders

Much of the literature on anxious traits and the *DSM* IDs can be attributed to the development of Clark and Watson's (1991) tripartite model, which posited that symptoms of NA and autonomic arousal would account for the substantial comorbidity that is observed among the anxiety and mood disorders. Whereas high NA was posited to be associated with all IDs, high autonomic arousal was believed to be uniquely associated with the anxiety disorders. Clark et al. (1994) broadened the scope of the model by introducing the possibility of predispositional and pathoplastic relations between trait-levels of NA and autonomic arousal with the anxiety and mood disorders. In an early confirmatory structural model of the tripartite model, Brown and colleagues (Brown, Chorpita, & Barlow, 1998) found that trait (i.e., "general") levels of NA accounted for nearly all of the covariance among five *DSM–IV* ID disorders (depression, panic disorder/agoraphobia, generalized anxiety disorder, social phobia, and obsessive-compulsive disorder). Moreover, whereas NA was significantly positively associated with all of the disorder outcomes (with particularly strong associations with generalized anxiety disorder and depression), autonomic arousal was uniquely related only to panic disorder/agoraphobia. In an independent sample of 295 patients, Brown and McNiff (2009) replicated the unique relationship between autonomic arousal ($\gamma = .36$, $p < .001$) and panic disorder/agoraphobia as well as the strong associations between NA and generalized anxiety disorder ($\gamma = .63$, $p < .001$; see Figure 14.1). Furthermore, this study extended earlier findings by also demonstrating that autonomic arousal has significant associations with posttraumatic stress disorder ($\gamma = .14$, $p < .05$).

In addition to studies examining the tripartite constructs of NA and autonomic arousal, a vast literature has looked at the associations between neuroticism and the IDs. This literature has consistently found nearly all of the internalizing disorders to be associated with high levels of neuroticism (see Kotov, Gamez, Schmidt, & Watson, 2010, for a meta-analysis). Fewer studies have examined how the lower order facet of anxiety is differentially related to the IDs. Evidence from epidemiological studies suggests individuals with any anxiety or mood disorder have higher levels of anxiousness than those without (Bienvenu et al., 2001, 2004). More recently, Rector, Bagby, Huta, and Ayearst (2012) examined facet-level differences across diagnoses in a sample of 610 outpatients and found that patients with panic disorder/agoraphobia, social phobia, obsessive-compulsive disorder, and depression had significantly higher levels of anxiousness than those with posttraumatic stress disorder. Furthermore, individuals with social phobia displayed the largest mean elevations in anxiousness (see Table 14.1). Although some of these

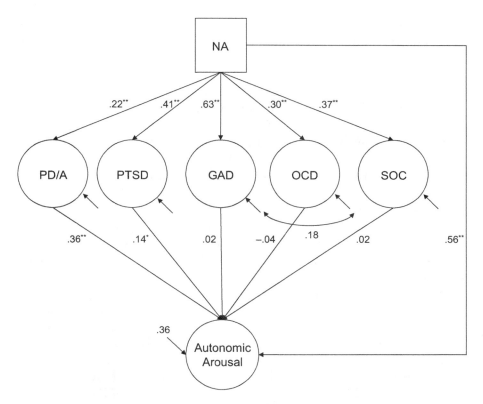

Figure 14.1. Latent structural model of the relationships between *DSM–IV* anxiety disorder constructs, negative affect, and autonomic arousal. AA = autonomic arousal; GAD = generalized anxiety disorder; NA = negative affect; OCD = obsessive-compulsive disorder; PD/A = panic disorder/agoraphobia; PTSD = posttraumatic stress disorder; SOC = social phobia. Completely standardized estimates are shown. From "Specificity of Autonomic Arousal to *DSM–IV* Panic Disorder and Posttraumatic Stress Disorder," by T. A. Brown and J. McNiff, 2009, *Behaviour Research and Therapy, 47*, p. 491. Copyright 2009 by Elsevier. Reprinted with permission.
*$p < .01$; **$p < .001$.

findings are at odds with studies of the tripartite model (e.g., posttraumatic stress disorder not being associated with high levels of anxiousness), they nonetheless confirm that the IDs display meaningful differential relationships with various constructs of anxious personality.

Although there is a longitudinal literature that suggests high levels of NA are associated with a more chronic course of internalizing disorder such as generalized anxiety disorder, depression, and social phobia, findings have not always supported such pathoplastic relationships (e.g., Clark, Vittengl, Kraft, & Jarrett, 2003; Naragon-Gainey, Gallagher, & Brown, 2013;

Spinhoven et al., 2011). One important methodological issue influencing these mixed findings is the possibility that the assessment of personality in patients with IDs is likely influenced by *mood-state distortion*; that is, NA and anxiousness likely consist of stable trait variance (i.e., vulnerability) as well as more transient state variance (e.g., general distress associated with having an ID). The development of trait–state–occasion latent variable modeling (Cole, Martin, & Steiger, 2005) has allowed researchers to isolate trait levels of NA in the prediction of the course of IDs. For example, Naragon-Gainey et al. (2013) used a longitudinal measurement model to show that 57% of the variance in NA/anxiousness (a latent variable composed of trait negative affect, neuroticism, and behavioral inhibition) was time-invariant. In addition, the time-invariant component of NA/anxiousness predicted fewer reductions in symptoms of depression and social phobia over a 1-year period. This study elucidates the mixed findings for the effects of NA/anxiousness on the course of IDs by suggesting that omission of the time-variant component of NA/anxiousness significantly increases the strength of its associations with the IDs.

With a few exceptions (e.g., Kasch, Rottenberg, Arnow, & Gotlib, 2002), longitudinal research on the IDs and lower order traits of anxiousness has tended to obtain more consistent results. For example, research on trait anxiety suggests that individuals with high baseline levels report significantly more symptoms of depression (Bromberger & Matthews, 1996; Parker, Wilhelm, Mitchell, & Gladstone, 2000) and greater ID comorbidity (Chambers, Power, & Durham, 2004) several years later. In regard to harm avoidance, high baseline levels have been shown to predict a more stable course of social phobia among young adults (Beesdo-Baum et al., 2012) and depression among inpatients (Richter, Eisemann, & Richter, 2000). Accordingly, although it seems reasonable that anxiousness would be influenced by mood-state distortion in similar ways as NA, the time-varying variance in anxiousness may not be substantial enough to preclude the detection of significant effects between baseline anxiousness and ID course. Nonetheless, additional longitudinal research using trait-state-occasion modeling is needed to determine the extent to which anxious personality is influenced by mood-state distortion.

Adaptive Features of Anxiousness

Although the majority of research has focused on the deleterious effects of anxiety (e.g., the maladaptive effects reviewed in the two preceding sections), there is a small but noteworthy literature on the potentially protective role of the personality trait of anxiousness. This research is based on the idea that individuals with high NA may be more likely to adaptively avoid or avert dangerous and threatening situations. Indeed, studies of decision-making processes have found high trait anxiety to be associated with increased avoidance of making risky decisions (e.g., Maner et al., 2007). Few studies have examined the adaptive features of anxiousness outside of the laboratory and with practically important outcomes. However, one population-based study found that high trait anxiety during adolescence was associated with fewer accidents and accidental deaths in early adulthood (Lee, Wadsworth, & Hotopf, 2006).

A related literature has also discussed the evolutionary benefits of experiencing anxiety symptoms and disorders. As reviewed by Bateson, Brilot, and Nettle (2011), for example, anxiety symptoms are adaptive so long as they maximize survival and reproduction, even in the case of such symptoms causing significant role impairment or distress (e.g., a *DSM* disorder). In fact, one study even found that depressed patients with comorbid anxiety disorders have poorer health and more disability but lower rates of mortality compared with patients without comorbid anxiety (Mykletun et al., 2009). Indeed, there is a clear survival function for many of the anxiety symptoms included in *DSM*: Increased heart rate prepares the body for action; insomnia allows one to be constantly alert and ready for danger; worrying thoughts allow individuals to anticipate potentially dangerous situations well before they occur.

CLINICAL IMPLICATIONS

Anxiousness and Treatment Response

As reviewed earlier, a number of studies have looked at anxious traits as predictors of depression course. A separate literature has also examined anxiousness as a specific predictor of depression treatment outcome. This research suggests that high pretreatment trait anxiety and harm avoidance are associated with poor outcome of both psychological and pharmacological interventions for depression (Kampman et al., 2012; Min, Lee, Lee, Lee, & Chae, 2012; Tome, Cloninger, Watson, & Isaac, 1997). High pretreatment harm avoidance has also been associated with poor response to cognitive-behavioral therapies for social phobia (Mörtberg & Andersson, 2014) and pharmacotherapy for panic disorder/agoraphobia (Marchesi, Cantoni, Fontò, Giannelli, & Maggini, 2006). Although additional research is needed to ascertain the relevance of anxious traits in predicting the course and treatment response of other IDs (e.g., posttraumatic stress disorder, obsessive-compulsive disorder), the extant longitudinal literature collectively suggests that there is useful prognostic value in assessing anxiousness at the start of treatment. This is in part why *DSM–5* now allows diagnosticians to attach the *anxious distress* specifier to a mood disorder.

Anxiousness and Classification

As previously mentioned, the differential associations observed between five-factor model personality traits (including the facet of anxiousness) and *DSM* PDs (Samuel & Widiger, 2008) have been used to justify a five-factor model approach to diagnosis and classification. For example, Miller (2013) discussed diagnosing the PDs using a five-factor model prototype matching approach that involves (a) assessing the personality profile of a patient (e.g., using the NEO instruments) and (b) matching the personality profile to a theoretically or empirically predetermined personality "prototype" (e.g., assigning a *DSM* category based on specific cutoff scores on different NEO domains and facets). In contrast, Section III of *DSM–5* outlines a criteria-based approach for PD diagnosis via its 25 personality trait facets. For the six PDs discussed in Section III, Criterion B captures their associated personality trait facet profile. Anxiousness is identified as a key pathological trait (i.e., required for Criterion B) for avoidant PD and a peripheral but related (i.e., not required) trait for borderline PD (see Table 14.1). Although quite different from what is proposed in *DSM–5* Section III, it is also noteworthy that *ICD–11* will likely adopt a dimensional approach to PD classification, including an emphasis on assessing the extent to which the higher order trait of negative affectivity results in functional impairment (Kim et al., 2014; Tyrer et al., 2014).

There has been much less discussion of personality-based diagnosis and classification of the IDs with a few notable exceptions (e.g., Brown & Barlow, 2009; Clark, 2005). These proposals have tended to focus broadly on integrating NA in ID diagnosis and nosology (i.e., based on purported predispositional and pathoplastic relations) rather than inclusion of specific lower order facets of anxious personality. For example, Brown and Barlow (2009) proposed a dimensional-categorical hybrid approach to classification in which dimensions of personality (e.g., NA) and transdiagnostic ID phenotypes are plotted into a "diagnostic profile." Although this proposal also underscores the importance of assessing autonomic arousal (i.e., to differentiate panic disorder/agoraphobia and posttraumatic stress disorder from other IDs with high NA), it is discussed primarily as a symptom-based dimension. Nonetheless, given the differential associations that have been observed between other anxious personality traits (e.g., trait anxiety, anxiousness) and the IDs (e.g., Rector et al., 2012), future research should further investigate the utility of integrating lower order anxiousness traits in the assessment and diagnosis of IDs.

Treatment of Anxious Personality

Although often conceptualized to be temporally stable, there is research to suggest that anxious personality traits change over time without intervention (Roberts & Mroczek, 2008) as well as with psychological (Jorm, 1989) or pharmacological treatments (Soskin, Carl, Alpert, & Fava, 2012). Using latent growth modeling, for example, Brown (2007) found that NA evidenced larger reductions than *DSM–IV* anxiety and mood disorder dimensions among treatment-seeking outpatients over a 2-year period. Reductions in NA were also significantly correlated with reductions in *DSM–IV* IDs. Indeed, several other studies have found similar reductions in lower order traits of anxiousness over the course of treatment. For instance, Hofmann and Loh (2006) found that group treatment for social phobia led to reductions in harm avoidance and that change in harm avoidance significantly predicted reductions in social phobia. Although the effects are small, findings from the pharmacological treatment literature also suggest that antidepressants may lead to reductions in levels of neuroticism (Soskin et al., 2012), trait anxiety (Nabi et al., 2013), and harm avoidance (Agosti & McGrath, 2002).

On the basis of empirical evidence that anxious personality traits (a) predict the course of several IDs and (b) may be modifiable via psychological and pharmacological treatments, the identification and development of treatments specifically aimed at reducing NA and its associated lower order trait of anxiousness has been suggested (Chambers et al., 2004). However, the corresponding treatment literature has tended to focus on interventions broadly targeting NA. Findings from pharmacological treatment studies suggests that selective serotonin reuptake inhibitors uniquely lead to reductions in NA (Harmer et al., 2009; Murphy, Yiend, Lester, Cowen, & Harmer, 2009), whereas noradrenergic and dopaminergic agents do not (McCabe, Mishor, Cowen, & Harmer, 2010; Tomarken, Dichter, Freid, Addington, & Shelton, 2004). Although little has been done in the realm of psychological treatments, Barlow's unified protocol for transdiagnostic treatment of emotional disorders (UP) is one exception (Barlow et al., 2011). The UP is a cognitive-behavioral intervention designed specifically to address core personality and temperamental processes in the IDs by broadly identifying and modifying negative emotional reactions associated with high NA. Although a large randomized controlled trial is currently underway, preliminary findings suggest that the UP produces small-to-moderate effects on NA over the course of treatment (Carl, Gallagher, Sauer-Zavala, Bentley, & Barlow, 2013).

CONCLUSIONS AND FUTURE DIRECTIONS

Several conclusions can be drawn from the literature on anxiousness in the PDs and IDs. First, although there is clear overlap among the various conceptualizations of anxious personality (e.g., anxiousness, autonomic arousal, trait anxiety, behavioral inhibition, harm avoidance), there is also evidence that different constructs of anxious personality have differential relationships with the PDs and IDs (e.g., NA having strong associations with generalized anxiety disorder; autonomic arousal having unique associations with panic disorder/agoraphobia and posttraumatic stress disorder; five-factor model anxiousness highest among those with social phobia, avoidant PD, dependent PD, and borderline PD). This pattern suggests the need for additional research examining the nomological network of anxious personality subfacets and how these subfacets relate to the PDs and IDs. Indeed, consistent with the multifaceted definition of *DSM–5* anxiousness, Gray and McNaughton's (1996) behavioral inhibition, and Cloninger's (1986) harm avoidance, anxious personality likely involves somewhat distinct subfacets of tension/panic (e.g., fight–flight, autonomic arousal) and worry/apprehension (e.g., anxiety).

Unfortunately, most of the PD and ID literature has focused more on higher order traits of NA or neuroticism rather than anxious personality. Moreover, psychopathology research that has examined the lower order trait of anxiousness has not examined nuanced associations with potential subfacets. Such pursuits could clarify differential relationships between anxious personality constructs and psychopathology in ways that could further bolster the inclusion of anxiousness in diagnostic assessment and classification, particularly for the IDs.

Furthermore, although anxious personality constructs appear to predict the course and treatment response of several IDs more consistently that NA, most of this research has focused on outcomes related to depression. Additional research is needed to ascertain the relevance of anxious traits in predicting the course and treatment response of other IDs (e.g., posttraumatic stress disorder, obsessive-compulsive disorder, panic disorder/agoraphobia, generalized anxiety disorder). As such, it is unclear to what extent anxiousness may be influenced by mood-state distortion; the assessment of anxiousness among individuals primarily experiencing depression is presumably less influenced by mood-state distortion than NA or neuroticism. Accordingly, longitudinal research using newer latent variable methodologies (e.g., trait–state–occasion modeling) would be useful in determining the extent to which anxious personality is composed of trait versus state variance, and the extent to which these components are differentially relevant to the prediction of ID course and treatment response (cf. Naragon-Gainey et al., 2013).

REFERENCES

Agosti, V., & McGrath, P. J. (2002). Comparison of the effects of fluoxetine, imipramine and placebo on personality in atypical depression. *Journal of Affective Disorders, 71*, 113–120. http://dx.doi.org/10.1016/S0165-0327(01)00393-7

American Psychiatric Association. (1980). *Diagnostic and statistical manual of mental disorders* (3rd ed.). Washington, DC: Author.

American Psychiatric Association. (1994). *Diagnostic and statistical manual of mental disorders* (4th ed.). Washington, DC: Author.

American Psychiatric Association. (2013). *Diagnostic and statistical manual of mental disorders* (5th ed.). Arlington, VA: Author.

Barlow, D. H., Ellard, K. K., Fairholme, C., Farchione, T. J., Boisseau, C., Allen, L., & Ehrenreich-May, J. (2011). *Unified protocol for the transdiagnostic treatment of emotional disorders*. New York, NY: Oxford University Press.

Bateson, M., Brilot, B., & Nettle, D. (2011). Anxiety: An evolutionary approach. *Canadian Journal of Psychiatry, 56*, 707–715.

Beesdo-Baum, K., Knappe, S., Fehm, L., Höfler, M., Lieb, R., Hofmann, S. G., & Wittchen, H. U. (2012). The natural course of social anxiety disorder among adolescents and young adults. *Acta Psychiatrica Scandinavica, 126*, 411–425. http://dx.doi.org/10.1111/j.1600-0447.2012.01886.x

Bell, R. C., & Jackson, H. J. (1992). The structure of personality disorders in *DSM–III*. *Acta Psychiatrica Scandinavica, 85*, 279–287. http://dx.doi.org/10.1111/j.1600-0447.1992.tb01470.x

Bienvenu, O. J., Nestadt, G., Samuels, J. F., Costa, P. T., Howard, W. T., & Eaton, W. W. (2001). Phobic, panic, and major depressive disorders and the five-factor model of personality. *Journal of Nervous and Mental Disease, 189*, 154–161. http://dx.doi.org/10.1097/00005053-200103000-00003

Bienvenu, O. J., Samuels, J. F., Costa, P. T., Reti, I. M., Eaton, W. W., & Nestadt, G. (2004). Anxiety and depressive disorders and the five-factor model of personality: A higher- and lower-order personality trait investigation in a community sample. *Depression and Anxiety, 20*, 92–97. http://dx.doi.org/10.1002/da.20026

Bromberger, J. T., & Matthews, K. A. (1996). A longitudinal study of the effects of pessimism, trait anxiety, and life stress on depressive symptoms in middle-aged women. *Psychology and Aging, 11*, 207–213. http://dx.doi.org/10.1037/0882-7974.11.2.207

Brown, T. A. (2007). Temporal course and structural relationships among dimensions of temperament and *DSM–IV* anxiety and mood disorder constructs. *Journal of Abnormal Psychology, 116*, 313–328. http://dx.doi.org/10.1037/0021-843X.116.2.313

Brown, T. A., & Barlow, D. H. (2009). A proposal for a dimensional classification system based on the shared features of the *DSM–IV* anxiety and mood disorders: Implications for assessment and treatment. *Psychological Assessment, 21*, 256–271. http://dx.doi.org/10.1037/a0016608

Brown, T. A., Chorpita, B. F., & Barlow, D. H. (1998). Structural relationships among dimensions of the *DSM–IV* anxiety and mood disorders and dimensions of negative affect, positive affect, and autonomic arousal. *Journal of Abnormal Psychology, 107,* 179–192. http://dx.doi.org/10.1037/0021-843X.107.2.179

Brown, T. A., & McNiff, J. (2009). Specificity of autonomic arousal to *DSM–IV* panic disorder and posttraumatic stress disorder. *Behaviour Research and Therapy, 47,* 487–493. http://dx.doi.org/10.1016/j.brat.2009.02.016

Campbell-Sills, L., Liverant, G. I., & Brown, T. A. (2004). Psychometric evaluation of the behavioral inhibition/behavioral activation scales in a large sample of outpatients with anxiety and mood disorders. *Psychological Assessment, 16,* 244–254. http://dx.doi.org/10.1037/1040-3590.16.3.244

Carl, J. R., Gallagher, M. W., Sauer-Zavala, S. E., Bentley, K. H., & Barlow, D. H. (2013). *A preliminary examination of the effects of the unified protocol on temperament.* Manuscript submitted for publication.

Carver, C. S., & White, T. L. (1994). Behavioral inhibition, behavioral activation, and affective responses to impending reward and punishment: The BIS/BAS scales. *Journal of Personality and Social Psychology, 67,* 319–333. http://dx.doi.org/10.1037/0022-3514.67.2.319

Caseras, X., Torrubia, R., & Farré, J. M. (2001). Is the behavioral inhibition system the core vulnerability for Cluster C personality disorders? *Personality and Individual Differences, 31,* 349–359. http://dx.doi.org/10.1016/S0191-8869(00)00141-0

Cattell, R. B., & Scheier, I. H. (1961). *The meaning and measurement of neuroticism and anxiety.* New York, NY: Ronald.

Chambers, J. A., Power, K. G., & Durham, R. C. (2004). The relationship between trait vulnerability and anxiety and depressive diagnoses at long-term follow-up of generalized anxiety disorder. *Journal of Anxiety Disorders, 18,* 587–607. http://dx.doi.org/10.1016/j.janxdis.2003.09.001

Clark, L. A. (2005). Temperament as a unifying basis for personality and psychopathology. *Journal of Abnormal Psychology, 114,* 505–521. http://dx.doi.org/10.1037/0021-843X.114.4.505

Clark, L. A., Vittengl, J., Kraft, D., & Jarrett, R. B. (2003). Separate personality traits from states to predict depression. *Journal of Personality Disorders, 17,* 152–172. http://dx.doi.org/10.1521/pedi.17.2.152.23990

Clark, L. A., & Watson, D. (1991). Tripartite model of anxiety and depression: Psychometric evidence and taxonomic implications. *Journal of Abnormal Psychology, 100,* 316–336. http://dx.doi.org/10.1037/0021-843X.100.3.316

Clark, L. A., Watson, D., & Mineka, S. (1994). Temperament, personality, and the mood and anxiety disorders. *Journal of Abnormal Psychology, 103,* 103–116. http://dx.doi.org/10.1037/0021-843X.103.1.103

Cloninger, C. R. (1986). A unified biosocial theory of personality and its role in the development of anxiety states. *Psychiatric Developments, 4,* 167–226.

Cole, D. A., Martin, N. C., & Steiger, J. H. (2005). Empirical and conceptual problems with longitudinal trait–state models: Introducing a trait–state–occasion model. *Psychological Methods, 10,* 3–20. http://dx.doi.org/10.1037/1082-989X.10.1.3

Costa, P. T., Jr., & McCrae, R. R. (1990). Personality disorders and the five-factor model of personality. *Journal of Personality Disorders, 4,* 362–371. http://dx.doi.org/10.1521/pedi.1990.4.4.362

Costa, P. T., Jr., & McCrae, R. R. (1992). *NEO PI–R professional manual: Revised NEO Personality Inventory (NEO PI–R) and NEO Five-Factor Inventory (NEO-FFI)*. Odessa, FL: Psychological Assessment Resources.

Digman, J. (1990). Personality structure: Emergence of the five-factor model. *Annual Review of Psychology, 41,* 417–440. http://dx.doi.org/10.1146/annurev.ps.41.020190.002221

Erdle, S., & Rushton, J. (2010). The general factor of personality, BIS–BAS, expectancies of reward and punishment, self-esteem, and positive and negative affect. *Personality and Individual Differences, 48,* 762–766. http://dx.doi.org/10.1016/j.paid.2010.01.025

Eysenck, H. J. (Ed.). (1981). *A model for personality*. New York, NY: Springer. http://dx.doi.org/10.1007/978-3-642-67783-0

Fossati, A., Beauchaine, T. P., Grazioli, F., Borroni, S., Carretta, I., De Vecchi, C., . . . Maffei, C. (2006). Confirmatory factor analyses of *DSM–IV* Cluster C personality disorder criteria. *Journal of Personality Disorders, 20,* 186–203. http://dx.doi.org/10.1521/pedi.2006.20.2.186

Fossati, A., Maffei, C., Bagnato, M., Battaglia, M., Donati, D., Donini, M., . . . Prolo, F. (2000). Patterns of covariation of *DSM–IV* personality disorders in a mixed psychiatric sample. *Comprehensive Psychiatry, 41,* 206–215. http://dx.doi.org/10.1016/S0010-440X(00)90049-X

Gray, J. A., & McNaughton, N. (1996). The neuropsychology of anxiety: A reprise. In D. A. Hope (Ed.), *Nebraska Symposium on Motivation: Vol. 43. Perspectives on anxiety, panic, and fear* (pp. 61–134). Lincoln: University of Nebraska Press.

Harmer, C. J., O'Sullivan, U., Favaron, E., Massey-Chase, R., Ayres, R., Reinecke, A., . . . Cowen, P. J. (2009). Effect of acute antidepressant administration on negative affective bias in depressed patients. *The American Journal of Psychiatry, 166,* 1178–1184. http://dx.doi.org/10.1176/appi.ajp.2009.09020149

Heubeck, B. G., Wilkinson, R. B., & Cologon, J. (1998). A second look at Carver and White's (1994) BIS/BAS scales. *Personality and Individual Differences, 25,* 785–800. http://dx.doi.org/10.1016/S0191-8869(98)00124-X

Hofmann, S. G., & Loh, R. (2006). The Tridimensional Personality Questionnaire: Changes during psychological treatment of social phobia. *Journal of Psychiatric Research, 40,* 214–220.

Hyler, S. E., & Lyons, M. (1988). Factor analysis of the *DSM–III* personality disorder clusters: A replication. *Comprehensive Psychiatry, 29,* 304–308. http://dx.doi.org/10.1016/0010-440X(88)90053-3

Jorm, A. F. (1989). Modifiability of trait anxiety and neuroticism: A meta-analysis of the literature. *Australian and New Zealand Journal of Psychiatry, 23,* 21–29. http://dx.doi.org/10.3109/00048678909062588

Jylhä, P., Ketokivi, M., Mantere, O., Melartin, T., Suominen, K., Vuorilehto, M., . . . Isometsä, E. (2013). Temperament, character, and personality disorders. *European Psychiatry, 28,* 483–491. http://dx.doi.org/10.1016/j.eurpsy.2013.06.003

Jylhä, P., Melartin, T., & Isometsä, E. (2009). Relationships of neuroticism and extraversion with Axis I and II comorbidity among patients with *DSM–IV* major depressive disorder. *Journal of Affective Disorders, 114,* 110–121. http://dx.doi.org/10.1016/j.jad.2008.06.011

Kampman, O., Poutanen, O., Illi, A., Setälä-Soikkeli, E., Viikki, M., Nuolivirta, T., & Leinonen, E. (2012). Temperament profiles, major depression, and response to treatment with SSRIs in psychiatric outpatients. *European Psychiatry, 27,* 245–249. http://dx.doi.org/10.1016/j.eurpsy.2010.07.006

Kasch, K. L., Rottenberg, J., Arnow, B. A., & Gotlib, I. H. (2002). Behavioral activation and inhibition systems and the severity and course of depression. *Journal of Abnormal Psychology, 111,* 589–597. http://dx.doi.org/10.1037/0021-843X.111.4.589

Keiser, H. N., & Ross, S. R. (2011). Carver and White's BIS/FFFS/BAS scales and domains and facets of the five factor model of personality. *Personality and Individual Differences, 51,* 39–44. http://dx.doi.org/10.1016/j.paid.2011.03.007

Kim, Y. R., Blashfield, R., Tyrer, P., Hwang, S. T., & Lee, H. S. (2014). Field trial of a putative research algorithm for diagnosing *ICD–11* personality disorders in psychiatric patients: 1. Severity of personality disturbance. *Personality and Mental Health, 8,* 67–78. http://dx.doi.org/10.1002/pmh.1248

Kotov, R., Gamez, W., Schmidt, F., & Watson, D. (2010). Linking "big" personality traits to anxiety, depressive, and substance use disorders: A meta-analysis. *Psychological Bulletin, 136,* 768–821. http://dx.doi.org/10.1037/a0020327

Krueger, R. F., Derringer, J., Markon, K. E., Watson, D., & Skodol, A. E. (2012). Initial construction of a maladaptive personality trait model and inventory for *DSM–5. Psychological Medicine, 42,* 1879–1890. http://dx.doi.org/10.1017/S0033291711002674

Krueger, R. F., Eaton, N. R., Clark, L. A., Watson, D., Markon, K. E., Derringer, J., . . . Livesley, W. J. (2011). Deriving an empirical structure of personality pathology for *DSM–5. Journal of Personality Disorders, 25,* 170–191. http://dx.doi.org/10.1521/pedi.2011.25.2.170

Lee, W. E., Wadsworth, M. E. J., & Hotopf, M. (2006). The protective role of trait anxiety: A longitudinal cohort study. *Psychological Medicine, 36,* 345–351. http://dx.doi.org/10.1017/S0033291705006847

Lenzenweger, M. F., Lane, M. C., Loranger, A. W., & Kessler, R. C. (2007). *DSM-IV* personality disorders in the National Comorbidity Survey Replication. *Biological Psychiatry, 62,* 553–564. http://dx.doi.org/10.1016/j.biopsych.2006.09.019

Maner, J. K., Richey, J. A., Cromer, K., Mallott, M., Lejuez, C. W., Joiner, T. E., & Schmidt, N. B. (2007). Dispositional anxiety and risk-avoidant decision-making.

Personality and Individual Differences, 42, 665–675. http://dx.doi.org/10.1016/j.paid.2006.08.016

Marchesi, C., Cantoni, A., Fontò, S., Giannelli, M. R., & Maggini, C. (2006). The effect of temperament and character on response to selective serotonin reuptake inhibitors in panic disorder. *Acta Psychiatrica Scandinavica, 114*, 203–210. http://dx.doi.org/10.1111/j.1600-0447.2006.00772.x

Matthews, G., & Gilliland, K. (1999). The personality theories of H. J. Eysenck and J. A. Gray: A comparative review. *Personality and Individual Differences, 26*, 583–626. http://dx.doi.org/10.1016/S0191-8869(98)00158-5

McCabe, C., Mishor, Z., Cowen, P. J., & Harmer, C. J. (2010). Diminished neural processing of aversive and rewarding stimuli during selective serotonin reuptake inhibitor treatment. *Biological Psychiatry, 67*, 439–445. http://dx.doi.org/10.1016/j.biopsych.2009.11.001

McCrae, R. R., & Costa, P. T., Jr. (1987). Validation of the five-factor model of personality across instruments and observers. *Journal of Personality and Social Psychology, 52*, 81–90. http://dx.doi.org/10.1037/0022-3514.52.1.81

Miller, J. D. (2013). Prototype matching and the five-factor model: Capturing the *DSM–IV* personality disorders. In T. A. Widiger & P. T. Costa, Jr. (Eds.), *Personality disorders and the five-factor model of personality* (3rd ed., pp. 249–267). Washington, DC: American Psychological Association. http://dx.doi.org/10.1037/13939-017

Min, J. A., Lee, N. B., Lee, C. U., Lee, C., & Chae, J. H. (2012). Low trait anxiety, high resilience, and their interaction as possible predictors for treatment response in patients with depression. *Journal of Affective Disorders, 137*, 61–69. http://dx.doi.org/10.1016/j.jad.2011.12.026

Moran, P., Coffey, C., Mann, A., Carlin, J. B., & Patton, G. C. (2006). Dimensional characteristics of *DSM–IV* personality disorders in a large epidemiological sample. *Acta Psychiatrica Scandinavica, 113*, 233–236. http://dx.doi.org/10.1111/j.1600-0447.2005.00739.x

Mörtberg, E., & Andersson, G. (2014). Predictors of response to individual and group cognitive behavior therapy of social phobia. *Psychology and Psychotherapy: Theory, Research and Practice, 87*, 32–43. http://dx.doi.org/10.1111/papt.12002

Murphy, S. E., Yiend, J., Lester, K. J., Cowen, P. J., & Harmer, C. J. (2009). Short-term serotonergic but not noradrenergic antidepressant administration reduces attentional vigilance to threat in healthy volunteers. *International Journal of Neuropsychopharmacology, 12*, 169–179. http://dx.doi.org/10.1017/S1461145708009164

Mykletun, A., Bjerkeset, O., Øverland, S., Prince, M., Dewey, M., & Stewart, R. (2009). Levels of anxiety and depression as predictors of mortality: The HUNT study. *The British Journal of Psychiatry, 195*, 118–125. http://dx.doi.org/10.1192/bjp.bp.108.054866

Nabi, H., Virtanen, M., Singh-Manoux, A., Hagger-Johnson, G., Pentti, J., Kivimäki, M., & Vahtera, J. (2013). Trait anxiety levels before and after antidepressant treatment: A 3-wave cohort study. *Journal of Clinical Psychopharmacology, 33*, 371–377. http://dx.doi.org/10.1097/JCP.0b013e31828b26c2

Naragon-Gainey, K., Gallagher, M. W., & Brown, T. A. (2013). Stable "trait" variance of temperament as a predictor of the temporal course of depression and social phobia. *Journal of Abnormal Psychology, 122,* 611–623. http://dx.doi.org/10.1037/a0032997

Parker, G., Wilhelm, K., Mitchell, P., & Gladstone, G. (2000). Predictors of 1-year outcome in depression. *Australian and New Zealand Journal of Psychiatry, 34,* 56–64. http://dx.doi.org/10.1046/j.1440-1614.2000.00698.x

Rector, N. A., Bagby, R. M., Huta, V., & Ayearst, L. E. (2012). Examination of the trait facets of the five-factor model in discriminating specific mood and anxiety disorders. *Psychiatry Research, 199,* 131–139. http://dx.doi.org/10.1016/j.psychres.2012.04.027

Reichborn-Kjennerud, T., Czajkowski, N., Neale, M. C., Ørstavik, R. E., Torgersen, S., Tambs, K., . . . Kendler, K. S. (2007). Genetic and environmental influences on dimensional representations of *DSM–IV* Cluster C personality disorders: A population-based multivariate twin study. *Psychological Medicine, 37,* 645–653.

Richter, J., Eisemann, M., & Richter, G. (2000). Temperament and character during the course of unipolar depression among inpatients. *European Archives of Psychiatry and Clinical Neuroscience, 250,* 40–47. http://dx.doi.org/10.1007/PL00007538

Roberts, B. W., & Mroczek, D. (2008). Personality trait change in adulthood. *Current Directions in Psychological Science, 17,* 31–35. http://dx.doi.org/10.1111/j.1467-8721.2008.00543.x

Ross, S. R., Keiser, H. N., Strong, J. V., & Webb, C. M. (2013). Reinforcement sensitivity theory and symptoms of personality disorder: Specificity of the BIS in cluster C and BAS in cluster B. *Personality and Individual Differences, 54,* 289–293. http://dx.doi.org/10.1016/j.paid.2012.09.020

Samuel, D. B., & Widiger, T. A. (2008). A meta-analytic review of the relationships between the five-factor model and *DSM–IV–TR* personality disorders: A facet level analysis. *Clinical Psychology Review, 28,* 1326–1342. http://dx.doi.org/10.1016/j.cpr.2008.07.002

Soskin, D. P., Carl, J. R., Alpert, J., & Fava, M. (2012). Antidepressant effects on emotional temperament: Toward a biobehavioral research paradigm for major depressive disorder. *CNS Neuroscience & Therapeutics, 18,* 441–451. http://dx.doi.org/10.1111/j.1755-5949.2012.00318.x

Spielberger, C. D., Gorsuch, R. L., Lushene, R. E., Vagg, P. R., & Jacobs, G. A. (1983). *Manual for the State-Trait Anxiety Inventory STAI (Form Y).* Palo Alto, CA: Consulting Psychologists Press.

Spinhoven, P., Elzinga, B. M., Hovens, J. G., Roelofs, K., van Oppen, P., Zitman, F. G., & Penninx, B. W. (2011). Positive and negative life events and personality traits in predicting course of depression and anxiety. *Acta Psychiatrica Scandinavica, 124,* 462–473. http://dx.doi.org/10.1111/j.1600-0447.2011.01753.x

Svrakic, D. M., Draganic, S., Hill, K., Bayon, C., Przybeck, T. R., & Cloninger, C. R. (2002). Temperament, character, and personality disorders: Etiologic, diagnostic, treatment issues. *Acta Psychiatrica Scandinavica, 106,* 189–195. http://dx.doi.org/10.1034/j.1600-0447.2002.02196.x

Tomarken, A. J., Dichter, G. S., Freid, C., Addington, S., & Shelton, R. C. (2004). Assessing the effects of bupropion SR on mood dimensions of depression. *Journal of Affective Disorders, 78,* 235–241.

Tome, M. B., Cloninger, C. R., Watson, J. P., & Isaac, M. T. (1997). Serotonergic autoreceptor blockade in the reduction of antidepressant latency: Personality variables and response to paroxetine and pindolol. *Journal of Affective Disorders, 44,* 101–109. http://dx.doi.org/10.1016/S0165-0327(97)00030-X

Tyrer, P. (2005). The anxious cluster of personality disorders: A review. In M. Maj, H. S. Akiskal, J. E. Mezzich, & A. Okasha (Eds.), *Personality disorders* (pp. 349–375). West Sussex, England: Wiley.

Tyrer, P., Crawford, M., Sanatinia, R., Tyrer, H., Cooper, S., Muller-Pollard, C., . . . Weich, S. (2014). Preliminary studies of the *ICD-11* classification of personality disorder in practice. *Personality and Mental Health, 8,* 254–263. http://dx.doi.org/10.1002/pmh.1275

World Health Organization. (1992). *International statistical classification of diseases and related health problems* (10th rev.). Geneva, Switzerland: Author.

15

DEPRESSIVITY AND ANHEDONIA

ELLEN M. KESSEL AND DANIEL N. KLEIN

Modern clinical psychiatry conceptualizes depression as a disorder primarily characterized by the presence of a markedly depressed mood and/or anhedonia, a diminished interest or pleasure in nearly all activities. As such, the term *depression* can be used to refer to either a profound sadness or to describe a manifestation of a clinical syndrome. This dual definition creates a paradoxical relationship between depression and anhedonia; anhedonia is, simultaneously, interchangeable with depression, a feature of depression, and a distinct entity from depression. This chapter explores the nature of that curious "and/or."

We first provide a historical background of the larger literature on the depressive personality. Then we examine the scanter literature on anhedonic personality. Although these literatures have developed largely independently from one another, we argue that both can be understood together in terms of more basic temperament dimensions. In the bulk of this chapter, we discuss how positive and negative emotionality may serve as building blocks for these

http://dx.doi.org/10.1037/14854-016

The Dark Side of Personality: Science and Practice in Social, Personality, and Clinical Psychology, V. Zeigler-Hill and D. K. Marcus (Editors)

personality styles. In doing so, we suggest the need for empirical inquiry into how depressivity and anhedonia influence each other over the course of time and development.

DEFINITION AND BACKGROUND

Depressivity

The recognition of a depressive personality style can be traced as far back as antiquity. Hippocrates, and later Galen, attributed an excess of black bile as the cause of the clinical state of melancholia, whereas a lesser and more stable imbalance of the four humors, predominated by black bile, undergird a melancholic disposition characterized by fear and sadness (Maher & Maher, 1994). More than a millennium later, the emergence of a clinical construct of depressive personality emerged when the classical European descriptive psychopathologists in the late 19th and early 20th centuries observed that many patients with mood disorders, as well as their relatives, exhibited premorbid personalities that appeared to be attenuated versions of their illnesses. Emil Kraepelin (1921) identified a constellation of traits characteristic of a "depressive temperament": joyless, despondent, insecure, guilt-prone, ruminative, indecisive, anxious, quiet and shy, and lacking in vitality and initiative. He postulated that these traits were constitutional in nature, early emerging, stable, and made up the *forme fruste*, or early antecedents, of major depressive illness. Major depressive states emerge as a by-product of the difficulties and disappointments in life that such traits elicit, and continue to wax and wane over time. At their extreme, however, these traits can be perpetually morbid without the appearance of a more severe delimited episode.

The rich literature on depressive personality that has emerged includes a multitude of accounts from diverse traditions. Although the majority of clinical descriptions bear significant resemblance to Kraepelin's, the literature is laden with ambiguity and multiplicity, illustrating the likely heterogeneity and etiological complexity of what has been conceptualized as depressive personality. For example, in contrast to Kraepelin's precursor model, Emil Kretschmer (1925) theorized a single continuum that ranged in severity from normative depressive personality through personality disorder to clinical depression. To Kurt Schneider (1958), a person with depressive temperament—which he termed the *depressive psychopath*—was an extreme variant of normal personality traits that were more common in males and did not share a biogenic link with affective illness. Schneider's depressive psychopath is gloomy and pessimistic, quiet and self-effacing, duty-bound, anxious, and lacking a capacity for frank enjoyment. He also noted that these individuals idealized suffering and viewed those with more exuberant and lighthearted qualities as inferior and superficial. Whereas Hubert Tellenbach (1961) placed greater emphasis on compulsive personality features, such as orderliness, conscientiousness, and achievement, Kretschmer (1925) believed that the essential and unifying element of this depressive spectrum was not a propensity toward sadness but rather a less joyous and cheerful disposition. Otto Kernberg (1984), the leading contemporary psychoanalytic theorist in this area, proposed a broader construct of depressive personality encompassing both masochistic and dependent traits. The defining features of this depressive-masochist personality was an excessively harsh superego that imposes unrealistic performance standards, and the tendency to be overly dependent, creating susceptibility to depressive episodes when faced with achievement failures or loss of love.

It was not until the early 1980s that researchers began studying depressive personality disorder (DPD) empirically. Largely drawing on the work of Schneider (1958), Akiskal (1983) proposed criteria for a depressive temperament, which later provided the foundation for the formal criteria for DPD in the *Diagnostic and Statistical Manual of Mental Disorders* (4th ed.; *DSM–IV*; American Psychiatric Association, 1994) Appendix as a condition requiring further study. These research criteria, in tandem with descriptive features found in the text of the *DSM–IV*, shaped contemporary clinical conceptualizations of DPD. Individuals with DPD, according to this perspective, exhibit a pervasive and enduring pattern of cognitive, affective, and interpersonal attributes that are apparent in most aspects of their lives. They tend to take everything seriously and lack a capacity for relaxation or enjoyment. When they do try to have a good time—which to the depressive can be synonymous with shirking obligations—they typically feel guilty and undeserving. Constant pessimism renders them gloomy and fearful of the future because they are certain that it will be as bleak as their present and past. They are plagued with pervasive feelings of self-contempt, inadequacy, worthlessness, and excessive remorse and regret, and believe others see them similarly. Negative judgments are not only projected inward; they often judge family members and friends harshly and critically as well. The *DSM–IV* suggests that these qualities often result in social impairment, and the lack of appeal to others of individuals with these traits may reinforce and exacerbate their maladaptive views about themselves, others, and the world.

Despite objections by some investigators (e.g., Huprich, 2012), DPD was dropped from the fifth edition of the *DSM* because of its conceptual overlap with several other personality disorders and, more notably, dysthymic disorder (DD), which was incorporated into a new category that combined various forms of chronic depression called *persistent depressive disorders*

(Ryder, Schuller, & Bagby, 2006). In the *International Classification of Diseases* (10th rev.; World Health Organization, 1992), depressive personality is subsumed under dysthymia. However, there is disagreement in the literature as to whether DPD and dysthymia are redundant constructs. Unlike persistent depressive disorders, depressive personality is conceptualized in terms of personality traits evident at least by early adulthood, rather than symptoms that can emerge at any age, and does not require a persistent depressed mood. Moreover, DD is a broad category and heterogeneous with respect to personality (Huprich, Defife, & Westen, 2014; Riso et al., 1996). Additionally, a diagnosis of DPD is not redundant with DD because the presence of a comorbid DPD diagnosis predicts a more pernicious course of DD (Laptook, Klein, & Dougherty, 2006).

Family, twin, and follow-up studies suggest that depressive personality is part of the mood disorder spectrum, with normative individual differences in depressive personality traits on one pole and persistent depressive disorders as their more severe variant on the opposite pole (Klein & Bessaha, 2009). Family studies indicate that individuals with depressive personality have an increased rate of persistent depressive disorders in their first-degree relatives (e.g., Klein & Miller, 1993), and patients with persistent depression have elevated levels of depressive personality traits in their first-degree relatives (Klein, 1999). Depressive personality also shares substantial genetic variance with major depressive disorder (MDD), although evidence also exists for unique genetic factors (Ørstavik, Kendler, Czajkowski, Tambs, & Reichborn-Kjennerud, 2007). The limited corpus of prospective longitudinal studies suggests that depressive personality may be a precursor to or increase vulnerability for depression. For example, Kwon et al. (2000) found that women with depressive personality and no comorbid mood and personality disorders had a significantly increased risk of developing DD (but not MDD) over time.

Researchers have also noted the possibility that the distinction between DPD and DD may be artificial. For some individuals, a low-grade chronic sad mood may be habitual, presumed to be normative, and thus ego-syntonic. As a result, depressive individuals may not recognize that there is anything remarkable about their mood and consequently fail to endorse depressed mood as a symptom. At the same time, the divide between DPD and DD could arise from differences in diagnostic algorithms (Klein & Bessaha, 2009). That is, individuals with a depressive personality may be unhappy without experiencing a sad mood and thus not meet criteria for dysthymic disorder. If criteria for persistent depressive disorder paralleled that of MDD and allowed anhedonia to substitute for depressed mood, it may lead to a greater overlap between depressive personality and dysthymia. Unfortunately, this possibility has not been examined.

Anhedonia

The French psychologist Theodule-Armand Ribot (1897) coined the term *anhedonia* to shift attention away from only the negative emotional states commonly associated with depression to describe the pleasure-related deficits. Since then, anhedonia has taken on an important role in schizophrenia and substance abuse disorders, in addition to mood disorders. The *DSM*, beginning with the third edition, broadened Ribot's definition by incorporating a loss of interest, and included it as a core symptom of depression.

Abraham Myerson (1944) described a personality style characterized by a persistent state of anhedonia that is crystallized by early childhood through a combination of inherited and environmental factors, which he termed the *constitutional anhedonic personality*. Individuals with Myerson's constitutional anhedonic personality are pessimistic, withdrawn, chronically fatigued, lack both a desire and drive for pleasure, and despite the former qualities, attribute great significance to and devote the majority of their time to work-related activities. To Myerson (1946), these traits were linked to a low-grade chronic depressive illness. Paul Meehl (1975) identified early emerging temperamental differences in the capacity to experience pleasure, which he referred to as *hedonic capacity*. Also like Myerson (1944), Meehl argued that a constitutionally low hedonic tone could be a precursor to low-grade chronic depressive illness. Hypohedonic individuals are unable to buffer the effects of negative affect, placing them at increased risk for depression. Years later, Loas (1996) proposed a model of vulnerability to depression that focused on trait anhedonia. In this model, interactions between low genetically determined hedonic capacity and the environment develop into a constitutionally low-grade chronic depression characterized by a high capacity to feel displeasure, introversion, autonomy, dysfunctional attitudes, low sensation seeking, passivity, perfectionism, and marked interest in work activity. When faced with stress, these individuals were hypothesized to develop endogenomorphic (i.e., melancholic) depression.

Empirically, anhedonic traits have been linked to risk for developing depression and are consistent with clinical models of the relationship between anhedonic temperament and MDD. Longitudinal studies have shown that observed anhedonic behavior in early adolescence predicted onset of depression later in life (van Os, Jones, Lewis, Wadsworth, & Murray, 1997). First-degree relatives of probands with MDD exhibited higher levels of trait anhedonia than relatives of healthy controls (Hecht, van Calker, Berger, & von Zerssen, 1998). Additionally, familial risk for depression was associated with attenuated striatal activity during both anticipation and receipt of reward in adolescent girls (Gotlib et al., 2010). Although these neural reward-processing abnormalities may not parallel anhedonic behavioral manifestations, a handful of neuroimaging studies have identified similar functional and structural abnormalities associated with MDD in individuals with trait anhedonia. In a nonclinical sample, Harvey, Pruessner, Czechowska, and Lepage (2007) found that individual differences in trait anhedonia were associated with reduced caudate and ventral striatum volumes, key reward-related brain regions. Consistent with this finding, Keller and colleagues (2013) found individuals with trait anhedonia but no history of mental illness to show reduced reactivity and connectivity of mesolimbic and related limbic and paralimbic systems involved in reward-processing in response to hedonic stimuli. However, no studies have examined whether trait anhedonia is a risk factor for anhedonic depression in particular.

A core criticism of modern clinical psychiatry's conceptualization of depression as a disorder characterized by depressed mood and/or anhedonia is that it is treated as a monolithic construct, despite evidence suggesting that anhedonia and depressivity are associated with distinct psychobiological systems (Carver, 2006). Nonetheless, the majority of clinically depressed individuals exhibit both a depressed mood and anhedonia (Lewinsohn, Rohde, & Seeley, 1998). A recent prospective study examining the stability and relationship between anhedonia and depressed mood from late childhood to adulthood indicated that there is a reciprocal relationship between the two: Each was equally predictive of the other. Additionally, the strength of the relationship between anhedonia and depressivity increased and became more stable over the course of development (Bennik, Nederhof, Ormel, & Oldehinkel, 2013).

The work on depressive and anhedonic temperament has been helpful to understanding the development of depressive disorders. However, it is unlikely that these traits actually reflect basic temperamental processes that originate in early childhood because their defining features include a number of developmentally complex cognitive and interpersonal characteristics. Instead, these temperament types are more likely to be intermediate outcomes that reflect the interaction of more basic temperament traits that are elaborated over development in conjunction with early socialization and other influences. Examining more basic temperament styles may shed further light on the development of anhedonia and depressivity and on the nature of their relationship.

Although DPD has historically been conceptualized within a categorical framework, taxometric analysis (e.g., Meehl, 1973) provides support for an underlying dimensional structure (Arntz et al., 2009). Indeed, in recent years, there has been increasing evidence that depressive personality is associated with several of the basic personality trait dimensions (Bagby, Watson, & Ryder, 2013), particularly positive emotionality and negative emotionality (Klein, 1990; Klein & Shih, 1998; Watson & Clark, 1995). Additionally, clinical descriptions of the anhedonic temperament describe low positive emotionality as a core feature. Temperamental dimensions may serve as the building blocks for the more cognitive and interpersonal characteristics comprising depressive and anhedonic temperaments.

Temperament, Depressivity, and Anhedonia

Temperament refers to early emerging, stable, and heritable differences in emotional reactivity and regulation (Rothbart & Bates, 2006) and is thought to, in tandem with the social milieu, influence the development and serve as the underpinnings of later personality (Caspi & Shiner, 2006). It is important to note that recent conceptualizations of temperament and personality do not support distinguishing between these constructs because most core personality traits exhibit all of the same characteristics of temperament (Kendler & Neale, 2010; Watson, Kotov, & Gamez, 2006). Moreover, like personality, temperament is a dynamic construct that, even in the first few years of life, can change as a function of development and is influenced by environmental experiences (Emde & Hewitt, 2001).

Two of the best-studied dimensions of temperament and personality are positive emotionality (PE) and negative emotionality (NE). These broadband dimensions are included as core features of almost all hierarchical models of personality that organize a number of narrow constructs into three to five higher order factors (Eysenck & Eysenck, 1985; Goldberg, 1990; Tellegen, 1985). The Big Five traits are Neuroticism, Extraversion, Conscientiousness, Agreeableness, and Openness. These five factors can be further reduced to the Big Three, which include PE, NE, and constraint (CN; referred to as Effortful Control in the child literature) versus disinhibition. PE and NE are for the most part analogous to Extraversion and Neuroticism, respectively. CN includes aspects of both Conscientiousness and Agreeableness, such as self-control, conformity, and harm avoidance.

PE subsumes lower order traits such as the propensity to experience cheerful, energetic, and enthusiastic affect; responsiveness to potential rewards; dominance and assertiveness; and engagement in social interactions. NE entails a tendency to experience sadness, fear, irritability, anger, and increased stress reactivity. It may also incorporate aspects of low agreeableness, such as aggression and hostility. Several theorists propose that the behaviors comprising PE and NE are governed by underlying biobehavioral motivation systems, which are fundamental to human functioning and survival. The behavioral approach system (Gray, 1994), also referred to as the behavioral activation system (Fowles, 1980), approach system (Davidson, 1992) and most recently the Research Domain Criteria's (RDoC) positive valence system (National Institute of Mental Health, 2011), is proposed to generate positive affect to facilitate and reinforce appetitive and goal-oriented behaviors (Depue &

Collins, 1999; Smillie, 2013). In contrast, the withdrawal (Davidson, 1992), behavioral inhibition (Gray, 1994), and RDoC's negative valence systems are characterized by sensitivity to signals of threat and punishment and give rise to dispositional negative affect.

The most influential contemporary model of temperament and depression was proposed by Watson and Clark (1995), who argued that low PE and high NE are precursors of, or predispose patients to, depressive disorders. They claimed that low PE is relatively specific to depression, whereas NE is associated with most forms of psychopathology but has the strongest influence on depressive and anxiety disorders. Empirically, associations between NE and the common mental disorders, including anxiety, mood, and substance disorders have been well established (for a meta-analysis, see Kotov, Gamez, Schmidt, & Watson, 2010). In contrast, the relation between PE and depression has been less consistent, and evidence suggests that low levels of PE are more characteristic of chronic forms of depression (Klein, Taylor, Dickstein, & Harding, 1988; Wiersma et al., 2011).

There is also evidence suggesting that the combination of both low PE and high NE is particularly important to depressive disorders (Gershuny & Sher, 1998; Joiner & Lonigan, 2000), but other studies have failed to find an interaction between low PE and high NE (Jorm et al., 2000; Kendler, Gatz, Gardner, & Pedersen, 2006). Interestingly, in one study examining associations between parental depression and temperament in a sample of preschool-age children, higher rates of parental depression were associated with particular temperament styles in children: High NE was found only in the presence of high PE, and low PE was found only in presence of low NE (Olino, Klein, Dyson, Rose, & Durbin, 2010). Corresponding to these findings, Bogdan and Pizzagalli (2009) found that genes that enhance perceived stress response also increased reward responsiveness. Conversely, individual-specific environmental factors that enhance perceived stress responses tend to diminish reward responsiveness. Although this relationship between stress and reward seemingly contradicts the notion that the combination of low PE and high NE poses risk to developing depression, it may be consistent with that idea from a developmental perspective. Heritable stress responses may lead to diminished reward responsiveness through environmentally mediated processes, constituting a temperament profile that ultimately converges on low PE and high NE over time.

PE and NE are typically discussed as independent constructs. However, the nature of the relationship of these constructs with each other and with depression is likely complex. There may be multiple developmental pathways through which early temperament can lead to depression and even to later personality styles. For instance, personality structures characterized by both low PE and high NE at any point in development may be the product of environmental influences interacting with or mediating early emerging low PE to increase later levels of NE or early emerging high NE to reduce later levels of PE. Thus, personality profiles across development may be characterized by equifinality—the notion that different causal pathways can converge on the same outcome—and etiological heterogeneity.

It follows that, counter to the presumed valence coupling of anhedonia with low PE and depressivity with high NE, the reverse may also be the case: NE may contribute to the later development of anhedonia, and low PE may contribute to depressivity. For example, the combination of temperamental NE and stress, either through stressful life events moderating heightened stress reactivity or mediating trait neuroticism (e.g., via the generation of stressful life events and interpersonal difficulties; Hammen, 2006) may produce clinical manifestations of anhedonia. Illustrating this pathway, there is growing evidence to suggest that both chronic and acute stressors—particularly those that are uncontrollable or inescapable—can induce anhedonia (e.g., Al'Absi, Nakajima, Hooker, Wittmers, & Cragin, 2012). Hedonic blunting and reductions in approach motivation are mediated by stress-induced disruptions in dopaminergic pathways leading to profound and persisting changes in brain systems supporting anticipatory and consummatory reward processing (McCabe, Cowen, & Harmer, 2009; Pizzagalli, 2014). Indeed, evidence suggests that exposing highly reactive individuals to laboratory stressors results in reductions in reward responsiveness and poorer reinforcement learning (Bogdan & Pizzagalli, 2006). Additionally, enhanced perceptions of stress associated with NE can be environmentally mediated through low perceived control and lead to anhedonia.

In a similar vein, low PE may influence the development of depressivity. According to Fredrickson's (1998) undoing hypothesis, PE buffers against the pernicious effects of stress, and evidence suggests that low PE is associated with increased biological susceptibility to stressors, as indexed by enhanced levels of cortisol shortly after awakening, an index of hypothalamic-pituitary-adrenal axis dysregulation (Dougherty, Klein, Olino, Dyson, & Rose, 2009). Furthermore, the propensity to experience PE is associated with responsivity to positive reinforcement. It has been theorized that individuals who are low on PE experience daily reinforcers intermittently and thus can be viewed as being on an extinction schedule (Meehl, 1975). It is postulated that these individuals are less capable of learning to anticipate pleasant events and perceive the world as unpredictable. Additionally, they fail to acquire skills and mastery behaviors and over time develop a sense of low perceived control over their environment (e.g., learned helplessness; Hamburg, 1998). As a result, stressful life events are perceived as more overwhelming and uncontrollable (Bogdan, Pringle, Goetz, & Pizzagalli, 2012), which may result in individuals becoming hopeless and filled with despair.

Interpersonally, children with lower PE may face increased difficulties in developing meaningful peer relations (Hayden, Klein, Durbin, & Olino, 2006). These difficulties may extend into the romantic sphere in adolescence. Interestingly, recent neural evidence suggests that individuals who are more socially anhedonic have greater self-relevant neural reactivity in response to mutual liking (Healey, Morgan, Musselman, Olino, & Forbes, 2014). Thus, romantic breakups may be particularly salient loss events linked to one's identity and lend themselves to depressivity (Keller, Neale, & Kendler, 2007).

ADAPTIVE AND MALADAPTIVE FEATURES OF ANHEDONIA AND DEPRESSIVITY

In their more extreme manifestations, depressive and anhedonic personalities are associated with higher levels of comorbidity, suicidality, suicide attempts, poorer social functioning, and higher rates of unemployment (McDermut, Zimmerman, & Chelminski, 2003). However, depressivity and anhedonia are not necessarily or exclusively pathological. They can actually be adaptive for a variety of reasons. This idea dates back to Aristotle (1971, pp. 953–954), who wrote that "all men who have attained excellence in philosophy, in poetry, in art and in politics, even Socrates and Plato, had a melancholic habitus; indeed some suffered even from melancholic disease" (Problemata; Book 30). Jamison (1993) updated this point, suggesting that individuals with mood disorders characterized by these temperament styles are "touched with fire" and are often highly artistic and creative. Qualities such as those that come with depressive personality can give rise to talents: A comedian such as the openly depressive Woody Allen spots things that other people cannot see and crafts them into humor. In the modern West, as scholars such as Michel Foucault (1964) have pointed out, the figure of the neurotic has often taken on the role of society's moral compass and source of regulation when it comes to social cues through this figure's extreme contrast with the "normal" person. Contemporary studies have corroborated the idea that, to some degree, depressives have a more realistic view of the world because they are lacking in an optimistic bias and tend to see through the superficial (Moore & Fresco, 2012).

The rank theory of depression suggests that it is an adaptive evolutionary strategy for facing defeat or loss of status, enabling the sufferer to alter his or her behavior and avoid subsequent defeat and potential damage to his or her survival (Stevens & Price, 2000). Other evolutionary theories further corroborate the potential adaptive benefits of depression and anhedonia. Nesse (2000), for instance, argued that depression facilitates terminating fruitless quests, whereas Allen and Badcock (2003) suggested that depression provides individuals with information that enables them to avoid becoming outcasts in their communities. Andrews and Thomson (2009), furthermore, suggested that depression is adaptive in fostering a particularly focused analytical rumination that enables people to prioritize analyzing and solving the most salient problems in their lives, while avoiding stimuli and activities that would distract from that priority. These perspectives emphasize the fundamental adaptiveness of depressive and anhedonic personality traits as key to forming a socially acceptable character. If we combine elements of the depressive personality with high levels of conscientiousness or agreeableness reminiscent of Schneider's (1958) depressive psychopath, the result is a high-functioning variant of these personality styles.

DIRECTIONS FOR FUTURE RESEARCH

There are a number of areas that should be explored in future research. First, more work is needed to examine the dynamic and interactive relationships between basic temperament traits over the course of development because they influence risk for depressive disorders. Second, identifying biomarkers of early temperament may be useful for tracing and understanding the processes and developmental trajectories through which early temperament creates risk for depression. However, it is important to be aware of the challenges in mapping relationships between the psychological and biological domains, given that psychological constructs such as temperament are unlikely to correspond simply and directly to neural processes. Third, research is needed to delineate the processes that mediate the links between early temperament traits and depressive disorders, including the development of broad biobehavioral systems such as reward and threat processing and stress sensitivity (Klein, Dyson, Kujawa, & Kotov, 2012). Fourth, it is important to examine how the environment influences pathways between temperament and mood disorder. Finally, potential protective factors should be explored to inform prevention and intervention efforts.

CLINICAL IMPLICATIONS

Understanding the dynamic etiological temperamental and environmental mechanisms of personality pathology, as well as the role of personality in the expression of depressive disorders, has the potential to enhance treatments in addition to early prevention efforts. Low PE and high NE have each been shown to predict poor responsiveness to treatment (Kennedy, Farvolden, Cohen, Bagby, & Costa, 2005; Tang et al., 2009). Thus, personalized treatments that specifically target underlying temperament may treat depressive disorders with more precision (Zinbarg, Uliaszek, & Adler, 2008). For example, in a recent clinical depression treatment trial, NE moderated treatment effects, such that depressed women with high NE were only responsive to particular medications that enhanced serotonergic, as opposed to dopaminergic, neurotransmission (Weissman et al., 2015). In addition, further research on early temperament may help identify which individuals are at risk, which environments promote resilience, and which environments exacerbate risk.

SUMMARY AND CONCLUSIONS

We have suggested that depressive and anhedonic personalities and their relationship with each other and with depressive disorders can be best understood by examining basic temperamental constructs within a developmental context. We question the traditional view that PE and NE are predominantly related to anhedonia and depressivity, respectively, and are inexorably orthogonal constructs. Depressivity and anhedonia can result from the same temperamental vulnerability, but both are likely to be heterogeneous constructs with respect to their etiological mechanisms. Examining the nuances of depressivity and anhedonia will ultimately shed light on the dark side of personality, reminding us that darkness comes in many shades.

REFERENCES

Akiskal, H. S. (1983). Dysthymic disorder: Psychopathology of proposed chronic depressive subtypes. *The American Journal of Psychiatry*, *140*, 11–20. http://dx.doi.org/10.1176/ajp.140.1.11

Al'Absi, M., Nakajima, M., Hooker, S., Wittmers, L., & Cragin, T. (2012). Exposure to acute stress is associated with attenuated sweet taste. *Psychophysiology*, *49*, 96–103. http://dx.doi.org/10.1111/j.1469-8986.2011.01289.x

Allen, N. B., & Badcock, P. B. T. (2003). The social risk hypothesis of depressed mood: Evolutionary, psychosocial, and neurobiological perspectives. *Psychological Bulletin*, *129*, 887–913. http://dx.doi.org/10.1037/0033-2909.129.6.887

American Psychiatric Association. (1994). *Diagnostic and statistical manual of mental disorders* (4th ed.). Washington, DC: Author.

Andrews, P. W., & Thomson, J. A., Jr. (2009). The bright side of being blue: Depression as an adaptation for analyzing complex problems. *Psychological Review*, *116*, 620–654. http://dx.doi.org/10.1037/a0016242

Aristotle. (1971). Problemata (E. S. Forster, Trans.). In W. D. Ross & J. A. Smith (Eds.), *The works of Aristotle translated into English: Vol. 7*. Oxford, England: Clarendon Press.

Arntz, A., Bernstein, D., Gielen, D., van Nieuwenhuyzen, M., Penders, K., Haslam, N., & Ruscio, J. (2009). Taxometric evidence for the dimensional structure of cluster-C, paranoid, and borderline personality disorders. *Journal of Personality Disorders, 23*, 606–628. http://dx.doi.org/10.1521/pedi.2009.23.6.606

Bagby, R. M., Watson, C., & Ryder, A. G. (2013). Depressive personality disorder and the five-factor model. In T. A. Widiger & P. T. Costa, Jr., (Eds.), *Personality disorders and the five-factor model of personality* (3rd ed., pp. 179–192). Washington, DC: American Psychological Association. http://dx.doi.org/10.1037/13939-012

Bennik, E. C., Nederhof, E., Ormel, J., & Oldehinkel, A. J. (2013). Anhedonia and depressed mood in adolescence: Course, stability, and reciprocal relation in the TRAILS study. *European Child & Adolescent Psychiatry, 23*, 579–586. http://dx.doi.org/10.1007/s00787-013-0481-z

Bogdan, R., & Pizzagalli, D. A. (2006). Acute stress reduces reward responsiveness: Implications for depression. *Biological Psychiatry, 60*, 1147–1154. http://dx.doi.org/10.1016/j.biopsych.2006.03.037

Bogdan, R., & Pizzagalli, D. A. (2009). The heritability of hedonic capacity and perceived stress: A twin study evaluation of candidate depressive phenotypes. *Psychological Medicine, 39*, 211–218. http://dx.doi.org/10.1017/S0033291708003619

Bogdan, R., Pringle, P., Goetz, E., & Pizzagalli, D. (2012). Perceived stress, anhedonia, and illusion of control: Evidence for two mediational models. *Cognitive Therapy and Research, 36*, 827–832. http://dx.doi.org/10.1007/s10608-011-9413-8

Carver, C. S. (2006). Approach, avoidance, and the self-regulation of affect and action. *Motivation and Emotion, 30*, 105–110. http://dx.doi.org/10.1007/s11031-006-9044-7

Caspi, A., & Shiner, R. L. (2006). Personality development. In N. Eisenberg, W. Damon, & W. M. Lerner (Eds.), *Handbook of child psychology: Vol. 3. Social, emotional, and personality development* (6th ed., pp. 300–365). Hoboken, NJ: Wiley.

Davidson, R. J. (1992). Emotion and affective style: Hemispheric substrates. *Psychological Science, 3*, 39–43. http://dx.doi.org/10.1111/j.1467-9280.1992.tb00254.x

Depue, R. A., & Collins, P. F. (1999). Neurobiology of the structure of personality: Dopamine, facilitation of incentive motivation, and extraversion. *Behavioral and Brain Sciences, 22*, 491–517. http://dx.doi.org/10.1017/S0140525X99002046

Dougherty, L. R., Klein, D. N., Olino, T. M., Dyson, M., & Rose, S. (2009). Increased waking salivary cortisol and depression risk in preschoolers: The role of maternal history of melancholic depression and early child temperament. *Journal of Child Psychology and Psychiatry, 50*, 1495–1503. http://dx.doi.org/10.1111/j.1469-7610.2009.02116.x

Emde, R. N., & Hewitt, J. K. (2001). *Infancy to early childhood: Genetic and environmental influences on developmental change.* New York, NY: Oxford University Press.

Eysenck, H. J., & Eysenck, M. E. (1985). *Personality and individual differences: A natural science approach.* New York, NY: Plenum. http://dx.doi.org/10.1007/978-1-4613-2413-3

Foucault, M. (1964). *Madness and civilization: A history of insanity in the age of reason* (R. Howard, Trans.). New York, NY: Pantheon Books.

Fowles, D. C. (1980). The three arousal model: Implications of Gray's two-factor learning theory for heart rate, electrodermal activity, and psychopathy. *Psychophysiology, 17,* 87–104. http://dx.doi.org/10.1111/j.1469-8986.1980.tb00117.x

Fredrickson, B. L. (1998). What good are positive emotions? *Review of General Psychology, 2,* 300–319. http://dx.doi.org/10.1037/1089-2680.2.3.300

Gershuny, B. S., & Sher, K. J. (1998). The relation between personality and anxiety: Findings from a 3-year prospective study. *Journal of Abnormal Psychology, 107,* 252–262. http://dx.doi.org/10.1037/0021-843X.107.2.252

Goldberg, L. R. (1990). An alternative "description of personality": The Big-Five factor structure. *Journal of Personality and Social Psychology, 59,* 1216–1229. http://dx.doi.org/10.1037/0022-3514.59.6.1216

Gotlib, I. H., Hamilton, J. P., Cooney, R. E., Singh, M. K., Henry, M. L., & Joormann, J. (2010). Neural processing of reward and loss in girls at risk for major depression. *Archives of General Psychiatry, 67,* 380–387. http://dx.doi.org/10.1001/archgenpsychiatry.2010.13

Gray, J. A. (1994). Framework for a taxonomy of psychiatric disorder. In S. H. M. van Goozen, N. E. Van de Poll, & J. A. Sergeant (Eds.), *Emotions: Essays on emotion theory* (pp. 29–59). Hillsdale, NJ: Erlbaum.

Hamburg, S. (1998). Inherited hypohedonia leads to learned helplessness: A conjecture updated. *Review of General Psychology, 2,* 384–403. http://dx.doi.org/10.1037/1089-2680.2.4.384

Hammen, C. (2006). Stress generation in depression: Reflections on origins, research, and future directions. *Journal of Clinical Psychology, 62,* 1065–1082. http://dx.doi.org/10.1002/jclp.20293

Harvey, P. O., Pruessner, J., Czechowska, Y., & Lepage, M. (2007). Individual differences in trait anhedonia: A structural and functional magnetic resonance imaging study in non-clinical subjects. *Molecular Psychiatry, 12,* 767–775. http://dx.doi.org/10.1038/sj.mp.4002045

Hayden, E. P., Klein, D. N., Durbin, C. E., & Olino, T. M. (2006). Positive emotionality at age 3 predicts cognitive styles in 7-year-old children. *Development and Psychopathology, 18,* 409–423. http://dx.doi.org/10.1017/S0954579406060226

Healey, K. L., Morgan, J., Musselman, S. C., Olino, T. M., & Forbes, E. E. (2014). Social anhedonia and medial prefrontal response to mutual liking in late adolescents. *Brain and Cognition, 89,* 39–50. http://dx.doi.org/10.1016/j.bandc.2013.12.004

Hecht, H., van Calker, D., Berger, M., & von Zerssen, D. (1998). Personality in patients with affective disorders and their relatives. *Journal of Affective Disorders, 51,* 33–43. http://dx.doi.org/10.1016/S0165-0327(98)00154-2

Huprich, S. K. (2012). Considering the evidence and making the most empirically informed decision about depressive personality disorder in *DSM–5*. *Personality Disorders: Theory, Research, and Treatment, 3,* 470–482. http://dx.doi.org/10.1037/a0027765

Huprich, S. K., Defife, J., & Westen, D. (2014). Refining a complex diagnostic construct: Subtyping Dysthymia with the Shedler–Westen Assessment Procedure—II. *Journal of Affective Disorders, 152–154*, 186–192. http://dx.doi.org/10.1016/j.jad.2013.09.008

Jamison, K. R. (1993). *Touched with fire: Manic-depressive illness and the artistic temperament*. New York, NY: Free Press.

Joiner, T. E., Jr., & Lonigan, C. J. (2000). Tripartite model of depression and anxiety in youth psychiatric inpatients: Relations with diagnostic status and future symptoms. *Journal of Clinical Child Psychology, 29*, 372–382. http://dx.doi.org/10.1207/S15374424JCCP2903_8

Jorm, A. F., Christensen, H., Henderson, A. S., Jacomb, P. A., Korten, A. E., & Rodgers, B. (2000). Predicting anxiety and depression from personality: Is there a synergistic effect of neuroticism and extraversion? *Journal of Abnormal Psychology, 109*, 145–149. http://dx.doi.org/10.1037/0021-843X.109.1.145

Keller, J., Young, C. B., Kelley, E., Prater, K., Levitin, D. J., & Menon, V. (2013). Trait anhedonia is associated with reduced reactivity and connectivity of mesolimbic and paralimbic reward pathways. *Journal of Psychiatric Research, 47*, 1319–1328. http://dx.doi.org/10.1016/j.jpsychires.2013.05.015

Keller, M. C., Neale, M. C., & Kendler, K. S. (2007). Association of different adverse life events with distinct patterns of depressive symptoms. *The American Journal of Psychiatry, 164*, 1521–1529. http://dx.doi.org/10.1176/appi.ajp.2007.06091564

Kendler, K. S., Gatz, M., Gardner, C. O., & Pedersen, N. L. (2006). Personality and major depression: A Swedish longitudinal, population-based twin study. *Archives of General Psychiatry, 63*, 1113–1120. http://dx.doi.org/10.1001/archpsyc.63.10.1113

Kendler, K. S., & Neale, M. C. (2010). Endophenotype: A conceptual analysis. *Molecular Psychiatry, 15*, 789–797. http://dx.doi.org/10.1038/mp.2010.8

Kennedy, S. H., Farvolden, P., Cohen, N. L., Bagby, R. M., & Costa, P. T., Jr. (2005). The impact of personality on the pharmacological treatment of depression. In M. Rosenbluth, S. H. Kennedy, & R. M. Bagby (Eds.), *Depression and personality: Conceptual and clinical challenges* (pp. 97–119). Arlington, VA: American Psychiatric Publishing.

Kernberg, O. F. (1984). *Severe personality disorders: Psychotherapeutic strategies*. New Haven, CT: Yale University Press.

Klein, D. N. (1990). Depressive personality: Reliability, validity, and relation to dysthymia. *Journal of Abnormal Psychology, 99*, 412–421. http://dx.doi.org/10.1037/0021-843X.99.4.412

Klein, D. N. (1999). Depressive personality in the relatives of outpatients with dysthymic disorder and episodic major depressive disorder and normal controls. *Journal of Affective Disorders, 55*, 19–27. http://dx.doi.org/10.1016/S0165-0327(98)00195-5

Klein, D. N., & Bessaha, M. (2009). Depressive personality disorder. In T. Millon, P. H. Blaney, & R. D. Davis (Eds.), *Oxford textbook of psychopathology* (2nd ed., pp. 738–751). New York, NY: Oxford University Press.

Klein, D. N., Dyson, M. W., Kujawa, A. J., & Kotov, R. (2012). Temperament and internalizing disorders. In M. Zentner & R. Shiner (Eds.), *Handbook of temperament* (pp. 541–561). New York: Guilford Press.

Klein, D. N., & Miller, G. A. (1993). Depressive personality in nonclinical subjects. *The American Journal of Psychiatry, 150*, 1718–1724. http://dx.doi.org/10.1176/ajp.150.11.1718

Klein, D. N., & Shih, J. (1998). Depressive personality: Associations with *DSM–III–R* mood and personality disorders and negative and positive affectivity, 30-month stability, and prediction of course of Axis I depressive disorders. *Journal of Abnormal Psychology, 107*, 319–327. http://dx.doi.org/10.1037/0021-843X.107.2.319

Klein, D. N., Taylor, E. B., Dickstein, S., & Harding, K. (1988). Primary early-onset dysthymia: Comparison with primary nonbipolar nonchronic major depression on demographic, clinical, familial, personality, and socioenvironmental characteristics and short-term outcome. *Journal of Abnormal Psychology, 97*, 387–398. http://dx.doi.org/10.1037/0021-843X.97.4.387

Kotov, R., Gamez, W., Schmidt, F., & Watson, D. (2010). Linking "big" personality traits to anxiety, depressive, and substance use disorders: A meta-analysis. *Psychological Bulletin, 136*, 768–821. http://dx.doi.org/10.1037/a0020327

Kraepelin, E. (1921). *Manic depressive insanity and paranoia.* Edinburgh, Scotland: Livingstone.

Kretschmer, E. (1925). *Physique and character.* New York, NY: Harcourt, Brace.

Kwon, J. S., Kim, Y. M., Chang, C. G., Park, B. J., Kim, L., Yoon, D. J., . . . Lyoo, I. K. (2000). Three-year follow-up of women with the sole diagnosis of depressive personality disorder: Subsequent development of dysthymia and major depression. *The American Journal of Psychiatry, 157*, 1966–1972. http://dx.doi.org/10.1176/appi.ajp.157.12.1966

Laptook, R. S., Klein, D. N., & Dougherty, L. R. (2006). Ten-year stability of depressive personality disorder in depressed outpatients. *The American Journal of Psychiatry, 163*, 865–871. http://dx.doi.org/10.1176/ajp.2006.163.5.865

Lewinsohn, P. M., Rohde, P., & Seeley, J. R. (1998). Major depressive disorder in older adolescents: Prevalence, risk factors, and clinical implications. *Clinical Psychology Review, 18*, 765–794. http://dx.doi.org/10.1016/S0272-7358(98)00010-5

Loas, G. (1996). Vulnerability to depression: A model centered on anhedonia. *Journal of Affective Disorders, 41*, 39–53. http://dx.doi.org/10.1016/0165-0327(96)00065-1

Maher, B. A., & Maher, W. B. (1994). Personality and psychopathology: A historical perspective. *Journal of Abnormal Psychology, 103*, 72–77. http://dx.doi.org/10.1037/0021-843X.103.1.72

McCabe, C., Cowen, P. J., & Harmer, C. J. (2009). Neural representation of reward in recovered depressed patients. *Psychopharmacology, 205*, 667–677. http://dx.doi.org/10.1007/s00213-009-1573-9

McDermut, W., Zimmerman, M., & Chelminski, I. (2003). The construct validity of depressive personality disorder. *Journal of Abnormal Psychology, 112*, 49–60. http://dx.doi.org/10.1037/0021-843X.112.1.49

Meehl, P. E. (1973). MAXCOV-HITMAX: A taxonomic search method for loose genetic syndromes. In P. E. Meehl (Ed.), *Psychodiagnosis: Selected papers* (pp. 200–224). Minneapolis: University of Minnesota Press.

Meehl, P. E. (1975). Hedonic capacity: Some conjectures. *Bulletin of the Menninger Clinic, 39,* 295–307.

Moore, M. T., & Fresco, D. M. (2012). Depressive realism: A meta-analytic review. *Clinical Psychology Review, 32,* 496–509. http://dx.doi.org/10.1016/j.cpr.2012.05.004

Myerson, A. (1944). Constitutional anhedonia and the social neurosis. *Journal of Nervous and Mental Disease, 99,* 309–312.

Myerson, A. (1946). The constitutional anhedonic personality. *The American Journal of Psychiatry, 102,* 774–779. http://dx.doi.org/10.1176/ajp.102.6.774

National Institute of Mental Health. (2011). Research Domain Criteria Matrix. Retrieved from http://www.nimh.nih.gov/research-priorities/rdoc/research-domain-criteria-matrix.shtml

Nesse, R. M. (2000). Is depression an adaptation? *Archives of General Psychiatry, 57,* 14–20. http://dx.doi.org/10.1001/archpsyc.57.1.14

Olino, T. M., Klein, D. N., Dyson, M. W., Rose, S. A., & Durbin, C. E. (2010). Temperamental emotionality in preschool-aged children and depressive disorders in parents: Associations in a large community sample. *Journal of Abnormal Psychology, 119,* 468–478. http://dx.doi.org/10.1037/a0020112

Ørstavik, R. E., Kendler, K. S., Czajkowski, N., Tambs, K., & Reichborn-Kjennerud, T. (2007). Genetic and environmental contributions to depressive personality disorder in a population-based sample of Norwegian twins. *Journal of Affective Disorders, 99,* 181–189. http://dx.doi.org/10.1016/j.jad.2006.09.011

Pizzagalli, D. A. (2014). Depression, stress, and anhedonia: Toward a synthesis and integrated model. *Annual Review of Clinical Psychology, 10,* 393–423. http://dx.doi.org/10.1146/annurev-clinpsy-050212-185606

Ribot, T. (1897). *The psychology of the emotions.* London, England: W. Scott.

Riso, L. P., Klein, D. N., Ferro, T., Kasch, K. L., Pepper, C. M., Schwartz, J. E., & Aronson, T. A. (1996). Understanding the comorbidity between early-onset dysthymia and cluster B personality disorders: A family study. *The American Journal of Psychiatry, 153,* 900–906. http://dx.doi.org/10.1176/ajp.153.7.900

Rothbart, M. K., & Bates, J. E. (2006). Temperament. In N. Eisenberg, W. Damon, & W. M. Lerner (Eds.), *Handbook of child psychology: Vol. 3. Social, emotional, and personality development* (6th ed., pp. 99–166). Hoboken, NJ: Wiley.

Ryder, A. G., Schuller, D. R., & Bagby, R. M. (2006). Depressive personality and dysthymia: Evaluating symptom and syndrome overlap. *Journal of Affective Disorders, 91,* 217–227. http://dx.doi.org/10.1016/j.jad.2006.01.008

Schneider, K. (1958). *Psychopathic personalities.* London, England: Cassell.

Smillie, L. D. (2013). Extraversion and reward processing. *Current Directions in Psychological Science, 22,* 167–172. http://dx.doi.org/10.1177/0963721412470133

Stevens, A., & Price, J. (2000). *Evolutionary psychiatry: A new beginning* (2nd ed.). London, England: Routledge.

Tang, T. Z., DeRubeis, R. J., Hollon, S. D., Amsterdam, J., Shelton, R., & Schalet, B. (2009). Personality change during depression treatment: A placebo-controlled trial. *Archives of General Psychiatry, 66,* 1322–1330.

Tellegen, A. (1985). Structures of mood and personality and their relevance to assessing anxiety, with an emphasis on self-report. In A. H. Tuma & J. D. Maser (Eds.), *Anxiety and the anxiety disorders* (pp. 681–706). Hillsdale, NJ: Erlbaum.

Tellenbach, H. (1961). *Melancholy: History of the problem, endogeneity, typology, pathogenesis, clinical considerations.* Pittsburgh, PA: Duquesne University Press. http://dx.doi.org/10.1007/978-3-662-12458-1

van Os, J., Jones, P., Lewis, G., Wadsworth, M., & Murray, R. (1997). Developmental precursors of affective illness in a general population birth cohort. *Archives of General Psychiatry, 54,* 625–631. http://dx.doi.org/10.1001/archpsyc.1997.01830190049005

Watson, D., & Clark, L. A. (1995). Depression and the melancholic temperament. *European Journal of Personality, 9,* 351–366. http://dx.doi.org/10.1002/per.2410090505

Watson, D., Kotov, R., & Gamez, W. (2006). Basic dimensions of temperament in relation to personality and psychopathology. In R. F. Krueger & J. L. Tackett (Eds.), *Personality and Psychopathology* (pp. 7–38). New York, NY: Guilford Press.

Weissman, M. M., Wickramaratne, P., Pilowsky, D. J., Poh, E., Batten, L. A., Hernandez, M., . . . Stewart, J. W. (2015). Treatment of maternal depression in a medication clinical trial and its effect on children. *The American Journal of Psychiatry, 172,* 450–459. http://dx.doi.org/10.1176/appi.ajp.2014.13121679

Wiersma, J. E., van Oppen, P., van Schaik, D. J. F., van der Does, A. J. W., Beekman, A. T. F., & Penninx, B. W. J. H. (2011). Psychological characteristics of chronic depression: A longitudinal cohort study. *Journal of Clinical Psychiatry, 72,* 288–294. http://dx.doi.org/10.4088/JCP.09m05735blu

World Health Organization. (1992). *The ICD–10 classification of mental and behavioural disorders: Clinical descriptions and diagnostic guidelines.* Geneva, Switzerland: Author.

Zinbarg, R. E., Uliaszek, A. A., & Adler, J. M. (2008). The role of personality in psychotherapy for anxiety and depression. *Journal of Personality, 76,* 1649–1688. http://dx.doi.org/10.1111/j.1467-6494.2008.00534.x

16

THE DARK SIDES OF HIGH AND LOW SELF-ESTEEM

VIRGIL ZEIGLER-HILL, CHRISTOPHER J. HOLDEN,
ASHTON C. SOUTHARD, AMY E. NOSER, BRIAN ENJAIAN,
AND NOAH C. POLLOCK

DEFINITION AND BACKGROUND

John Milton is believed to have coined the term *self-esteem* in 1642 (Jordan, 2001), and he even used it in his epic poem *Paradise Lost* ("Ofttimes nothing profits more / Than self-esteem, grounded on just and right / Well managed"; Milton, 1674/2004, Book VIII, Lines 571–573). This construct was introduced to the field of psychology more than two centuries later by William James (1890), who described self-esteem as the sense of positive self-regard that develops when individuals consistently meet or exceed the important goals in their lives. Today, self-esteem is defined as the evaluative aspect of self-knowledge that reflects the extent to which individuals like themselves and believe they are competent (e.g., Brown & Marshall, 2006; Tafarodi & Swann, 1995). Individuals with high self-esteem have relatively positive attitudes toward themselves, whereas those with low self-esteem have either

http://dx.doi.org/10.1037/14854-017

The Dark Side of Personality: Science and Practice in Social, Personality, and Clinical Psychology, V. Zeigler-Hill and D. K. Marcus (Editors)

negative attitudes about themselves or are uncertain about their feelings of self-worth (Campbell, 1990). However, as discussed later in this chapter, high self-esteem also has its dark side, and low self-esteem can be adaptive in some ways. There are also ways to conceptualize self-esteem outside of the high–low dynamic. Therefore, this chapter considers other important factors, such as the security or fragility of self-esteem (i.e., whether one's evaluation of self is stable and realistic).

Self-esteem is one of the most widely investigated topics in contemporary psychology, with thousands of publications concerning its potential causes, consequences, and correlates (Zeigler-Hill, 2013). The importance of self-esteem has been debated in recent years; some researchers have argued that it has limited utility (e.g., Baumeister, Campbell, Krueger, & Vohs, 2003; Boden, Fergusson, & Horwood, 2007, 2008; Scheff & Fearon, 2004; Seligman, 1993), whereas other scholars have argued that self-esteem is a valuable construct (e.g., Swann, Chang-Schneider, & Larsen McClarty, 2007; Trzesniewski et al., 2006; Zeigler-Hill, 2013). Consistent with the view that self-esteem is a useful psychological construct, research has shown that high levels of self-esteem are associated with a variety of desirable outcomes including subjective well-being (Diener & Diener, 1995; Furnham & Cheng, 2000), psychological adjustment (Goldman, 2006), interpersonal relationship functioning (Murray, 2006), and academic outcomes (Zeigler-Hill, Li, et al., 2013), whereas low levels of self-esteem are associated with negative outcomes, such as poor health (e.g., Stinson et al., 2008; Trzesniewski et al., 2006), criminal behavior (Donnellan, Trzesniewski, Robins, Moffitt, & Caspi, 2005), and limited economic prospects (Trzesniewski et al., 2006). In addition, several longitudinal studies suggest that self-esteem level can predict later outcomes, such as depressive symptoms (e.g., Orth, Robins, & Roberts, 2008; Orth, Robins, Trzesniewski, Maes, & Schmitt, 2009; Shahar & Henrich, 2010), but the extent to which self-esteem plays a causal role in these associations is still a matter of debate.

Self-esteem is usually assessed through self-report instruments (e.g., the Rosenberg Self-Esteem Scale; Rosenberg, 1965) that directly ask individuals to rate how they feel about themselves using items such as, "I feel that I'm a person of worth, at least on an equal plane with others." This approach is reasonable given that self-esteem is a subjective evaluation of the self that cannot be adequately captured with objective criteria (Baumeister, 1998). However, this measurement strategy is based on two underlying assumptions: (a) individuals know how they feel about themselves and (b) individuals are willing to report honestly how they feel about themselves (for a review, see Zeigler-Hill & Jordan, 2010). These assumptions are problematic because they may often be violated. For example, Myers and Zeigler-Hill (2012) found that narcissistic individuals appeared to inflate their self-esteem under traditional self-report conditions but admitted to having relatively low levels of self-esteem when they believed others would know if they were lying via a bogus pipeline task (participants in the experimental condition were connected to physiological equipment, including a polygraph, and told that the experimenter would be able to detect any deception). It is unlikely that narcissistic individuals are the only people who distort their self-reported feelings of self-worth, so it is important that researchers carefully consider the meaning of responses to self-report instruments rather than simply assume they are accurately capturing the intended constructs.

REVIEW OF THE RELEVANT LITERATURE

A number of demographic differences have emerged for self-esteem. For example, meta-analyses have shown that men and boys report slightly higher levels of self-esteem than women and girls (e.g., Kling, Hyde, Showers, & Buswell, 1999). However, the size of this effect is generally small, and it changes across the lifespan. Boys and girls do not differ in their levels of self-esteem until adolescence, which is the point when boys begin reporting higher levels of self-esteem than girls (e.g., Kling et al., 1999). It is also during adolescence when this sex difference is the largest. The reason for this divergence in self-esteem during adolescence is unclear, but it has been argued that one factor may be changes in body image that accompany puberty (e.g., boys express greater satisfaction than girls with bodily changes during puberty because they interpret these changes as characterizing masculinity, whereas girls interpret these changes as deviations from societal ideals; Lamb, Jackson, Cassiday, & Priest, 1993; Nolen-Hoeksema & Girgus, 1994). Furthermore, there are reliable age differences in self-esteem level such that self-esteem declines from childhood to adolescence, increases during the transition to adulthood, reaches a peak in middle adulthood, and decreases in old age (for a review, see Trzesniewski, Donnellan, & Robins, 2013).

Another demographic feature that is associated with self-esteem is racial/ethnic background. It is often assumed that members of stigmatized groups, such as certain racial/ethnic minority groups, internalize negative societal views of their group, which leads to low self-esteem. This idea is referred to as the *internalization of stigma hypothesis* (e.g., Zeigler-Hill, Wallace, & Myers, 2012). Although there is considerable support for this idea, one of the most notable exceptions to this pattern is that Black individuals consistently report higher levels of self-esteem than White individuals despite their stigmatized status in the United States (for meta-analyses, see Gray-Little & Hafdahl, 2000; or Twenge & Crocker, 2002). Attempts to explain this pattern have argued that membership in a stigmatized group may protect self-esteem to the extent that it allows individuals to attribute their negative experiences to prejudice rather than their own characteristics or behavior (e.g., Crocker & Major, 1989).

Although this explanation is appealing, it has important limitations, including that it only seems to apply to certain stigmatized groups (e.g., Hispanic individuals are also stigmatized in the United States, but they do not report high levels of self-esteem). Another possibility is that the high levels of self-esteem reported by Black individuals may be, at least in part, a defensive response to the stigma surrounding their racial/ethnic group. This possibility was supported by the results of a recent study that used a bogus pipeline procedure, similar to that used by Myers and Zeigler-Hill (2012), and found that Black individuals with high levels of self-esteem reported more modest feelings of self-worth in the bogus pipeline condition than in the control condition, whereas the feelings of self-worth reported by White participants with high self-esteem did not change in the bogus pipeline condition (Zeigler-Hill et al., 2012). These results suggest that it is important to consider impression management when examining the self-esteem levels reported by members of stigmatized groups.

Why Is Self-Esteem Associated With Important Life Outcomes?

There is support for the link between self-esteem and important life outcomes (e.g., subjective well-being, psychological adjustment), but these associations are modest, and it is unclear whether self-esteem is a cause or a consequence of these outcomes (Zeigler-Hill, 2013). Various models have been proposed to explain the connection that low self-esteem has with these outcomes (for a review of the models linking low self-esteem with depression, see Orth & Robins, 2013). One explanation is the *vulnerability model of low self-esteem*, which suggests that low levels of self-esteem serve as a causal risk factor for negative outcomes such as psychopathology. The link between self-esteem level and depression may provide the clearest illustration of this model. Low self-esteem is thought to play a causal role in the development of depressive symptoms through both intrapsychic processes (e.g., ruminative tendencies) and interpersonal strategies (e.g., excessive reassurance seeking; Orth et al., 2008). Recent longitudinal studies using cross-lagged regression models have provided support for the vulnerability model (e.g., Orth et al., 2008, 2009; Shahar & Henrich, 2010). Another explanation for the connection between self-esteem and depression is the *scar model*, which argues that low self-esteem is actually a consequence of depression rather than a cause. According to this model, depression leaves "scars" on individuals that erode their feelings of self-worth over time (e.g., Coyne, Gallo, Klinkman, & Calarco, 1998). It is important to note that the vulnerability model and the scar model are not mutually exclusive, and they may work in conjunction such that low self-esteem may contribute to the development of depression at the same time that depression contributes to low self-esteem. A recent meta-analysis of longitudinal studies (Sowislo & Orth, 2013) found support for both of these models, but the effect for the vulnerability model ($\beta = -.16$) was considerably stronger than the effect for the scar model ($\beta = -.08$).

An important extension of the vulnerability model suggests that low self-esteem may be linked with negative outcomes in the wake of stressful experiences. That is, individuals with low self-esteem lack the positive feelings of self-worth necessary to buffer against the deleterious consequences of negative experiences such as failure or rejection. This idea is often referred to as the *diathesis-stress model of low self-esteem* or the *stress-buffering model of high self-esteem* (Brown, 2010). Individuals with low self-esteem are often more affected by negative events and tend to recover from them more slowly than those with high self-esteem (e.g., Brown, 2010; Sedikides, Rudich, Gregg, Kumashiro, & Rusbult, 2004). For example, Brown (2010) found that individuals with high self-esteem were more resilient than those with low self-esteem when confronted with negative social feedback (i.e., receiving a negative evaluation from a confederate) or negative achievement feedback (i.e., receiving bogus negative feedback about their performance on an intellectual task). This pattern led Brown to argue that "high self-esteem functions primarily to enable people to fail without feeling bad about themselves" (p. 1389). One explanation for this pattern is that individuals with high self-esteem perceive themselves more positively in various areas of life than those with low self-esteem, which may provide them with more self-affirmation resources to draw on when their feelings of self-worth are threatened (Spencer, Josephs, & Steele, 1993). Consistent with this explanation, individuals with high self-esteem tend to focus on their personal strengths and suppress thoughts about their weaknesses after failure, whereas those with low self-esteem focus on their weaknesses (Dodgson & Wood, 1998). The tendency for individuals with high levels of self-esteem to focus on their strengths after failure may also lead to problems because they may ignore critical feedback and miss opportunities for self-improvement.

The Interpersonal Nature of Self-Esteem

Individuals who feel valued and accepted by others generally report higher levels of self-esteem than those who do not (e.g., Leary & Baumeister, 2000). This observation is at the core of the sociometer model that was developed by Leary, Tambor, Terdal, and Downs (1995) to explain the function of self-esteem. According to the sociometer model, self-esteem has a *status-tracking property* such that the feelings of self-worth possessed by an individual depend on the level of relational value that the individual believes he or she possesses. This model argues that self-esteem is an evolutionary adaptation that allows individuals to monitor the degree to which they believe they are valued by others. The basic sociometer model has been extended by others to include domains beyond relational value (e.g., dominance, prestige, mate value; Kirkpatrick

& Ellis, 2001, 2006). More recently, Zeigler-Hill and his colleagues (Zeigler-Hill, 2012; Zeigler-Hill & Myers, 2009, 2011) have proposed a *status-signaling model of self-esteem* that complements the sociometer model by addressing the possibility that self-esteem influences how individuals present themselves to others and alters how those individuals are perceived by their social environment. The existing data support this basic idea by showing that individuals who are believed to possess low self-esteem are generally evaluated less positively than those who are believed to possess high self-esteem (e.g., Zeigler-Hill, Besser, Myers, Southard, & Malkin, 2013; Zeigler-Hill & Myers, 2009, 2011). However, there are limits to the advantages of possessing high self-esteem because those who are believed to possess inflated views of their own self-worth are often seen as being pompous or snobbish (Leary, Bednarski, Hammon, & Duncan, 1997).

Various interpersonal experiences are linked with self-esteem, but the connections between experiences in romantic relationships and self-esteem appear to be particularly important. Self-esteem is associated with a wide range of outcomes connected to romantic relationships such that individuals with high levels of self-esteem generally report more positive relational outcomes than do those with low levels of self-esteem (e.g., Murray, 2006). One reason why self-esteem is important for understanding behavior in romantic relationships is that feelings of self-worth influence how individuals respond to events that are potentially threatening (Murray, Holmes, & Griffin, 2000). This is an important issue because close relationships require that individuals leave themselves open to the possibility of rejection to form a deep, meaningful relationship with another person (e.g., Murray, Holmes, & Collins, 2006). Self-esteem level is related to the willingness of individuals to allow themselves to be vulnerable to potential hurt during the initiation of relationships as well as how they respond to problems that occur during the course of their established relationships (for a review, see Murray, 2008). The basic pattern that has emerged from previous research is that individuals with high self-esteem often seek to enhance their connections with their relationship partners after negative events that occur either within the relationship (e.g., having an argument with a romantic partner) or outside of the relationship (e.g., getting fired from a job) because they expect their partners to be accepting and responsive to their needs (e.g., Baldwin & Sinclair, 1996). In contrast, those with low self-esteem tend to withdraw from their relational partners after negative events because their fear of rejection makes them unwilling to assume the risks associated with seeking deeper connections (e.g., Murray, Rose, Bellavia, Holmes, & Kusche, 2002). These results suggest that individuals with low self-esteem may process information about rejection differently from those with high self-esteem, which is consistent with the idea that low self-esteem makes individuals vulnerable to negative outcomes. The sensitivity of individuals with low self-esteem to rejection may manifest quite early in the processing of these experiences such that these individuals are more likely than those with high self-esteem to anticipate rejection (Downey & Feldman, 1996), devote more attentional resources to potential rejection cues (Li, Zeigler-Hill, Luo, Yang, & Zhang, 2012; Li, Zeigler-Hill, Yang, et al., 2012), fail to engage in strategies to prevent rejection (Sommer & Baumeister, 2002), and react more strongly when rejection actually occurs (Murray et al., 2002).

ADAPTIVE AND MALADAPTIVE FEATURES

Individuals generally show a preference for high levels of self-esteem under most conditions (e.g., Sedikides, 1993) and even prefer receiving self-esteem enhancements more than engaging in other pleasant activities (e.g., eating a favorite food, engaging in a favorite sexual activity) when given a choice (Bushman, Moeller, & Crocker, 2011). Although it is clear from past research that individuals generally want to feel good about themselves, this does not necessarily mean that high self-esteem is always beneficial. In fact, high levels of self-esteem have been found to be associated with a number of negative outcomes including narcissism (Brown & Zeigler-Hill, 2004; see also Chapter 1, this volume), prejudice (Crocker, Thompson, McGraw, & Ingerman, 1987), aggression (Baumeister, Smart, & Boden, 1996), and a variety of self-protective or self-enhancement strategies (e.g., Baumeister, Heatherton, & Tice, 1993). These findings suggest that high self-esteem has a "dark side." To gain a clearer understanding of how high self-esteem could be associated with such a range of both positive and negative outcomes, researchers have suggested that high self-esteem is a heterogeneous construct with two forms: *secure* high self-esteem and *fragile* high self-esteem (e.g., Kernis, 2003). The secure form of high self-esteem reflects positive attitudes toward the self that are realistic, well anchored, and resistant to threat. In contrast, the fragile form of high self-esteem refers to feelings of self-worth that are vulnerable to challenge, need constant validation, and frequently require some degree of self-deception (for a review, see Jordan & Zeigler-Hill, 2013). This distinction has allowed researchers to understand the sometimes weak and inconsistent associations that self-esteem level has with certain outcomes. For example, individuals with secure high self-esteem are perceived as less aggressive than those with fragile high self-esteem or low self-esteem (Zeigler-Hill, Enjaian, Holden, & Southard, 2014). These findings suggest that the fragility of high self-esteem has important implications for whether feelings of self-worth are associated with positive or negative outcomes. Although much of the research concerning fragile and secure self-esteem has focused on distinguishing between different forms of high self-esteem, it is important to note that similar distinctions can be drawn between forms of low self-esteem with "secure" low self-esteem indicating *true* low self-esteem and "fragile" low self-esteem indicating *uncertain* low self-esteem (e.g., Zeigler-Hill, Clark, & Beckman, 2011).

It is relatively easy to identify the negative outcomes that accompany low self-esteem. Low self-esteem is a risk factor for a variety of negative outcomes, including depression (Sowislo & Orth, 2013), and individuals who are believed to possess low self-esteem are perceived to be less competent (Zeigler-Hill & Myers, 2009) and less attractive (Zeigler-Hill & Myers, 2011). However, low self-esteem is not without some benefits: Individuals with low self-esteem often perform better on tasks in which a single "best" solution must be identified because these individuals appear to be more cautious and gather more information about possible solutions before implementing them (Knight & Nadel, 1986; Weiss & Knight, 1980). To put it another way, individuals with high self-esteem tend to be confident in their ability to deal with problems, which leads them to feel less need to seek information concerning their performance (for a review of overconfidence, see Chapter 12, this volume). Importantly, this confidence, which is sometimes unwarranted, often persists even when they are receiving negative feedback (e.g., Knight & Nadel, 1986). In contrast, individuals with low self-esteem are more willing to seek out feedback and are more responsive to this information. In essence, individuals with low self-esteem seem to be more humble than those with high self-esteem.

Another advantage for individuals with low self-esteem is that they are often more likable than those with high self-esteem after aversive events. For example, Heatherton and Vohs (2000) had naive dyads participate in structured conversations. For half of the dyads, one of the participants received an ego threat before the interaction (e.g., bogus performance feedback on a test of intellectual ability). Across two studies, threatened participants who possessed high self-esteem were rated as less likable than threatened participants with low self-esteem. This pattern of results appears to be because individuals with high self-esteem tended to behave in a more antagonistic fashion after a potential threat to their feelings of self-worth. Although high self-esteem is often advantageous, there are exceptions.

DIRECTIONS FOR FUTURE RESEARCH

Some directions for future research concerning self-esteem include (a) refining the measurement of self-esteem, (b) understanding the etiology of self-esteem, (c) using domain-specific forms of self-esteem when considering particular outcomes (e.g., measuring academic self-esteem when considering academic outcomes), (d) returning to a focus on actual behaviors that are associated with self-esteem rather than relying on self-reported behaviors, (e) giving more attention to the physiological features associated with self-esteem (e.g., activity in specific brain regions, cardiovascular reactivity, hormonal activity, genetic influences), and (f) continuing to examine the differences between secure and fragile forms of self-esteem. This is just a sample of the important issues that scholars interested in self-esteem should consider, and each of these issues deserves more attention than can be provided in this chapter. However, a direction for future research that deserves special mention is the need to gain a better understanding of whether self-esteem plays a causal role in important life outcomes or whether it is an epiphenomenon that is merely indicative of positive experiences (e.g., success, social acceptance). This issue is especially important because self-esteem is associated with a broad range of phenomena, but relatively little of the existing work suggests that self-esteem actually causes many of these outcomes. Some of the available longitudinal studies suggest that low self-esteem is a risk factor for negative outcomes such as depression (Sowislo & Orth, 2013) and poor health outcomes (Trzesniewski et al., 2006), but the exact mechanisms linking self-esteem with these outcomes need to be clarified. It is possible that the connections that self-esteem has with some important life outcomes may be reciprocal such that self-esteem may have elements of being both a cause and a consequence of these outcomes. This pattern may explain the results of the meta-analysis of longitudinal studies conducted by Sowislo and Orth (2013), which found support for the vulnerability model of low self-esteem (low self-esteem is a cause of depression) as well as the scar model (low self-esteem is simply a consequence of depression). It is also important to note that not all longitudinal studies have found that self-esteem has strong associations with outcomes later in life (e.g., Boden et al., 2008).

CLINICAL IMPLICATIONS

Individuals with high self-esteem tend to experience greater subjective well-being and better psychological adjustment than those with low self-esteem (e.g., Diener & Diener, 1995). There is also a clear link between self-esteem and various forms of psychopathology that is evident in the fifth edition of the *Diagnostic and Statistical Manual of Mental Disorders* (American Psychiatric Association, 2013) and in the 10th revision of the *International Statistical Classification of Diseases and Related Health Problems* (World Health Organization, 1992), which contain numerous references to self-esteem and related terms (e.g., "feelings of worthlessness"). The inclusion of self-esteem as a diagnostic criterion or an associated feature of these disorders is consistent with research showing that low self-esteem is associated with clinical and subclinical features of psychopathology. A partial list of the forms of psychopathology that have been found to be associated with low self-esteem includes depression, social anxiety, anorexia, bulimia, body dysmorphic disorder, and borderline personality features (for a review, see Zeigler-Hill, 2011). The link between low self-esteem and psychopathology is clear, but there has been considerable debate concerning the reason for this connection (e.g., Zeigler-Hill, 2011). Furthermore, high self-esteem has also been found to be associated with particular forms of psychopathology. For example, high levels of self-esteem are consistently observed for individuals with narcissistic personality features (e.g., Brown & Zeigler-Hill, 2004). However, the high self-esteem displayed by narcissistic individuals may not be entirely genuine because it is possible that this grandiose facade may serve as a disguise for underlying feelings of self-loathing and self-doubt (for reviews, see Chapter 1, this volume, and Zeigler-Hill & Jordan, 2011).

SUMMARY AND CONCLUSIONS

Self-esteem has been the focus of a tremendous number of studies in psychology, and it has been shown to be associated with a range of outcomes (e.g., depression, relationship satisfaction, subjective well-being). The general pattern that has emerged from these studies is that low self-esteem is often linked with negative outcomes, and high self-esteem is associated with positive outcomes. However, low self-esteem is not always detrimental because it is accompanied by some advantages, such as being more responsive to performance feedback and being friendlier in certain contexts. Also, high self-esteem is not always beneficial—especially the fragile form of high self-esteem—because it is sometimes linked with aversive outcomes, such as aggression. Although a great deal is known about the connections that self-esteem has with other constructs, the precise mechanisms underlying these associations remain poorly understood. Basic questions such as whether self-esteem is a cause or a consequence (or both) of important life outcomes remain largely unanswered. Furthermore, it is important that future studies adopt a more nuanced perspective concerning self-esteem. A rich body of research has clearly demonstrated that there is more to self-esteem than simply whether it is high or low, yet most studies of self-esteem continue to focus exclusively on self-esteem level without attending to other important features, such as its fragility.

REFERENCES

American Psychiatric Association. (2013). *Diagnostic and statistical manual of mental disorders* (5th ed.). Arlington, VA: Author.

Baldwin, M. W., & Sinclair, L. (1996). Self-esteem and "if . . . then" contingencies of interpersonal acceptance. *Journal of Personality and Social Psychology, 71,* 1130–1141. http://dx.doi.org/10.1037/0022-3514.71.6.1130

Baumeister, R. F. (1998). The self. In D. T. Gilbert, S. T. Fiske, & G. Lindzey (Eds.), *Handbook of social psychology* (4th ed., pp. 680–740). New York, NY: McGraw-Hill.

Baumeister, R. F., Campbell, J. D., Krueger, J. I., & Vohs, K. D. (2003). Does high self-esteem cause better performance, interpersonal success, happiness, or healthier lifestyles? *Psychological Science in the Public Interest, 4,* 1–44. http://dx.doi.org/10.1111/1529-1006.01431

Baumeister, R. F., Heatherton, T. F., & Tice, D. M. (1993). When ego threats lead to self-regulation failure: Negative consequences of high self-esteem. *Journal of Personality and Social Psychology, 64,* 141–156. http://dx.doi.org/10.1037/0022-3514.64.1.141

Baumeister, R. F., Smart, L., & Boden, J. M. (1996). Relation of threatened egotism to violence and aggression: The dark side of high self-esteem. *Psychological Review, 103,* 5–33. http://dx.doi.org/10.1037/0033-295X.103.1.5

Boden, J. M., Fergusson, D. M., & Horwood, L. J. (2007). Self-esteem and violence: Testing links between adolescent self-esteem and later hostility and violent behavior. *Social Psychiatry and Psychiatric Epidemiology, 42,* 881–891. http://dx.doi.org/10.1007/s00127-007-0251-7

Boden, J. M., Fergusson, D. M., & Horwood, L. J. (2008). Does adolescent self-esteem predict later life outcomes? A test of the causal role of self-esteem. *Development and Psychopathology, 20,* 319–339. http://dx.doi.org/10.1017/S0954579408000151

Brown, J. D. (2010). High self-esteem buffers negative feedback: Once more with feeling. *Cognition and Emotion, 24,* 1389–1404. http://dx.doi.org/10.1080/02699930903504405

Brown, J. D., & Marshall, M. A. (2006). The three faces of self-esteem. In M. H. Kernis (Ed.), *Self-esteem issues and answers: A source book of current perspectives* (pp. 350–358). New York, NY: Psychology Press.

Brown, R. P., & Zeigler-Hill, V. (2004). Narcissism and the nonequivalence of self-esteem measures: A matter of dominance? *Journal of Research in Personality, 38,* 585–592. http://dx.doi.org/10.1016/j.jrp.2003.11.002

Bushman, B. J., Moeller, S. J., & Crocker, J. (2011). Sweets, sex, or self-esteem? Comparing the value of self-esteem boosts with other pleasant rewards. *Journal of Personality, 79,* 993–1012. http://dx.doi.org/10.1111/j.1467-6494.2011.00712.x

Campbell, J. D. (1990). Self-esteem and clarity of the self-concept. *Journal of Personality and Social Psychology, 59,* 538–549. http://dx.doi.org/10.1037/0022-3514.59.3.538

Coyne, J. C., Gallo, S. M., Klinkman, M. S., & Calarco, M. M. (1998). Effects of recent and past major depression and distress on self-concept and coping. *Journal of Abnormal Psychology, 107,* 86–96. http://dx.doi.org/10.1037/0021-843X.107.1.86

Crocker, J., & Major, B. (1989). Social stigma and self-esteem: The self-protective properties of stigma. *Psychological Review, 96,* 608–630. http://dx.doi.org/10.1037/0033-295X.96.4.608

Crocker, J., Thompson, L. L., McGraw, K. M., & Ingerman, C. (1987). Downward comparison, prejudice, and evaluations of others: Effects of self-esteem and threat. *Journal of Personality and Social Psychology, 52,* 907–916. http://dx.doi. org/10.1037/0022-3514.52.5.907

Diener, E., & Diener, M. (1995). Cross-cultural correlates of life satisfaction and self-esteem. *Journal of Personality and Social Psychology, 68,* 653–663. http:// dx.doi.org/10.1037/0022-3514.68.4.653

Dodgson, P. G., & Wood, J. V. (1998). Self-esteem and the cognitive accessibility of strengths and weaknesses after failure. *Journal of Personality and Social Psychology, 75,* 178–197. http://dx.doi.org/10.1037/0022-3514.75.1.178

Donnellan, M. B., Trzesniewski, K. H., Robins, R. W., Moffitt, T. E., & Caspi, A. (2005). Low self-esteem is related to aggression, antisocial behavior, and delinquency. *Psychological Science, 16,* 328–335. http://dx.doi.org/10.1111/ j.0956-7976.2005.01535.x

Downey, G., & Feldman, S. I. (1996). Implications of rejection sensitivity for intimate relationships. *Journal of Personality and Social Psychology, 70,* 1327–1343. http://dx.doi.org/10.1037/0022-3514.70.6.1327

Furnham, A., & Cheng, H. (2000). Perceived parental behavior, self-esteem, and happiness. *Social Psychiatry and Psychiatric Epidemiology, 35,* 463–470. http:// dx.doi.org/10.1007/s001270050265

Goldman, B. M. (2006). Making diamonds out of coal: The role of authenticity in healthy (optimal) self-esteem and psychological functioning. In M. H. Kernis (Ed.), *Self-esteem issues and answers: A source book of current perspectives* (pp. 132–140). New York, NY: Psychology Press.

Gray-Little, B., & Hafdahl, A. R. (2000). Factors influencing racial comparisons of self-esteem: A quantitative review. *Psychological Bulletin, 126,* 26–54.

Heatherton, T. F., & Vohs, K. D. (2000). Interpersonal evaluations following threats to self: Role of self-esteem. *Journal of Personality and Social Psychology, 78,* 725–736. http://dx.doi.org/10.1037/0022-3514.78.4.725

James, W. (1890). *The principles of psychology.* Cambridge, MA: Harvard University Press. http://dx.doi.org/10.1037/11059-000

Jordan, C. H., & Zeigler-Hill, V. (2013). Fragile self-esteem: The perils and pitfalls of (some) high self-esteem. In V. Zeigler-Hill (Ed.), *Self-esteem* (pp. 80–98). London, England: Psychology Press.

Jordan, M. (2001). *Milton and modernity: Politics, masculinity, and* Paradise Lost. New York, NY: Palgrave.

Kernis, M. H. (2003). Toward a conceptualization of optimal self-esteem. *Psychological Inquiry, 14,* 1–26. http://dx.doi.org/10.1207/S15327965PLI1401_01

Kirkpatrick, L. A., & Ellis, B. J. (2001). Evolutionary perspectives on self-evaluation and self-esteem. In G. Fletcher & M. Clark (Eds.), *The Blackwell handbook of social psychology: Vol. 2. Interpersonal processes* (pp. 411–436). Oxford, England: Blackwell.

Kirkpatrick, L. A., & Ellis, B. J. (2006). The adaptive functions of self-evaluative psychological mechanisms. In M. H. Kernis (Ed.), *Self-esteem issues and answers: A sourcebook of current perspectives* (pp. 334–339). New York, NY: Psychology Press.

Kling, K. C., Hyde, J. S., Showers, C. J., & Buswell, B. N. (1999). Gender differences in self-esteem: A meta-analysis. *Psychological Bulletin, 125,* 470–500. http://dx.doi.org/10.1037/0033-2909.125.4.470

Knight, P. A., & Nadel, J. I. (1986). Humility revisited: Self-esteem, information search, and policy consistency. *Organizational Behavior and Human Decision Processes, 38,* 196–206. http://dx.doi.org/10.1016/0749-5978(86)90016-6

Lamb, C. S., Jackson, L. A., Cassiday, P. B., & Priest, D. J. (1993). Body figure preferences of men and women: A comparison of two generations. *Sex Roles, 28,* 345–358. http://dx.doi.org/10.1007/BF00289890

Leary, M. R., & Baumeister, R. F. (2000). The nature and function of self-esteem: Sociometer theory. In M. P. Zanna (Ed.), *Advances in experimental social psychology* (Vol. 32, pp. 1–62). New York, NY: Academic Press.

Leary, M. R., Bednarski, R., Hammon, D., & Duncan, T. (1997). Blowhards, snobs, and narcissists. In R. M. Kowalski (Ed.), *Aversive interpersonal behaviors* (pp. 111–131). New York, NY: Springer. http://dx.doi.org/10.1007/978-1-4757-9354-3_6

Leary, M. R., Tambor, E., Terdal, S., & Downs, D. L. (1995). Self-esteem as an interpersonal monitor: The sociometer hypothesis. *Journal of Personality and Social Psychology, 68,* 518–530. http://dx.doi.org/10.1037/0022-3514.68.3.518

Li, H., Zeigler-Hill, V., Luo, J., Yang, J., & Zhang, Q. (2012). Self-esteem modulates attentional responses to rejection: Evidence from event-related brain potentials. *Journal of Research in Personality, 46,* 459–464. http://dx.doi.org/10.1016/j.jrp.2012.02.010

Li, H., Zeigler-Hill, V., Yang, J., Jia, L., Xiao, X., Luo, J., & Zhang, Q. (2012). Low self-esteem and the neural basis of attentional bias for social rejection cues: Evidence from the N2pc ERP component. *Personality and Individual Differences, 53,* 947–951. http://dx.doi.org/10.1016/j.paid.2012.03.004

Milton, J. (2004). *Paradise lost* (3rd rev. ed.; G. Teskey, Ed.). New York, NY: Norton. (Original work published 1674)

Murray, S. L. (2006). Self-esteem: Its relational contingencies and consequences. In M. H. Kernis (Ed.), *Self-esteem issues and answers: A source book of current perspectives* (pp. 350–358). New York, NY: Psychology Press.

Murray, S. L. (2008). Risk regulation in relationships: Self-esteem and the if-then contingencies of interdependent life. In J. V. Wood, A. Tesser, & J. G. Holmes (Eds.), *The self and social relationships* (pp. 3–25). New York, NY: Psychology Press.

Murray, S. L., Holmes, J. G., & Collins, N. L. (2006). Optimizing assurance: The risk regulation system in relationships. *Psychological Bulletin, 132,* 641–666. http://dx.doi.org/10.1037/0033-2909.132.5.641

Murray, S. L., Holmes, J. G., & Griffin, D. W. (2000). Self-esteem and the quest for felt security: How perceived regard regulates attachment processes. *Journal of Personality and Social Psychology, 78,* 478–498. http://dx.doi.org/10.1037/0022-3514.78.3.478

Murray, S. L., Rose, P., Bellavia, G. M., Holmes, J. G., & Kusche, A. G. (2002). When rejection stings: How self-esteem constrains relationship-enhancement processes. *Journal of Personality and Social Psychology, 83,* 556–573. http://dx.doi.org/10.1037/0022-3514.83.3.556

Myers, E. M., & Zeigler-Hill, V. (2012). How much do narcissists really like themselves? Using the bogus pipeline procedure to better understand the self-esteem of narcissists. *Journal of Research in Personality, 46,* 102–105. http://dx.doi.org/10.1016/j.jrp.2011.09.006

Nolen-Hoeksema, S., & Girgus, J. S. (1994). The emergence of gender differences in depression during adolescence. *Psychological Bulletin, 115,* 424–443. http://dx.doi.org/10.1037/0033-2909.115.3.424

Orth, U., & Robins, R. W. (2013). Understanding the link between low self-esteem and depression. *Current Directions in Psychological Science, 22,* 455–460. http://dx.doi.org/10.1177/0963721413492763

Orth, U., Robins, R. W., & Roberts, B. W. (2008). Low self-esteem prospectively predicts depression in adolescence and young adulthood. *Journal of Personality and Social Psychology, 95,* 695–708. http://dx.doi.org/10.1037/0022-3514.95.3.695

Orth, U., Robins, R. W., Trzesniewski, K. H., Maes, J., & Schmitt, M. (2009). Low self-esteem is a risk factor for depressive symptoms from young adulthood to old age. *Journal of Abnormal Psychology, 118,* 472–478. http://dx.doi.org/10.1037/a0015922

Rosenberg, M. (1965). *Society and the adolescent self-image.* Princeton, NJ: Princeton University Press.

Scheff, T. J., & Fearon, D. S. (2004). Cognition and emotion? The dead end in self-esteem research. *Journal for the Theory of Social Behaviour, 34,* 73–90. http://dx.doi.org/10.1111/j.1468-5914.2004.00235.x

Sedikides, C. (1993). Assessment, enhancement, and verification determinants of the self-evaluation process. *Journal of Personality and Social Psychology, 65,* 317–338. http://dx.doi.org/10.1037/0022-3514.65.2.317

Sedikides, C., Rudich, E. A., Gregg, A. P., Kumashiro, M., & Rusbult, C. (2004). Are normal narcissists psychologically healthy? Self-esteem matters. *Journal of Personality and Social Psychology, 87,* 400–416. http://dx.doi.org/10.1037/0022-3514.87.3.400

Seligman, M. E. R. (1993). *What you can change and what you can't: The complete guide to successful self-improvement.* New York, NY: Fawcett.

Shahar, G., & Henrich, C. C. (2010). Do depressive symptoms erode self-esteem in early adolescence? *Self and Identity, 9,* 403–415. http://dx.doi.org/10.1080/15298860903286090

Sommer, K. L., & Baumeister, R. F. (2002). Self-evaluation, persistence, and performance following implicit rejection: The role of trait self-esteem. *Personality and Social Psychology Bulletin, 28,* 926–938. http://dx.doi.org/10.1177/01467202028007006

Sowislo, J. F., & Orth, U. (2013). Does low self-esteem predict depression and anxiety? A meta-analysis of longitudinal studies. *Psychological Bulletin, 139,* 213–240. http://dx.doi.org/10.1037/a0028931

Spencer, S. J., Josephs, R. A., & Steele, C. M. (1993). Low self-esteem: The uphill struggle for self-integrity. In R. F. Baumeister (Ed.), *Self-esteem: The puzzle of low self-regard* (pp. 21–36). New York, NY: Plenum. http://dx.doi.org/10.1007/978-1-4684-8956-9_2

Stinson, D. A., Logel, C., Zanna, M. P., Holmes, J. G., Cameron, J. J., Wood, J. V., & Spencer, S. J. (2008). The cost of lower self-esteem: Testing a self- and social-bonds model of health. *Journal of Personality and Social Psychology, 94*, 412–428. http://dx.doi.org/10.1037/0022-3514.94.3.412

Swann, W. B., Jr., Chang-Schneider, C., & Larsen McClarty, K. (2007). Do people's self-views matter? Self-concept and self-esteem in everyday life. *American Psychologist, 62*, 84–94. http://dx.doi.org/10.1037/0003-066X.62.2.84

Tafarodi, R. W., & Swann, W. B., Jr. (1995). Self-liking and self-competence as dimensions of global self-esteem: Initial validation of a measure. *Journal of Personality Assessment, 65*, 322–342. http://dx.doi.org/10.1207/s15327752jpa6502_8

Trzesniewski, K. H., Donnellan, M. B., Moffitt, T. E., Robins, R. W., Poulton, R., & Caspi, A. (2006). Low self-esteem during adolescence predicts poor health, criminal behavior, and limited economic prospects during adulthood. *Developmental Psychology, 42*, 381–390. http://dx.doi.org/10.1037/0012-1649.42.2.381

Trzesniewski, K. H., Donnellan, M. B., & Robins, R. W. (2013). Development of self-esteem. In V. Zeigler-Hill (Ed.), *Self-esteem* (pp. 60–79). London, England: Psychology Press.

Twenge, J. M., & Crocker, J. (2002). Race and self-esteem: Meta-analyses comparing Whites, Blacks, Hispanics, Asians, and American Indians and comment on Gray-Little and Hafdahl (2000). *Psychological Bulletin, 128*, 371–408.

Weiss, H. M., & Knight, P. A. (1980). The utility of humility: Self-esteem, information search, and problem-solving efficiency. *Organizational Behavior & Human Performance, 25*, 216–223. http://dx.doi.org/10.1016/0030-5073(80)90064-1

World Health Organization. (1992). *International statistical classification of diseases and related health problems* (10th rev.). Geneva, Switzerland: Author.

Zeigler-Hill, V. (2011). The connections between self-esteem and psychopathology. *Journal of Contemporary Psychotherapy, 41*, 157–164. http://dx.doi.org/10.1007/s10879-010-9167-8

Zeigler-Hill, V. (2012). The extended informational model of self-esteem. In S. De Wals & K. Meszaros (Eds.), *Handbook on psychology of self-esteem* (pp. 211–226). Hauppauge, NY: Nova.

Zeigler-Hill, V. (2013). The importance of self-esteem. In V. Zeigler-Hill (Ed.), *Self-esteem* (pp. 1–20). London, England: Psychology Press.

Zeigler-Hill, V., Besser, A., Myers, E. M., Southard, A. C., & Malkin, M. L. (2013). The status-signaling property of self-esteem: The role of self-reported self-esteem and perceived self-esteem in personality judgments. *Journal of Personality, 81*, 209–220. http://dx.doi.org/10.1111/j.1467-6494.2012.00790.x

Zeigler-Hill, V., Clark, C. B., & Beckman, T. E. (2011). Fragile self-esteem and the interpersonal circumplex: Are feelings of self-worth associated with interpersonal style? *Self and Identity, 10,* 509–536. http://dx.doi.org/10.1080/15298868.2010.497376

Zeigler-Hill, V., Enjaian, B., Holden, C. J., & Southard, A. C. (2014). Using self-esteem instability to disentangle the connection between self-esteem level and perceived aggression. *Journal of Research in Personality, 49,* 47–51. http://dx.doi.org/10.1016/j.jrp.2014.01.003

Zeigler-Hill, V., & Jordan, C. H. (2010). Two faces of self-esteem: Implicit and explicit forms of self-esteem. In B. Gawronski & B. K. Payne (Eds.), *Handbook of implicit social cognition: Measurement, theory, and applications* (pp. 392–407). New York, NY: Guilford Press.

Zeigler-Hill, V., & Jordan, C. H. (2011). Behind the mask: Narcissism and implicit self-esteem. In W. K. Campbell & J. Miller (Eds.), *Handbook of narcissism and narcissistic personality disorder: Theoretical approaches, empirical findings, and treatment* (pp. 101–115). Hoboken, NJ: Wiley. http://dx.doi.org/10.1002/9781118093108.ch9

Zeigler-Hill, V., Li, H., Masri, J., Smith, A., Vonk, J., Madson, M. B., & Zhang, Q. (2013). Self-esteem instability and academic outcomes in American and Chinese college students. *Journal of Research in Personality, 47,* 455–463. http://dx.doi.org/10.1016/j.jrp.2013.03.010

Zeigler-Hill, V., & Myers, E. M. (2009). Is high self-esteem a path to the White House? The implicit theory of self-esteem and the willingness to vote for presidential candidates. *Personality and Individual Differences, 46,* 14–19. http://dx.doi.org/10.1016/j.paid.2008.08.018

Zeigler-Hill, V., & Myers, E. M. (2011). An implicit theory of self-esteem: The consequences of perceived self-esteem for romantic desirability. *Evolutionary Psychology, 9,* 147–180. http://dx.doi.org/10.1177/147470491100900202

Zeigler-Hill, V., Wallace, M. T., & Myers, E. M. (2012). Racial differences in self-esteem revisited: The role of impression management in the Black self-esteem advantage. *Personality and Individual Differences, 53,* 785–789. http://dx.doi.org/10.1016/j.paid.2012.06.007

17

INTERPERSONAL DEPENDENCY

ROBERT F. BORNSTEIN

On December 1, 1989, 4-year-old James Novy died from injuries sustained over a period of several days. He was covered with bruises, bleeding internally, and his skull had been fractured in two places. On January 12, 1990, James Novy's stepmother, Kimberly Novy, was charged with first-degree murder in the death of her stepson. She was eventually found guilty, but the charge was reduced to involuntary manslaughter based on an unusual mitigating circumstance: Kimberly Novy suffered from dependent personality disorder (DPD)—an overreliance on other people for external support and validation—and she claimed that as a result, she was unable to resist her husband's demands that she punish her stepson severely for various offenses, real and imagined. The court held that Kimberly Novy's DPD was sufficient to diminish her culpability for the death of James Novy and shift much of the accountability to her husband, the boy's father, Keith Novy.

http://dx.doi.org/10.1037/14854-018

The Dark Side of Personality: Science and Practice in Social, Personality, and Clinical Psychology, V. Zeigler-Hill and D. K. Marcus (Editors)

Invoking the presence of DPD as a mitigating circumstance in criminal defense, although rare, is not unheard of; as Jaffe, Goller, and Friedman (2012) noted, documentation of a defendant's strong underlying dependency needs has occurred in several criminal cases, most involving child abuse or neglect. This defense strategy does in fact have some empirical support: When Bornstein (2005b) conducted a meta-analytic review of research on the link between parental dependency and child abuse, he found that, on average, perpetrators of child abuse had significantly higher levels of trait dependency and DPD than did matched nonabusing controls ($d = 0.43$). These patterns held for both mothers and fathers and were consistent across different dependency assessment modalities (i.e., questionnaire, interview, performance-based test).

Such findings are often surprising to clinicians, who tend to regard dependent psychotherapy patients as relatively easy to work with. Although dependent patients are described by practitioners as anxious, clingy, and needy, they are also seen as being compliant, conscientious, and eager to please (Bornstein, 2007). Dependent patients' desire to strengthen ties to figures of authority helps them form a strong working alliance early in treatment (Overholser, 1997; Paris, 1998), and relative to patients with borderline, antisocial, paranoid, or narcissistic pathology, patients with DPD seem unlikely to act out in aggressive or self-destructive ways.

Like many long-standing clinical "truths," clinicians' perception of dependent patients as compliant, acquiescent, and generally "low risk" is only partially correct. Consistent with clinical lore, studies confirm that in many situations, dependent adults are indeed agreeable and amiable, readily acceding to others' demands and expectations (Lowe, Edmundson, & Widiger, 2009). However, there is another side to dependency as well—a darker side—and evidence indicates that patients with high levels of trait dependency or DPD engage in a variety of behaviors that harm themselves and others (e.g., Bornstein, 2012; Wilberg, Karterud, Pedersen, & Urnes, 2009). Dependency is a more complex personality style than many psychologists realize, and it is important that clinicians and researchers have an accurate and nuanced view that encompasses all aspects of dependency, active as well as passive, negative as well as positive.

DEFINITION AND BACKGROUND

Pathological dependency has a long history in psychology and psychiatry, forming an integral component of many early descriptive nosologies (e.g., Kraepelin, 1913; Schneider, 1923) and playing a central role in Freud's classical psychoanalytic theory (Freud, 1905/1953), as well as in subsequent trait frameworks (Leary, 1957), circumplex models (Wiggins, 1991), and cognitive models (Beck & Freeman, 1990). In recent years, a consensus has emerged regarding how best to conceptualize dependency and describe its core elements: Bornstein (1993, 2005a), Pincus (e.g., Pincus & Gurtman, 1995; Pincus & Wilson, 2001), and others (e.g., Cogswell, 2008; Fiori, Consedine, & Magai, 2008) agree that interpersonal dependency may be broadly defined as the tendency to rely on other people for nurturance, guidance, protection, and support, even in situations in which autonomous functioning is possible.

Bornstein (1993, 2005a), Pincus and Gurtman (1995), Gardner and Helmes (2007), and Fiori et al. (2008) further suggested that interpersonal dependency and DPD comprise four primary components: (a) *motivational* (a marked need for guidance, help, support, and approval), (b) *cognitive* (a perception of oneself as powerless and ineffectual, coupled with the belief that others are comparatively confident and competent), (c) *affective* (a tendency to become anxious when required to function autonomously, especially when one's efforts may be evaluated by figures of authority), and (d) *behavioral* (use of a broad array of strategic self-presentation strategies to strengthen ties to potential caregivers). Discussions of the inter- and intrapersonal dynamics of these four components of dependency are provided by Bornstein (1993, 2005a, 2007, 2011a).

Three factors contribute to the development of a dependent personality orientation. First, overprotective and authoritarian parenting, alone or in combination, foster the development of pathological dependency by causing the child to internalize a schema of the self as vulnerable and weak—a helpless self-concept. Several dozen retrospective and prospective studies have documented the role of these two parenting styles in the etiology of dependency, and findings suggest that overprotective and authoritarian parenting, alone or in combination, are associated with increased risk for DPD as well (Baker, Capron, & Azorlosa, 1996; Bamelis, Renner, Heidkamp, & Arntz, 2011).

Cultural factors also play a role in the development of dependency. Several investigations have shown that sociocentric cultures (i.e., cultures that value interpersonal relatedness over individual achievement) are more tolerant of dependent behavior in adults than are individualistic cultures (i.e., cultures that emphasize competition and achievement over group harmony; see Neki, 1976). Not surprisingly, adults in India and Japan (cultures that have traditionally been relatively sociocentric) report higher levels of interpersonal dependency than do adults in Great Britain and America (cultures that are among the most individualistic). As traditionally sociocentric cultures become Westernized and incorporate individualistic values and norms, self-reported dependency levels tend to decrease, and adults in those cultures—especially men—become increasingly conflicted regarding how best to integrate dependent urges with strivings for autonomy and independence (Yamaguchi, 2004).

Like culture, gender role socialization helps shape the experience and expression of dependency. In most Western societies dependent behavior is regarded as less acceptable in boys (and men) than in girls (and women). As a result, men tend to be more reluctant than women to express dependency needs openly. By late childhood significant gender differences in self-reported dependency emerge and remain relatively stable through later adulthood, at which time men's dependency scores increase and the gender gap closes. Meta-analyses confirm that women in early and middle adulthood score higher than men on every questionnaire and interview measure of interpersonal dependency and DPD for which reliable gender-difference data are available, with a mean gender difference effect size (d) of 0.41 (Bornstein, 1995). Studies also show that women receive DPD diagnoses at significantly higher rates than men do in inpatient and outpatient settings (Bornstein, 2011b).

ADAPTIVE AND MALADAPTIVE DEPENDENCY

Some of the more well-established adaptive features of interpersonal dependency include decreased delay in seeking treatment following the onset of a physical symptom (Greenberg & Fisher, 1977) and conscientious adherence to treatment regimens once intervention has begun (Poldrugo & Forti, 1988). Dependent college students obtain higher grade point averages than do matched nondependent students, even when scholastic aptitude is controlled for statistically, in part because dependent students are more willing than nondependent students to seek help from professors when they are struggling with class material (Bornstein & Kennedy, 1994). High levels of interpersonal dependency are also associated with increased sensitivity to subtle verbal and nonverbal cues emitted by roommates, professors, and therapists (Masling, Johnson, & Saturansky, 1974; Masling, Shiffner, & Shenfeld, 1980). Presumably the dependent person's desire to strengthen ties with potential caregivers leads him or her to become sensitive to others' needs and expectations—an adaptive skill in cultivating and maintaining close ties with others.

High levels of interpersonal dependency are also associated with some significant negative consequences. These include increased risk for several forms of psychopathology, most notably mood disorders (Nietzel & Harris, 1990), anxiety disorders (Ng & Bornstein, 2005), and eating disorders (Narduzzi & Jackson, 2000). Dependent people are at increased risk for physical illness as well, including colds and flu, as well as more significant illnesses such as heart disease and cancer (Bornstein, 1998; Greenberg & Dattore, 1981). Evidence suggests that dependent people are particularly upset by interpersonal stressors (e.g., relationship conflict), which, over time, taxes the immune system and increases the risk of illness. Studies further indicate that even when heath status is controlled for statistically, dependent people use health services at higher rates than do nondependent people with similar backgrounds (Porcerelli,

Bornstein, Markova, & Huprich, 2009). Dependent people accumulate higher overall health care costs than do nondependent people, have longer hospital stays, and make more emergency room visits. In inpatient settings, dependent adults are referred by their attending physician for more consultations and medical tests and receive a greater number of medication prescriptions than do nondependent patients with similar diagnoses (R. M. O'Neill & Bornstein, 2001).

Along somewhat different lines, high levels of interpersonal dependency are associated with an array of difficulties in close relationships. Dependent people (children and adults alike) tend to show an insecure attachment style (Feeney & Noller, 1990; Pincus & Wilson, 2001). As a result, dependent schoolchildren score low on indices of sociometric status, being perceived by their peers as clingy and needy (Bornstein, 1993). Dependent college students have difficulties adjusting during the first semester away from home, reporting increased levels of loneliness and depression and increased roommate conflict (Joiner & Metalsky, 2001). High levels of interpersonal dependency are associated with elevated risk for perpetration of partner abuse in men (Bornstein, 2006), and, as noted, with increased risk for perpetration of child abuse in both women and men (Bornstein, 2005b). Contrary to clinical lore, high levels of dependency in women are not associated with increased likelihood of victimization by a partner, but they are linked with increased tolerance of abuse, in part because dependent women have more difficulty terminating abusive relationships than do nondependent women (Watson et al., 1997).

Conceptualizing Dependency-Related Adaptation and Dysfunction

Researchers have used two general strategies to conceptualize and examine dependency's adaptive and maladaptive features. Some have used a dispositional approach to understand variations in underlying and expressed dependency, positing that certain people are able to express dependency needs in relatively adaptive ways, whereas others express dependency in ways that lead to more negative consequences. Although there is relatively little research on the psychological processes that distinguish healthy from unhealthy expressions of dependency, preliminary evidence suggests that the ability to modulate affect and anxiety effectively and to make judicious choices regarding when (and how) to ask for help and support are both associated with more adaptive manifestations of dependency (see Bornstein, 2012; Bornstein & Languirand, 2003).

Other researchers have adopted an interactionist view of dependency-related adaptation and dysfunction, hypothesizing that certain correlates and components of dependency (e.g., a need to please other people) can lead to positive outcomes in certain situations, and negative outcomes in others (e.g.,

Besser & Priel, 2005; Fiori et al., 2008). In the following sections, evidence bearing on the dispositional and interactionist perspectives is reviewed.

The Individual Differences Perspective: Dispositional Approaches

Three independent streams of research have documented stable individual differences in adaptive versus maladaptive manifestations of dependency. These research programs are not only useful in understanding traitlike individual differences in the expression of underlying dependency needs but also provide psychometrically sound measures that can be used to elucidate the correlates and consequences of healthy and unhealthy dependency in future studies and assess different manifestations of dependency in clinical settings.

The Depressive Experiences Questionnaire

Blatt, D'Afflitti, and Quinlan's (1976) Depressive Experiences Questionnaire (DEQ) was originally designed to assess personality styles that place people at risk for depression and to help predict the form depression will take if it occurs (i.e., dependent/anaclitic vs. self-critical/introjective). The DEQ has been used successfully in an array of populations during the past several decades, including psychiatric inpatients, outpatients, college students, and community adults. A separate version of the DEQ for adolescents has also been developed (DEQ-A; Blatt, Schaffer, Bers, & Quinlan, 1992).

As research involving the DEQ accumulated, it became apparent that the anaclitic subscale was not unitary but in fact tapped two separate dependency styles (or "levels of relatedness"; see Blatt, Zohar, Quinlan, Zuroff, & Mongrain, 1995). Scores on one subset of DEQ items, labeled *immature dependence* or *neediness*, were associated with fears of abandonment, low self-esteem, and increased risk for depression; scores on the other subset of items, labeled *mature dependence* or *relatedness*, were associated with a more flexible desire for interpersonal closeness, healthy connectedness, and intimacy (Blatt, Zohar, Quinlan, Luthar, & Hart, 1996). Subsequent investigations have extended these results, demonstrating differential relationships of DEQ neediness and relatedness scores to risk for various symptom disorders (Cogswell & Alloy, 2006), risk for postpartum depression in women (Vliegen, Luyten, Meurs, & Cluckers, 2006), mortality concerns in older adults (Besser & Priel, 2005), and psychosocial adjustment across a broad range of interpersonal and professional domains (Luyten & Blatt, 2013).

The 3-Vector Dependency Inventory

Pincus and Gurtman's (1995) 3-Vector Dependency Inventory (3-VDI) was created by combining items from an array of existing measures, including the Interpersonal Dependency Inventory (Hirschfeld et al., 1977), Sociotropy-Autonomy Scale (Beck, Epstein, Harrison, & Emery, 1983), and DEQ (Blatt et al., 1976). Circumplex analyses were used to identify three clusters of test items that ultimately proved to have differential relationships with an array of outcome variables. These three clusters (which form the three subscales of the 3-VDI) were labeled *submissive dependence*, *exploitable dependence*, and *love dependence*.

Evidence confirms that the first two 3-VDI subscales are associated with negative outcomes, whereas the third represents a more adaptive expression of dependency (see Pincus & Gurtman, 1995; Pincus & Wilson, 2001; Roche, Pincus, Hyde, Conroy, & Ram, 2013). Individuals who score high on exploitable dependence are more willing than others to tolerate mistreatment in close relationships, show a fearful/insecure attachment style, and engage in a pattern of compulsive care-seeking. Those who score high on submissive dependence are suggestible, have difficulty resisting external influence, and score high on measures of neuroticism and fearful attachment. In contrast to submissive and exploitable dependents, individuals who score high on love dependence show a strong desire for intimacy, a secure attachment style, and confidence in their ability to develop and sustain close ties to others in friendships and romantic relationships.

The Relationship Profile Test

The Relationship Profile Test (RPT; Bornstein & Languirand, 2003) yields three subscale scores: *destructive overdependence*, *dysfunctional detachment*, and *healthy dependency*. Thus, the RPT not only distinguishes healthy from unhealthy dependency but also yields a separate score for problematic "underdependence" (i.e., detachment; see Denckla, Mancini, Bornstein, & Bonanno, 2011). Scores on the three RPT subscales show the expected patterns of gender differences, with women scoring higher than men on destructive overdependence and healthy dependency, and men scoring higher than women on dysfunctional detachment (Bornstein et al., 2003). Preliminary evidence suggests that RPT scores also vary as expected across culture, with adults raised in sociocentric cultures scoring higher on healthy dependency than those from more individualistic cultures.

Considerable evidence has accumulated demonstrating that RPT destructive overdependence and healthy dependency scores are associated with theoretically predicted variables in psychiatric inpatients, psychiatric outpatients, medical patients, college students, and community adults. High destructive overdependence scores are associated with insecure attachment, low self-esteem, poor affect regulation, and increased risk for depression (Bornstein, Geiselman, Eisenhart, & Languirand, 2002; Bornstein et al., 2003), as well as with use of dysfunctional interaction strategies in close relationships (Bornstein, Porcerelli, Huprich, & Markova, 2009), and excessive health service use (Porcerelli et al., 2009). High healthy dependency scores, in contrast, are associated with a secure attachment style, interdependent self-construal, and high levels of life satisfaction (Bornstein et al., 2003, 2009). High healthy dependency scores are also associated with good psychological functioning in older adults (Fiori et al., 2008) and with low levels of interpersonal distress in psychiatric inpatients (Haggerty, Blake, & Siefert, 2010).

The Interactionist Perspective: Context-Driven Variability

The interactionist perspective on healthy and unhealthy dependency is derived from Mischel's (1979, 1984) social-cognitive framework, which posits that the locus of stability in personality is rooted in core beliefs and affective responses that are consistent across context and setting. These core beliefs and affect patterns may lead to different behavioral outcomes depending on the contingencies, opportunities, and risks that characterize different situations (see Mischel, Shoda, & Mendoza-Denton, 2002). Bornstein (2005a, 2011a) used these principles to develop a cognitive-interactionist (C/I) model of interpersonal dependency, which contends that whereas dependency-related cognitions (a perception of oneself as vulnerable and weak) and affective responses (fear of abandonment) remain stable over time and across situations, dependent people use a diverse array of social influence strategies to strengthen ties to potential caregivers. These range from the more accommodating strategies typically associated with dependency and DPD (e.g., supplication, ingratiation) to more active—even aggressive—strategies (e.g., intimidation) that are used to preclude abandonment by a valued other when less intrusive strategies fail.

These variable behavioral patterns were initially identified in the mid-1980s, when an unexpected experimental result called into question the universality of the long-standing dependency–passivity link. In this investigation, Bornstein, Masling, and Poynton (1987) created same-sex dyads of college students, each consisting of one dependent and one nondependent person, and asked the two members of each dyad to debate an issue on which they had previously disagreed. In line with previous findings, it was expected that the dependent participants would yield in the majority of dyads, but the opposite occurred: In 70% of dyads, the nondependent participant yielded to the opinion of the dependent participant. Postexperiment interviews revealed that many dependent participants chose not to yield because they hoped to impress the professor conducting the study, whom they believed would be scrutinizing their results. In other words, when forced to choose between impressing a figure of authority by holding their ground or accommodating a peer by yielding, the dependent participants opted to impress the authority figure. These findings suggested that dependency-related passivity, when it occurs, is not an automatic, reflexive response but a mindful, deliberate self-presentation strategy aimed at strengthening ties with those most able to provide help and support.

In a follow-up experiment in which the presence (vs. absence) of an authority figure was varied systematically across dyads (Bornstein, Riggs, Hill, & Calabrese, 1996), these initial results were confirmed: Dependent students competed aggressively with another student on a mock creativity task when told that a professor would be evaluating their performance at the end of the experiment, but they acquiesced passively (and performed relatively poorly) when told that only the undergraduate experimenter would have access to their data. When given the opportunity to rate the other student's creativity test performance on a series of evaluative scales, dependent students actively undermined the peer to impress the professor, denigrating the peer's competence by assigning low ratings to the other student's work.

These situational variations in dependency-related behavior have since been documented in an array of real-world settings; in each instance a common underlying process has been shown to lead to a negative outcome in certain contexts and a positive outcome in others. For example, dependent people's fear of abandonment causes them to be perceived by others as friendly, warm, and agreeable (Lowe et al., 2009), but it also leads them to tolerate mistreatment and exploitation when involved in a dysfunctional friendship or romantic relationship (Watson et al., 1997). The same interpersonal sensitivity that helps dependent people decipher subtle verbal and nonverbal cues (e.g., Masling et al., 1980) causes them to be particularly sensitive to relationship conflict, leading to increased illness risk (Bornstein, 1998). In medical settings, the dependent person's desire to be cared for by a protective authority figure leads to decreased delay in seeking treatment after illness onset (Greenberg & Fisher, 1977), but it also leads to overuse of medical services and increased pseudo-emergencies (Porcerelli et al., 2009).

CLINICAL IMPLICATIONS

The present review has implications for the assessment, diagnosis, and treatment of dependent patients. The fact that researchers have been able to identify an array of positive and negative features of interpersonal dependency in laboratory, clinical, and field settings suggests that in patients for whom dependency-related issues are salient, assessment of both the adaptive and maladaptive elements of dependency may be warranted. The existence of relatively brief, psychometrically sound measures of healthy and unhealthy dependency (i.e., the DEQ, 3-VDI, and RPT) can facilitate these efforts. Recommendations for interpreting the results of these dependency scales and integrating results across assessment modalities (e.g., questionnaire vs. performance-based) are provided by Bornstein (2005a, 2009); Huprich (2011); and Cogswell, Alloy, Karpinski, and Grant (2010).

With respect to diagnosis, empirical evidence has repeatedly demonstrated that high levels of trait dependency and DPD are associated with an array of negative consequences, including increased risk for psychopathology and physical illness, increased risk for perpetration of partner and child abuse, overuse of health (and mental health) services, and increased health care costs (for a review, see Bornstein, 2012). Although the Personality and Personality Disorders (PPD) work group proposed eliminating DPD from the fifth edition of the *Diagnostic and Statistical Manual of Mental Disorders* (*DSM–5*; American Psychiatric Association, 2013), the American Psychiatric Association (2012) Board of Trustees rejected this proposal. Given compelling evidence that DPD leads to significant psychosocial impairment and an array of negative health and mental health outcomes, it should remain as a separate diagnostic category in the sixth edition of the *DSM* and beyond (see also Bornstein, 2011b, for a review of evidence documenting the clinical utility of DPD diagnoses). The diagnostic criteria for DPD in the current edition of the *International Classification of Diseases* (10th ed.; *ICD–10*; World Health Organization, 2004) are very similar to those in the *DSM–5*, and preliminary proposals for reconceptualizing personality disorders in the eleventh revision of the *ICD* using dimensional criteria in lieu of categorical diagnoses retain maladaptive dependency as a core dimension of personality pathology (see Crawford, Koldobsky, Mulder, & Tyrer, 2011).

Beyond assessment and diagnosis, this review has noteworthy treatment implications. As a number of clinicians have noted, the traditional goals in therapeutic work with dependent patients have been to (a) help the patient gain insight into the origins and dynamics of his or her problematic dependency (Luborsky & Crits-Christoph, 1990), (b) reframe situations that represent dependency "triggers" so that dependency urges can be modulated more effectively (Overholser & Fine, 1994), and (c) use behavioral interventions to extinguish self-defeating dependent behavior (Turkat, 1990; Turkat & Carlson, 1984). In addition to these long-standing therapeutic techniques derived from traditional treatment models, two other strategies may be helpful, alone or in combination.

First, it would be useful to develop proactive interventions aimed at reducing the likelihood that an individual will develop dysfunctional dependency. Although approximately 30% of the variance in trait dependency and DPD is attributable to genetic factors (Torgersen et al., 2000) and it is likely that infantile temperament plays some role in prompting dependency-fostering behaviors in parents (e.g., a timid infant will tend to evoke parental over-protectiveness), family members can be made aware of parenting practices likely to increase their child's dependency and taught alternative ways of responding that instead foster autonomy and secure attachment. Often, problematic dependency first becomes apparent when the child is immersed in a peer group (e.g., in day care or preschool), typically manifested as separation anxiety and school refusal; child care staff can be informed regarding these early indicators of problematic dependency in children so that interventions are implemented early.

Beyond proactive measures, a system-focused approach is needed at the onset of problematic dependency. Because they are sensitive to interpersonal cues and skilled at meeting others' needs, dependent patients often surround themselves with individuals who support their pathology. Over time, family members, romantic partners, and friends may become invested in maintaining the patient's dependency (e.g., if a parent's dependency enables a spouse or child to act out in various ways, then that person may covertly undermine treatment). Marital and family therapy are useful in elucidating aspects of the patient's social network that foster unhealthy behavior, and even in those situations where formal marital or family treatment is not feasible, an understanding of the dependency-fostering features of the patient's interpersonal milieu is crucial for long-term growth and positive change. Beyond the family system, attention to community forces (e.g., peer group norms) and the patient's cultural background and identity are crucial for contextualizing dependent behavior and implementing interventions that are likely to yield positive results over the long term.

DIRECTIONS FOR FUTURE RESEARCH

Although dependency has long been a topic of interest to clinical, personality, developmental, and social psychologists, a number of issues remain unresolved. Three of these unresolved issues stand out.

Etiology of Adaptive and Maladaptive Dependency

Although there have been numerous studies documenting the parenting practices and other early experiences that foster unhealthy dependency, there has been comparatively little research assessing directly those factors that contribute to healthy, flexible dependency (see Bornstein & Languirand, 2003). Researchers speculate that parental behaviors that encourage children to regard help seeking as a strategy to be used selectively, as a means of gaining skills that will enable them to function more effectively (rather than as a means of avoiding challenge), may contribute to the development of a healthy dependent personality orientation (see Clark & Ladd, 2000; Cross & Madson, 1997). Continued research on healthy connectedness and interdependence may enhance our understanding of the family dynamics and cultural factors that lead to adaptive dependency.

A Lifespan Perspective: Dependency and Aging

Research on late-life dependency has tended to emphasize changes in functional dependency that affect older adults' ability to carry out activities of daily living rather than focusing on trait dependency or DPD. In one of the few research programs to take a broader, more integrative view, Baltes (1996) found that older adults' levels of trait dependency are only modestly predictive of functional dependency, although high levels of trait dependency (operationalized by Baltes as *emotional dependency*) in nursing home residents are associated with a difficult treatment course and negative perceptions by treatment staff. Studies of the evolution of DPD across adulthood—also relatively rare—suggest that it is one of the more stable forms of personality pathology in later life. The evolving manifestations of dependency during middle and later adulthood warrant further study.

The Relationship Spectrum: Dependency and Detachment

A third area that warrants continued attention from researchers is detachment. Due in part to the individualistic values that characterize many Western societies, high levels of dependency in adults have typically been seen as problematic in formal diagnostic classification systems, whereas excessive independence and self-reliance have been regarded as more normative, especially in men (Colgan, 1987; J. M. O'Neil, 2008). In fact, evidence suggests that marked underdependence can be as problematic as overdependence (see Denckla et al., 2011; Pace & Zappulla, 2013), and it would be worthwhile to assess more systematically the factors that contribute to pathological detachment, both early in life and as individuals mature.

SUMMARY AND CONCLUSIONS

Clinicians and laypersons alike associate interpersonal dependency with passivity, compliance, and acquiescence, but evidence suggests that this view is only partially correct. Dependency-related passivity is not universal, and it usually reflects the dependent person's efforts to strengthen ties to others and preclude abandonment when it occurs. Dependent people are capable of behaving assertively as well, even becoming aggressive when important relationships are threatened and alternative social influence strategies prove ineffective.

Underlying this behavioral variability is a fundamental consistency: Contrasting expressions of dependency are invariably rooted in the dependent person's perception of himself or herself as vulnerable and weak, and the belief that he or she cannot survive without the guidance and support of others. This core belief—the helpless self-schema—leads to maladaptive behaviors in certain contexts, and adaptive behaviors in others. Therapeutic work with dependent patients need not always aim to reduce dependent urges and strivings but may instead focus on replacing unhealthy expressions of dependency with healthier ones.

REFERENCES

American Psychiatric Association. (2012, December 1). *American Psychiatric Association Board of Trustees Approves* DSM–5. News Release No. 12-43. Washington, DC: Author.

American Psychiatric Association. (2013). *Diagnostic and statistical manual of mental disorders* (5th ed.). Arlington, VA: Author.

Baker, J. D., Capron, E. W., & Azorlosa, J. (1996). Family environment characteristics of persons with histrionic and dependent personality disorders. *Journal of Personality Disorders, 10,* 82–87. http://dx.doi.org/10.1521/pedi.1996.10.1.82

Baltes, M. M. (1996). *The many faces of dependency in old age.* Cambridge, England: Cambridge University Press.

Bamelis, L. L. M., Renner, F., Heidkamp, D., & Arntz, A. (2011). Extended Schema Mode conceptualizations for specific personality disorders: An empirical study. *Journal of Personality Disorders, 25,* 41–58. http://dx.doi.org/10.1521/pedi.2011.25.1.41

Beck, A. T., Epstein, N., Harrison, R. P., & Emery, G. (1983). *Development of the Sociotropy-Autonomy Scale: A measure of personality factors in psychopathology.* Unpublished manuscript, University of Pennsylvania School of Medicine, Philadelphia.

Beck, A. T., & Freeman, A. (1990). *Cognitive therapy of the personality disorders.* New York, NY: Guilford Press.

Besser, A., & Priel, B. (2005). Interpersonal relatedness and self-definition in late adulthood depression: Personality predispositions and protective factors. *Social Behavior and Personality, 33,* 351–382. http://dx.doi.org/10.2224/sbp.2005.33.4.351

Blatt, S. J., D'Afflitti, J. P., & Quinlan, D. M. (1976). Experiences of depression in normal young adults. *Journal of Abnormal Psychology, 85,* 383–389. http://dx.doi.org/10.1037/0021-843X.85.4.383

Blatt, S. J., Schaffer, C. E., Bers, S. A., & Quinlan, D. M. (1992). Psychometric properties of the Depressive Experiences Questionnaire for adolescents. *Journal of Personality Assessment, 59,* 82–98. http://dx.doi.org/10.1207/s15327752jpa5901_8

Blatt, S. J., Zohar, A., Quinlan, D. M., & Luthar, S. (1996). Levels of relatedness within the dependency factor of the Depressive Experiences Questionnaire for Adolescents. *Journal of Personality Assessment, 67*, 52–71. http://dx.doi.org/10.1207/s15327752jpa6701_4

Blatt, S. J., Zohar, A. H., Quinlan, D. M., Zuroff, D. C., & Mongrain, M. (1995). Subscales within the dependency factor of the Depressive Experiences Questionnaire. *Journal of Personality Assessment, 64*, 319–339. http://dx.doi.org/10.1207/s15327752jpa6402_11

Bornstein, R. F. (1993). *The dependent personality.* New York, NY: Guilford Press.

Bornstein, R. F. (1995). Sex differences in objective and projective dependency tests: A meta-analytic review. *Assessment, 2*, 319–331. http://dx.doi.org/10.1177/1073191195002004003

Bornstein, R. F. (1998). Interpersonal dependency and physical illness: A meta-analytic review of retrospective and prospective studies. *Journal of Research in Personality, 32*, 480–497. http://dx.doi.org/10.1006/jrpe.1998.2230

Bornstein, R. F. (2005a). *The dependent patient: A practitioner's guide.* http://dx.doi.org/10.1037/11085-000

Bornstein, R. F. (2005b). Interpersonal dependency in child abuse perpetrators and victims: A meta-analytic review. *Journal of Psychopathology and Behavioral Assessment, 27*, 67–76. http://dx.doi.org/10.1007/s10862-005-5381-1

Bornstein, R. F. (2006). The complex relationship between dependency and domestic violence: Converging psychological factors and social forces. *American Psychologist, 61*, 595–606.

Bornstein, R. F. (2007). Dependent personality disorder: Effective time-limited therapy. *Current Psychiatry, 6*, 37–45.

Bornstein, R. F. (2009). Heisenberg, Kandinsky, and the heteromethod convergence problem: Lessons from within and beyond psychology. *Journal of Personality Assessment, 91*, 1–8. http://dx.doi.org/10.1080/00223890802483235.

Bornstein, R. F. (2011a). An interactionist perspective on interpersonal dependency. *Current Directions in Psychological Science, 20*, 124–128. http://dx.doi.org/10.1177/0963721411403121

Bornstein, R. F. (2011b). Reconceptualizing personality pathology in *DSM–5*: Limitations in evidence for eliminating dependent personality disorder and other *DSM–IV* syndromes. *Journal of Personality Disorders, 25*, 235–247. http://dx.doi.org/10.1521/pedi.2011.25.2.235

Bornstein, R. F. (2012). From dysfunction to adaptation: An interactionist model of dependency. *Annual Review of Clinical Psychology, 8*, 291–316. http://dx.doi.org/10.1146/annurev-clinpsy-032511-143058

Bornstein, R. F., Geiselman, K. J., Eisenhart, E. A., & Languirand, M. A. (2002). Construct validity of the Relationship Profile Test: Links with attachment, identity, relatedness, and affect. *Assessment, 9*, 373–381. http://dx.doi.org/10.1177/1073191102238195

Bornstein, R. F., & Kennedy, T. D. (1994). Interpersonal dependency and academic performance. *Journal of Personality Disorders, 8,* 240–248. http://dx.doi.org/10.1521/pedi.1994.8.3.240

Bornstein, R. F., & Languirand, M. A. (2003). *Healthy dependency.* New York, NY: Newmarket Press.

Bornstein, R. F., Languirand, M. A., Geiselman, K. J., Creighton, J. A., West, M. A., Gallagher, H. A., & Eisenhart, E. A. (2003). Construct validity of the Relationship Profile Test: A self-report measure of dependency-detachment. *Journal of Personality Assessment, 80,* 67–74. http://dx.doi.org/10.1207/S15327752JPA8001_15

Bornstein, R. F., Masling, J. M., & Poynton, F. G. (1987). Orality as a factor in interpersonal yielding. *Psychoanalytic Psychology, 4,* 161–170. http://dx.doi.org/10.1037/h0079129

Bornstein, R. F., Porcerelli, J. H., Huprich, S. K., & Markova, T. (2009). Construct validity of the Relationship Profile Test: Correlates of overdependence, detachment, and healthy dependency in low income urban women seeking medical services. *Journal of Personality Assessment, 91,* 537–544. http://dx.doi.org/10.1080/00223890903228406

Bornstein, R. F., Riggs, J. M., Hill, E. L., & Calabrese, C. (1996). Activity, passivity, self-denigration, and self-promotion: Toward an interactionist model of interpersonal dependency. *Journal of Personality, 64,* 637–673. http://dx.doi.org/10.1111/j.1467-6494.1996.tb00525.x

Clark, K. E., & Ladd, G. W. (2000). Connectedness and autonomy support in parent–child relationships: Links to children's socioemotional orientation and peer relationships. *Developmental Psychology, 36,* 485–498. http://dx.doi.org/10.1037/0012-1649.36.4.485

Cogswell, A. (2008). Explicit rejection of an implicit dichotomy: Integrating two approaches to assessing dependency. *Journal of Personality Assessment, 90,* 26–35. http://dx.doi.org/10.1080/00223890701468584

Cogswell, A., & Alloy, L. B. (2006). The relation of neediness and Axis II pathology. *Journal of Personality Disorders, 20,* 16–21. http://dx.doi.org/10.1521/pedi.2006.20.1.16

Cogswell, A., Alloy, L. B., Karpinski, A., & Grant, D. A. (2010). Assessing dependency using self-report and indirect measures: Examining the significance of discrepancies. *Journal of Personality Assessment, 92,* 306–316. http://dx.doi.org/10.1080/00223891.2010.481986

Colgan, P. (1987). Treatment of dependency disorders in men: Toward a balance of identity and intimacy. *Journal of Chemical Dependency Treatment, 1,* 205–227. http://dx.doi.org/10.1300/J034v01n01_12

Crawford, M. J., Koldobsky, N., Mulder, R., & Tyrer, P. (2011). Classifying personality disorder according to severity. *Journal of Personality Disorders, 25,* 321–330. http://dx.doi.org/10.1521/pedi.2011.25.3.321

Cross, S. E., & Madson, L. (1997). Models of the self: Self-construals and gender. *Psychological Bulletin, 122,* 5–37. http://dx.doi.org/10.1037/0033-2909.122.1.5

Denckla, C. A., Mancini, A. D., Bornstein, R. F., & Bonanno, G. A. (2011). Adaptive and maladaptive dependency in bereavement: Distinguishing prolonged and resolved grief trajectories. *Personality and Individual Differences, 51,* 1012–1017. http://dx.doi.org/10.1016/j.paid.2011.08.014

Feeney, J. A., & Noller, P. (1990). Attachment style as a predictor of adult romantic relationships. *Journal of Personality and Social Psychology, 58,* 281–291. http://dx.doi.org/10.1037/0022-3514.58.2.281

Fiori, K., Consedine, N., & Magai, C. (2008). The adaptive and maladaptive faces of dependency in later life: Links to physical and psychological health outcomes. *Aging & Mental Health, 12,* 700–712. http://dx.doi.org/10.1080/13607860802148863

Freud, S. (1953). Three essays on the theory of sexuality. In J. Strachey (Ed. & Trans.), *The standard edition of the complete psychological works of Sigmund Freud* (Vol. 4, pp. 125–248). London, England: Hogarth. (Original work published 1905)

Gardner, D., & Helmes, E. (2007). Development of the interpersonal dependency scale for older adults. *Australasian Journal on Ageing, 26,* 40–44. http://dx.doi.org/10.1111/j.1741-6612.2007.00204.x

Greenberg, R. P., & Dattore, P. J. (1981). The relationship between dependency and the development of cancer. *Psychosomatic Medicine, 43,* 35–43. http://dx.doi.org/10.1097/00006842-198102000-00005

Greenberg, R. P., & Fisher, S. (1977). The relationship between willingness to adopt the sick role and attitudes toward women. *Journal of Chronic Diseases, 30,* 29–37. http://dx.doi.org/10.1016/0021-9681(77)90049-2

Haggerty, G., Blake, M., & Siefert, C. J. (2010). Convergent and divergent validity of the Relationship Profile Test: Investigating the relationship with attachment, interpersonal distress and psychological health. *Journal of Clinical Psychology, 66,* 339–354.

Hirschfeld, R. M. A., Klerman, G. L., Gough, H. G., Barrett, J., Korchin, S. J., & Chodoff, P. (1977). A measure of interpersonal dependency. *Journal of Personality Assessment, 41,* 610–618. http://dx.doi.org/10.1207/s15327752jpa4106_6

Huprich, S. K. (2011). Contributions from personality- and psychodynamically oriented assessment to the development of the DSM–5 personality disorders. *Journal of Personality Assessment, 93,* 354–361. http://dx.doi.org/10.1080/00223891.2011.577473

Jaffe, A. M., Goller, H., & Friedman, A. F. (2012). Psychology and the law: Dependent personality disorder as an affirmative defense. *Journal of Forensic Psychology Practice, 12,* 189–210. http://dx.doi.org/10.1080/15228932.2012.676325

Joiner, T. E., Jr., & Metalsky, G. I. (2001). Excessive reassurance seeking: Delineating a risk factor involved in the development of depressive symptoms. *Psychological Science, 12,* 371–378. http://dx.doi.org/10.1111/1467-9280.00369

Kraepelin, E. (1913). *Psychiatrie: Ein lehrbuch* [Psychiatry: A textbook]. Leipzig, Germany: Barth.

Leary, T. (1957). *Interpersonal diagnosis of personality*. New York, NY: Ronald.

Lowe, J. R., Edmundson, M., & Widiger, T. A. (2009). Assessment of dependency, agreeableness, and their relationship. *Psychological Assessment, 21*, 543–553. http://dx.doi.org/10.1037/a0016899

Luborsky, L., & Crits-Christoph, P. (1990). *Understanding transference: The core conflictual relationship theme method*. New York, NY: Basic Books.

Luyten, P., & Blatt, S. J. (2013). Interpersonal relatedness and self-definition in normal and disrupted personality development: Retrospect and prospect. *American Psychologist, 68*, 172–183. http://dx.doi.org/10.1037/a0032243

Masling, J. M., Johnson, C., & Saturansky, C. (1974). Oral imagery, accuracy of perceiving others, and performance in Peace Corps training. *Journal of Personality and Social Psychology, 30*, 414–419. http://dx.doi.org/10.1037/h0036900

Masling, J. M., Shiffner, J., & Shenfeld, M. (1980). Client perception of the counselor and orality. *Journal of Counseling Psychology, 27*, 294–298. http://dx.doi.org/10.1037/0022-0167.27.3.294

Mischel, W. (1979). On the interface of cognition and personality: Beyond the person–situation debate. *American Psychologist, 34*, 740–754. http://dx.doi.org/10.1037/0003-066X.34.9.740

Mischel, W. (1984). Convergences and challenges in the search for consistency. *American Psychologist, 39*, 351–364. http://dx.doi.org/10.1037/0003-066X.39.4.351

Mischel, W., Shoda, Y., & Mendoza-Denton, R. (2002). Situation-behavior profiles as a locus of consistency in personality. *Current Directions in Psychological Science, 11*, 50–54. http://dx.doi.org/10.1111/1467-8721.00166

Narduzzi, K. J., & Jackson, T. (2000). Personality differences between eating-disordered women and a nonclinical comparison sample: A discriminant classification analysis. *Journal of Clinical Psychology, 56*, 699–710. http://dx.doi.org/10.1002/(SICI)1097-4679(200006)56:6<699::AID-JCLP1>3.0.CO;2-K

Neki, J. S. (1976). An examination of the cultural relativism of dependence as a dynamic of social and therapeutic relationships. I. Socio-developmental. *British Journal of Medical Psychology, 49*, 1–10. http://dx.doi.org/10.1111/j.2044-8341.1976.tb02348.x

Ng, H. M., & Bornstein, R. F. (2005). Comorbidity of dependent personality disorder and anxiety disorders: A meta-analytic review. *Clinical Psychology: Science and Practice, 12*, 395–406. http://dx.doi.org/10.1093/clipsy.bpi049

Nietzel, M. T., & Harris, M. J. (1990). Relationship of dependency and achievement/autonomy to depression. *Clinical Psychology Review, 10*, 279–297. http://dx.doi.org/10.1016/0272-7358(90)90063-G

O'Neil, J. M. (2008). Summarizing 25 years of research on men's gender role conflict using the Gender Role Conflict Scale: New research paradigms and clinical implications. *The Counseling Psychologist, 36,* 358–445. http://dx.doi.org/10.1177/0011000008317057

O'Neill, R. M., & Bornstein, R. F. (2001). The dependent patient in a psychiatric inpatient setting: Relationship of interpersonal dependency to consultation and medication frequencies. *Journal of Clinical Psychology, 57,* 289–298. http://dx.doi.org/10.1002/jclp.1012

Overholser, J. C. (1997). Treatment of excessive interpersonal dependency: A cognitive-behavioral model. *Journal of Contemporary Psychotherapy, 27,* 283–301. http://dx.doi.org/10.1023/A:1025614524578

Overholser, J. C., & Fine, M. A. (1994). Cognitive-behavioral treatment of excessive interpersonal dependency: A four-stage psychotherapy model. *Journal of Cognitive Psychotherapy, 8,* 55–70.

Pace, U., & Zappulla, C. (2013). Detachment from parents, problem behaviors, and the moderating role of parental support among Italian adolescents. *Journal of Family Issues, 34,* 768–783. http://dx.doi.org/10.1177/0192513X12461908

Paris, J. (1998). *Working with traits: Psychotherapy of personality disorders.* Northvale, NJ: Aronson.

Pincus, A. L., & Gurtman, M. B. (1995). The three faces of interpersonal dependency: Structural analyses of self-report dependency measures. *Journal of Personality and Social Psychology, 69,* 744–758. http://dx.doi.org/10.1037/0022-3514.69.4.744

Pincus, A. L., & Wilson, K. R. (2001). Interpersonal variability in dependent personality. *Journal of Personality, 69,* 223–251. http://dx.doi.org/10.1111/1467-6494.00143

Poldrugo, F., & Forti, B. (1988). Personality disorders and alcoholism treatment outcome. *Drug and Alcohol Dependence, 21,* 171–176. http://dx.doi.org/10.1016/0376-8716(88)90066-X

Porcerelli, J. H., Bornstein, R. F., Markova, T., & Huprich, S. K. (2009). Physical health correlates of pathological and healthy dependency in urban women. *Journal of Nervous and Mental Disease, 197,* 761–765. http://dx.doi.org/10.1097/NMD.0b013e3181b97bbe

Roche, M. J., Pincus, A. L., Hyde, A. L., Conroy, D. E., & Ram, N. (2013). Within-person variation of agentic and communal perceptions: Implications for interpersonal theory and assessment. *Journal of Research in Personality, 47,* 445–452. http://dx.doi.org/10.1016/j.jrp.2013.01.007

Schneider, K. (1923). *Die psychopathischen personlichkeiten* [The psychopathic personalities]. Vienna, Austria: Deuticke.

Torgersen, S., Lygren, S., Øien, P. A., Skre, I., Onstad, S., Edvardsen, J., . . . Kringlen, E. (2000). A twin study of personality disorders. *Comprehensive Psychiatry, 41,* 416–425. http://dx.doi.org/10.1053/comp.2000.16560

Turkat, I. D. (1990). *The personality disorders: A psychological approach to clinical management.* New York, NY: Pergamon Press.

Turkat, I. D., & Carlson, C. R. (1984). Data-based versus symptomatic formulation of treatment: The case of a dependent personality. *Journal of Behavior*

Therapy and Experimental Psychiatry, 15, 153–160. http://dx.doi.org/10.1016/0005-7916(84)90011-9

Vliegen, N., Luyten, P., Meurs, P., & Cluckers, G. (2006). Adaptive and maladaptive dimensions of relatedness and self-definition: Relationship with postpartum depression and anxiety. *Personality and Individual Differences, 41*, 395–406. http://dx.doi.org/10.1016/j.paid.2005.11.029

Watson, C. G., Barnett, M., Nikunen, L., Schultz, C., Randolph-Elgin, T., & Mendez, C. M. (1997). Lifetime prevalences of nine common psychiatric/personality disorders in female domestic abuse survivors. *Journal of Nervous and Mental Disease, 185*, 645–647. http://dx.doi.org/10.1097/00005053-199710000-00011

Wiggins, J. S. (1991). Agency and communion as conceptual coordinates for the understanding and measurement of interpersonal behavior. In D. Cicchetti & W. M. Grove (Eds.), *Thinking clearly about psychology: Essays in honor of Paul E. Meehl* (Vol. 2, pp. 89–113). Minneapolis: University of Minnesota Press.

Wilberg, T., Karterud, S., Pedersen, G., & Urnes, Ø. (2009). The impact of avoidant personality disorder on psychosocial impairment is substantial. *Nordic Journal of Psychiatry, 63*, 390–396. http://dx.doi.org/10.1080/08039480902831322

World Health Organization. (2004). *International statistical classification of diseases and related health problems* (10th rev.). Geneva, Switzerland: Author.

Yamaguchi, S. (2004). Further clarifications of the concept of *amae* in relation to dependence and attachment. *Human Development, 47*, 28–33. http://dx.doi.org/10.1159/000075367

V

CURRENT AND FUTURE ISSUES

18

UNDERSTANDING THE DARK SIDE OF PERSONALITY: REFLECTIONS AND FUTURE DIRECTIONS

DAVID K. MARCUS AND VIRGIL ZEIGLER-HILL

The primary aim of this volume was to provide an overview of the current conceptualizations of a diverse array of personality traits that may have socially aversive, destructive, or dark features. We hoped that this volume would expand the appreciation that researchers and clinicians have for what constitutes dark personality traits beyond the ubiquitous Dark Triad (i.e., narcissism, psychopathy, and Machiavellianism; see Furnham, Richards, & Paulhus, 2013, for a review). Consequently, we cast a wide net when identifying potentially dark personality traits that were worthy of review. Despite this diversity of subject matter, a number of common themes, questions, and directions for future research emerged from these reviews. In this concluding chapter, we consider some of these issues and ways to advance the understanding of dark personality features.

http://dx.doi.org/10.1037/14854-019
The Dark Side of Personality: Science and Practice in Social, Personality, and Clinical Psychology, V. Zeigler-Hill and D. K. Marcus (Editors)

MAGNITUDE, CONTEXT, FLAVOR, AND INTERACTIONS: WHEN DOES A TRAIT TURN DARK?

Although each chapter included discussions of the adaptive or positive qualities associated with the traits being reviewed, there are a few traits that are dark or interpersonally toxic most all of the time (e.g., sadism, callousness). To borrow a phrase from Ralph Nader (1965), these traits may be considered "unsafe at any speed." In contrast, most of the traits included in the current volume may only be dark and destructive under particular circumstances. One of the most common themes is that many of these traits are only problematic at extreme levels. For example, Gratz, Dixon-Gordon, and Whalen (Chapter 13, this volume) suggested that the association between emotional lability and impairment was curvilinear. Extremely high levels of emotional lability are associated with a range of psychological disorders and problems, including borderline personality disorder, eating disorders, and aggressive behavior. However, extremely low levels of emotional lability (or "emotional inertia") are linked to depression, low self-esteem, and reduced creativity. This curvilinear relation between a trait and impairment is not unique to emotional lability. High levels of anxiety are debilitating, moderate levels of anxiety are adaptive, and the absence of anxiety can lead to risky decisions and even an increased risk of accidental death (Rosellini & Brown, Chapter 14, this volume). Similarly, whereas a lack of self-confidence is associated with underachievement, relatively accurate levels of self-confidence that may be slightly higher than are warranted can contribute to resilience in the face of minor failure, and extreme levels of overconfidence can be fatal (Ehrlinger & Eichenbaum, Chapter 12, this volume). Other traits reviewed in this volume that are likely to fit this curvilinear model include dependency, self-esteem, sensation seeking, and perfectionism.

Whether a trait is considered to be dark and destructive may also depend on the aptitude and traits of the possessor and the context in which it is displayed. Overall, higher levels of fearless dominance are associated with a more successful presidency (Lilienfeld et al., 2012). However, other individual differences and context may moderate this association. Consider the presidencies of Franklin Roosevelt and George W. Bush, both of whom were rated as having above average levels of fearless dominance (Lilienfeld et al., 2012). High levels of fearless dominance may have contributed to one of these presidents ending the Great Depression, spearheading the New Deal, and defeating the Axis powers in World War II, whereas in the other case, it may have contributed to the United States blundering into a disastrous Middle Eastern war and following fiscal policies that nearly resulted in a second Great Depression. Similarly, high levels of sensation seeking may have very different consequences if the situation requires running into a burning building to save a child or presents the opportunity to "hook up" with a stranger who may have a sexually transmitted disease (STD; Maples-Keller, Berke, Few, & Miller, Chapter 7, this volume). If the person were to get an STD, high levels of interpersonal dependency may make it more likely that the person would seek medical assistance in a timely fashion, although if this person were to suspect that the STD resulted from his or her partner's infidelity, the person might also be more likely to abuse his or her partner (Bornstein, Chapter 17, this volume). Even spitefulness, which is typically associated with destructive or vindictive behaviors (e.g., spending excessive amounts of money on attorney fees during divorce battles) may have some prosocial benefits in the right context. For example, a former faculty colleague of ours secured a "ticket book" from the campus police and was allowed to issue parking tickets to college students who parked in the lots that were designated for faculty parking. The act was clearly spiteful—he wasted his time engaging in an activity that was not part of his job in order to harm others—yet his behavior also helped to enforce parking regulations and incrementally improved the parking situation for his colleagues.

A number of the personality traits reviewed in this volume have a multidimensional structure, with some dimensions being darker than others (i.e., these traits may come in various "flavors"). With respect to narcissism (Dowgwillo, Dawood, & Pincus, Chapter 1, this volume), grandiose narcissism is associated with a variety of both positive (e.g., greater health and well-being, ability to foster a positive first impression) and negative external correlates (e.g., low agreeableness, aggressive behavior), whereas vulnerable narcissism is darker and solely associated with negative correlates (e.g., self-injury, impulsivity). Similarly, as described by Flett, Hewitt, and Sherry (Chapter 10, this volume), each dimension of perfectionism appears to be dark but in different ways. Although self-oriented perfectionism may be exhausting and associated with work addiction, socially prescribed perfectionism appears to be the dimension that is most strongly associated with suicidality (Flett, Hewitt, & Heisel, 2014). Further, other-oriented perfectionism, which involves holding others to exceedingly high standards, is the dimension that is most strongly associated with blame, hostility, and aggression directed at others.

One of the most interesting themes to emerge from these chapters was the possibility that some of these traits may become darker—or may only be dark—when they interact with other traits or characteristics. As described by Lilienfeld, Smith, and Watts (Chapter 3, this volume), fearless dominance provides a clear example of such a putative interaction. Sure, high levels of fearless dominance may be associated with higher levels of risky sexual behavior, but it is quite possible that fearless dominance is often adaptive and may even be associated with admirable behavior. For example, fearless dominance is associated with decreased depression and anxiety, higher levels of extraversion and positive affect, and even everyday acts of heroism and altruism. The colorful description of Chuck Yeager's heroic exploits that was provided by Lilienfeld and colleagues—which included his bravery as a World War II fighter pilot and his having broken the sound barrier as a test pilot—vividly demonstrated the positive impact that a person with high levels of fearless dominance can have. However, if high levels of this dimension co-occur with deficient executive functioning or high levels of impulsivity—or perhaps with high levels of callousness or coldheartedness—then heroism may be replaced by psychopathy. Although only a limited number of studies have examined these interactions with fearless dominance, and so far the evidence has been mixed, this hypothesis that the interaction between fearless dominance and other characteristics can turn the "right stuff" into the "wrong stuff" remains intriguing.

In addition to fearless dominance, there are a number of other traits in which their dark nature may be amplified by the presence of other characteristics or experiences. Emotional lability predicts aggressive behavior when paired with high negative urgency, but not when individuals are low in negative urgency (Gratz et al., Chapter 13, this volume). Stalking behavior is predicted by the interaction of narcissistic vulnerability and a reported history of childhood sexual abuse (Dowgwillo et al., Chapter 1, this volume). Sensation seeking better predicts risky sexual behavior when combined with high levels of impulsivity (Maples-Keller et al., Chapter 7, this volume). Although interaction effects can be notoriously difficult to replicate, we believe that one of the most promising avenues for future research on the dark side of personality will be studies examining how these various traits interact with one another.

A TAXONOMY OF DARK PERSONALITY TRAITS: WHEN TO SPLIT AND WHEN TO LUMP

As previously noted, one of our aims was to cast a wide net when generating a list of dark traits for review. Consequently, our inclination was to split traits that might be related rather than to aggregate them into higher order constructs. However, a number of the traits included in this volume are both conceptually and empirically related to one another. At what point do different trait names identify related but distinct constructs, and when might different trait names simply be minor variations on the same latent construct? For example, do urgency (Cyders, Coskunpinar, & VanderVeen, Chapter 8, this volume) and emotional lability (Gratz et al., Chapter 13, this volume) describe distinct constructs, or is this distinction an artifact of these terms having been developed from different research traditions? The extent to which some of the differing trait names represent distinctions without any real underlying differences remains an open empirical question for future research.

Consider the three related traits of sadism, callousness, and spitefulness. Buckels, Jones, and Paulhus (2013) reported relatively large correlations between self-reported sadism and a measure of psychopathy that has a strong callousness component (rs ranging between .58 and .62). Similarly, Marcus, Zeigler-Hill, Mercer, and Norris (2014) found high correlations between self-reported spitefulness and callous affect (rs ranging from .65 to .71). Although researchers have yet to assess the association between sadism and spitefulness, it is likely that these two constructs are also strongly related. Paulhus and Dutton (Chapter 5, this volume) argued that callousness is the common factor underlying all of the Dark Tetrad traits, including sadism. If this argument is accurate, then sadism is a subtype of callousness, and one could be callous without being sadistic, but to be sadistic, one must be callous. Accordingly, there would be a benefit to distinguishing between these two traits because assessing sadism would provide additional information beyond what is captured when assessing callousness. We are currently examining whether measuring spitefulness predicts spiteful behavior in an Ultimatum Game above and beyond more general measures of callousness and antagonism. Ultimately, these distinctions will be worth making if they can account for unique variance in predicting relevant outcomes.

Conversely, some of the traits included in this volume may be opposite ends of the same dimension. For example, are fearless dominance and anxiousness merely opposites? Self-reported fearless dominance is negatively correlated with a variety of measures of internalizing symptoms, including anxiety and depression. Further, fearless dominance is negatively correlated with measures of various anxiety disorders (Lilienfeld et al., Chapter 3, this volume). However, the magnitude of these negative correlations is not nearly as large as the correlations among the aforementioned antagonism traits. Furthermore, although anxious individuals (especially people who are socially anxious) typically display an innocuous social manner (Barlow, 2004), the social potency aspect of fearless dominance likely addresses a component of this trait that is not simply the absence of anxiety. Similarly, it is possible that low self-esteem and narcissism occupy opposite ends of a continuum. However, as discussed by Zeigler-Hill et al. (Chapter 16, this volume) and Dowgwillo et al. (Chapter 1, this volume), the actual link between self-esteem and narcissism is likely far more nuanced. Grandiose narcissism may be positively associated with self-esteem level, but vulnerable narcissism is actually negatively associated with self-esteem. Thus, although researchers have occasionally created composite measures that combine multiple dark personality traits into a single score (e.g., Jonason, Li, Webster, & Schmitt, 2009), we encourage researchers to continue to examine potentially subtle differences among these various dark traits.

The myriad connections among the dark personality traits may be more interesting than the question of whether certain traits identify the same latent construct. Especially interesting are the possible connections that might not have been readily apparent. For example, although it is not surprising that perfectionism and narcissism are associated traits, the link between other-oriented perfectionism and authoritarianism (Flett et al., Chapter 10, this volume) may not have been expected. Another possibly unexpected connection was between distractibility and overconfidence (Barry, Fisher, DiSabatino, & Tomeny, Chapter 9, this volume): Distractibility may contribute to overconfidence because distractible individuals may be less attentive to corrective feedback (i.e., they do not notice when they get things wrong).

MEASUREMENT ISSUES

A large majority of the research reported in this volume was based on self-report measures. Self-report measures have a number of strengths including that they are the most economical way to collect personality data and the reporter is most likely the person who knows the subject of the report best. However, the myriad limitations of self-report measures have also been well documented, including the possibility that the reporter may lack self-awareness, respond carelessly, engage in various self-presentational strategies to appear more socially desirable, or simply respond dishonestly (see Lilienfeld & Fowler, 2006, for a detailed discussion of these issues with respect to the self-report assessment of psychopathy). All of these issues may become more acute when attempting to assess negative personality traits, especially when a lack of self-awareness may be a component of the trait. For example, individuals with narcissistic personality disorder self-report lower levels of narcissism than is reported by peer ratings and this self-other agreement between patients and peers is lower in narcissistic personality disorder than in other personality disorders (for a review, see Pincus & Lukowitsky, 2010).

Some of the most interesting and exciting research reviewed in this volume involved innovative alternatives to self-report instruments. Paulhus and Dutton (Chapter 5, this volume) described some creative methods for assessing sadism in the laboratory using a task in which participants work for the opportunity to crush bugs in a bug-crunching machine or, in another study, to blast an innocent victim with a loud noise. In both studies, participants who scored higher on a self-report measure of sadism worked harder for the opportunity to harm bugs or people. Thus, not only did these methods provide an alternative to self-report assessments, but they also helped validate the self-report measures of sadism. Additionally, Zeigler-Hill and colleagues (Chapter 16, this volume) described the use of a bogus pipeline technique to assess self-esteem more accurately. Offering people a large financial incentive to accurately judge their performance on a task is also an inventive way to assess overconfidence (Ehrlinger & Eichenbaum, Chapter 12, this volume). Distractibility is one of the few traits reviewed in the current volume in which self-report has played a limited role. Instead, computerized tasks, neuropsychological assessments, and reports provided by parents and teachers (when children are being assessed) have been the primary methods for assessing distractibility. In contrast, Jones (Chapter 4, this volume) described the challenges of developing a valid peer-report measure of Machiavellianism. We encourage researchers who study dark personality traits to continue to develop innovative methods that supplement (and may even help validate) standard self-report measures.

TRAITS OR TYPES?

The chapters in the current volume were written with the assumption that each of the dark personality traits is a dimensional construct (i.e., that it exists on a continuum). This assumption is probably correct for all—or nearly all—of these dark personality traits. However, this assumption is inconsistent with how many of these traits are discussed in both everyday discourse and scientific writing. It is not uncommon to refer to *psychopaths*, *sadists*, and *perfectionists*. The study of authoritarianism has its origins in attempts to identify individuals with an authoritarian personality (Ludeke, Chapter 11, this volume). Furthermore, some of these dark traits are represented by categorical psychiatric diagnoses, such as narcissistic and dependent personality disorders. Do these terms refer to individuals at the far end of a continuum, or are there genuine types (qualitatively distinct groups) hidden among these traits?

Taxometric methods (Ruscio, Haslam, & Ruscio, 2006; Waller & Meehl, 1998) can be used to examine the latent structure (i.e., taxonic or dimensional) of a construct. So far, only some of these dark personality traits have been the subject of taxometric analyses. Narcissism appears to be dimensional (Foster & Campbell, 2007; although see Fossati et al., 2005, for a study that may have found that narcissistic personality disorder is taxonic). Psychopathy (including fearless dominance) is most likely dimensional (e.g., Marcus, John, & Edens, 2004), as is perfectionism (Broman-Fulks, Hill, & Green, 2008). Sexual sadism among sex offenders also appears to be dimensional (Mokros, Schilling, Weiss, Nitschke, & Eher, 2014), but there have not been any taxometric analyses of the "everyday sadism" discussed by Paulhus and Dutton (Chapter 5, this volume). Although no taxometric analyses have specifically examined distractibility or emotional lability, taxometric analyses of their related disorders—attention-deficit disorder (Marcus & Barry, 2011) and borderline personality disorder (Edens, Marcus, & Ruiz, 2008), respectively—both yielded dimensional findings.

Knowing whether each these dark personality traits has a dimensional or taxonic latent structure can inform etiological models of these traits and can guide research methods and analyses. Whereas a dimensional trait is likely due to the combination of multiple causal factors, a taxonic construct may be due to a single causal factor or may be explained by a tipping point model in which the combination of multiple causal factors result in a qualitative change. If any of these dark personality features actually represent types, then assessment instruments that sort individuals by group membership will be needed. Additionally, group designs in which taxon members are compared with those who do not have the taxonic feature would need to replace the more common use of correlational designs. Conversely, in the absence of evidence of a taxon, the use of continuous measures and correlational designs remains preferable to attempts at artificial dichotomization (MacCallum, Zhang, Preacher, & Rucker, 2002).

CLINICAL IMPLICATIONS

Given the range of dark personality features addressed in the current volume, there is no one standard set of recommendations that can apply to all of these traits. Some of the traits are represented by specific *Diagnostic and Statistical Manual of Mental Disorders* (DSM) or *International Classification of Diseases* (ICD) diagnoses (e.g., depressivity, narcissism, dependency). Others serve as symptoms of one or more psychological disorders (e.g., emotional liability, anxiousness, callousness, distractibility). Even though they are dark and likely to result in problematic interpersonal outcomes, some of these traits are unlikely to be the subject of clinical evaluations or interventions for a variety of reasons. For example, overconfident individuals are by definition unaware that they are overconfident. Machiavellian and sadistic individuals are also unlikely to identify these traits as problems that require treatment. Additionally, those individuals who are high in authoritarianism are often reluctant to seek mental health treatment (Ludeke, Chapter 11, this volume). However, each of these traits, along with many of the other traits reviewed in the current volume, may influence the course and treatment of particular psychological disorders. An example of one such "aptitude by treatment interaction" (Smith & Sechrest, 1991) is the finding that depressed clients who are high in impulsivity benefit more from cognitive therapy, whereas depressed clients low in impulsivity benefit more from supportive therapy (Beutler et al., 1991). Furthermore, a number of these traits may serve as negative treatment indicators or contribute to therapy-interfering behaviors (e.g., distractibility reducing the likelihood that the client will remember to complete therapy homework assignments). Furthermore, those high in callousness are less likely to develop a therapeutic alliance with their therapists and are more likely to drop out of treatment (Pardini & Ray, Chapter 2, this volume), and high levels of sensation seeking predict poorer outcomes among patients addicted to cocaine (Maples-Keller et al., Chapter 7, this volume).

The questions of the stability and malleability of these dark traits may be one of the most pertinent from a clinical perspective. Are individuals with high levels of these traits destined to remain this way, and are there clinical interventions that can diminish these traits? Although a number of chapters in this volume, including those on callousness (Pardini & Ray, Chapter 2), anxiousness (Rosellini & Brown, Chapter 14), depressivity (Kessel & Klein, Chapter 15), and dependency (Bornstein, Chapter 17) reviewed the research on the stability of these traits, most noted that additional longitudinal research was needed. This absence of data may be especially true for those traits that are not directly identified with *DSM* or *ICD* diagnoses. For example, perfectionism appears to be relatively stable over a roughly 4-month time period among college students (Rice & Aldea, 2006) and over a 2.5-year period among middle-age women (Procopio, Holm-Denoma, Gordon, & Joiner, 2006), but little is known about the vicissitudes of perfectionism over the life course. Far less is known about the stability of other dark traits such as spitefulness, overconfidence, sadism, and Machiavellianism.

Long-term research on the course of personality disorders suggests that the personality traits associated with these disorders (e.g., suspiciousness, anxiousness) are more stable than either the diagnoses (e.g., whether a patient continues to meet the diagnostic criteria for borderline personality disorder) or the presence of specific behavioral symptoms, such as self-harm (for a review, see Morey & Hopwood, 2013). This pattern of data suggests that many of the traits reviewed in the current volume are likely to be relatively stable, but this extrapolation from the personality disorder literature should not replace long-term studies examining the stability of these dark traits. Although the psychotherapy outcome literature is vast and far beyond the scope of the current volume, it is worth noting that, based on their review and previous meta-analyses, Westen, Novotny, and Thompson-Brenner (2004) concluded that time-limited psychotherapies are more effective at reducing specific problematic symptoms or behaviors (e.g., panic attacks, binging and purging) than at changing more stable personality traits such as anxiousness (represented by generalized anxiety disorder) and emotional lability (associated with borderline personality disorder). This conclusion is consistent with the findings from the longitudinal studies of personality disorders and again suggests that many of these dark traits are likely to be relatively stable.

FINAL THOUGHTS

Our hope is that this volume will help stimulate research into the dark side of personality. Only by understanding our worst traits and impulses can we begin to modify and channel them. Many of these traits—perhaps all of them—are presumed to have been shaped by evolutionary processes and are not simply the result of deficits or abnormalities. Being anxious, spiteful, dependent, callous, and overconfident, to name just a few, may be adaptive in some circumstances and may have their origins in our shared evolutionary history. Yet there are also large individual differences in whether and how people manifest these dark traits. In their own research, each of the authors who contributed to this volume has added to our understanding of how these traits function, the roles of nature and nurture in shaping these traits, and the interpersonal consequences of acting in accordance with these traits.

REFERENCES

Barlow, D. H. (2004). *Anxiety and its disorders: The nature and treatment of anxiety and panic* (2nd ed.). New York, NY: Guilford Press.

Beutler, L. E., Engle, D., Mohr, D., Daldrup, R. J., Bergan, J., Meredith, K., & Merry, W. (1991). Predictors of differential response to cognitive, experiential, and self-directed psychotherapeutic procedures. *Journal of Consulting and Clinical Psychology, 59*, 333–340. http://dx.doi.org/10.1037/0022-006X.59.2.333

Broman-Fulks, J. J., Hill, R. W., & Green, B. A. (2008). Is perfectionism categorical or dimensional? A taxometric analysis. *Journal of Personality Assessment, 90*, 481–490. http://dx.doi.org/10.1080/00223890802248802

Buckels, E. E., Jones, D. N., & Paulhus, D. L. (2013). Behavioral confirmation of everyday sadism. *Psychological Science, 24*, 2201–2209. http://dx.doi.org/10.1177/0956797613490749

Edens, J. F., Marcus, D. K., & Ruiz, M. A. (2008). Taxometric analyses of borderline personality features in a large-scale male and female offender sample. *Journal of Abnormal Psychology, 117*, 705–711. http://dx.doi.org/10.1037/0021-843X.117.3.705

Flett, G. L., Hewitt, P. L., & Heisel, M. J. (2014). The destructiveness of perfectionism revisited: Implications for the assessment of suicide risk and the prevention of suicide. *Review of General Psychology, 18*, 156–172. http://dx.doi.org/10.1037/gpr0000011

Fossati, A., Beauchaine, T. P., Grazioli, F., Carretta, I., Cortinovis, F., & Maffei, C. (2005). A latent structure analysis of *Diagnostic and Statistical Manual of Mental Disorders, Fourth Edition*, narcissistic personality disorder criteria. *Comprehensive Psychiatry, 46*, 361–367.

Foster, J. D., & Campbell, W. K. (2007). Are there such things as "narcissists" in social psychology? A taxometric analysis of the Narcissistic Personality Inventory. *Personality and Individual Differences, 43*, 1321–1332. http://dx.doi.org/10.1016/j.paid.2007.04.003

Furnham, A., Richards, S. C., & Paulhus, D. L. (2013). The dark triad of personality: A 10-year review. *Social and Personality Psychology Compass, 7*, 199–216. http://dx.doi.org/10.1111/spc3.12018

Jonason, P. K., Li, N. P., Webster, G. D., & Schmitt, D. P. (2009). The dark triad: Facilitating a short-term mating strategy in men. *European Journal of Personality, 23*, 5–18. http://dx.doi.org/10.1002/per.698

Lilienfeld, S. O., & Fowler, K. A. (2006). The self-report assessment of psychopathy: Problems, pitfalls, and promises. In C. J. Patrick (Ed.), *Handbook of the psychopathy* (pp. 107–132). New York, NY: Guilford Press.

Lilienfeld, S. O., Waldman, I. D., Landfield, K., Watts, A. L., Rubenzer, S., & Faschingbauer, T. R. (2012). Fearless dominance and the U.S. presidency: Implications of psychopathic personality traits for successful and unsuccessful political leadership. *Journal of Personality and Social Psychology, 103*, 489–505. http://dx.doi.org/10.1037/a0029392

MacCallum, R. C., Zhang, S., Preacher, K. J., & Rucker, D. D. (2002). On the practice of dichotomization of quantitative variables. *Psychological Methods, 7*, 19–40. http://dx.doi.org/10.1037/1082-989X.7.1.19

Marcus, D. K., & Barry, T. D. (2011). Does attention-deficit/hyperactivity disorder have a dimensional latent structure? A taxometric analysis. *Journal of Abnormal Psychology, 120*, 427–442.

Marcus, D. K., John, S. L., & Edens, J. F. (2004). A taxometric analysis of psychopathic personality. *Journal of Abnormal Psychology, 113*, 626–635. http://dx.doi.org/10.1037/0021-843X.113.4.626

Marcus, D. K., Zeigler-Hill, V., Mercer, S. H., & Norris, A. L. (2014). The psychology of spite and the measurement of spitefulness. *Psychological Assessment, 26*, 563–574. http://dx.doi.org/10.1037/a0036039

Mokros, A., Schilling, F., Weiss, K., Nitschke, J., & Eher, R. (2014). Sadism in sexual offenders: Evidence for dimensionality. *Psychological Assessment, 26*, 138–147. http://dx.doi.org/10.1037/a0034861

Morey, L. C., & Hopwood, C. J. (2013). Stability and change in personality disorders. *Annual Review of Clinical Psychology, 9*, 499–528. http://dx.doi.org/10.1146/annurev-clinpsy-050212-185637

Nader, R. (1965). *Unsafe at any speed: The designed-in dangers of the American automobile.* New York, NY: Grossman.

Pincus, A. L., & Lukowitsky, M. R. (2010). Pathological narcissism and narcissistic personality disorder. *Annual Review of Clinical Psychology, 6*, 421–446. http://dx.doi.org/10.1146/annurev.clinpsy.121208.131215

Procopio, C. A., Holm-Denoma, J. M., Gordon, K. H., & Joiner, T. E., Jr. (2006). Two–three-year stability and interrelations of bulimotypic indicators and depressive and anxious symptoms in middle-aged women. *International Journal of Eating Disorders, 39*, 312–319. http://dx.doi.org/10.1002/eat.20242

Rice, K. G., & Aldea, M. A. (2006). State dependence and trait stability of perfectionism: A short-term longitudinal study. *Journal of Counseling Psychology, 53,* 205–213. http://dx.doi.org/10.1037/0022-0167.53.2.205

Ruscio, J., Haslam, N., & Ruscio, A. (2006). *Introduction to the taxometric method: A practical guide.* Mahwah, NJ: Erlbaum.

Smith, B., & Sechrest, L. (1991). Treatment of aptitude × treatment interactions. *Journal of Consulting and Clinical Psychology, 59,* 233–244. http://dx.doi.org/10.1037/0022-006X.59.2.233

Waller, N. G., & Meehl, P. E. (1998). *Multivariate taxometric procedures: Distinguishing types from continua.* Newbury Park, CA: Sage.

Westen, D., Novotny, C. M., & Thompson-Brenner, H. (2004). The empirical status of empirically supported psychotherapies: Assumptions, findings, and reporting in controlled clinical trials. *Psychological Bulletin, 130,* 631–663. http://dx.doi.org/10.1037/0033-2909.130.4.631

INDEX

Gambling, 144–145
Gardner, D., 343
Geis, F., 87, 98
Gender differences
    in callous personality features, 53
    in distractibility, 194
    in interpersonal dependency, 343–344
    in self-esteem, 327
    in spitefulness, 127–128
    in STEM field, 255
Generalized anxiety disorder (GAD),
    33, 199, 292, 293
"General neurotic syndrome," 290
Genetic heritability
    of callous personality features, 49
    of distractibility, 192
    of emotional lability, 270–271
    of Machiavellianism, 99
    of sadism, 115
    of sensation seeking, 140
Gilbert, D. T., 197
Glenn, A. L., 89–90
Goller, H., 341
Gomà-i-Freixanet, M., 141, 142
Gottlieb, R. M., 129
Graf, M., 214
Grandiosity, 27–35
Grand Theft Auto, 112
Grant, A. M., 77
Grant, D. A., 350
Gray, J. A., 68, 288
Great Depression, 364
Grossman, P. J., 128
Groupthink, 256–257
Guilt, 89, 96
Gurtman, M. B., 343

Hall, P. A., 219–220
Hamilton, W. D., 123
Harm avoidance, 288, 294
Hartmann, T., 196
Haruvi-Catalan, L., 36
Harvey, P. O., 312
Hawley, P. H., 88
Healy, P. J., 252
Heart disease, 344
Heatherton, T. F., 332
Helmes, E., 343
Henrich, J., 128

Heritability. *See* Genetic heritability
Heroism, 75
Hewitt, P. L., 214, 215, 219–221
HEXACO model, 8, 115, 221
Hibbing, J. R., 236
Hicks, B. M., 70, 71
Hill, R. W., 218
Hippocrates, 308
Hipwell, A. E., 129
Histrionic personality disorder, 146,
    219
Hitler, Adolf, 217
Hittner, J. B., 146
Hofmann, S. G., 297
Horney, K., 214, 216–217
Hostility
    with Dark Triad traits, 6
    and narcissism, 33
    perfectionism in, 217–218
    on Personality Inventory for the
      DSM–5, 8
    and spite, 129
Humor, 143
Huprich, S. K., 350
Huta, V., 292
Hyperkinetic disorder, 190. *See also*
    Attention-deficit/hyperactivity
    disorder

Iacono, W. G., 71
ICD–10. See International Classification
    of Diseases
IDs. *See* Internalizing disorders
Ignorance of incompetence
    phenomenon, 198
Immature dependence, 346
Impulse control disorders, 167–176
Impulsive noncomformity, 69, 70
Impulsivity
    and Machiavellianism, 90–91
    and narcissism, 31
    and sensation seeking, 145
    and urgency, 157–158
Inattentiveness, 190. *See also*
    Distractibility
Infancy, 49–50
Intelligence, 254–255
Internal distractibility, 191
Internalization of stigma hypothesis, 327

ABOUT THE EDITORS

Virgil Zeigler-Hill, PhD, is an associate professor and the director of graduate training for the Department of Psychology at Oakland University, Rochester, Michigan. His primary research interests are in three interrelated areas: (a) dark personality features (e.g., narcissism, spitefulness), (b) self-esteem, and (c) interpersonal relationships. He has written more than 120 journal articles and book chapters that focus on these topics. Dr. Zeigler-Hill has edited two previous books: *Self-Esteem* and *Evolutionary Perspectives on Social Psychology*. He is currently an associate editor for *Self and Identity*, *Journal of Personality Assessment*, and *Evolutionary Psychology*.

David K. Marcus, PhD, is a professor and the chair of the Department of Psychology at Washington State University, Pullman. He is the author of more than 75 journal articles. Much of his work focuses on psychopathy and antisocial behavior, but his research interests are diverse and include studies on spitefulness, hypochondriasis, psychotherapy outcomes and processes, and interpersonal perception. He is currently the editor of *Group Dynamics* and serves on the editorial boards of *Psychological Assessment* and the *Journal of Social and Clinical Psychology*.